Industrial Relations,
the Economy, and Society

Industrial Relations,
the Economy, and Society

Fourth Edition

John Godard

Captus Press

Industrial Relations, the Economy, and Society
Fourth Edition

Captus Press Inc.
Units 14 & 15
1600 Steeles Avenue West
Concord, Ontario   L4K 4M2
Telephone: (416) 736–5537
Fax: (416) 736–5793
Email: info@captus.com
Internet: http://www.captus.com

Library and Archives Canada Cataloguing in Publication
Godard, John
Industrial relations, the economy, and society / John Godard. -- 4th ed

Includes bibliographical references and index.
ISBN 978-1-55322-235-4

1. Industrial relations--Canada--Textbooks. I. Title.

HD8106.5.G63 2011   331'.0971   C2010-907071-2

Canada   *We acknowledge the financial support of the Government of Canada through the Canada Book Fund for our publishing activities.*

0 9 8 7 6 5 4 3 2
Printed in Canada

to Mary Ellen

Contents

CONTENTS

CONTENTS

CONTENTS

Preface

Textbooks on industrial relations have traditionally focused on the institutions of labour unionism, labour law, and collective bargaining, and been primarily descriptive in nature. In recent years, this focus has expanded somewhat, to include increased attention to employer practices. However, there has been a tendency to discuss these institutions and practices largely in isolation from broader political and economic issues having to do with the nature of work and employment in Canada. In contrast, the present book adopts a broader "political economy" approach. As with more conventional approaches, this approach includes extensive coverage of labour unions, labour law, and collective bargaining. It also includes extensive coverage of employer practices. But these topics are addressed in the context of ongoing debates about industrial relations and their implications for the broader issues of economy and society. The approach adopted in this book is also more critical in orientation than is the case for most industrial relations texts, as this book explores various problems associated with established institutional arrangements and identifies alternatives for the future. The book covers a number of topics often paid only limited attention in these texts. These topics include: theories of industrial relations, the economy and society (chapter two), understanding conflict in industrial relations (chapter three), the social functions of unions (chapter seven), the political-economy of employer practices (chapter six), the role of the state (chapter nine), understanding the state (chapter ten), and broader issues, developments, and alternatives (chapter sixteen).

In adopting a political economy approach, this book also proceeds from an "educative" orientation (Godard, 1992a). In other words, in addition to providing a "working knowledge" of industrial relations, the focus on various issues, debates, and problems is intended to provide readers with a deeper understanding of industrial relations, ideally challenging them to think critically and develop their own perspective on the subject matter. This book *does* develop and proceed from its own particular perspective on industrial relations, one that stresses the sources of conflict underlying the relationship between labour and management. But this understanding is meant to provide the thread or "storyline" that holds the book together. Readers are provided with considerable "space" to think critically and hence to disagree with any arguments advanced and conclusions drawn.

This Edition

This edition largely updates its predecessor. The main changes are to: (1) chapter three, where the statistics have been updated; (2) chapter four, where I have lengthened the discussion of the crisis in the 1970s and added a section addressing the relevant developments of the past decade; (3) chapter five, where I have altered the discussion of autonomic/consociative practices (e.g., the high performance model) and both shortened and updated the discussion of the research into these practices; and (4) chapter sixteen, where I have dropped the discussion of whether there has been a "transformation" of work and employment practices (too dated) and instead inserted a (brief) discussion of "shifting sands" that includes workplace changes, but also other changes that pose a challenge to the current system. There have been no major structural changes from the previous edition.

As for the previous edition, this edition is written so that any chapter (with the exception of chapter one) may be skipped without affecting the ability of students to understand subsequent chapters. The intention is to make the book as flexible as possible, enabling instructors to pick and choose those chapters that they consider most suited to their course. I have also written most chapters so that entire sections may be skipped, allowing instructors to use only those portions of a chapter that are most consistent with their course objectives.

I again thank Clive Gilson, Kurt Wetzel, Brian Williams, Roy Adams, Hilda Gowans, Rodney Rawlings, and Gail Marsden for their assistance with the first edition and everyone at Captus Press, especially Jason Wormald, Pauline Lai, and Lily Chu for their help and support with this edition and its two predecessors. In addition, a great many people, but especially my wife Mary, my daughter Christy, her partner Karel, and my parents, deserve thanks for their tolerance over the years (even if it has been limited at times). Ben, Dave, Robyn, and Tyler also again deserve mention. At least one of them will, I hope, at some point, take a course in industrial relations and possibly even use this book, helping to line their Uncle John's pockets. Once more, congratulations to Leanne, for making it to university and excelling against the odds, and to Patrick (the Matrix), for (I hope) hanging in there, again against the odds. But most important, as I write this, Samuel is experiencing his second day after birth. This book will likely be long out of print by the time he will be old enough to read it. However, my great hope is that, along with all of the work I have done over the past two decades, it will in some way have helped to make things just a little bit better by the time he is. In the meantime, it will be great just to have him around.

Foundations
Concepts, Issues, and Debates

1

Industrial relations play an important role in the Canadian economy, with critical implications for workers, for employers, and for society in general. For workers, the terms of their employment, the nature of their work, and the treatment they receive from their employer in large part determine their standard of living, their opportunity for personal growth, their sense of dignity and self-respect, their physical and mental health, and ultimately, "who they are." For employers, worker performance, loyalty, and wage and benefit levels can have critical implications for efficiency, labour costs, product quality, and ultimately the employer's survival and growth. For society in general, the relations between workers and their employers have implications for economic growth, inflation, unemployment, the level and distribution of income and wealth, and, more generally, the overall quality of life.

In view of this importance, it is not surprising that the study of industrial relations has traditionally given rise to a number of issues and debates. For example, some have argued that these relations involve fundamental conflicts, with workers at an inherent disadvantage and labour unions unable to protect them from employer exploitation. Yet others have argued that allowing workers to join labour unions serves to remedy any such disadvantage, enabling them to confront their employers as equals. Still others have argued that there is no such disadvantage to begin with, and that unions only result in lower productivity and artificially high wages, with negative consequences for everyone over the long run.

These issues and debates, coupled with the importance of industrial relations for workers, employers and society, mean that the study of industrial relations requires more than simply learning about various rules, processes, or techniques, whether these involve labour laws, collective bargaining, grievance handling, or specific employer practices. Although these topics are important and are covered in subsequent chapters, there is also a need to develop a more basic understanding of the nature of industrial relations and of related issues and debates. Indeed, the study of these topics is otherwise likely to be inadequate. The starting point for developing such an understanding is, first, to establish a conceptual definition for thinking about industrial relations, then to identify competing perspectives, or ways of thinking, about industrial relations. The purpose of this chapter is to accomplish these two objectives, beginning with the former. Throughout, key terms and concepts appear in bold face — a convention that is followed in subsequent chapters as well. For ease of reference, all such terms and concepts also appear in the Glossary at the end of the book.

I. STUDYING INDUSTRIAL RELATIONS: A CONCEPTUAL FOUNDATION

There have been a number of attempts to define the subject matter of industrial relations as a field of study. Perhaps the broadest definition is "the study of all aspects of people at work" (Kochan, 1980: 1).[1] Yet most texts define the subject matter of industrial relations far narrower than this, focusing almost entirely upon labour law, labour unionism, and collective bargaining. For present purposes, we will adopt a definition, which falls in between the broad and the narrow, as the study of the *relations* between *labour* and *management*. In order to provide a conceptual foundation for studying about Canadian industrial relations, it will be useful to expand at some length upon the components of this definition, beginning with the term "labour".

Who Is "Labour"?

Though somewhat difficult to define precisely (see Arthurs et al., 1993: 213), the term "**labour**" generally refers to all of those working Canadians who are in an employment relation and do *not* exercise substantive authority, but are instead in a position of subordination to those who do. "Substantive" authority includes not only authority over others, but also authority with regard to organizational decisions in

---

[1] See Adams, 1993a, for an excellent discussion of the development and content of the field based upon this definition.

general, provided that it is exercised independently, in a managerial capacity.[2] Under this definition, the term "labour" thus encompasses not only manual workers, but also a great many non-manual and professional workers — including nurses, office workers, teachers, police, social workers, technicians, and other groups sometimes considered to be part of the "middle class". It can even include low level supervisors, provided their function is only to supervise and allocate work and does not involve the actual issuance of commands or the exercise of rewards and punishments. Finally, it encompasses both union and non-union workers.

Though the term "labour" refers to both union and non-union workers, it also encompasses the organizations to which workers, *as workers*, belong. These can be labour unions, independent non-union employee associations, or professional associations. But labour unions are by far and away the principal form of worker organization in Canada. Most simply, **labour unions** are organizations of workers intended primarily to represent and advance the interests and values of their members. While this can encompass a number of functions, labour unions are not legally recognized as such in Canada unless one of their primary purposes is to represent their members through formal negotiations with management representatives, or what is normally referred to as **collective bargaining**.

Union density, or the percent of non-agricultural paid workers who are members of a union, was estimated to be 29.6 percent as of 2010 (Statistics Canada, 2010a). This represents a drop of from 4 to 8 percentage points since union density reached its peak in the early 1980s, depending on the data source one relies on (Godard, 2003a). As one might expect, density is higher for workers in larger workplaces. As of 2010, it was estimated to be 41 percent in workplaces with between 100 and 500 employees, and 54 percent in those with over 500 employees. Density is also estimated to be much higher in the public sector. As of 2010, it was 71 percent in this sector, compared to 16 percent in the private sector. Finally, women now account for half of all union members in Canada (Statistics Canada, 2010a).

It is common to hear the terms "**labour movement**" and "**organized labour**". These terms refer not just to labour unions and their members, but also to **labour federations**. Labour federations are associations of unions, established primarily to represent, coordinate, and

---

[2] Under the law, this serves as the primary distinction between managerial and non-managerial employees and hence as a primary basis for determining whether employees are eligible for union representation rights under the law (see Arthurs et al., 1993: 213).

provide services to member unions at the provincial and national levels. The largest national federation in Canada, whose member unions account for 7 in 10 of all union workers, is the **Canadian Labour Congress** or CLC. However, Canada has a number of smaller national federations, the largest of which is the Quebec-based Confederation of National Trade Unions (CNTU), whose member unions account for roughly one in every fifteen union workers.

Finally, in addition to being affiliated with a national federation, many unions are also affiliated with provincial ones, named after the province in which they are established (e.g., the Manitoba Federation of Labour, or MFL).

Who Is Management?

If labour can be considered to encompass all employed Canadians who do not exercise substantive authority, management can be considered to encompass all employed Canadians who do exercise such authority. Ultimately, managerial authority derives from legal rights attaching to the ownership of work organizations, generally referred to as property rights. With the exception of work organizations managed solely by one or a few individuals, these rights are usually delegated downwards, with authority at each level exercised subject to the authority of those in superordinate positions. Thus, we can think of management as hierarchical, with authority at each level overarching authority at lower levels. This view of management has important implications, for, with the exception of those in the most senior positions, managers typically find themselves in positions of subordination as well as superordination. In other words, in addition to exercising authority over others, others exercise authority over them. Indeed, managers are more often than not employees rather than owners of the organization for which they work. In this sense, they are little different from their non-managerial counterparts working for the same **employer** (the term used to refer to an organization in which people work in return for economic compensation). Yet their job is not just to exercise substantive authority, but to do so on behalf of those who legally own or control the employer, not those over whom it is exercised. This is why the distinction between labour and management is at the core of our conceptual definition.

As for unions, management is often represented by one or more associations. These are especially pervasive in the private sector, and include such broad-based organizations as the Canadian Council of Chief Executives, the Canadian Manufacturers Association (CMA), the

Canadian Federation of Independent Business, and local Chambers of Commerce, to name a few. They can also include narrower-based industry and trade organizations and associations in which a number of employers combine to negotiate a common collective agreement with the union or unions representing their workers. Except in the latter case, these associations do not directly involve themselves *in* labour–management relations, but they often engage in extensive political activities, advocating policies and legal reforms with important implications *for* labour–management relations (e.g., changes in labour law).

What Do We Mean by Relation?

The relationship between labour and management is both an economic and a social one. It is an economic relation because workers in effect sell their ability to work to management, subject to agreed upon terms and conditions of employment. It is a social relation because, in so doing, they agree to submit to managerial authority, complying with managerial rules and directives in the day-to-day performance of their work.

As a social relation, the labour–management relation involves an interplay of cooperation, conflict, power, and authority. It involves **cooperation** in the sense that both parties function jointly to produce particular goods or services, acting largely in accordance with a system or "web" of rules which each party expects the other to adhere to.[3] These rules can be unilaterally imposed by management, or they can be formally negotiated and written into a collective agreement (or individual employment contract), or they can be informally established over time and unwritten, reflecting a "psychological contract" as to the rights and obligations of each party, what is fair and what is not fair, and so forth.[4] They can also involve both matters of substance,

---

[3] The emphasis upon rules has a long history under the institutionalist approach to industrial relations, beginning a century ago in the writings of Sydney and Beatrice Webb (1897). Most notable, however, was John Dunlop's "systems theory" (1958), where the web of rules is defined as the core subject matter of industrial relations. The present discussion, though influenced by Dunlop's systems theory, defines the web of rules more broadly than does this theory, and does not proceed from the same assumptions as do most versions of systems theory.

[4] Perhaps the clearest discussion of the development and role of informal rules and understandings in industrial relations continues to be found in chapter four of Hyman and Brough (1975) and chapter two of Fox (1971). For a discussion of the importance

including how much workers are paid, the amount of effort expected, and the type of discipline meted out for various offences, and matters of procedure, such as how disagreements are to be resolved, the processes by which disciplinary matters are to be handled, and how promotions are to be decided.

The existence of a web of rules provides a basis for cooperation between labour and management. Yet the interests, goals, or expectations of one party can still often differ from those of the other. When they do, and when one party intentionally acts in a way that negatively affects the outcomes of the other, we can say that **conflict** has taken place. For reasons discussed in chapter three, conflict is usually explored with reference to the actions of workers or their unions. Going on strike is probably the most evident form of such conflict, but conflict may also be said to occur when workers engage in various forms of recalcitrance on a day-to-day basis, including absenteeism, slacking, and even sabotage. Quitting or "exit behaviour" may also be viewed as a form of conflict, because it normally entails costs for management. But although conflict is most associated with the actions of workers, management can also engage in various acts of conflict, including forcing a strike or "locking out" workers (i.e., if negotiations break down with the union), disciplining workers for recalcitrant behaviour, and laying workers off. All of these actions tend to reflect conflicting interests and negatively affect workers.

Power can be of central importance in determining how conflicting interests, goals, or expectations are addressed. Though power can be defined in a variety of ways (see Isaac, 1988), the most useful definition for the present is simply "the ability to influence the outcomes of others." Following from this definition, it is useful to distinguish between **labour market power** and **relational power**. Workers can be considered to have high labour market power to the extent that employers in general (i.e., in the labour market) place a high value on their skills and abilities. They can be considered to have high relational power to the extent that what they do once *in* the employment relation can affect employer outcomes. Relational power varies with the extent to which quitting, going on strike, or engaging in recalcitrant behaviour (e.g., slacking) at work entail costs for the employer, as reflected in hiring and training expenses, lost sales, or lower produc-

---

of these rules and understandings as they apply to organizational life in general, see Mills and Murgatroyd (1991). Finally, for a discussion of the "psychological contract" see Rousseau (1995).

tivity. For example, workers in a nuclear power plant can be expected to have considerable relational power, because replacements require extensive training, strikes can be extremely costly due to high levels of capital investment involved, and slacking or sabotage by one or a few individuals can have catastrophic results. In contrast, workers in a low skill garment assembly plant can be expected to have little relational power, because they typically require little training, are readily replaced during a strike, and slacking and sabotage have only a minor effect. Thus, *other things being equal*, we might expect employers to treat the former much more favourably, because the costs of exits, strikes, or recalcitrance which can result from not doing so can be much higher.

Management also has varying amounts of both labour market and relational power. It has labour market power to the extent that the jobs it offers are in demand by job seekers in the labour market, a reflection of the extent to which comparable alternatives are scarce. It has relational power to the extent that it controls outcomes that are of value to workers once they are in the relationship such as pay levels, benefits, job assignments, and hours worked.

Authority entails authorization to make decisions on behalf of those who legally own or control the organization. Most important to the labour–management relationship is managerial authority to issue directives and exact obedience from workers, backed up by the right to exercise sanctions. Yet managerial authority is much broader than this, enabling managers to influence worker behaviour and outcomes in a variety of ways. In particular, management can (and often does) devote considerable resources in an attempt to enhance worker commitment and performance. As discussed in chapter five, this can include workplace design and participation programs intended to elicit more positive work attitudes, recruitment and hiring practices intended to ensure the "appropriate" values and work orientations, and a variety of other practices intended to induce workers to voluntarily act in accordance with managerial purposes. Managerial authority also entails the right to make broader decisions having to do with product development and design, investments in plant and equipment, operating budgets, and other considerations that can have major implications for the growth and viability of a workplace and hence for workers employed in that workplace.

Because of its authority, management is in a dominant position vis-à-vis workers, at least *within* the employment relation. Yet it is important to recognize that this dominance is by no means total. Nor is it unquestioned. If workers do not consider the exercise of authority to be *legitimate*, or in accordance with established rules, understandings, and fairness perceptions, they are more likely to exit, go on strike (if there is a union), or engage in workplace recalcitrance. But whatever the case, the effective exercise of managerial authority generally requires some level of "consent" from workers as well as the threat of discipline (Burawoy, 1979). Thus, the legitimacy of authority is of considerable importance.

Most would agree that cooperation, conflict, power, and authority all play some role in labour–management relations. Where disagreement arises is over the extent to which each is important and why. As noted earlier, there has been considerable debate over the relationship between labour and management in developed economies, with various perspectives on this relationship assigning different levels of importance to various components of this relationship and their implications for workers, management, and ultimately, society. Thus, while our conceptual definition of the subject matter of industrial relations may be useful as a starting point, it is important to be familiar with this debate and the issues it raises.

II.   PERSPECTIVES ON LABOUR–MANAGEMENT RELATIONS

The debate over industrial relations involves competing perspectives or **ideologies**, defined for present purposes as "frameworks of interconnected values, beliefs, and assumptions upon which individuals draw in order to assess the functioning and legitimacy of established institutional arrangements (e.g., labour law) and the desirability of reforms" (Godard, 1992c). In the *study* of industrial relations, these different ideologies tend to be reflected in different "schools" of theory and research, each of which tends to be dominated by a common set of assumptions and beliefs. In the *practice* of industrial relations, they tend to be reflected in the actions of the parties, with important implications for the type of relationship which develops between labour and management over time. However, in this book, concern is primarily with ideological differences in the *study* of industrial relations, for these differences often lie at the heart of various debates to be referred to throughout — whether they involve the development of the economy (chapter two), the nature of management decision-making (chapter six), the functions and effects of unions (chapter seven), government policy-making (chapter nine), the effects of "high performance" management practices (chapter five), or alternatives for the future (chapter sixteen).

At risk of oversimplification, it is possible to identify five different ideological perspectives, each of which can be located along a continuum ranging from "right wing" to "left wing": (1) the neoliberal, (2) the managerialist, (3) the orthodox-pluralist, (4) the liberal-reformist, and (5) the radical. These perspectives all recognize that workers and management can have different goals or interests, but they differ over *the extent to which* this is the case and the ease with which these differences are resolved in a market economy. They also differ over the role of power and conflict, particularly the extent to which conflict is fundamental to industrial relations and either labour or management are at an inherent power disadvantage vis-à-vis the other. Finally, they differ over the impact and effectiveness of labour unions and the need for changes to the current system.

These perspectives will serve as valuable points of reference for addressing various issues and disagreements throughout the remainder of this book and they will be elaborated upon with respect to specific topics as the book proceeds. As such, *it is essential that the reader be familiar with each*. To aid in this task, some of the essential arguments and assumptions of each are outlined in Table 1–1. This table distinguishes between these perspectives on seven characteristics: (1) the primary concern of scholars associated with each; (2) their primary analytical focus; (3) the importance they attribute to power; (4) their assumptions about the extent to which conflict is inherent; (5) their assessment of the need for and impact of unions under collective bargaining; (6) their prescriptions for improving labour–management relations; and (7) their location on the political spectrum, from "right wing" to "left wing".

The Neoliberal Perspective

The neoliberal perspective (see Reynolds, 1984) is most adhered to by conventional economists.[5] The primary concern of these scholars is the maximization of economic efficiency, and their primary analytical focus is on the role of market forces. According to neoliberals, market forces not only drive management to pursue maximum efficiency, they also ensure that workers are fairly and equitably treated.

---

[5] The term "neoliberal" can be confusing, especially because it is normally adhered to by people who support conservative causes and vote for conservative political parties. It may be especially confusing in North America, because in politics the term "liberal" often refers to people who are "left-of-centre", believing in strong unions, employment standards and social programs. In Canada, there is also the Liberal Party, which tends to be

TABLE 1-1 Perspectives on Industrial Relations

Topic/Perspective	Neoliberal	Managerialist	Orthodox Pluralist	Liberal Reformist	Radical
Primary Concern	Maximizing Efficiency	Maximizing Worker Loyalty	Balancing Efficiency and Equity	Elimination of Inequalities and Injustices	Elimination of System-Wide Power Imbalances
Primary Focus	Labour Markets	Managerial Policies and Practices	Labour Unions, Labour Law, and Collective Bargaining	Social Issues/Problems of Workers	Conflict and Control
Importance of Power	Not Important — Remedied by Market Forces	Minor Importance if Management Adopts Progressive Practices	Moderate Importance	Considerable Importance; Primary Source of Inequality	Fundamental Importance; System Wide Power Imbalance Between "Labour" and "Capital"
Extent to Which Conflict is Inherent	Not At All — Remedied by Market Forces	Very Little if Management Adopts Progressive Practices	Moderate; Limited by Overarching Commonalities of Interest	Depends: Low in the "Core"; High in the "Periphery"	Fundamental, Though Varies According to Worker Power
Assessment of Unions under Collective Bargaining	Negative Economic and Social Consequences	Ambivalent; Depends on Willingness of the Parties to Cooperate	Positive "Social" Effects, Neutral Or Even Positive Economic Effects	Ineffective in "Periphery"; Limited Effectiveness in "Core"	Inherently Limited Effectiveness under Capitalism
Prescription	Reduce Government and Union Interference in Markets	Promote Progressive Managerial Practices and Labour–Management Cooperation	Protect Right of Workers to Bargain Collectively; Minimum Standards Legislation	Increased Government Intervention/Labour Law Reforms	Radical Structural Change; Employee Ownership and Control
Political Position	← "RIGHT WING"				"LEFT WING" →

Neoliberals generally view the labour–management relationship as a free and equal exchange between two rational economic actors with different yet compatible goals. According to neoliberals, the forces of supply and demand operate over the long run so as to ensure that neither party is at a disadvantage in relation to the other. Workers are able to obtain terms and conditions of employment commensurate with their skills, abilities, and effort, and ultimately with their productivity. It is possible for workers to receive wages and benefits which exceed what most other employers might offer in the external labour market, but employers offer above-market rates because it induces workers to work harder, thus enhancing efficiency (Akerlof and Yellon, 1986). Employers may also use various incentive devices (e.g., tying pay to performance) in order to achieve this outcome (Lazear, 1986; 1992). But provided that the operation of labour markets and the exercise of managerial authority are not interfered with, and each party fulfills its duties and obligations to the other, efficiency and productivity are maximized. The net effect is that both parties benefit — management through higher profits, and workers through better wages, benefits, and job security.

Because labour market forces ensure that neither party is at a disadvantage, power and conflict should play little role. Where workers are underpaid or treated unfairly, they are always free to quit and find another job. As a result, there is little role for unions. Indeed, unions only upset this relationship, in effect constituting a monopoly which prevents management from dealing with workers individually. This upsets the balance of labour market forces so that management is at a power disadvantage, with unions artificially inflating wages (and hence prices), interfering with management authority, and ultimately harming the competitive position of the employer and hence the job security of workers.[6]

---

centrist even if it is not always clear exactly what it stands for. But the term "liberal" has traditionally referred to the belief that there should minimal government involvement in the economy, allowing markets and private decision makers to operate without outside interference. It has also been closely associated with "laisser faire" or "neoclassical" economics. "Neo" simply refers to "new", so neoliberal refers to the most recent version of this perspective. In turn, the term "liberal reformist" (see below) is in this book used to refer to a "left-of-centre" perspective. This is consistent with the common, political usage of the term "liberal".

[6] This, of course, applies to the private sector. In the public sector, the ultimate result, according to neoliberals, is higher taxation and/or deficits.

In addition, employment standards, such as the minimum wage, only have negative effects because they either interfere with efficiency or force employers to pay workers more than they are worth (as determined by market forces), ultimately lowering the ability of such workers to find a job.

The Managerialist Perspective

The managerialist perspective is adhered to by most organizational behaviour and human resource management specialists. While neo-liberals concern themselves primarily with the operation of markets, believing that markets ensure both efficiency for employers and equitable treatment for employees, managerialists are more concerned with maximizing worker motivation and commitment once in the employment relation. To this end, their primary focus is on managerial policies and practices towards workers.

Managerialists typically argue that it is possible to achieve high levels of motivation and commitment if management adopts the appropriate policies and practices. As is discussed more fully in chapter five, these policies and practices include the provision of good wages and benefits, ensuring that workers are treated fairly and equitably, and implementing various workplace participation and job redesign practices. If these policies and practices are properly implemented, management can expect high productivity, low quit rates and absenteeism, and the eradication of various other behavioural "problems". Thus, the interests of workers and management are generally harmonious.

Managerialists tend to be ambivalent towards both unions and employment standards. They seem to believe that unions should be avoided because they can threaten managerial authority and introduce uncertainty and adversariness into the labour–management relationship. But they also seem to believe that, where unions are established, management should accept them as a fact of life and seek to establish a cooperative relationship with union leaders. They have also increasingly argued that traditional, "adversarial" unionism is obsolete, and that only those unions that are willing to adopt a cooperative approach are likely to survive in the future.

With regard to employment standards, managerialists generally believe that these should be minimal because it is in the interests of employers to treat workers fairly. Where established, they should be designed to encourage voluntary compliance and should allow for as much flexibility as is possible.

The Orthodox-Pluralist Perspective

The orthodox-pluralist perspective has traditionally been adhered to by economists and industrial relations scholars adopting a traditional institutionalist approach[7] (see Katz and Kochan, 1992: 2–9) and reflects the traditional philosophy underlying labour law in North America (see chapter eleven). The primary concern of orthodox pluralists is to find a balance between the need for efficiency in the economy and the need for equity and fairness in employment relations (see Meltz, 1989), and their primary focus has traditionally been on the institutions of labour law, labour unionism, and collective bargaining (see, for example, Peirce, 2000).

Orthodox pluralists place greater emphasis on conflict than do managerialists, arguing that the concerns of workers for equitable and fair treatment can conflict with the concerns of management for efficiency and organizational effectiveness (Kochan and Katz, 1988: 6–7; Meltz, 1989). At the same time, they also tend to believe that conflict is limited to a "subset of issues" (e.g., income and job security) and that the parties have "a common overarching interest in successfully resolving issues arising from their conflicting interests" (Kochan and Katz, 1988: 7).

The problem is that, as individuals, workers often find themselves at a power disadvantage relative to management, for they often confront a "scarcity of opportunities" in the labour market and often have limited choice as to the type of job they take and few alternatives if they quit. Labour unions and collective bargaining help to remedy this imbalance, enabling workers to confront their employers as equals, and creating a form of "industrial democracy" (Leiserson, 1973). Not only is this desirable on moral grounds, it also has positive implications for worker morale and hence ultimately for turnover and productivity, thus helping to offset the higher wages and benefits which unions win for their members (Freeman and Medoff, 1984). Thus, labour unions and collective bargaining should represent the primary means through which workers can achieve equity and fairness at work. There is also need of minimum employment standards. But these should be limited and play a secondary role, designed to ensure minimum levels

---

[7] Because it is most associated with the institutionalist approach, many refer to this as the "institutionalist" perspective. However, the term institutionalist has come over the years to refer to a number of different perspectives, primarily because it also refers to a particular approach to the analysis of the economy (see, for example, Hodgson, 1988). Accordingly, in this book, it refers to an approach rather than a perspective.

of equity and fairness for those who, for one reason or another, do not have union representation.

The Liberal-Reformist Perspective

The liberal-reformist perspective is adhered to by more critical, reform-oriented academics and activists concerned with reducing or eliminating inequalities and injustices in the treatment afforded workers (see, for example, Bowles, Gordon, and Weisskopf, 1983; Drache and Glasbeek, 1992; Adams, 1995). It is perhaps the least cohesive of the five perspectives, but it generally entails a focus on such problems as discrimination, inequality, layoffs and plant closings, inadequate wages and benefits, hazardous working conditions, and weaknesses in the established system of labour law and collective bargaining. In focusing on these problems, liberal reformists adopt a more critical orientation than do adherents to the former three perspectives, who typically view these problems as either less important or less pervasive than do liberal reformists. For liberal reformists, the continued existence of a large number of jobs in which workers are subject to poor wages and working conditions is evidence that the arguments advanced under each of these perspectives just do not hold up in practice — regardless of how good they may sound in theory.

Liberal-reformists tend to be highly supportive of labour unions and collective bargaining, but they are at the same time often highly critical of the system within which unions currently operate. Their general argument is that, under this system, unions tend to be least effective in workplaces where workers are most in need of assistance. In these workplaces, worker power is typically low, and employers are often unable to grant substantial concessions because of competitive conditions. Thus, unions meet with intensive management opposition and are often unable to achieve many gains for their members. Yet liberal reformists also view unions as of limited effectiveness even in larger, more dominant firms, arguing that they too often fail to win strong enough rights and protections for their members or a real say in decisions which critically affect them. They have become especially concerned about this in recent years, as globalization has enabled major employers to close up shop and move if they become unhappy with wage and benefit or performance levels.

For liberal reformists, the only solution is government policies and strong employment standards that ensure decent terms and conditions of employment for all workers. This would include, for example, a strengthening of minimum wage laws, better health and safety standards, and stronger protections against unfair, arbitrary, or discriminatory treatment at work. Unions would continue to play a central role, but this role would be as much one of helping to implement and enforce these standards as of negotiating improved terms and conditions of employment.

The Radical Perspective

The radical perspective is even more critical than the liberal-reformist perspective. Radicals share many of the same concerns as do liberal reformists, though they focus much more on the role of broader sources of conflict believed to be fundamental to all capitalist economies and the implications of these sources for industrial relations (Braverman, 1974; Edwards, 1979; Hyman, 1987; Kelly, 1998). They also believe that the problems identified by liberal reformists are virtually endemic to capitalist economies and hence that liberal reforms, though laudable, can be of only limited effectiveness.

Radicals maintain that, in the economy in general, the interests of "**labour**", as represented by workers, and those of "**capital**", as represented by those who own and manage work organizations, are, on the whole, diametrically opposed. This opposition is especially apparent in labour–management relations, where it is in the interests of capital to exploit workers, extracting a maximum of effort for a minimum cost, and where workers find themselves at an inherent disadvantage due to their limited opportunities. Thus, conflict underlies the labour–management relationship, and is far more fundamental than proponents of other perspectives assume, extending beyond narrow issues having to do with income and job security to the workplace itself and ultimately to broader labour-capital conflicts in the economy as a whole.

In order to reduce labour costs and maximize worker effort and conformity, management designs and structures the workplace so as to reduce the skills required of workers and minimize their discretion — at least to the extent possible given the nature of the product or service produced and the available technologies (Braverman, 1974). Management also seeks to control the behaviour of workers through a combination of manipulation and coercion (Burawoy, 1979). In this respect, "progressive" policies and practices simply reflect a more sophisticated strategy of control than do more traditional authoritarian methods (Friedman, 1977; Fantasia, Clawson, and Graham, 1988; Wells, 1987). These policies are seldom totally effective, for the very reason that conflict always underlies the labour–management relationship. However, they tend to be reinforced by implicit pro-capital biases in the media and educational systems, thus creating a capitalist "hegemony" (dominance) through which workers accept the legitimacy of the established system, thus forestalling any serious or widespread challenge to this system. Conflict thus tends to be limited and is confined largely to the workplace.

According to radicals, unions are of only limited effectiveness as long as they attempt to work within the confines of a capitalist economic system (see Hyman, 1975: 94–121). While they may win a number of improvements for workers, these can never be very great. With respect to smaller employers, union gains are limited by competitive constraints. Larger employers are less constrained in this respect, but always possess the ability to close down and relocate operations if union demands get out of hand. Moreover, individual unions can do little to protect workers against technological changes and international competition, which are often based more upon labour cost advantages than productivity per se. For unions to make a real difference, it is necessary for them to raise worker consciousness as to their rights and potential alternatives, and in so doing build a broader "oppositional" movement which can ultimately challenge the dominance of capital. One author has referred to this as "movement unionism" (Gindin, 1997).

Finally, radicals tend to believe that strong employment standards would be desirable, but that governments are unduly influenced by employers (see chapter nine), with the result that these standards are too often weak and poorly enforced. They also believe that, even if strong standards could be established, they would fall far short of the sorts of changes necessary to achieve a truly egalitarian and democratic society.

Implications

It should be clear that the debate over labour–management relations raises a number of important issues, including the efficacy of market forces, the nature of the labour–management relationship, the role and effectiveness of managerial policies, the desirability and impact of labour unions, and the need for government policy and law reforms. It is unlikely that these issues can ever be fully resolved, for they typically involve deeply engrained values and beliefs not readily amenable to change. Nonetheless, each perspective can contribute to our understanding of labour relations, by alerting us to and focusing upon different aspects of these relations: neoliberals focus primarily on market forces; managerialists on management practices; orthodox pluralists on the institutions of labour law, labour unionism and collective bargaining; liberal reformists on power inequalities within and across firms; and radicals upon the importance of underlying conflicts. Thus, these perspectives all have important implications for the study of industrial relations.

The Assumptions Underlying This Book

Although the five perspectives identified above will be referred to extensively throughout the remainder of the book, the book *does* develop certain arguments and conclusions of its own. These are as follows:

1. When Canadians enter into an employment relation, they subordinate themselves to the authority of those who own or control the organization. Their status becomes that of a "human" resource, but a resource nonetheless, to be employed as an instrument for employer ends. As a result, the nature of the employment relation gives rise to problems of trust and commitment and to possible conflicts over the terms and conditions of employment, including over how employer authority is exercised. This can be manifest through quitting, strike activity, and recalcitrant behaviour, such as insubordination, slacking on the job, sabotage, and high levels of voluntary absenteeism (see chapter three). Although the extent to which this is the case can vary considerably, problems of trust and commitment, and the sources of conflict associated with them, always underlie the employment relation. They tend to be worsened by "contextual" sources of conflict, including economic insecurity and stress, inequalities in wealth and income, and other problems.

2. Managerial policies and practices can make an important difference in the attainment of worker trust and commitment and hence in achieving harmonious labour–management relations. But they cannot eliminate the problems of trust and commitment or the sources of conflict that arise from the nature of the employment relation, and their effectiveness is, partly as a result, often lower than their proponents assume.

3. The extent to which it is within the capacity or interests of employers to adopt progressive policies and practices can vary

considerably, depending in large measure on the extent to which workers have high levels of labour market and relational power. Where employers require highly qualified workers with skills that are in short supply, and where dissatisfied employees are able to impose high costs on the employer through quitting, striking, or performing poorly, it is more likely to be in the employer's interest to adopt these policies and practices. But to the extent that these conditions do not hold, employers are less likely to provide favourable terms and conditions of employment.

4. Unions can and do serve a number of functions in the economy beyond simply improving the wages and benefits of their members. Of particular importance is the provision of democratic rights and protections at work, helping to ensure that their members have meaningful representation in the determination of the terms and conditions of their employment and that they are treated fairly by their employer. Although unions may also have negative economic effects, the extent to which this is the case varies. Any such effects do not appear to outweigh the positive functions of unions. The real problem is that the Canadian system of labour law and collective bargaining tends to foster unduly adversarial relations between unions and management and to often limit the effectiveness of unions. In addition, only three in ten Canadian workers are currently represented by a union. Within the Canadian context, this means that a majority of workers lack the kind of rights and protections that one would expect of an advanced democracy.

5. There is need for governments to establish stronger rights and protections for workers. Although many employers already provide their employees with relatively good terms and conditions of employment, and although labour unions play an important role in ensuring that such terms and conditions are established, too many Canadians continue to be subject to poverty-level wages, with few, if any, benefits, and to often coercive employer practices. Employees should not in any case have to rely on their employer or on a union to ensure that they have basic rights and protections at work. Rather, these rights and protections should be enshrined in law and apply to virtually all workers, regardless of who they work for or whether they have a union. They should include a minimum wage that equals or exceeds the poverty level, rights to decent benefits (e.g., pensions, holidays), universal grievance and arbitration rights in the event of unfair treatment,

participation and consultation rights and, most important, collective representation in some form to ensure that these and other rights are effectively realized.

It should be stressed that these positions represent a particular understanding of industrial relations. They are intended not to impose a singular point of view but rather to provide a frame of reference against which the reader can develop his or her own understanding of the subject matter. Thus, rather than passively accepting these positions, the reader is encouraged to think about them critically, accepting, rejecting or modifying them accordingly.

III. CONCLUSIONS

This chapter has provided a foundation for the study of industrial relations. First, it has provided a conceptual definition intended to familiarize readers with the primary actors (labour and management), the relationship between them, and both the nature and importance of the context within which this relationship occurs. Second, it has identified and briefly described five different perspectives brought to bear in the study of labour–management relations, and outlined the assumptions underlying this book. The following chapter picks up where this one leaves off, addressing the broader debate over the nature and development of industrial relations, the economy, and society.

The Broader Debate
Three Theses on the Nature and Development of Industrial Relations, the Economy, and Society

2

The preceding chapter outlined five competing perspectives for studying industrial relations. In doing so, emphasis was placed upon the *relationship* between labour and management, especially the amount of conflict underlying this relationship, the balance of power between the parties, and the effects and effectiveness of labour unions and collective bargaining. This chapter will go beyond the debate over labour–management relations per se to the broader debate over the nature and development of western economies as a whole. This debate is important because it focuses upon the broader context within which labour–management relations take place and provides important insights into why they have developed as they have over the past century. Discussing this debate also sets the stage for chapters three and four, the former of which establishes a foundation for understanding labour–management relations, and the latter addresses the history and development of labour–management relations in Canada.

As is the case for the competing perspectives discussed in chapter one, a number of theories or schools can be identified within the broader debate over the nature and development of western economies, each of which suffers its own internal disagreements. However, the present purpose is best served by confining the discussion to three schools, presenting a particular version of each, and downplaying internal disagreements. These schools can be referred to as: (1) the capitalism thesis, (2) the industrialism thesis, and (3) the industrial capitalism thesis. As their names suggest, the capitalism thesis attributes the nature and development of western economies primarily to the underlying nature of capitalism, and, in particular, to the private ownership of work organizations; the industrialism thesis attributes it primarily to the processes of industrialization over the past century or so, making little reference to the role of capitalism in these processes; and the industrial capitalism thesis attributes it to the nature of capitalism and to processes of industrialization combined, viewing both as important to explaining the nature and development of western economies.

Each of these theses has a long tradition in social thought, largely drawing from the works of Karl Marx, Emile Durkheim, and Max Weber, respectively. Much of the discussion below follows from the work of these authors: though all three wrote at or before the turn of the twentieth century, the basic themes advanced by each continue to be reflected in debates about contemporary economic and social developments and their implications for industrial relations — as shall become apparent in later chapters. They also form the intellectual backdrop within which the competing perspectives outlined in the preceding chapter have developed. Generally, the capitalism thesis is reflected in the radical perspective, the industrialism thesis in both the orthodox pluralist and the managerial perspectives, and the industrial capitalism thesis in the liberal-reformist perspective.

Of note, none of the three theses discussed in this chapter is reflected in the neoliberal perspective. That perspective *does* have a long intellectual tradition, beginning primarily with Adam Smith's *Wealth of Nations*, first published in 1776. Central to this tradition is the general assumption that capitalism brings with it steadily improving standards of living provided that "free" competition is encouraged and there are few restrictions on the exercise of management authority. Yet this assumption falls short of providing a well developed general thesis on the nature and development of the economy and of society (see Swedberg, Himmelstrand, and Brulin, 1990).[1]

I.   KARL MARX AND THE CAPITALISM THESIS

Though there has been a large number of contributors to the capitalism thesis, Karl Marx is without question its founder. Marx's major works were completed in the mid-nineteenth century, often in collabo-

---

[1]   There have been a number of attempts to explain how and why the economy has developed as it has which are in many respects sympathetic to the general assumptions of the neoliberal tradition. Most notable is the work of Alfred Chandler (1977) and of Oliver Williamson (1975). However, these do not provide general theses as to the nature and development of the economy and society, serving more as explanations for the emergence of large scale organizations within the economy. They also fall outside of neoclassical economics, and as such are variously referred to as the "new institutional economics" and the "economics of organizations". Indeed, they in some respects bear closer ties with the industrialism thesis. Thus, they do not provide a distinctive thesis of the sort considered in this chapter.

ration with his friend and associate, Frederick Engels. In many ways, these works reflect an outrage against the deplorable living and working conditions of large segments of the British working class[2] (see in particular, Marx, 1967 [1867]: 654–712), and a commitment to the revolutionary overthrow of the capitalist institutions which Marx blamed for these conditions. As a result, Marx's name has been associated with a variety of revolutionary causes over the past century and a half, and there are many who dismiss his work on the grounds that it is misguided, outdated, or subversive. Yet it is important to disentangle that which Marx actually wrote from that which is often assumed under his name. It is also important to separate (to the extent possible) the moral from the analytical components of Marx's work, for there is much of analytical value to be garnered from the work of Marx and subsequent analyses in the Marxist tradition. Thus, the focus below is on the analytical contribution of Marx's work. It is this contribution which continues to provide the foundation of the capitalism thesis.[3]

Class and Class Conflict

At the core of Marx's work — and the work of most subsequent contributors to the capitalism thesis — is the belief that two basic classes define capitalism: the working class or "proletariat", and the capitalist class or "bourgeoisie". The distinction between these classes is relatively simple: members of the capitalist class own or control productive assets or the "means of production", while members of the working class do not, and hence are coerced to sell their labouring capacity to capitalists if they are to earn a living. Other "classes" can of course also exist under capitalism (e.g., landed aristocracy, farmers), but it is the relationship between these two classes which constitutes the central driving force underlying the nature and development of capitalist societies (see Harvey, 1982: 24ff).[4]

---

[2] Though Marx was German, rigid censorship forced him to leave Germany, first, for France, and then, for England, where he completed most of his major works.

[3] In doing so I will avoid what has come to be referred to as "post-Marxism" and the debate surrounding it (see Wood, 1986).

[4] Proponents of the capitalism thesis have had some difficulty establishing how managers fit within this two class distinction, for they appear to be in a "contradictory" position (Wright, 1985), not owning the means of production yet exercising authority on behalf of those who do. Some argue that they can for simplifying purposes be viewed as "agents" of capitalists, while others argue that their contradictory position has important implications for how they exercise authority. The actual purposes to which managerial authority are exercised has been a source of considerable disagreement more generally, and will be

According to Marx, the relationship between the capitalist and the working class is one of contradiction. Each is dependent upon the other — indeed, the very existence of each presupposes the existence of the other (see Marx and Engels, 1958 [1847]). Yet there is a fundamental conflict between the interests of capitalists and those of workers: where it is in the interests of capitalists to minimize wages while extracting a maximum amount of labour from workers, the interests of workers are just the opposite. Thus, we can see that, within capitalism, there are forces which push workers and capitalists together (their mutual dependence) and forces which at the same time pull them apart (their conflicting interests).

Exploitation

Equally important, workers are at a fundamental disadvantage vis-à-vis capitalists, for unemployment is endemic to capitalism, creating an "industrial reserve army" of workers (Marx, 1967 [1867]: 487, 632), who, as a result, must compete with one another for employment, enabling employers to bid down wages to the minimum, socially established level necessary for workers and their families to function in society.[5] The result is that workers are inherently exploited, for the wages necessary to sustain them are substantially less than the value of their labour. The famous illustration of this, as advanced by Marx, is that, when the worker comes into work, his or her first three or four hours on the job produce enough value to pay for his or her wages; for the rest of the working day he or she produces value that is appropriated by the employer (1967 [1867]: 217). This value is what Marxists refer to as "surplus value", for it is what is "left over" after the costs of production are subtracted from the proceeds. Its extraction from workers is a necessary condition of capitalism, for without surplus

---

discussed more fully in the next section of this chapter, as well as in chapters three and six.

[5] A common understanding of Marx is that he believed workers would always earn only enough for a bare subsistence. *The Communist Manifesto*, written by Marx and Engels in 1848, does suggest that this is the case (1972 [1848]: 347). However, this was a polemical work directed at the working class, and most scholars dismiss it as such. In his major scholarly work, *Capital*, Marx was quite aware that the living standards of workers could improve over the course of capitalism. For Marx, this would reflect socially established expectations about the minimum level of consumption acceptable. However, wages would still fall below the productive or "exchange" value of a worker's output, and there would be a widening of the gap between the wages of workers and the income of capitalists, reflecting an increase over time in the rate of "relative exploitation". See Marx, 1967 [1867]: 171–72; 523–24.

value, capitalists would not realize a return on their investments and hence the "raison d'être" of capitalism — the pursuit of profit — would not exist.

Of course, to make this argument in this way is somewhat oversimplified, for the wages of workers are not the only costs of production: there are also costs of machinery and equipment, energy, and so forth. According to Marx, however, these other factors of production embody "dead" or "indirect" labour, for they too are produced by workers — even if these workers are employed by other capitalists. Thus, within the economy as a whole, surplus value represents the difference between the proceeds from production and the costs of labour (1967 [1867]: 208).

Alienation

In addition to being exploited, workers are also alienated, lacking a sense of meaning or purpose in life and feeling estranged from both their inner selves and their fellow human beings. This happens for two basic reasons.[6] The first has to do with the requirement that they sell their labour in order to earn a living. According to Marx, the unique characteristic or "essence" of human beings — that which sets them apart from other forms of life — is their ability to create, and it is through productive labour that they are able to realize this ability and hence to develop and express themselves as unique human beings (Marx, 1959 [1844]: 68). Ideally, therefore, what individuals produce is very much an extension of their selves. But under capitalism, workers must sell their productive capacity in the labour market, as if it is like any other commodity or object external to them. Because of this, their labour is no longer their own, and their creative capacity becomes alien to them. Thus, they become alienated from their selves:

> ...in his (sic) work, [the worker] does not affirm himself but denies himself, does not feel content but unhappy, does not develop freely his physical and mental energy but mortifies his body and ruins his mind. The worker therefore feels himself outside his work, and **in his work feels outside himself** ... His labour is therefore not voluntary, but coerced ... It belongs to another, **it is his loss of his self** (1959 [1844]: 66, emphasis added).

---

6 Marx's writings on alienation appear throughout his work, though in his later works (e.g., *Capital*) he often refers to the "degradation" of labour instead. Perhaps as a result, there have been a number of different versions of Marx's understanding of alienation — perhaps the most sophisticated of which is Ollman, 1971. The understanding presented here is much less sophisticated and is perhaps most consistent with Giddens, 1971.

The second reason for alienation has to do with work itself. Here, Marx distinguishes between "**formal subordination**" and "**real subordination**" (1967 [1867]: 510). Under the former, workers are formally under the authority of capitalists, but may retain considerable control over the process by which they perform their work. Under the latter, this control is lost, with capitalists dictating both how they are to perform their work and at what pace. According to Marx, attempts by capitalists to increase the amount of labour extracted from workers — referred to as the "**intensification of the labour process**" (1967 [1867]: 409) — heighten the degree of real subordination. The alienation of workers is thus heightened, with the division of labour serving "to mutilate [the worker] into a fragment of a man (sic), degrade him to the level of an appendage of a machine, destroy the content of work by his agony, and alienate him from the intellectual potentialities of the labour process (1967 [1867]: 645)."[7]

These two sources of alienation mean that workers not only become estranged from their selves, they also develop a sense of meaninglessness in their work and their lives, a feeling of powerlessness about their ability to "make a difference", and a sense of isolatedness from their fellow human beings. These four conditions — self-estrangement, meaninglessness, powerlessness, and isolatedness — are in essence the subjective or social psychological manifestations of alienation, becoming increasingly prevalent throughout the development of capitalism.

Labour Unions, the State, and Ideology

To portray workers as both exploited and alienated is not, of course, to portray them as entirely passive. But according to Marx and subsequent proponents of the capitalism thesis, their ability to improve upon their condition is severely constrained within capitalism (Hyman, 1975: 94–120). Unions, for example, can help workers guard against further "encroachments" by capital (Marx, 1958 [1965]: 443), and they can provide a basis for broader working class movements. But as long as capitalism exists, workers remain at a serious disadvantage: it is workers who "go hungry" in the event of a strike, not capitalists. Moreover, capital is much more transformable than is the labour of workers: it

---

[7]   Adam Smith, whose *Wealth of Nations* is a major progenitor of the neoliberal perspective, arrived at a similar conclusion almost a century earlier, as Marx discusses at some length. See Marx, 1967 [1867]: 362.

can be converted into financial instruments and moved into alternative forms of investment if need be. Thus, for workers to seek more than minor concessions from employers is akin to shooting themselves in the foot, for they will eventually find themselves out of a job.

Government is of little help here, for the state is essentially an instrument of the capitalist class, serving to protect and reinforce the property rights of capitalists (Marx and Engels, 1972 [1848]: 151).[8] Though the state can and often does introduce reforms which improve the working and living conditions of workers, these reforms are typically weak and do not substantially threaten the interests of the capitalist class, for this class controls the "life blood" of the economy (investment).

Perhaps equally important is the ownership and control by capitalists of the media, enabling them to ensure that the point of view presented is conducive to the interests of the capitalist class, and that public opinion is shaped accordingly. As Marx and Engels phrase it, "the class which has the means of material production at its disposal has control at the same time over the means of intellectual production, so that thereby, generally speaking, the ideas of those who lack the means of intellectual production are subject to it" (cited in Giddens, 1971: 41). Marx also argues that "[i]n the course of capitalist production, there comes into existence a working class which, by education, tradition, and custom, is induced to regard the demands of [the capitalist] method of production as self evident laws of nature" (cited in Fox, 1974: 219). This in turn helps to ensure public policies consistent with capitalist interests, while misleading workers into believing that attempts to alter the status quo are ultimately against their better interests.

Unfortunately for members of the capitalist class, as Marx sees it, they are living on borrowed time. There are two related reasons for this: the first is the gradual polarization of class relations, while the second is the tendency of capitalist economies towards recurring economic crises.

The Polarization of Classes

According to Marx, there are at least four reasons for the polarization of classes over time. First, because large firms are more powerful eco-

---

[8] Marx did not have a great deal to say about the state, and there has been a considerable amount of debate among Marxist scholars as to the role and functioning of the state (see Orum, 1988). Part of this debate is discussed in chapter ten.

nomically and enjoy certain economies of scale, they are able to drive smaller competitors out of business. Not only does this further the concentration of power, it also means that smaller capitalists are driven into the ranks of the working class (Marx, 1967 [1867]: 625–28). As such, the capitalist class becomes both smaller in size and comprised of an increasingly wealthy membership.

Second, as the capitalist factory system expands and becomes dominated by large capitalists, workers find themselves increasingly concentrated into large workplaces. As a result, they become increasingly conscious of themselves as a distinctive class.

Third, in order to maximize their profits, capitalists are always seeking ways to improve productivity through the introduction of more capital intensive machinery and the intensification of the labour process (Marx, 1967 [1867]: 387). As a result, there is a tendency for skill differences to decline within the working class, as a growing number of workers find themselves displaced from manufacturing and performing lower-skilled "unproductive" labour in the service sector, and as those remaining in the manufacturing sector find themselves tending machines rather than performing more skilled trade work:

> The life-long specialty of handling one and the same tool now becomes the life-long specialty of serving one and the same machine. In this way, not only are the expenses of his [the worker's] reproduction considerably lessened, but at the same time his helpless dependence on the factory as a whole, and therefore upon the capitalist, is rendered complete (Marx, 1967 [1867]: 422).

By eliminating the need for skilled trades workers and hence the skill differences within the working class as a whole, the potential for a unified working class is further enhanced.

Fourth, though increases in productivity may, over time, come to be reflected in increases in the standard of living for the working class as a whole, these are smaller than are corresponding increases in the surplus value extracted by capitalists (Marx, 1967 [1867]: 523). Thus, the gap between workers and capitalists is widened further, again furthering the polarization of classes.

According to Marx, growing class polarization sets the stage for working class unrest and ultimately for a revolution. But though class polarization is an ongoing tendency of capitalist economies, it becomes especially pervasive during economic downturns. In this respect, Marx argues that capitalist economies are prone to economic crises, and that these crises become worse over time, ultimately creating the conditions for the demise of capitalism.

The Economic Crises of Capitalism

Marx's theory of crisis is a complex and controversial one, but it in essence argues that there is a chronic excess of supply over demand in capitalist economies. This stands to reason, as the working class is paid for and hence can purchase only part of what it produces. The surplus accruing to capitalists can be disposed of in a number of profitable ways, but eventually it comes to be realized in the form of surplus production capacity. When this occurs, the returns to capital (i.e., profits) decline, and smaller, financially weaker firms either fail or are substantially devalued and taken over by their larger, more powerful counterparts. But even larger firms are not immune to the effects of economic downturns, and, because of this, these downturns also pressure these capitalists to find ways to enhance the surplus value extracted per worker. As a result, they spur an increase in the rate at which machines are adopted and induce capitalists to reorganize the labour process so as to raise the degree of real subordination and lower worker skill requirements more rapidly than would otherwise be the case.

The results of these adjustments are both short- and long-term. Over the short term, surplus capacity is reduced and per unit labour costs are lowered, thereby generating the conditions for profitable growth and ending the crisis: to use contemporary management verbiage, firms are "leaner and meaner". But the long-run effects are less happy ones: the absorption of small capitalists by large ones results in a growing concentration of economic power in the hands of a smaller and smaller capitalist elite, while the progressive "rationalization" of the labour process reduces worker wage and skill differentials, thereby breaking down internal working class divisions. Equally important, each crisis grows worse and worse, as capitalists find it increasingly difficult to find new ways of enhancing profits (Marx, 1953 [1858]: 749–50). Ultimately, the system reaches a state of permanent crisis, at which point a unified working class emerges out of the labour movement, and revolution — either peaceful or violent — becomes inevitable. In Marx's words, "the knell of private property sounds. The expropriators are expropriated" (Marx, 1967 [1867]: 763).

Implications

This is an oversimplified account of the capitalism thesis, especially because subsequent authors adhering to this thesis have offered a number of different interpretations, critiques, and modifications to Marx's work. Of particular note is the work of "regulation" and "social-structures of accumulation" theorists, both of whom have attempted to explain why capitalist economies entered into a period of relative stability and substantially improved living standards in the post-World War II era, a development which appears contrary to Marx's crisis theory (see Aglietta, 1979; Lipietz, 1987; Kotz, McDonough, and Reich, 1994). Also of note is a burgeoning debate on the "capitalist state" (see Wood, 1986; Jessop, 1990). Finally, and perhaps most relevant for the study of industrial relations, is a now massive literature on managerial attempts to "de-skill" and enhance their control over workers in the "labour process", sparked primarily by Harry Braverman's *Labor and Monopoly Capital*, published in 1974. This literature will be returned to in subsequent chapters. At present, the purpose has been to familiarize students with the general content of the capitalism thesis and to illustrate its value as one explanation for why conflict and worker alienation often seem to pervade labour–management relations, how these "problems" are linked to the broader political economy of capitalism, and what the implications of these linkages are for the present and future. Yet, as shall become clear, the industrialism thesis provides quite a different understanding of contemporary arrangements.

II. EMILE DURKHEIM AND THE INDUSTRIALISM THESIS

The industrialism thesis coincides with a long tradition of thought in western societies. Sometimes referred to as "structural functionalism", this tradition assumes that (i) societies develop in ways that are functional for all of their members, and (ii) order and progress, rather than conflict and stagnation, represent the natural course of economic and social development (e.g., see Parsons and Smelser, 1956). Emile Durkheim, a French sociologist writing at the turn of the twentieth century, can be considered as a major contributor to this tradition. Particularly important is his *Division of Labour in Society*, published in 1893. But though this book can be viewed as an important precursor to the industrialism thesis, this thesis was not to become fully developed until the mid-twentieth century, long after Durkheim's death. Thus, while Marx's work can be equated with the capitalism thesis, Durkheim's cannot be equated with the industrialism thesis, and hence will be considered separately, before elaborating on the industrialism thesis itself.

Emile Durkheim and the Division of Labour

In *The Division of Labour*, Durkheim in essence argues that the growth of working class movements and the emergence of class conflict during the nineteenth century reflected problems associated with the transition from a pre-industrial to an industrial society. In pre-industrial society, the division of labour is low and hence there is little differentiation between people (Durkheim, 1964 [1893]: 70). In any given community, individuals generally perform similar activities and undergo similar life experiences. As a result, they develop a common identity and "collective conscience", consisting of a "totality of beliefs and sentiments common to average citizens" (1964 [1893]: 79). It is through this collective conscience that social order is maintained, resulting in a condition referred to as "mechanical solidarity". As society industrializes, however, there is a growing division of labour, and, as a result, people become increasingly differentiated in both status and occupation. With this differentiation, their life experiences become increasingly dissimilar and they tend to develop a "personal conscience", thereby eroding the collective conscience and hence the basis for mechanical solidarity (1964 [1893]: 172). Yet, individuals also find themselves increasingly interdependent, relying more and more on the goods and services of others (1964 [1893]: 228). Because of this interdependence, there is need for coordination and cooperation, and society becomes much more like a biological organism or "system of organs, each of which has a special role and which are themselves formed of differentiated parts" (1964 [1893]: 190–93). This provides the basis for a new form of social order, referred to by Durkheim as "organic solidarity".

According to Durkheim, therefore, it is "normal" for organic solidarity to supplant mechanical solidarity. But this transition is not always a smooth one, particularly if "external inequalities", or inequalities attributable to social and economic background rather than "internal" characteristics (e.g., intelligence), are allowed to persist. To the extent that this is the case, the division of labour is "forced", for less advantaged individuals are unable to realize their innate potential (1964 [1893]: 375). As a result, a "pervasive egoism" develops, in which individuals and groups pursue only their own interests, with little concern for the interests or needs of others. Accompanying this egoism is a state of "anomie" or normlessness, under which individuals have little sense of belongingness or moral purpose in life.

For Durkheim, class conflict is a manifestation or "pathology" of the forced division of labour and the concomitant breakdown of mechanical solidarity associated with the transformation from pre-industrial to industrial society. In other words, it is not attributable to the institutions of capitalism, but rather is a transitory phenomenon attributable to the industrialization process. Once external inequalities are reduced, the stage is set for a new era of organic solidarity, one in which the individual is able to realize his/her true potential and develop a sense of meaning and moral purpose within the social whole. Particularly important in this respect is the emergence and development of occupational groups and associations, which provide individuals with a source of identity and serve as a basis for moral regulation. These groups and associations essentially mediate between the individual and what would otherwise be an impersonal, mass society.

Durkheim's optimism about the development of industrial societies has been echoed by a large number of authors throughout the twentieth century. Indeed, by the 1950s and 1960s, the industrialism thesis[9] — as it came to be known — was widely accepted, with many authors maintaining that the problems experienced by western capitalist societies earlier in the century had by-and-large been resolved. There are two general variants of this thesis, referred to for present purposes as "the industrial society" thesis and the "post-industrial society" thesis. Below, each is considered in turn.

The Industrial Society Thesis

The industrial society thesis has had a number of contributors, and a number of arguments can be identified with it. For present purposes, three primary arguments — each with important implications for labour–management relations — can be identified.

The first general argument is that, contrary to the capitalism thesis, the traditional working class-capitalist class dichotomy has become outmoded (Dahrendorf, 1957: 246–79). In support of this claim, it is argued that the twentieth century has brought affluence to virtually all members of society and has witnessed the emergence of a burgeoning "middle class" of white-collar, managerial, and professional

---

[9] This term is perhaps most closely identified with *Industrialism and Industrial Man*, particularly as developed in the final chapter. First published in 1960, this book was written by four prominent industrial relations scholars: Clark Kerr, John Dunlop, Fred Harbison, and Charles Myers. Notably, however, it has received far less attention from industrial relations scholars than it has from sociologists.

workers, reflecting a shift towards a more "meritocratic" society in which external inequalities have been minimized (Kerr et al., 1964: 230). Moreover, "citizenship rights" have increased substantially, with all individuals — regardless of economic or social position — enjoying equality before the law, the right to vote, and a variety of legal protections and entitlements (e.g., welfare, minimum wage, unemployment insurance; see Lipset, 1960). Finally, society has become increasingly differentiated both occupationally and socially, thereby giving rise to a multitude or "plurality" of interest groups with cross-cutting concerns and goals (Kerr et al., 1964; Lipset, 1960: 65). Instead of engaging in class conflict, interdependencies between these groups lead them to seek constructive, positive-sum solutions to conflicts. Accordingly, where, in earlier times, workers may have had considerable cause for discontent, bringing this discontent with them to the workplace in the form of class consciousness, they now have become beneficiaries of and equal partners in society, with every reason to cooperate and contribute:

> Consensus develops wherever industrialization is successful. The labor force becomes committed to and settled into industrial life. It accepts the pace of work, the web of rules, and the surrounding culture (Kerr et al., 1964: 228).

The second argument is that the growth of large scale corporations has resulted in a separation between the ownership of firms and their management, and that ownership has become so widely diffused — with few shareholders controlling more than a small percentage of stock — that owners no longer exert much effective control over the way corporations are run (Berle and Means, 1932; Dahrendorf, 1957; Berle, 1959). The implications are quite revolutionary: because managers are no longer subject to ownership pressures, and because they have little or no ownership stake in the firm, they have no a priori reason to maximize profits. Instead, as professionals, they seek to maximize operational efficiency, while at the same time satisfying the often competing goals and expectations of workers, consumers, investors, suppliers, and other interest groups with a stake in the organization. As two prominent theorists phrase it:

> It makes only slightly more sense to say that the goal of the corporation is to maximize the income of shareholders than it does to say that it is to maximize the income of Sam Smith, the janitor (Cyert and March, 1963: 10).

With respect to labour relations, this does not necessarily mean an end to conflict, for managerial attempts to achieve efficiency and to satisfy the goals of other interest groups can conflict with the goals and expectations of workers (as orthodox pluralists argue). Indeed, there can be considerable conflict within management, as different factions attempt to serve different goals (Chamberlain and Kuhn, 1965). But it does mean an end to the harsh, exploitive treatment often afforded workers in earlier times, with management instead seeking to accommodate worker interests and concerns to the extent possible without jeopardizing the firm's long-run survival and growth.

The third argument has to do with the growth of labour unionism and collective bargaining in post-war years. Again, consistent with the orthodox-pluralist perspective, proponents of the industrial society thesis generally believe that labour unionism and collective bargaining enable workers to confront management as equals and hence introduce democracy into the workplace. In turn, this not only helps to foster industrial stability, it also prevents conflict from becoming channelled into mass political movements and protests. In effect, therefore, labour unionism and collective bargaining serve to "institutionalize" and contain conflict within the economic sphere (Dahrendorf, 1957: 276). According to proponents of the industrialism thesis, this has also been accompanied by greater "maturity" in the labour movement, characterized by more temperate and business-like labour leaders, concerned not with effecting widespread economic and political reform but rather with winning improvements in the wages and working conditions of their members (Lester, 1958: 120).

The three arguments considered so far suggest that the major problems of industrialization have, in effect, been resolved, and that any remaining problems are simply matters of fine tuning. This is particularly the case with respect to labour–management relations: broader, class-based sources of conflict have virtually disappeared, firms are no longer managed strictly in the interests of owners, and mechanisms for the orderly resolution of remaining conflicts are well established. These three assumptions have been central to the orthodox-pluralist perspective, and came to be virtually taken-for-granted by most industrial relations scholars throughout the post-World War II era — so much so that the arguments underlying them were often left unstated. This is especially true with respect to the exercise of management authority: it became rare to find any mention of the profit motive in prominent industrial relations texts (e.g., Kochan and Katz, 1988).

The Post-Industrial Society Thesis

Though the industrial society thesis paints a highly optimistic picture of industrial society, it was clear by the late 1950s and early 1960s that all of the problems attributed to industrialization had not been resolved. Of particular relevance to industrial relations is the concern which arose over worker alienation and its economic and social consequences. It was at this time that a further argument emerged.

Sometimes referred to as the Woodward/Blauner thesis, after its two major exponents, Joanne Woodward (1958, 1965) and Robert Blauner (1964), it was argued that the widespread adoption of mass production technologies in the first half of this century had resulted in highly fragmented and routinized work, typically requiring little skill and giving rise to impersonal, bureaucratic workplaces within which workers lack control over the way work is performed. This, in turn, gave rise to widespread worker alienation, with workers developing negative work orientations and expressing their dissatisfaction in a variety of ways, from insubordination and sabotage to exorbitant wage and benefit demands and strike activity. Yet, as technology continues to develop, becoming increasingly automated and capital intensive, these problems should disappear. Machines (e.g., robots) will do most of the physical work, eliminating the most boring and monotonous tasks, and leaving workers with the job of controlling and monitoring the work process. Levels of skill will increase, and, due to the complexity of the technology and the higher levels of capital investment per worker, management will concern itself more with the smooth and continuous operation of the work process than with labour costs and individual worker productivity. The overall result will be favourable wages and working conditions, more cooperative, team-like relations in the workplace, and lower conflict (Woodward, 1965).

The Woodward/Blauner thesis forms part of the basis for what has come to be known as the "**post-industrial society**" thesis.[10] As its name suggests, this thesis argues that we are moving into a "post-industrial" era, where traditional blue-collar/industrial work (as we know it) virtually disappears and large, bureaucratic organizations give

---

[10] There have been a number of variants of this thesis, some of which have been "outside" of the industrialism thesis tradition (e.g., Tourraine, 1971; Block, 1987). The variant considered here is, however, from within this tradition, and is perhaps most associated with the work of Daniel Bell (1967, 1973). More recent variants, emergent in the past few years and associated with the "flexibility" debate, will be considered in chapter sixteen. They are also discussed in some detail in Smart (1992), especially chapters two and three.

way to smaller, more participative "adhocracies", characterized by high levels of flexibility and adaptiveness (Bennis, 1967; Toffler, 1972). In this society, the economy centres around the provision of services rather than the production of goods, and the possession of information and knowledge skills become more important sources of power and status than the possession of capital and material wealth (Bell, 1973). Moreover, workers enjoy high levels of affluence, and, along with this, increased opportunities for leisure. Finally, where workers once received their sense of identity and belongingness from their family, their church, and their local community, they now receive it from their work organizations and associations.

Rather than forming a distinctive tradition, the post-industrial society thesis is clearly an extension of the industrial society variant, and for this reason each can be considered as a variant. Perhaps the major difference is in its degree of optimism: where industrial society theorists *generally* acknowledge legitimate (though limited) interest conflicts in labour–management relations and hence consider labour unions and collective bargaining important components of developed industrial societies, post-industrial society theorists seem to assume the end of interest conflicts, with unions playing a very limited role, serving primarily to foster cooperation and provide economic services for workers. Thus, where the industrial society variant of the industrialism thesis largely conforms with the ideals of the orthodox-pluralist perspective, the post-industrial society variant conforms more to the ideals of the managerialist perspective. Indeed, many of the panaceas long advocated by proponents of the managerialist perspective — from job enrichment and teamwork to worker participation and profit-sharing (see chapter five) are at the heart of the post-industrial society thesis.

Implications

In essence, the post-industrial society thesis posits the realization of Durkheim's organic solidarity, with work organizations and associations serving the same function as Durkheim's occupational groups. In doing so, it paints a rather comforting view of society in general (Naisbitt, 1982; Drucker, 1989) and industrial relations in particular (Heckscher, 1988) — one in which most of the problems faced by workers during the industrialization process have been conquered, ending the need for "adversariness" and ushering in a new era, characterized by much more "positive sum" or harmonious relations between labour and management. Of course, many proponents of the industrial society thesis *do* acknowledge that a number of problems remain and that labour–

management relations continue to be adversarial in some settings. But they argue that these problems reflect outdated values and beliefs rather than fundamental limitations to the system itself.

III. MAX WEBER AND THE "INDUSTRIAL CAPITALISM" THESIS

The industrial capitalism thesis, as its name implies, in many respects provides a middle ground between the capitalism and the industrialism thesis, though, as shall become apparent, it is in many respects more pessimistic than either of them. As is the case for the capitalism thesis, it is primarily associated with the work of a single author — in this case, Max Weber, who was a German sociologist writing at the turn of the twentieth century (circa 1890–1919). Focus is thus on his work.

Calculative Rationality and the Spread of Bureaucracy

Weber is perhaps most widely known for his concern over the growing predominance of calculative rationality and the growth of large-scale "bureaucratic" organizations. According to Weber (1968 [1922]: 24–26), it is possible to identify four different bases or reasons for economic and social actions: tradition (i.e., what is customary), values (i.e., what is moral), affect (i.e., how one feels), and rational calculation (i.e., the most efficient means to a given end). The distinguishing characteristic of modern capitalism is that the latter of these bases — rational calculation — becomes increasingly predominant, as does bureaucracy, which is the very embodiment of calculative rationality. According to Weber "the purely bureaucratic type of administrative organization is, from a purely technical view, capable of attaining the highest degree of efficiency and is in this sense formally the most rational known means of exercising authority over human beings (Weber, 1968 [1922]: 223)". Elaborating on this at another point, Weber states:

> Precision, speed, unambiguity, knowledge of the files, continuity, discretion, unity, strict subordination, reduction of friction and of material and personal costs — these are raised to the optimum point in the strictly bureaucratic administration (Weber, 1968 [1922]: 973).

What is Weber's model of bureaucracy? He identifies a number of characteristics, but in its purest form, bureaucracy is characterized primarily by a high degree of specialization in the way work is performed, a clearly established hierarchy of authority, a well developed system of rules and procedures, selection and promotion based upon impersonal standards (qualifications, merit, seniority), and lifetime employment with career advancement opportunities (Weber, 1968 [1922]: 220, 956–63). Perhaps most important, however, is that bureaucracies are run by professional managers rather than owners or politicians (1968 [1922]: 224), and that authority is exercised impersonally, based on the ethos of rational calculation and sustained by a system of rational law. In contrast to earlier periods, where the legitimacy of authority was based either upon tradition (i.e., inheritance) or upon a ruler's personality (i.e., "charisma"), rational calculation and law form the basis from which the legitimacy of authority derives in modern capitalism. In this respect, Weber refers to authority as "legitimate domination"; if the legitimacy of authority is weakened, then it becomes increasingly difficult to exert dominance over others (1968 [1922]: 954). Thus, in modern capitalism, it is important that managerial authority is exercised rationally and that the legal system is viewed as legitimate (1968 [1922]: 36); otherwise, those in positions of subordination (e.g., workers) are likely to respond unfavourably. Contrary to the industrialism thesis, however, Weber views profit as the primary determinant of rationality and hence as the primary criterion underlying the exercise of managerial authority (1968 [1922]: 90–100).

Weber identifies a number of factors that are associated with the development of bureaucracy and the ethos upon which it is based (see Collins, 1986: 83–94). One is the "spirit of capitalism", which he attributes to the Protestant ethic of "hard work and self denial"; according to Weber, the secularization of this ethic in large part accounts for the predominance of rational calculation in modern capitalism (Weber, 1930 [1905]). Another is the development of modern cost accounting methods, which are critical to the attainment of efficiency in large-scale work organizations. Still another is the existence of competitive market forces which ultimately ensure that less rational forms of organization fail. But of even greater relevance to the present discussion is the existence of a "free" labour market.

Labour Markets and the Employment Relation

According to Weber, the existence of capitalist enterprise is predicated upon the existence of a free labour market, within which individuals are disenfranchised from ownership of the means of production and hence effectively coerced to submit to employer authority — whether they view it as legitimate or not — if they wish to earn a livelihood.

Finding themselves at a disadvantage in the labour market, workers are in turn driven by the "whip of hunger" (1961 [1922]: 209) to accept the terms and conditions imposed on them:

> The formal right of a worker to enter into any contract whatsoever with any employer whatsoever does not in practice represent for the employment seeker even the slightest freedom in the determination of his own conditions of work and it does not guarantee him any influence in this process. It rather means ... that the more powerful party in the market, i.e. normally the employer, has the possibility to set the terms; to offer the job, "take it or leave it", and given the normally more pressing economic need of the worker, to impose his own terms upon him (Weber, 1968 [1922]: 729).

It would thus appear that, while Weber considers legitimacy to be important, he considers managerial dominance to be based upon economic coercion as much as it is on consent.

Class and Class Conflict

Weber also recognizes that the interests of workers and of capitalists are conflicting — a position similar to that of Marx. But Weber does not consider the widespread manifestation of this conflict to be inevitable; indeed, his discussion of bureaucracy suggests that its superiority as a form of organization rests as much upon its effectiveness for maintaining control and stability as upon its technical efficiency. Moreover, where conflict occurs, it does not take the form of "class" conflict, but is instead directed against management, as it is management, not capitalists, with whom workers are directly involved:

> It is not the rentier, the shareholder, and the banker who suffer the ill will of the worker, but almost exclusively the manufacturers and the business executives who are direct opponents of workers in wage conflicts (Weber, 1968 [1922]: 931).

In fact, Weber rejects Marx's concept of class, adopting a more hierarchical, stratified conception of society, characterized by a multitude of classes and status groups.[11] As is the case under the liberal-reformist perspective, Weber believes economic power plays a central role in determining one's "life chances" and level of attainment. He also argues that "property and lack of property are the basic categories

---

[11] Many subsequent writers in the Weberian tradition jettison the concepts of class and status group almost altogether, at least as analytical concepts (see Parkin, 1982: 93).

of all class situations" (1968 [1922]: 927). But he also believes that, within these categories, class situation is further differentiated depending upon a number of additional considerations — including one's ability and education. Moreover, economic power and level of attainment do not determine one's status alone. Thus, one's position in the economic order is not to be equated with one's position in the social order (1968 [1922]: 938).

The Paradox of Consequences

In essence, therefore, Weber considers the economy, and ultimately society, as becoming increasingly hierarchical, characterized by large scale bureaucracies, an ethos of rational calculation, a multitude of classes and status groups, and limited industrial conflict, confined largely to the economic sphere. What are the economic and social outcomes? For Weber and subsequent writers in the Weberian tradition, there is a "paradox of consequences". On the one hand, society comes to enjoy high levels of efficiency, relative economic and social stability, and ultimately, rising standards of living. On the other hand, the material benefits of industrial capitalism are accompanied by a number of deleterious social and cultural consequences. At least four such consequences can be identified.

First, the predominance of large bureaucratic organizations results in a concentration of power in the hands of an increasingly small elite — an elite which includes union and government officials as well as business leaders. The power of these individuals derives not just from their positions of authority, but also from the effectiveness of bureaucracy as a method of controlling those in subordinate positions (Weber, 1968 [1922]: 987).

Second, is a weakening of democracy (1968 [1922]: 984–94). Members of the bureaucratic elite control information and channels of communication in their organizations and in society in general. This, coupled with the size and formal structure of bureaucracies, places the average citizen in a position of relative powerlessness, lacking both the knowledge and the influence to "make a difference" in political affairs (1968 [1922]: 951–52).[12]

---

[12] This argument was developed more fully by Weber's colleague, Robert Michels, who advanced the "iron law of oligarchy". This will be discussed more fully in chapter eight, for it has often been drawn upon to argue that unions are characterized by an inherent bias against democracy.

Third, work itself becomes increasingly devoid of meaning or fulfilment. Bureaucracy entails high levels of specialization, standardization, and formalization: individual jobs are therefore narrow in scope, and they allow little discretion or opportunity for initiative. Indeed, the essence of bureaucracy in its purest form is that it eliminates human variability, with everyone working as an indistinguishable cog in a large, impersonal machine.

The fourth consequence, and the one which constitutes Weber's major concern, encompasses but goes beyond the first three. According to Weber the growth of calculative rationality as a predominant ethos results in a culture that is cold, depersonalized, and devoid of meaning or moral purpose — a state which Weber referred to as "cultural disenchantment". Bureaucracy comes to pervade almost every aspect of life, with the result that individuals find themselves trapped within the "iron cage of bureaucracy", not just in their employment, but in society in general.

All in all therefore, the industrial capitalism thesis is a pessimistic one, in which processes of bureaucratization and rationalization render individuals increasingly powerless and unable to find meaning in their lives. What makes this vision especially pessimistic is that Weber does not consider radical change to be inevitable. Thus, Weber is even more pessimistic than is Marx, who is optimistic about the development of a socialist epoch once capitalism has been overthrown. Indeed, Weber considers socialism as only making matters worse, hastening the growth of bureaucracy and providing it with its ultimate triumph.

Implications

The implications of the industrial capitalism thesis for industrial relations should be quite clear. On the one hand, industrial conflict (e.g., strikes), though ultimately a reflection of broader conflicts between investors and workers, takes the form of labour–management conflict, played out in accordance with a well-established system of rules and procedures. In addition, workers enjoy relatively favourable living standards, have high levels of job security, and enjoy considerable opportunity for career advancement. In this respect, the industrial capitalism thesis suggests an industrial relations system which largely conforms to the core or primary sector of the economy, as identified by proponents of the liberal-reformist perspective (chapter one). It is also, *in this respect*, largely consistent with the industrialism thesis.

On the other hand, workers find themselves dominated by large bureaucratic employers, unions, and government agencies. They also find little opportunity for meaning or purpose in their work, developing largely cynical, instrumental orientations towards their tasks, and passively accepting the reality within which they find themselves. It is because of this that critics of Weber maintain that bureaucracy is not efficient, but for Weber, the essence of bureaucracy is that individual motivation is unimportant: passive adherence to established rules and procedures ensures, rather than impairs, efficiency.

As we shall see in later chapters, contemporary conventional wisdom is that, in a world characterized by high levels of change and uncertainty, bureaucracy is outmoded, and must be replaced by more adaptive forms of organization in which individual motivation and commitment is key. Whether this is the case or not, there can be little question that the industrial capitalism thesis contributes considerably to our understanding of developments throughout the twentieth century — as shall become especially apparent in chapter four.

IV. COMPARING THE THREE THESES

As should now be evident, the three theses considered in this chapter have important implications for how one thinks about the nature and development of modern societies, and these implications are, in turn, highly relevant to the study of industrial relations. Table 2–1 provides a comparison of these three theses on a number of dimensions. While this table is oversimplified and does not provide a full representation of the various arguments and ideas associated with each, it does enable us to identify some major differences between them.

In essence, Table 2–1 indicates that the capitalism and the industrialism theses are polar opposites. Under the capitalism thesis, the primary social formation is class and the underlying developmental logic is class conflict. The employment relation is based primarily upon coercion and is largely exploitive in nature, with work becoming increasingly unskilled and alienating. Finally, the prognosis for the future is one of class polarization and growing instability. In contrast, under the industrialism thesis, cross-cutting interest groups constitute the primary social formation and the underlying developmental logic entails consensus. The employment relation is based primarily on consent and is largely cooperative in nature, with work becoming increasingly skilled and fulfilling. The prognosis for the future is one of progress and stability.

The industrial capitalism thesis essentially falls in between these two opposites. Under this thesis, modern society is hierarchical, charac-

TABLE 2–1   The Broader Debate: Three Theses on Industrial Relations, The Economy and Society

	Capitalism Thesis	Industrialism Thesis	Industrial Capitalism Thesis
Primary Explanation	Capitalist Institutions	Industrialization Processes	Capitalist Industrialization Processes
Primary Contributors	Karl Marx	Emile Durkheim and Others	Max Weber
Corresponding IR Perspectives†	Radical	Orthodox Pluralist / Managerial	Liberal Reformist
Primary Social Formation	Class	Cross-Cutting Interest Groups	Hierarchical: Multiple Classes and Status Groups
Underlying Developmental Dynamic	Class Conflict	Consensus	Rationalization, Bureaucratic Domination
Primary Basis of the Employment Relation	Coercion	Consent	Coercion and Consent
The Primary Purpose of Management	Maximization of Surplus Value (Profit) through Exploitation	Efficiency and Effectiveness	Maximization of Profit through Calculative Rationality
Nature and Development of Work	De-skilled, Alienating	Upskilled, Fulfilling	Highly Formalized and Specialized, Unfulfilling
Prognosis for the Future	Class Polarization and Growing Instability	Progress and Stability	Economic Progress, but Cultural Disenchantment

† The neoliberal perspective does not correspond to any well-developed thesis on the nature and development of the economy and of society. See p. 23 of text.

terized by multiple classes and status groups rather than a two class dichotomy or a plurality of equal interest groups. Society comes to be characterized by a high degree of rationalization and bureaucratic domination rather than by either class conflict or consensus per se. The employment relation is based on a combination of coercion and consent rather than one or the other, and it is characterized by calculative or "instrumental" worker and management orientations rather than either exploitative or purely cooperative ones. Work itself becomes highly specialized and formalized rather than highly skilled and fulfilling (as the industrialism thesis argues), but it is not de-skilled and alienating, at least to the extent predicted by Marx. The prognosis is for economic progress but at the expense of widespread cultural disenchantment.

Who Is Right?

The debate represented in these three theses has raged in one form or another for over a century, and various sources of evidence can be brought to bear in support of each. It is not possible within the confines of this book to attempt to resolve this debate or to review all of the relevant evidence. However, each of the three theses provides a number of insights. More important, the differences between them raise a number of issues which go beyond those considered in the discussion of competing perspectives in the preceding chapter, yet have clear implications for the study of industrial relations. As depicted in rows four to nine of Table 2–1, these range from issues of social formation (i.e., class) to prognoses for the future. These issues will be referred to at various points throughout the remainder of this book. But they are especially important to any attempt to *understand* industrial relations, as shall become apparent in the next chapter.

V.   CONCLUSIONS

This chapter has outlined three general theses on the nature and development of industrial capitalism. Each provides important insights about labour–management relations and their relationship to the broader "political economy" of western societies. Each also raises issues that have important implications for industrial relations, as should be especially apparent in the next chapter.

Understanding Labour–Management Relations

3

If there is anything which appears to define industrial relations to the casual observer, it is conflict. Regardless of the form this conflict takes, it is often portrayed as economically irrational and illegitimate, reflecting unduly adversarial attitudes, poor work values, or inadequate understandings of economic reality. Yet, such a portrayal fails to consider the underlying reasons that conflict occurs. When these are understood, the surprising thing may not be that we have conflict, but rather that we do not have more of it. Indeed, when walking through any workplace, what is perhaps most evident is not the level of conflict, but rather the level of cooperation. Nonetheless, there can be little doubt that various sources of conflict are pervasive in industrial relations, even though these may not always be manifest in obvious ways. An in-depth understanding of industrial relations thus requires an in-depth understanding of these sources of conflict, the sources of cooperation which prevent conflict from being more widespread, and the ways in which conflict is manifest given the sources of cooperation. The task of this chapter is to provide such an understanding.

I. THE SOURCES OF CONFLICT

In discussing the sources of conflict, it is useful to distinguish between those sources which appear to be fundamental to the labour–management relation in contemporary capitalist economies, and those which appear to be more variable, depending on the organization, industry, region, or country concerned. The former can be called the **underlying sources** of conflict, while the latter can be referred to as the **contextual sources**.

The Underlying Sources of Conflict

Four underlying sources of conflict may be identified: (1) legal alienation, (2) objective interest conflicts, (3) the nature of the employment relation, and (4) the nature of the employment contract.

Legal Alienation. The Canadian economy is a *capitalist* market economy. That is, it is based primarily on the principle of private ownership and control of economic enterprises. At least since 1776, when Adam Smith described Britain as a "nation of shopkeepers" in his *Wealth of Nations,* one of the principal justifications for such an economy has been that individuals can be expected to work harder when working for themselves rather than someone else.

The problem is that most people do not work for themselves. In recognition of this, Karl Marx was to argue, almost a century after the publication of Smith's treatise, that capitalist market economies are based on an important division, between the capitalist class and the working class (see chapter two). While members of the former own or control the means of production and derive their income largely through this ownership and control, members of the latter do not, instead having to sell their labour to capitalists in order to earn a livelihood. Although Marx's distinction between these two classes may seem oversimplified, it is useful in at least one respect: the defining characteristic of modern capitalism is that most labour market participants (in excess of 85 percent in Canada) do indeed work for someone else. Indeed, this is the defining characteristic of the employment *relation* in contemporary capitalist economies.

Because individuals do not work for themselves, they do not have *legal* ownership or control over, and hence are *legally alienated* from, the *means* by which they do their work (e.g., materials, equipment), the *process* by which they do their work (i.e., how the work is done), the *product* or output of their work, and the *proceeds* from their work (i.e., when the product is sold). As discussed more fully later in this chapter, workers may still identify with their work and work harder than they have to in order to keep their job. But, other things being equal, they have little *objective* reason to do so, simply because the means, process, product, and proceeds of their work are not legally their own, but instead belong to someone else.[1] This, in itself, creates

---

[1]   By "objective", I mean they have little to gain. Note also that this does not mean that workers *should not* work harder than they have to. But whether they should or should

a problem for management. But this problem is heightened by the second underlying source of conflict: the purposes to which employer authority is exercised.

Objective Interest Conflicts. A further tenet of capitalist market economies is that firms are managed so as to maximize profits. According to neoliberals this, in turn, helps to ensure that efficiency and innovation, and ultimately the "wealth of nations", are maximized. Yet, efficiency and innovation are not the only ways of maximizing profit. Although there may be a number of alternative ways, the one most cited by critics and most relevant to the present analysis is through the "exploitation" of workers. This argument is again traditionally most associated with the work of Karl Marx. As discussed in the preceding chapter, Marx argued that all value in an economy is ultimately created through productive work.[2] Thus, if employers were to collectively reward workers in accordance with the value of this work, there would be nothing left-over for profits, thereby eliminating any incentive to invest and ultimately resulting in economic collapse.[3] As a result, the very existence of capitalism depends on the ability of capitalists to exploit workers, made possible by a chronic over-supply of labour (i.e., unemployment) placing workers at a power disadvantage and hence enabling employers to pay them less than the true value of their labour.

Whether one accepts the exploitation argument or not, the pursuit of profit means that there is a basic, underlying conflict between the interests of employers and those of workers. *Other things being equal*, it is in an employer's interest to minimize what they pay workers and maximize the amount of work they obtain from them. This conflicts directly with the interests of employees, which, again *other things being equal*, are to maximize their pay and benefits and to do as little work as they have to in order to keep their job. In this regard, conflict goes beyond issues having to do with pay and benefits to include the

---

not is a normative question and hence of little relevance to understanding why conflict occurs.

[2] For example, although machines used by workers may be owned by the employer, they were ultimately produced by workers somewhere else.

[3] Of course, profits may also appear to come from other functions provided by capitalists or their agents, including risk taking, organizing and coordinating skills, and innovative ideas. But, under Marx's logic, these entail intellectual work and hence are not strictly returns to capital itself. For capitalism to survive, there must be a pure return to capital, above and beyond returns to these functions.

design of work itself, because employers have an interest in designing work so that it entails lower skill levels than otherwise (enabling them to pay lower wages) and maximizes worker effort and output levels. This may undoubtedly be "efficient" from an employer's point of view, but it clearly may not be from the point of view of the worker.

This is not to suggest that it is necessarily in an employer's interest to pay low wages or to design jobs that have little or no skill content. Employers must pay enough to be able to attract and retain workers of sufficient skill given the nature of the work to be performed and available technologies. It may even be in an employer's interest to pay somewhat more than this if the costs of doing so are outweighed by resulting performance gains — due, for example, to better worker morale, lower turnover, or higher quality workers. But it is not in an employer's interest to pay any more than the minimum necessary subject to this proviso, which is why the use of the term "other things being equal" in the above paragraph. A similar logic applies with regard to job design and, for that matter, a whole host of additional issues, including the provision of job security, employee benefits, seniority rights, and so forth (see chapter fifteen). It is in this sense that underlying interest conflicts can be said to exist.

Of course, the extent to which underlying conflicts are actually manifest in the behaviour of workers or management varies, as discussed more fully later in this chapter. For example, employers may decide it is in their interests to adopt highly progressive practices towards workers, while workers may develop high levels of commitment to management, with the result that there is little, if any, conflictual behaviour. Even where this is not the case, workers and management may in some, or even many, cases have certain interests in common (e.g., in the survival of the employer), and there may be certain issues on which both can benefit. But this has little to do with whether interest conflicts *underlie* the labour–management relationship, which is the concern here.

More relevant at present is the extent to which employers actually seek to maximize profits and the strategies they adopt to do so. For example, it is sometimes argued that, in countries like Germany and Japan, managers are under less pressure than otherwise to maximize profits. In Germany, this is in theory because firms tend to be controlled by large banks which view their role as maximizing the long-term welfare of German society (Streeck, 1997). In Japan, it is in theory because firms are members of enterprise groups in which there are considerable "cross-holdings", so that firms are accountable to other firms within their group rather than to investors per se (e.g.,

Dore, 1997). To the extent that these arguments hold, the underlying conflict between labour and management may be substantially lessened.

As discussed in chapter two, the "managerial revolution" thesis suggests a similar circumstance in North America, based primarily on the argument that firm ownership has become so diffused that individual shareholders no longer exert any real pressure on managers. Yet this argument was largely a product of the 1940s and 1950s. Although the intensity with which Canadian managers do so may vary, there can be little question that the rational pursuit of profit is the primary motive guiding their decisions (see chapter six). Indeed, it is widely believed that changes in financial markets over the past few decades have placed increased pressure on management not only to maximize profits, but to do so over the short term, through a strategy of cost-cutting and work intensification (e.g., Porter, 1992; Hutton, 1995; Fligstein, 2001).

A similar ethos would appear to have spread to the public sector, as pressures to eliminate deficits and reduce taxation levels, coupled with widespread vilification of public sector workers, have induced public sector managers to increasingly base decisions on impersonal economic calculations consistent with the profit motive and to give short shrift to the interests of employees, unless employee disaffection is likely to generate costs that equal or exceed any savings from lower pay or higher work loads. Thus, while the sources of pressure to which public sector employers are subject may be different and possibly not as strong as in the private sector, the implications are basically the same. Important conflicts underlie the labour–management relation in the public as well as the private sector.

The Nature of the Employment Relation. Recall from chapter one that employer authority is delegated downwards within work organizations, in the form of hierarchically overarching relations of subordination and superordination. This authority derives from the property rights of owners, so in the absence of specific laws to the contrary, workers in conventionally owned organizations have no legal right to elect or appoint either their immediate superordinates or those in senior positions of authority, and neither their superordinates nor senior managers are legally accountable to them. Workers do, of course, possess varying amounts of power, and they can attempt to negotiate restrictions on the exercise of management authority. But in Canada, worker power is largely reactive, for workers have few, if any, legal rights to actually participate in the exercise of managerial authority. In most cases, they can only react to this exercise, by quitting, striking, filing a grievance, or engaging in some other form of job-related conflict.

It follows that, in this sense at least, work organizations are to a large extent analogous to an authoritarian state: those who "rule" (senior management) are neither elected by nor accountable to those over whom they rule (workers and both lower and middle management). Of course, such an analogy should not be taken too far, for work organizations in Canada exist within a broader political democracy and market system, and there are important legal constraints on the way authority is exercised. Moreover, even though work organizations are *legally* authoritarian, the *exercise* of authority is by no means necessarily authoritarian; it can be highly progressive, involving considerable consultation with workers. But drawing such an analogy serves to highlight the underlying nature of organizations and employment relations — something that is too often paid insufficient due.

This analogy underscores the dominant position typically enjoyed by management by virtue of its position of authority. More important at present, however, it points to a further source of conflict in labour–management relations. In a society that values individual freedom and democracy, workers can generally be expected to resent their position of subordination, and this can, in and of itself, serve as a source of conflict (Watson, 1987: 219). But it is especially important given that authority is exercised not in the interests of workers, but rather in those of owners (i.e., profit). As such, issues of trust and legitimacy are always problematic. Employers may go to considerable lengths to attempt to win the trust of workers, but as long as workers are aware (or simply perceive) that employer decisions are ultimately made in the interests of owners, and that these interests may often differ from their own, distrust is always likely to lie beneath the surface of the employment relation.

The Nature of the Employment Contract. If it were possible for employers and individual workers to enter into a highly specific contract detailing the exact duties or outputs required from workers and the exact rewards workers can expect, then the three sources of conflict above would be less important. Unless one party failed to live up to its side of the contract, the only time that conflicts would occur would be at such time that the two parties decided to renegotiate the contract. Yet one reason why employers hire workers and ultimately why work organizations exist at all is that the work required is often difficult to specify clearly in advance and the output difficult to measure (Williamson, 1975).[4]

As a result, the employment contract is typically non-specific or diffuse (Offe, 1985; Edwards, 1979). Often, nothing is even formally written down, beyond (perhaps) an initial written job offer by the employer. But even where a formal contract exists (as for example, in a union workplace), much remains unwritten, consisting of expectations and understandings that have developed over time. This "**psychological contract**", as it was referred to in chapter one, typically revolves around a "**wage-effort bargain**" (Baldamus, 1961), or the level of pay workers can expect for a given level of effort. But it tends to be much broader than this, involving the entire web of rules also referred to in chapter one. For example, it can include worker expectations as to job security, promotion opportunities, and work assignments on the one hand, and employer expectations as to worker loyalty and commitment on the other hand.

The problem is that these understandings and expectations are often both complex and ambiguous, so there is always room for disagreement on a day-to-day basis as to what is fair or legitimate. For the same reason, attempts to specify formal contracts can themselves engender considerable conflict, and there may still be considerable room for disagreement over what these contracts actually mean and how they should be applied, as evidenced by problems which arise in the negotiation and interpretation of collective agreements in union workplaces.

The diffuse nature of the employment contract thus makes for another important underlying source of conflict. This is especially so given the interest conflicts underlying the labour–management relation and the nature of the relation itself, which enhance the likelihood of disagreement, misunderstanding, and mistrust as to each side's legitimate role and obligations. In particular, employers are able to violate the psychological contract by introducing changes or issuing directives unilaterally, without consulting with employees. When this occurs, employees often have little legal recourse short of quitting. Under these circumstances, it should not be surprising that workers (and union leaders) often seem unduly insecure, distrustful, and even adversarial.

---

[4] Otherwise, it would conceivably be possible to replace work organizations with networks of contracts involving self-employed individuals or teams, thus generating the modern day equivalent of Adam Smith's nation of shopkeepers. Although it has been fashionable in recent years for organizations to attempt to mimic such networks, this almost invariably occurs within, and subject to, an authority hierarchy.

The Contextual Sources of Conflict

In addition to the underlying sources of conflict are more contextual ones. For the present, three such sources may be identified: (1) broader societal inequalities, (2) the labour market experience, and (3) the experience of work itself.

Broader Societal Inequalities. The income of the average Canadian family has increased dramatically over the years. For example, it is now more than two-and-a-half times what it was in the early 1950s (after controlling for inflation). In a 2002 survey of over 2000 Canadians by Ekos Research Associates, 47 percent considered their salary adequate to meet their basic needs (e.g., food, shelter, a second-hand car), 36 percent considered it to be moderately adequate, and only 17 percent considered it inadequate (CCSD, 2003: 8). This is important, because it is sometimes argued, especially by proponents of the industrialism thesis (see chapter two), that economic deprivation is an important cause of labour–management conflict, and that while such deprivation explains the growth of unions and industrial conflict throughout much of the past century, it has sufficiently diminished that there is less need of unions and less reason for conflict.

A problem with this argument is that individuals can still experience deprivation *relative* to others, especially if there are widespread disparities in wealth and income. This is important because such disparities continue to be substantial and may have even been on the increase in recent years. In Canada, the wealthiest twenty percent accounts for three quarters (75 percent) of all wealth, while the middle twenty percent accounts for only one-ninth (11 percent). The bottom forty percent accounts for only one one-hundredth (1 percent). These differences have actually been on the increase since the mid-1980s, when the wealthiest twenty percent accounted for "only" seven tenths (69 percent) of all wealth (Morisette and Zhang, 2007). From 1984 to 2005, the median wealth of the top twenty percent increased by 64 percent, while the wealth of the bottom forty percent actually declined, by 11 percent (Statistics Canada, 2006c). There is little reason to think that this trend has changed since 2005.

In addition, as of 2004, those in the top twenty percent of the income distribution accounted for half of all income (53.0 percent), while those in the middle twenty percent accounted for one-eighth (13.9 percent), and those in the bottom forty percent accounted for only one-tenth (10.4 percent). The top 1 percent actually accounted for more than the entire bottom forty percent (Murphy et al., 2007: 10).

Income inequality has also been on the increase over the past thirty years. From 1980 to 2008, upper- and upper middle-income families enjoyed increases of 28 percent and 11 percent, respectively. Low-income families enjoyed a 13 percent increase. But middle and lower middle-income families enjoyed increases of only 3 and 4 percent, respectively. For the latter two groups in particular, these increases only came after substantial declines during the 1980s and 1990s (CANSIM 202-0701; also Table 16–1).

The purpose in identifying these considerations is not to make a moral statement. Rather, it is to help explain why conflict occurs. The "promise" of capitalist market economies has always been one of *growing* affluence for the population in general. It appears that this promise has for the most part been broken. Workers have watched those for whom they work grow better off, yet found it increasingly difficult to get ahead themselves. This can generate resentment: the question is whether this resentment translates into workplace conflict, or whether it translates into a generalized sense of hostility toward other individuals and groups.

The Labour Market Experience. Since the early decades of this century, workers have seen much improved labour market and employment conditions. In addition to improved incomes, working hours are shorter,[5] and managerial authority is probably on the whole less coercively and arbitrarily exercised. Moreover, the right to join unions and negotiate with employers introduces an element of democracy into the workplace, for workers are represented by duly elected union officials in the determination of the terms and conditions of their employment (as is discussed more fully in chapter seven). Unions also enable workers to negotiate a number of rights and protections vis-à-vis management, thus protecting them against the arbitrary or unfair exercise of managerial authority. In addition, workers are protected by an extensive system of employment standards legislation, occupational health and safety laws, and most recently, human rights and employment equity provisions (as discussed in chapter nine). Finally, of course, there is now in place an extensive system of social assistance and health care programs. By the mid-1990s, this system began to be substantially eroded due to government cut-backs, and homelessness became a growing problem, as did the need for food banks. But the

---

[5] For example, in 1870 a work week of 64 hours was the norm in manufacturing. By 1996, the norm for full-time workers was 42 hours (Krahn and Lowe, 1998: 78–80).

overall importance of these advances should not be underestimated, for they ensure that the labour market experiences of workers are considerably less oppressive and coercive than in the past (consistent with the industrialism thesis, as discussed in chapter two).

At the same time, workers continue to face a number of problems in the labour market. Throughout the early and middle 1990s, unemployment rates equalled or exceeded 10 percent. This meant that, for every 90 employed Canadians, there were, on average, at least 10 who were either on temporary lay-off, between jobs, or unable to find work despite actually seeking it. By the late 1990s and early 2000s, unemployment had dropped, and hovered around 6 percent by 2006, before returning to over 8 percent in 2008. But a 1999 study found that such estimates may be more than double when one includes those who have either given up looking for work or have been unable to obtain full-time, permanent employment.[6] Meanwhile, employment insurance benefits were slashed in the 1990s. Only four in ten of those who are officially unemployed now qualify for these benefits at any point in time, and, when they do, they receive only 55 percent of their regular pay, up to 447 dollars per week.

In view of these statistics, it is perhaps not surprising that large numbers of Canadians feel insecure about their jobs. For example, the 2002 Ekos poll referred to earlier, conducted when unemployment was hovering around 7.5 percent, found that a quarter of employed Canadians agreed at least somewhat with the statement that they stood "a good chance of losing their job over the next few years", while only six in ten disagreed (the rest neither agreed nor disagreed; CCSD, 2003: 11).[7] Only a quarter of Canadians were confident that they could count on government support programs to adequately sustain them while they looked for a job (CCSD, 2003: 15). A more

---

[6] Using Statistics Canada data, Burke and Shields (1999: 16) estimated the "structural exclusion" rate to be 20.3 percent as of May 1998. To calculate this rate, they included persons who were: (1) unemployed but actively seeking work (8.4 percent), (2) discouraged workers, who would like to work but have given up looking for work (0.5 percent), (3) involuntary part-time workers, who are in part-time jobs (less than 30 hours per week) even though they have been seeking, but unable to obtain, full-time employment (1.8 percent), (4) discouraged involuntary part-time workers, who are in part-time jobs even though they would prefer, but have given up trying to obtain, full-time employment (3.2 percent), (5) workers who have only a temporary job and earn under ten dollars an hour (3.4 percent), (6) persons who are self-employed with no paid employees and working under 35 hours a week (3.0 percent).

[7] The 1996 Angus Reid poll discussed in chapter one reveals that there has been an improvement since the mid 1990s: it found that 37 percent were somewhat or very worried about losing their job (Lipset and Meltz, 1998: 16).

recent Prairie Research Associates (PRA) survey of 750 employed Canadians outside of Quebec, conducted in 2003 and 2004, found that 3 in 10 respondents worried to some, a considerable, or a great extent that they could soon find themselves out of job (Godard, 2004d). This was prior to the insecurity created by the economic crisis of 2008.

Health and safety problems also remain pervasive. A long-term shift away from traditional blue-collar work, coupled with recent provincial government efforts to strengthen their health and safety regimes, have meant a decline in time lost due to workplace injury (see Breshin et al., 2006; McDonald, 2010). Perhaps for this reason, surveys documenting the nature and extent of health and safety problems have been increasingly difficult to come by. Yet, in an Ekos survey of 1,345 employed Canadians conducted in 2002, a third of respondents reported that they thought their health or safety was at risk because of their work (CPRN, 2003: 38).

Women would appear to bear a disproportionate share of hardship in the labour market. The average hourly wage for women is only 83 percent of their male counterparts (Drolet, 2011), and they continue to experience a number of problems in the labour market, from inadequate day-care facilities to sexual harassment at work. With respect to the latter, a 1993 survey found that 6 percent of employed women aged 18 or over had experienced at least one form of sexual harassment in the previous 12 months (Johnson, 1994). Whether this has changed since is unclear.

Most significant, however, may be earnings levels. Not only have the earnings of middle income families been stagnant (as noted earlier), the median earnings of full-year, full-time workers in Canada were only 2 percent higher in 2008 than in 1976 (CANSIM 202-0101), despite an improvement in labour productivity of roughly 50 percent during that period (CANSIM 383-0008; also Russell and Dufour, 2007). As of 2004, almost one in four full-year, full-time workers in Canada earned less than two-thirds of the median level, which is a standard cut-off used to measure low pay (LaRochelle-Côté and Dionne, 2009). One in seven full-time, full-year employees earned below the Statistics Canada Low Income Cut-off (LICO) for a single individual, which has traditionally been considered a measure of the poverty level in Canada (Statistics Canada, 2006b). Matters may have improved somewhat after 2004 (the 2008 economic crisis notwithstanding). But such low levels of income not only mean an inability to properly support oneself without assistance from others, they also tend to be degrading and harmful to personal dignity — especially for adult workers with significant labour force experience.

As for the discussion of broader societal inequalities, the purpose in identifying these problems is not to make a moral statement (though one can certainly be made), but rather to identify a further set of reasons for conflict. Though the extent to which these problems directly manifest themselves in conflict behaviour is not readily established, they can be expected to contribute to a sense of inequity and injustice, thus fostering considerable resentment and insecurity, with important implications for labour–management relations.

The Nature of Work Itself. Under the radical perspective, employers have an interest in minimizing skill requirements so as to minimize labour costs and maximize control over workers. They also have an interest in "intensifying" work in order to maximize worker output. The result is not only increased stress and work overload, but also subjectively alienating, highly individualized work, in which workers perform narrow and often menial tasks. Yet, more optimistic commentators associated with the "industrialism thesis" (see chapter two) have traditionally argued that arduous and alienating work is largely a by-product of mass production (e.g., assembly line) technologies and factory occupations and should dissipate over time as more complex, automated technologies and service occupations requiring higher skill levels, problem solving, and team work, become increasingly prevalent (Blauner, 1964; Woodward, 1965; Bell, 1973). This argument has since become increasingly popular, as reflected in the widespread use of the term "the knowledge economy".

Although difficult to establish, existing research findings suggest that there has been some upgrading of skill levels, at least since the 1940s. But most of this took place prior to the 1970s. Subsequent upgrading has been relatively slight (Livingston, 1999: 134–48). As for the nature of work itself, perhaps the most direct indicator is the extent to which workers report that they are satisfied or dissatisfied with their jobs. Most studies find that a high percentage of workers report that they are somewhat or very satisfied with their jobs. Perhaps the largest recent survey to ask about job satisfaction in recent years was the 2001 Statistics Canada Workplace and Employee Survey, which included over 20,000 respondents. Fifty-six percent reported that they were "satisfied", and 34 percent that they were "very satisfied" (Statistics Canada, 2004). A 2003–4 telephone survey of 750 Canadian workers outside of Quebec conducted by Prairie Research Associates (PRA) (see Godard, 2009a) found even higher levels of "very satisfied" workers: 56 percent gave this response, while 29 percent indicated that they were "somewhat satisfied".[8] The PRA survey is of particular interest, however, because unlike most other general workforce surveys it also contained a large number of questions addressing a number of dimensions of the actual experience of work. These questions, and worker responses to them, appear in Table 3–1.

The responses in Table 3–1 reveal that Canadian workers generally view the characteristics of their jobs favourably. For example, 88 percent agreed (somewhat or strongly) that their job is challenging, and 82 percent that their job has lots of variety. Yet one-third to one-half also agreed with statements suggesting that they feel powerless in their job. For example, 47 percent agreed that what happens to them and their co-workers is pretty much out of their control and that they have little choice but to go along with things, even if they disagree with them. Work coercion, stress, and after-work fatigue would also appear to be widespread. For example, seven in ten agreed that they are expected to adopt employer goals and values as their own, even though they may not be. Seven in ten also agreed that they are under constant pressure to perform well and that their job is stressful. Two in three agreed that they are worn out by the end of the day, while four in ten agreed that, after working, they are too tired to do things with others and that they only want to rest when at home.

It follows that concerns about the content of work itself, and particularly about workplace alienation, may no longer be valid. Yet it would also appear that the context of work is a problem. Many employed Canadians are in jobs where they experience powerlessness, coercion, stress, and fatigue. It is possible that some Canadians actually choose such jobs, either because they pay well or because they find them challenging. Depending on one's perspective, it can also be argued that some of these characteristics — for example, having to adopt employer values and goals — are not necessarily bad, especially if they result in higher performance. Nonetheless, these characteristics can be expected to have a number of consequences for labour–management relations, not the least of which may, once again, be enhanced conflict in the workplace.

---

[8] The somewhat different results likely reflect changes in economic conditions combined with different questions and response formats. However, the PRA results seem to be closer to those of previous surveys. For example, a 1989 Statistics Canada survey found 56 percent to be "very satisfied" and 32 percent to be "somewhat satisfied" (Statistics Canada, 1992: 114). They are also almost identical to those from a 1997 PRA survey.

TABLE 3–1 The Work Experience

	strongly disagree	disagree somewhat	neutral	agree somewhat	strongly agree
Job Characteristics					
Your job requires a high level of skill.	6	9	3	30	52
Your job is challenging.	5	6	2	27	61
Your job makes you keep learning new things.	6	8	2	25	61
Your job requires lots of mental effort.	6	8	1	24	61
There is a lot of variety in the kinds of things you do in your job.	7	9	3	27	55
Powerlessness					
What happens to you and your co-workers is pretty much beyond your control.	24	23	7	20	27
There is little point for you and your co-workers in trying to affect the way things are done.	37	23	4	17	20
You and your co-workers have little choice but to go along with things at work, even if you disagree with them.	27	22	4	22	25
You and your co-workers have little choice but to do what you are told at work.	30	23	3	21	23
It does little good to speak up about things at work.	42	21	4	17	17

Continued....

TABLE 3–1 (continued)

	strongly disagree	disagree somewhat	neutral	agree somewhat	strongly agree
Coerciveness					
You are expected to not just do your job well, but also to demonstrate a high degree of loyalty to management.	5	9	8	33	45
It is not a good idea to question or criticize a management decision or policy.	23	31	4	22	20
You are expected to adopt employer goals and values as if they are your own, even though they may not be.	11	15	6	36	34
There is constant pressure to perform at high levels.	9	14	4	31	42
There is pressure to go to work even if you are feeling unwell.	34	22	4	17	24
Stressfulness					
Your job is stressful.	15	13	3	38	32
In your job, you are often confronted with problems you can't do much about.	28	25	4	26	18
You have little time to think and contemplate on your job.	35	30	5	18	12
You have conflicting demands placed on you on your job.	24	21	4	32	20
Some days you feel like you can't continue any longer at your job.	39	20	4	20	18
Fatigue					
You are often worn out by the end of the day.	14	17	3	37	30
After working, you are too tired to do things with others.	26	29	4	25	16
When at home, all you want to do is rest.	29	25	3	24	19

Source: PRA Survey (see Godard, 2009a).

Summing Up

The discussion to this point identifies a number of sources of conflict, from legal alienation to the nature of work. Each of these sources, whether underlying or contextual, can in-and-of itself be expected to have important implications for worker behaviour and labour–management relations.[9] However, their effects are probably much greater in *combination* than they are individually. That is, the problem is not so much that workers are legally alienated, or that management pursues maximum profit, or that workers are in positions of subordination, or that the employment contract is diffuse, or that many workers are in stressful jobs. Rather, the problem is that these sources of conflict exist in combination, with each feeding upon the other. The question, then, becomes not one of why conflict occurs, but rather one of why it is not more widespread. It is here that the sources of cooperation are important.

II. THE SOURCES OF COOPERATION

The sources of cooperation involve both "coercion" and "consent". Workers are coerced to cooperate in the sense that, as individuals, they have little effective choice but to enter into an employment relation if they wish to earn a living, and if they act in ways which are contrary to employer interests or expectations they can be subject to a variety of sanctions, including dismissal. Even where workers are unionized and act collectively, lengthy strikes or other forms of conflict can not only result in a considerable loss of income, they can also ultimately result in job loss — either because the employer goes out of business or because the employer shuts down and relocates operations. Indeed, workers depend on their employer for their livelihood. As such they have a strong interest in helping to ensure not only that their workplace remains viable, but also that it flourishes over the long run, enhancing their job security and possibly enabling them to obtain better wages and benefits. In this respect at least, there exist important commonalities as well as conflicts of interest between labour and management, as orthodox pluralists argue.

---

[9] These sources are important not only because they help explain conflict in the workplace, but also because they may have broader societal implications. For example, both Blackburn and Mann (1975) and Kohn (1979) have found a linkage between low discretion work and the development of "left leaning" ideologies.

As for consent, workers generally believe in the legitimacy of our economic system and in the right of management to exercise authority. One explanation for this may be that workers come to be socialized to accept the status quo as more or less given and to be "team players" rather than "trouble makers". This is the argument sometimes advanced by proponents of the radical perspective, who maintain that capitalists are able to impose their values and beliefs through both the media and the educational system, thus reducing the likelihood that workers will develop a "class consciousness" (Gramsci, 1971; Bowles and Gintis, 1976; Haiven, McBride, and Shields, 1991). Yet while there is probably a certain amount of truth to this argument, a second, less sinister explanation may be that most workers are simply realistic, seeing no viable alternative to contemporary arrangements and believing that, on the whole, the present system has functioned reasonably well.[10] Complementing this explanation is a third explanation: the knowledge that there are "worse" jobs means that workers are often happy just to have the job they have. Workers in this respect often have limited expectations, comparing their situation to others with similar qualifications, and believing that as long as they are doing well in this comparison, they have little to complain about.

Perhaps more important, there are also positive aspects to most jobs. As discussed earlier, the overwhelming majority of Canadian workers appear to have high levels of job satisfaction and to evaluate the content of their work favourably. Thus, even where they experience stress, coercion, or powerlessness, they may continue to be highly motivated. Closely related are work values and the notion of the psychological contract referred to earlier. While there is often room for disagreement over the psychological contract, workers tend to believe that they have a duty to live up to their side of the bargain at least until such time that the employer is perceived as violating its side. Finally, although the policies and practices advocated by managerialists do not appear to be as widespread as they would like (see chapter five), employers often do appear to find it in their interest to adopt practices addressing some of the sources of conflict and reinforcing some of the sources of cooperation. There are many "good" employers, and these are often able to win the trust and commitment of their employees.

---

[10] This realism may itself reflect socialization processes, but to argue this risks implying that workers (or the public in general) are somehow "cultural dopes", unable to think for themselves.

These sources of cooperation generally give rise to a far more acquiescent workforce than one would expect in view of the sources of conflict identified earlier. Indeed, in the 2003–4 PRA survey of 750 Canadian workers referred to earlier, respondents not only expressed high levels of job satisfaction, they also expressed high levels of commitment. For example, 88 percent agreed strongly or somewhat with the statement "you are loyal to the person who manages or is in charge of the place where you work." It seems, then, that most workers want to be able to do their jobs as well as possible and are generally loyal to the person they work for. But even in the absence of some of the sources of cooperation identified above, this would not be all that surprising. As Karl Marx long ago recognized, productive work is a central life activity, and although this work may be done outside of the employment relation (e.g., child rearing), the employment relation plays a critical role for most labour market participants. Indeed, one's job is often central to one's identity and self-image, perhaps so much so that one is willing to turn a blind eye to the sources of conflict, accepting and adjusting to the situation as best he or she can.

The problem is that, despite all of the sources of cooperation, and despite the apparent desire of workers to view their jobs positively, the sources of conflict remain. While the sources of cooperation may in part balance off the sources of conflict, it is probably most accurate to view these sources as in a *contradictory* relationship to each other. In other words, the sources of cooperation may mute or suppress the sources of conflict, much like one's conscience and sense of reality may mute or suppress one's impulses and desires. But they do not in any way eliminate them. Workers often have complex and contradictory feelings about their jobs, on the one hand expressing high levels of commitment, yet on the other harbouring a number of complaints and fears. While the former may reflect the sources of cooperation, the latter may reflect the sources of conflict, with each in effect standing in opposition to the other (see Fantasia, 1988: 4–7). So while high levels of trust and cooperation may be achieved, this trust and cooperation tends to be fragile, breaking down as soon as the employer is perceived as violating the psychological contract or engaging in some act which threatens employee interests (e.g., Fantasia, 1988). Even where this is not the case, the sources of conflict may be manifest in a number of ways, many of which are not obvious. Moreover, even for those that are obvious, the reasons for the conflict may be deeper and more complex than at first appears. Thus, it is useful to consider some of the ways in which underlying conflicts are manifest.

III. THE MANIFESTATION OF CONFLICT

Strikes

Strikes represent the most obvious manifestation of conflict. Because they entail costs for both sides, they can appear quite irrational. But to consider strikes only in economic terms is to misunderstand the broader rationale often underlying strike activity (see Hyman, 1977: 106ff). Strikes can, and often do, reflect and serve as an outlet for underlying hostilities, hostilities that arise out of the various sources of conflict identified above. Strikes can also involve matters of principle, especially if management has violated rules and understandings (i.e., the psychological contract) that have become established over time. In other words, the strike does not just serve as an economic instrument brought to bear against employers in order to win better wages and working conditions. As is also discussed in chapter thirteen, it also serves as a mechanism of "collective voice", where workers are able to express their discontent and "fight back" against what they believe to be unfair or illegitimate actions by management.

It follows that, while striking may appear irrational from the point of view of the economist, it may be perfectly rational from the point of view of the worker (Hyman, 1977). Indeed, while a strike may appear to be over economic issues, the economic demands of union representatives and the resolve with which they are pursued can reflect pent-up hostilities, serving as a vehicle through which these hostilities can be articulated. This may be especially so where management is considered to have acted illegitimately. Where this is the case, management's actions may serve to trigger otherwise suppressed or "latent" hostilities, providing workers with a moral basis for acting in ways which they would normally consider to be uncalled for. But even where this is not so, a strike may serve as the only meaningful outlet for collective discontent.

Alternative Forms of Conflict

Though striking is the most obvious form of conflict, it is not always a viable option. This is especially so given the conditions that must be met in order to engage in a legal strike. In Canada, workers may legally strike only if they are members of a union, the existing union contract (if there is one) has expired, and union and management representatives have been unable to negotiate a new one. Workers may, of course, ignore these conditions and engage in an illegal or "**wildcat**" strike. But doing so can result in substantial disciplinary penalties from management, and would at the present appear to be relatively rare. Instead of striking, employees may engage in a variety of alternative forms of conflict (see Morrill et al., 2003). Most obvious are various forms of "recalcitrant" behaviour, such as "slacking" or "the withdrawal of efficiency" (Veblen, 1921), sabotage, and voluntary absenteeism (Hodson and Sullivan, 1990: 109–12). None of these forms of behaviour need necessarily reflect a conscious attempt to express underlying conflicts nor even an awareness of these conflicts. Moreover, they often appear as isolated incidents, and can vary considerably not only with the conditions of work, but also with the personality characteristics of individuals. But they typically reflect the ways in which different individuals and groups adapt and adjust to the situation in which they find themselves, and ultimately to the contradictions between the sources of conflict and those of cooperation they experience in this situation. For example, "hiding out" or "goofing off" on the job may appear to be motivated by a simple desire to "take it easy". Yet these behaviours may also serve as attempts to "get away with something" and hence as acts of defiance against managerial authority (see Ackroyd and Thompson, 1999). Thus, while these forms of conflict might continue if the underlying sources of conflict identified earlier did not exist, their incidence would in all likelihood be far lower.

The same is true with respect to "exit" behaviour or quitting. Under conventional economic models, workers are viewed as rational decision-makers, seeking out the best paying job they can find. Thus, they quit because they have succeeded in finding a better job elsewhere. Yet, people often quit their jobs not because they have a better job lined up, but rather because they are fed up with their employer or the nature of their job. Where this is the case, quitting becomes the ultimate act of both "getting back" at the employer and restoring one's sense of dignity and pride.

The Negotiation of Order

Another, less obvious way in which the sources of conflict are manifest is in the day-to-day interactions between workers and their supervisors. Because of the sources of conflict in the employment relation, worker-supervisory relations can become highly political (Burawoy, 1985), with supervisors trying to elicit higher levels of performance from workers, and workers either offering resistance or going along with supervisory wishes only if the supervisor is prepared to reciprocate. For example, workers may speed up the pace of their work so that a shipment can be sent out on time, but in return they may expect a more relaxed work pace or even an informal work break afterwards. The supervisor who is not prepared to reciprocate in this or a similar way is unlikely to elicit such cooperation.

It is in part through this give-and-take that the psychological contract referred to earlier is formed. In this respect, it is useful to think of this contract as involving a "negotiated order", reflecting ongoing processes of give-and-take between workers and management (see Reed, 1985: 535–35). Management can of course unilaterally impose its will or violate established understandings, relying extensively upon the use of disciplinary sanctions, yet this can give rise to as many problems as it solves. These problems can involve any number of the forms of conflict behaviour identified above, including work slowdowns, sabotage of the work process, wildcat strikes, increased absenteeism, and even an increased level of quitting. Where a union is not established, workers may decide to organize one; where a union is established, there may be a sharp increase in grievances and even a "work-to-rule", where workers refuse to do anything not explicitly allowed for in the contract. It can also greatly increase the willingness of workers to go out on strike in subsequent contract negotiations, or even to engage in a wildcat strike.

Coping Behaviours

There can be little question that the above forms of conflict are important in labour relations, but perhaps equally important are the ways in which workers cope with the situation in which they find themselves. For example, it is not uncommon to observe repeated incidents of horseplay in the workplace (Roy, 1959; Applebaum, 1981). This may involve pranks against co-workers, or it may involve mock fighting, or even actual play fights with paper clips, tape balls, or whatever is at hand. It is also not uncommon to observe lengthy and often repetitive "chatter", interlaced with frequent swearing and various forms of "macho" behaviour (especially in predominantly male workplaces) and griping about supervisors, other workers, or, in service jobs, customers (Sugiman, 1984). This kind of behaviour can seem immature and illegitimate to the outsider, but it can serve as an important outlet for underlying tensions and frustrations arising from the nature of the employment relation, enabling workers to get through the work day.

While these forms of coping may be relatively benign in their effects, one which is more serious is alcohol and drug use, both on and off the job. On the job, workers may have bottles hidden, or they might look for opportunities to sneak outside and "smoke up". Off the job, it is not uncommon for leisure activities to be structured around drinking, whether this involves a few beers after work or meeting at the pub for drinks after some sporting event. The costs of substance abuse can be enormous, not just for workers and their families, but also for both employers and society in general. Not only does job performance suffer, injury rates and absenteeism are much higher. Of course, it would be wrong to attribute substance abuse solely to the nature of the employment experience. But it would be equally wrong to think that this experience is not an important contributing factor.

IV. ACCOUNTING FOR VARIATION IN CONFLICT

To this point, the sources of conflict and cooperation have been identified, the contradictions between them noted, and the behavioural manifestations of these contradictions addressed. Yet it would be wrong to leave the impression that either the experiences of workers or the manifestation of these experiences are uniform, for both can vary considerably across individual jobs, across firms, and across industries and occupations. What determines this variation?

On the surface, variation in the experiences and behaviour of workers can be explained by "cultural" considerations, including both the values and beliefs workers bring to the workplace (Gallie, 1978) *and* the attitudes and norms developed over time *within* the workplace (Gouldner, 1954; Edwards and Whitson, 1989). In other words, much depends upon the way in which workers perceive and interpret the reality in which they find themselves and the forms of behaviour that they consider acceptable.[11] Thus, if workers come from a conservative culture, in which obedience and deference to authority are strongly encouraged, and if the culture in the workplace is one where workers are highly committed and defiance or sabotage are frowned upon, then the level of conflict and work avoidance is likely to be relatively low, and most managerial actions are likely to be interpreted in a positive light. But if workers come from an "oppositional" culture, in which militancy and defiance to managerial authority are viewed as accept-

---

[11] This argument is consistent with "hermeneutic" or "subjectivist" approaches to social science, which generally stress that behaviour is not determined by objective circum

able, and if the culture in the workplace is one where workers are highly adversarial and deference is frowned upon, the opposite is likely to be the case.

At the same time, cultural factors cannot be considered in isolation from more "objective" circumstances, for they come over time to reflect these circumstances — at least in part. For example, research studies repeatedly find that workers are more likely to feel alienated from management and engage in acts of conflict in large establishments (Hodson, 1984; Godard, 1992b) They also indicate that the nature and conditions of work may make an important difference (Kohn, 1979; Kohn et al., 1990; Godard, 1999a, 2001), for reasons that should be evident from the discussion above. Perhaps even more important are managerial policies and practices in the workplace. As managerialists argue, these can significantly affect levels of job satisfaction, trust, and commitment. Finally, more "macro" economic conditions (e.g., unemployment levels) and government policies (e.g., unemployment benefits) may make an important difference, because they can affect the extent to which workers are effectively "coerced to cooperate" and hence their attitudes and expectations (see Burawoy, 1985; Godard, 1997a).

Identifying these objective sources of variation is not meant to suggest that they in any sense determine variation in the experiences and behaviour of workers. Instead, they should be seen as forming the conditions in which workplace cultures develop and norms of behaviour emerge, subject to social processes involving workers, managers, and other relevant actors. Under some conditions, certain attitudes and behaviours are more *likely* to develop than others, but whether in fact they do is by no means a certainty. More important, identifying the sources of variation should not be allowed to obscure the broader point: even though they may vary in a number of ways, the sources of conflict and cooperation identified in this chapter are fundamental to labour–management relations, with important implications for understanding these relations.

---

stances, but instead reflects the meanings actors attach to these circumstances (see Godard, 1993b). As it applies to the study of workplace behaviour, it is perhaps most effectively developed in Pfeffer and Salancik (1978).

V.   SOME IMPLICATIONS

The analysis in this chapter has at least two major implications. The first has to do with managerial attempts to ensure high levels of worker loyalty and job commitment through **progressive HRM practices**. These attempts are discussed more fully in chapter five, but they can be understood essentially as attempts to reduce the contextual sources of conflict and to enhance the sources of cooperation. For example, these policies can entail designing the work process so that workers have greater discretion and opportunity for fulfilment, minimizing status differentials between workers and management, providing safe and pleasant working conditions, establishing consultation and information-sharing programs, locating in areas characterized by conservative values, and a whole host of practices designed to maintain good "human relations". Yet these attempts cannot eliminate the underlying sources of conflict. Thus, while it *may* be possible to achieve high levels of loyalty and commitment, this loyalty and commitment may be far more difficult to achieve and sustain than proponents typically assume. This may be an important reason why these policies are not as widely adopted as managerialists would like and why their effectiveness is often limited, as discussed in chapter five.

The second major implication has to do with the effects of labour unions and collective bargaining on conflict. A common argument, especially by proponents of the neoliberal perspective, is that unions drive an artificial wedge between labour and management and hence act as an unnecessary cause of conflict. However, conflict underlies the labour–management relationship whether a union is established or not. While unions can no doubt give rise to increased levels of conflict, they are in many respects also a reflection of this conflict, providing a vehicle for its expression rather than causing it per se. Indeed, as pluralists in particular have argued, collective bargaining and the grievance arbitration process serve as mechanisms for its orderly resolution, and as such may provide workers with alternatives to the more "hidden" yet insidious forms of conflict identified above.

VI.   CONCLUSION

This chapter has provided a foundation for understanding labour–management relations in contemporary Canada. It has done so by establishing the sources of both conflict and cooperation in industrial relations, the contradictory relations between them, and the implications of these relations for the ways in which the sources of conflict tend to be manifest. It has also briefly identified the reasons for variation in conflict and the implications of underlying conflicts in particular for understanding unions and for employer practices in industrial relations. Yet, understanding the sources of conflict and cooperation and their interrelations only provides a starting point for understanding industrial relations. How these sources are manifest, and the outcomes which result, depend in considerable measure on the actions of employers, of unions, and of the state. In turn, these actions are very much the product of historical processes, which continue to develop and unfold. Thus, to really understand industrial relations, it is important to address their historical development. This is the task of the following chapter.

Work and Industrial Relations in Historical Perspective

4

This chapter addresses the historical development of industrial capitalism and its implications for industrial relations in Canada. Doing so is important in two respects. First, contemporary arrangements and developments do not represent an unchanging or pre-given "natural order of things", but are instead part and parcel of often complex historical processes. Thus, in order to understand labour–management relations in Canada at present and in the future, it is essential to be familiar with the past from which these relations came and of which they represent a continuation. Second, historical analysis can serve as an excellent vehicle for introducing various facets of labour law, labour unions, and management practices as they exist at present. Indeed, many of the remaining chapters in this text begin where the present one leaves off.

I.   UNDERSTANDING LABOUR HISTORY

The historical development of industrial relations can, for the most part, be viewed as reflecting historical processes of rationalization and bureaucratization, processes which have increasingly come to be manifest in the structure of, and the relations between, business, labour, and government. There are many who believe that this process reached its zenith in the 1970s, and that we have since been witnessing the emergence of a new era, in which bureaucratic institutions are giving way to more flexible ones. But few would disagree that, as firms became increasingly large in scale and as mass production technologies became increasingly predominant throughout the past century, work and labour–management relations became increasingly bureaucratized, as did the labour movement, government, and work organizations in general.

To an extent, these processes evolved gradually. But this evolution was punctuated by periods of disequilibrium and change, as the economy passed through periods of expansion and contraction, and as workers pushed for basic rights and protections. It was also far from pre-determined: though rationalization and bureaucratization increasingly came to define developed capitalist economies in general by the 1950s and 1960s, each country — including Canada — had its own specific national variant, reflecting institutions and value structures unique to that country as well as the conscious and unconscious choices of various "players", whether they were groups of workers, labour leaders, employers, or governments.

The punctuated nature of historical development is in large part attributable to the contradictions between the sources of conflict and those of cooperation (see chapter three) as these have developed and changed over time. In reflection of these contradictions, labour–management relations in Canada have historically oscillated between periods of substantial conflict, typically accompanied by more rapid growth in the labour movement (and working class organizations in general), and longer periods of relative calm and limited growth (or even decline). Consistent with these oscillations, the labour movement has had to struggle between the impulse to seek radical change and widespread reforms, reflecting the sources of conflict discussed in the preceding chapter, and the practical reality of limited worker power and aspirations, reflecting the sources of cooperation.

Various contradictions have also come to be reflected in the actions of employers who, on the one hand, have sought to maximize profitability through the design and organization of work, and on the other, have found themselves continually subject to the various forms of conflict identified in chapter three. Of particular importance have been attempts by workers to protect their wages, jobs, and working conditions in the face of employer attempts to introduce changes which (intentionally or unintentionally) threaten skill levels and/or intensify the pace of work. But even where this has not been the case, "problems" of turnover, absenteeism, workplace recalcitrance, and strike activity have always existed, although perhaps to varying degrees. As such, management has had to be concerned with the "political" problem of motivating and controlling workers as much as it has with the "technical" problem of maximizing efficiency per se. Indeed, the political and the technical have often conflicted with one another, as is discussed in chapter six.

Governments in Canada have faced a similar dilemma. On the one hand, they have traditionally sought to maintain the status quo, often with the collusion of employers (e.g., Jamieson, 1968). But on the other hand, to achieve this objective they have often had to respond to the demands of workers and their unions by providing rights and protections that have, in turn, altered the status quo. It is largely for this reason that the various rights and protections enjoyed by workers in the post-World War II era came into being — though to explain these rights and protections solely in these terms would, of course, be oversimplified (as shall become apparent in chapter ten). Nonetheless, the need to alter the status quo in order to preserve it has been an important factor underlying governmental actions.

It is not possible within the confines of a single chapter to fully draw out the importance of these considerations. In fact, the analysis can only concentrate on major events and developments of relevance to present-day industrial relations. However, it is important to keep them in mind. In addition, the reader may wish to refer to Table 4–1, which documents union membership, union density, and strike activity from the early decades of the twentieth century. For union membership and density, those numbers appearing in bold in this table reflect years of substantial increase (by 5 percent or more for total union membership and one percentage point or more for union density). For strike activity, they reflect years in which days lost due to strike exceeded .25 percent of total hours worked in the economy.

II. THE EARLY INDUSTRIALIZATION ERA: THE 1870s TO THE EARLY 1900s[1]

In the early nineteenth century, Canada was largely a pre-industrial society, with a small population concentrated along the eastern coast and along major inland waterways. Though there was some manufacturing (see Palmer, 1992: 37–39), fish, furs, timber, and wheat were the only goods produced in quantity for trade.

By the 1850s, things had begun to change. The construction of railways and canals linked the scattered rural villages, providing the infrastructure for expanded trade and an increased division of labour. Many craftsmen expanded their workshops into "manufactories" employing both skilled and unskilled workers, and merchants began to find that it was in their interests to set up factories rather than

---

[1] This and the following sections draw extensively from Rinehart (1996), Heron (1989), Russell (1990), and Palmer (1992).

TABLE 4–1 Strike Activity and Union Growth in Canada, 1911–2009

Year	Union membership (thousands)	Union density (membership as a percentage of non-agricultural paid workers)	Days lost due to strikes and lockouts as a percentage of total working time
1911	133	—	—
1912	**160**	—	—
1913	**176**	—	—
1914	166	—	—
1915	143	—	—
1916	**160**	—	—
1917	*205*	—	—
1918	**249**	—	—
1919	**378**	—	**0.60**
1920	374	—	0.14
1921	313	16.0	0.22
1922	277	13.6	**0.32**
1923	278	13.2	0.13
1924	261	12.2	**0.26**
1925	271	12.3	0.23
1926	275	12.0	0.05
1927	290	12.1	0.03
1928	301	12.1	0.04
1929	*319*	12.6	0.02
1930	322	13.1	0.01
1931	311	**15.3**	0.04
1932	283	15.3	0.05
1933	286	**16.7**	0.07
1934	281	14.6	0.11
1935	281	14.5	0.05
1936	**323**	**16.2**	0.05
1937	**383**	**18.2**	0.15
1938	382	18.4	0.02
1939	359	17.3	0.04
1940	362	16.3	0.04
1941	**462**	**18.0**	0.06
1942	**578**	**20.6**	0.05
1943	**665**	**22.7**	0.12
1944	**724**	**24.3**	0.06
1945	711	24.2	0.19
1946	**832**	**27.9**	**0.54**
1947	**912**	**29.1**	**0.27**
1948	**978**	**30.3**	0.10
1949	1,006	29.5	0.11
1950	n/a	n/a	0.15
1951	1,029	28.4	0.09
1952	**1,146**	**30.2**	**0.29**
1953	**1,220**	**33.0**	0.14
1954	1,268	33.8	0.15
1955	1,268	33.7	0.19
1956	**1,352**	33.3	0.11
1957	1,368	32.4	0.13
1958	1,454	34.2	0.25
1959	1,459	33.3	0.19
1960	1,459	32.3	0.06
1961	1,447	31.6	0.11
1962	1,423	30.2	0.11
1963	1,449	29.8	0.07
1964	1,493	29.4	0.11
1965	1,589	29.7	0.17

Continued....

TABLE 4–1 (continued)

Year	Union membership (thousands)	Union density (membership as a percentage of non-agricultural paid workers)	Days lost due to strikes and lockouts as a percentage of total working time
1966	**1,736**	**30.7**	**0.34**
1967	**1,921**	**32.3**	0.25
1968	**2,010**	33.1	**0.32**
1969	2,975	32.5	**0.46**
1970	2,173	**33.6**	**0.39**
1971	2,231	32.4	0.16
1972	**2,371**	**33.9**	**0.43**
1973	**2,591**	**35.4**	**0.30**
1974	**2,732**	35.3	**0.46**
1975	**2,884**	35.6	**0.53**
1976	**3,042**	**36.9**	**0.55**
1977	3,149	36.3	0.15
1978	3,278	37.1	**0.34**
1979	n/a	n/a	**0.34**
1980	3,397	35.7	**0.38**
1981	3,487	35.4	**0.37**
1982	3,617	35.7	**0.25**
1983	3,563	36.4	0.19
1984	3,651	**37.2**	0.16
1985	3,666	36.4	0.13
1986	3,730	36.0	**0.28**
1987	3,782	35.2	0.15
1988	3,841	34.8	0.18
1989	3,944	34.5	0.13
1990	4,031	**36.2**	0.17
1991	4,068	34.7	0.09
1992	4,089	**35.7**	0.07
1993	4,071	35.8	0.07
1994	4,078	35.6	0.06
1995	4,003	34.3	0.05
1996	4,033	33.9	0.11
1997	4,074	34.1	0.12
1998	3,938	**32.5***	0.08
1999	4,010	32.6	0.08
2000	4,058	31.9	0.05
2001	4,111	31.3	0.07
2002	4,174	31.1	0.09
2003	4,178	30.4	0.05
2004	4,261	30.5	0.09
2005	4,381	30.7	0.11
2006	4,441	30.7	0.02
2007	4,480	30.3	0.05
2008	4,592	30.4	0.02
2009	4,605	29.9	0.06

For union membership, bold text indicates years in which there has been an increase of 5.0 percent or more over the preceding year. For density, bold text indicates years in which density increased by 1 percent or more. For strike activity, bold text indicates years in which strike activity has exceeded .25 of working time.

* This drop may in part reflect a change in data collection methods. See chapter sixteen.

Sources: For union membership: from 1911 to 1970, J.K. Eaton (1975); from 1971–1998, Labour Canada, *Directory of Labour Organizations in Canada,* various years; from 1999 to 2009, HRSDC, the *Workplace Gazette* 6(3): 41. For strike activity: from 1919 to 1988, *Strikes and Lockouts in Canada*; from 1989 to 1998, HRDC, the *Workplace Gazette* 6(3): 41; from 1999 to 2009, HRSDC, Labour Program, website.

import commodities. But it was not until the 1870s and 1880s that the industrialization process really got under way in Canada. This period witnessed a widespread growth in factory work, and with it the emergence of both the "coercive drive system" and the modern labour movement. As shall become apparent, the former is of note because it was the precursor of "scientific management" and because it has a number of parallels to developments of the past few decades. The latter is of note because it essentially established the form of union-management relations that was to become dominant within North America throughout the twentieth century.

The Coercive Drive System

Prior to the 1870s, most manufacturing was carried out in small workshops in accordance with traditional craft methods, and most skilled work remained under the control of workers themselves. In general, relations between employers and employees remained informal, and workers enjoyed considerable discretion and autonomy on the job. Indeed, instead of attempting to assert direct control over their employees, many employers found it more practical to subcontract work to skilled tradespeople who, in turn, would hire their own assistants (Heron, 1989: 15). But by the 1870s and 1880s, factories were becoming increasingly large in size, with a growing division of labour and increased mechanization.

As a result, owners found it necessary to hire a middle strata of supervisors and gang bosses, providing these employees with almost total authority over the hiring, disciplining, and payment of workers under their direction (Stone, 1975). Often, these supervisors and gang bosses were paid on the basis of output and hence had every incentive to extract as much labour from workers as possible at as low a cost as possible. This latter development in particular, coupled with economic pressures of the time, led to what has come to be referred to as the **coercive drive system**.

As documented by the Royal Commission on the Relations Between Capital and Labour of 1889, this system entailed increasingly long hours, oppressive working conditions, and harsh and arbitrary treatment — especially for unskilled male workers, women, and children, who could not effectively "fight back" (Kealey, 1973; Rinehart, 1996: 32–34). Workers came to be treated more as commodities to be exploited than as human beings to whom employers bore a responsibility. Workers often found themselves working ten to twelve hours per day six days a week, with little or no economic security beyond that of support from their relatives if employers deemed them to be no longer of value and dismissed them. Thus, the term "coercive drive".

The coercive drive system appears to have been of only limited effectiveness for employers. Not only did it seem to heighten worker resistance and alienation (see Rinehart, 1996: 34–37), it also failed to address problems of planning, organizing, and coordinating work that had arisen with the growth in factory size and concomitant increases in the division of labour. A lack of rational management techniques meant that workplaces were often chaotic, with workers continuing to exercise considerable control over the pace of work and hence the quantity of output produced (Taylor, 1947; Gordon, Edwards, and Reich, 1982: 96–97). Workers were quick to learn that, if they all held the pace of production down, supervisors could not single out individuals for failing to do a "fair day's work" — especially if supervisors themselves did not understand the actual process by which work was performed. Intentionally holding down the pace of production, or what Frederick Taylor referred to as "systematic soldiering" (Taylor, 1947: 32), both protected individuals who were not capable of producing at a faster rate, and enabled workers to avoid exhausting themselves or putting themselves at undue risk of injury.

The Emergence of the Modern Labour Movement

Accompanying the growth of the coercive drive system was the growth of labour unions. The earliest unions in Canada can be traced back as far as 1798 (Palmer, 1992: 56). But they consisted largely of "mutual benefit societies", providing members or their families with economic benefits in the case of injury or death. It was not really until the 1870s that working class organizations really began to become established in Canada,[2] and not until the 1880s that the modern labour *movement* was to emerge.

The harsh working conditions associated with the coercive drive system undoubtedly played a key role in the growth of unions during this period. But at least two related factors may also be considered

---

[2] There were a number of important developments in the 1870s. For example, the Nine Hour Movement was formed in the early 1870s to fight (unsuccessfully) for a reduction in the length of the working day. The early 1870s also saw the formation of the Workingman's Political Party, the publication of Canada's first labour-oriented newspaper (the *Ontario Workman*), and the birth of the Canadian Labour Union (CLU), which was to represent workingmen's concerns at the political level, but working class organizations by-and-large languished throughout most of this decade (Heron, 1989: 18).

important. First, with the growth in firm size, the more informal, personal relations between employers and their workers characteristic of earlier times began to break down. Workers felt an increased psychological distance from owners, which was undoubtedly heightened by the use of gang bosses (Edwards, 1979: 29). Second, traditional craft methods and skills came to be increasingly threatened, as employers sought to bypass craft standards in order to lower costs, and to reduce dependence on expensive skilled labour. Underlying interest conflicts became increasingly apparent as a result, with craft workers resisting employer attempts to introduce new technologies and work methods, and workers in general becoming increasingly aware of the need to band together. The result was not only a growth in unions, but also the emergence of labour federations. Three are particularly worthy of note: the Knights of Labor, the Trades and Labour Congress, and the American Federation of Labor.

The Knights of Labor. The Knights of Labor was predominantly a U.S.-based organization founded in Philadelphia in 1869 and growing to a worldwide membership of roughly one million by 1886. The Knights are of interest in two respects.

First, the Knights possessed a very different philosophy than the one that was to become dominant within the North American labour movement throughout the twentieth century: they did not believe in workplace level struggle or strike activity. Instead, they sought a moral and political transformation of capitalism, advocating moral and legal restraints on the exercise of managerial authority and a greater sense of mutual obligation and cooperation between managers and the managed. To this end, they placed considerable emphasis on educating workers in the principles of what they referred to as "Labour Reform" and concomitantly on the election of politicians sympathetic to their cause (see Palmer, 1992: 138–42; Heron, 1989: 23–25). But they also sought to curb the power of the banks, which they believed to be largely responsible for many economic problems. Also noteworthy, they experimented (unsuccessfully) with producer and consumer cooperatives, in the belief that these would be conducive to the kind of economic and social order they envisioned.

Second, was the virtual collapse of the Knights of Labour in the United States after 1887, and with it their broad-based, reform-oriented philosophy. Though the reasons for their collapse are a matter of some debate (see Palmer, 1992: 149–54), a major reason would appear to be that the Knights were too idealistic, and perhaps even naive. To think that they could effect widespread change primarily through education rather than through economic and political struggle was to underestimate the power and influence of employers, who were essentially able to defeat the Knights through a major counterattack (Voss, 1993). Moreover, by focusing at the political level and attempting to avoid workplace level confrontation, the immediate, concrete concerns of workers were left unaddressed (Heron, 1989: 27). In fact, while the leaders of the Knights *did* authorize strikes, they did so only as a last resort. As a result, workers became frustrated and disillusioned, often striking against the wishes of their leaders and without leadership support (see Kealey and Palmer, 1986).

The Trades and Labour Congress (TLC). In Canada, the demise of the Knights occurred much later and somewhat more slowly than in the United States, probably because Canada was slower to industrialize. In fact, the Knights of Labour merged in 1886 with the predominantly craft-based Toronto Trades and Labour Council to form the **Trades and Labour Congress (TLC)**. The TLC had only a small staff, and its primary purpose was to serve as a vehicle for annual meetings of worker representatives from across the country. These representatives would, in turn, pass various policies advocating legislative reforms and then would lobby the federal and provincial governments to adopt these policies. However, it would appear that their success was limited: they do not seem to have significantly influenced government policies or legislation (Morton, 1989: 159). Perhaps the more important development was the formation in the United States of the American Federation of Labor (AFL), also in 1886. The philosophy and approach associated with the AFL was to become the predominant one in North America throughout the twentieth century.

The American Federation of Labor. The formation of the American Federation of Labor in part reflected the problems faced by the Knights. The AFL consisted primarily of **craft unions**, which are organized on the basis of skills (e.g., carpenters, machinists). While initially supportive of broader social and political reforms (Perlman, 1949 [1928]; Forbath, 1991), it came to adopt a more defensive, "job conscious" philosophy, sometimes referred to as "business" or "bread and butter" unionism. Though this philosophy did not oppose political action, it focused primarily upon establishing stable collective bargaining relationships with employers and negotiating formal, mutually binding, written contracts. It also engendered a much more bureaucratic style of unionism, characterized by higher dues, more full-time officials and organizers, more centralized power over strike funds and benefit plans, and strict craft lines defining the jurisdictions of member unions (Heron, 1989: 34–35).

Of particular importance, the AFL outlawed "dual unionism", said to occur where two or more unions claimed jurisdiction over the same workers or where one attempted to cut across craft lines. This meant the general exclusion of **industrial unions**, so named because they attempted to organize all workers within an industry and, as such, often attempted to claim jurisdiction over skilled workers already claimed by craft unions. As a result, the AFL accepted industrial unions only if they organized in industries that did not have traditional skilled workers or if they agreed to exclude skilled workers from their membership.

Though based primarily in the United States, AFL member unions began to accelerate their attempts to organize Canadian craft workers in the 1890s, primarily so as to prevent the development of a cheap, non-union labour force north of the border, thus eradicating a major possible source of pressure upon U.S. employers to reduce wages and violate craft standards in order to remain competitive (Heron, 1989: 36). By 1902, leaders of the AFL were able to have the last remnants of the Knights of Labor, several French-Canadian locals, and a few independent Canadian unions expelled from the TLC, in effect marking the beginning of over half a century of domination in Canada of U.S.-based **"international" unions**.

The exclusionary policies of the AFL and its unions were to portend a major split in both the U.S. and Canadian labour movements in the 1930s and 1940s, as the industrial union movement emerged and grew in strength. But the important point here is that the 1880s and 1890s witnessed the emergence of a narrower and more bureaucratic labour movement, one that was dominated by the international unions of the AFL. While this was to create some serious long-run problems for the Canadian labour movement, it strengthened craft unionism in this country considerably in the late 1890s and early 1900s.

In short, therefore, the period from 1870s to the early 1900s witnessed the rise of the factory system and the development of the capitalist employment relation: traditional bonds between employees and employers diminished, interest conflicts became increasingly apparent, work organizations became increasingly hierarchical, questions concerning a "fair day's work" began to arise, and work became increasingly fragmented and routinized. All of these factors were identified in chapter three as underlying sources of conflict, and so it is not surprising that management faced not only growing problems of disorganization, but also growing worker resistance and, most important, the emergence and early development of the labour movements in both the United States and Canada, with formative implications for the complexion of industrial relations throughout the twentieth century.

III. THE MANAGEMENT ERA: 1900 TO 1929

In essence, the late 1800s can be viewed as "labour's era". Even though the plight of a great many workers was by no means a satisfactory one and their organizations were still fledgling ones, workers often fought back both in the workplace and through their organizations in an attempt to maintain their dignity and living standards. Over the next few decades, however, management responded to the challenges confronting it, doing so in essentially three ways: (1) adopting increasingly coercive union avoidance practices, (2) developing techniques for rationalizing and gaining control over the work process, and (3) adopting progressive practices in an attempt to re-establish relations of trust and loyalty characteristic of the pre-industrialization era.

Coercive Union Avoidance Practices

Coercive union avoidance policies were essentially extensions of the coercive drive approach, and had their beginnings in the late nineteenth century, when employers often fired, blacklisted, and even beat workers for participating in union activities.[3] But these practices became increasingly sophisticated in the early 1900s. Of particular note was the hiring of spies, detectives, and "spotters" to infiltrate the workplace, ferret out union activists, and/or (in some cases) encourage more militant workers to engage in acts of violence, thereby discrediting the union. In a number of instances, employers hired private police and obtained local or provincial police assistance in putting down strikes. Where possible, employers would also hire strikebreakers, bringing these individuals in to perform the jobs of workers on strike. A common practice of the times was also to require workers to sign, as a condition of employment, a "yellow dog contract" pledging that they were not members of a union and would not join one. Finally,

---

[3] For a discussion of these practices, see Bernstein (1972). They are also noted in Palmer (1992: 163).

where a union was established, it was not uncommon for management to simply violate the negotiated agreement. Especially important in this respect were employer attempts to violate union rules governing the training and use of apprentices, in the hope of breaking the power of skilled craft workers and hence of their union.

The Rationalization of Work

Attempts to rationalize the workplace often complemented union avoidance policies, for they appear to have been directed as much at reducing worker skill levels and enhancing employer control over the process of work as they were at reducing disorganization and enhancing efficiency in the technical sense of this term. Most notorious in this respect was the "**scientific management**"[4] movement associated with Frederick Taylor.

Frederick Winslow Taylor was from an old and respected Philadelphia family. In keeping with his background, he was originally slated to attend Harvard University, but was prevented from doing so due to eye problems (which appear to have been psychosomatic). Instead, he entered into a craft apprenticeship as a pattern-maker and machinist at the age of eighteen, in 1874. Four years later, after completing his apprenticeship, he took a job as a labourer at Midvale Steel in Philadelphia (which was owned by close family friends), eventually working his way up to the position of gang boss, then foreman, and, finally, chief engineer.

During this time, Taylor was struck by both the disorganization and chaos he observed in the workplace and by the recalcitrance of workers. But he also came to believe that these problems could be readily overcome by the application of scientific principles to both the design of work and the resolution of labour–management disagreements. Most notable in this respect are Taylor's "**time and motion**" studies, through which trained experts systematically observe the activities of workers, break them down into specific tasks and motions, and time how long it takes to do each one. Work is then redesigned so as to eliminate those motions that are "inefficient" and to narrow the number of tasks performed by each worker — in effect increasing the level of specialization and hence the division of labour. Next, workers

---

[4] See in particular chapters four and five of Braverman (1974). Though Braverman's discussion of the long-term effects of Taylorism has been taken to task by a number of authors, his discussion of the principles of scientific management and the rationale underlying it is excellent.

are assigned a daily quota, based upon the expert's conception of how much work they are capable of doing in a day, or "a fair day's work". To overcome resistance, workers are then provided with a substantial bonus each time they meet or exceed their quota.

In theory, Taylor's ideas not only enhanced efficiency, they also entailed the scientific resolution of conflict. During this era, much conflict was over what constituted a "fair day's work". By applying Taylor's principles, it would be possible for neutral "experts" to scientifically establish just how much workers could be expected to produce in a day. It would also be possible to resolve disputes over the most efficient methods by which to perform work.

In practice, it is likely that Taylor's methods did have positive efficiency implications. Yet scientific management has been widely criticized as resulting in the growth of narrow, repetitive tasks with little discretion throughout much of the twentieth century. It has also been argued that the real effect of Taylor's ideas was not to enhance efficiency per se, but rather to enable employers to undermine craft skills and wrest control of the work process away from workers (Braverman, 1974). Under this argument, time and motion studies allowed management to penetrate trade secrets and thereby "externalize" what hither-to had been the internal knowledge base and exclusive preserve of skilled workers. This not only enabled management to simplify and divide up work so that it could be done by unskilled workers, it also enabled employers to circumvent union apprenticeship systems by implementing "scientific" training methods.

Indeed, at the heart of Taylor's work was something that has come to be known as the "**think-do dichotomy**". According to Taylor, it is unfair to expect workers to think, for their job is simply to "do". It is management's job to think. As such, scientific management was in essence directed at the separation of "conception" (thinking) from "execution" (doing), thereby totally subordinating workers to their tasks and denying them any opportunity for mastery and control (Braverman, 1974).

Finally, the notion that work could be scientifically designed and a "fair day's work" scientifically established so as to eliminate workplace conflicts came to be advanced as an anti-union ideology, for if the issues typically under dispute could be scientifically resolved, all unions could do was get in the way (see Bendix, 1956). Although the extent to which Taylor himself believed this to be the case is a matter of some debate (Nyland, 1998), it would appear that Taylorism became an important device for marginalizing unions and rendering workers mute.

The extent to which all of Taylor's ideas were ever adopted in practice has been a matter of some debate,[5] as is the extent to which they served to undermine craft skills. But they clearly portended a general transformation in the nature of work, and have been applied in one form or another by industrial engineers throughout much of the past century (Soule, 1952; Clawson, 1980), finding their mechanical counterpart in mass production, and particularly the moving assembly line. First introduced by Henry Ford in 1914, the traditional assembly line not only entailed a minute division of labour, leaving workers with virtually no discretion over how the work is performed, it also determined the pace at which output is produced, leaving workers with virtually no discretion over the speed at which they worked.

While the success of managerial attempts to rationalize the work process undoubtedly met with some measure of success, they failed to address problems (at least, from management's point of view) associated with worker discontent, and in fact may have made these problems worse (Edwards, 1979). This was true even of the moving assembly line, where it was possible for workers to sabotage the production process and, indeed, to shut down the production line altogether. In addition, of course, despite Taylor's claim that the performance and pace of work could be scientifically determined by experts, these "experts" were management personnel, and so the notion of what constituted a fair day's work was very much a managerial one — as was the notion of what constituted a fair day's pay. Thus, trust and loyalty remained problematic for management.

Paternalistic Management Practices

To restore trust and loyalty, management in a number of firms began to adopt progressive measures. These measures are often referred to as **paternalistic management practices**, for they were based on the pre-industrial assumption that management has a responsibility to look after the welfare of workers and determine what was in their best interests — much as a father (or mother) would do for his (or her) children. They first began to be adopted in the early 1900s, though they did not become widespread until the 1920s, largely in response to massive labour unrest immediately after World War I (this will be

---

[5] A 1928 survey by the federal Department of Labour revealed that scientific management was widespread in Canada. However, the definition of scientific management used in this survey was far broader than Taylor's, and included a number of practices associated more with paternalistic management, as will be discussed below (Lowe, 1984: 166).

returned to later). Thus, while their early adoption may in part have been motivated by moral concerns of employers, the era of "**welfare capitalism**", as the 1920s are often referred to, seems to have arisen almost entirely for pragmatic reasons.

Paternalistic management essentially entailed the emergence of the personnel/human resources management function, and in many respects is the forerunner of the "new" human resources management and the "high performance" paradigms, which have become increasingly popular over the past few decades. Indeed, many of the practices associated with paternalistic management have become part and parcel of this paradigm and continue to be practised in today's economy (see Jacoby, 1997). Paternalistic management practices included:[6]

1. Joint labour–management "**works councils**", consisting of worker and management representatives meeting periodically to discuss various issues and problems; these were also referred to as "**company unions**", for they served as substitute unions largely controlled by the company.

2. Profit and/or "gain" sharing plans, where workers receive some form of bonus tied to the firm's profitability or productivity.

3. Provision of pensions, holidays, and other benefits for workers.

4. **"Open door" policies**, where individuals are free to take their concerns or grievances directly to senior management officials, whose "door is always open".

5. Elaborate safety and health programs, intended to convey a concern for employee well-being.

6. Counselling and assistance programs for workers with personal (e.g., alcohol-related) or family problems.

7. Provision of long-term job security, accompanied by a no-layoffs policy.

8. Formal recognition of employees for lengthy service and/or outstanding performance.

9. Company sponsored recreational and social events, including company picnics and Christmas parties.

10. Company subsidized stores and housing.

---

[6] For good discussions of these practices in the United States see Nelson (1975), chapter five; Edwards (1979), chapter six; and Jacoby (1997). For Canada, see Lowe (1979), and Storey (1987).

These practices were widely popularized as the wave of the future in both the press and the management literature, in much the same way that their modern day counterparts associated with the high performance paradigm have been over the past few decades. They also appear to have met with some success. Yet they were fully adopted only in a relatively small number of firms, accounting for no more than a fifth of the labour force in the United States (see Jacoby, 1997: 20), and probably less in Canada.

Paternalistic practices also did little to alter the nature of the labour–management relationship, at least not in any meaningful way. Though workers might have had the right to elect works council representatives and to take any concerns they might have to senior managers, these rights were granted by management at management's discretion. Workers had no legal recourse if dissatisfied with the outcome and, in the case of the open door policy, they had little protection against retribution from supervisors and lower level managers if they went over their heads. In addition, workers often did not automatically qualify for many of the benefits offered, but instead had to remain with the employer and demonstrate their loyalty over a given length of time (Edwards, 1979: 92–93; Jacoby, 1997: 15). And, even once they did qualify, they had little legal claim to the benefits. As such, any demonstration of disloyalty (real or imagined) could lead to disqualification or even dismissal. Thus, these benefits were a double-edged sword, in effect coercing workers to be loyal as much as inducing loyalty voluntarily.

Whither Conflict?

Whatever the inadequacies of the managerial response, the overall growth in the labour movement appears to have been minimal from the early 1900s through to the early 1930s. The first two decades of this period did, however, witness a considerable amount of conflict (see Palmer, 1992: 170ff). For example, from 1900 to 1911, there were over 1,300 strikes in Canada (Craven, 1980: 13).[7] Moreover, this conflict did result in some legislative response. Of particular note was a lengthy coal strike in autumn of 1906 in Western Canada, which served as a major impetus to the federal government's enactment of the **Industrial Disputes and Investigation Act (IDIA)** in 1907.

---

[7] For an excellent discussion of the nature and rationale of a number of these strikes, see Heron and Palmer (1987).

Intended to foster greater order and stability in key industries, the IDIA compelled all unions and employers in the transportation, resource, and utilities industries to go before an ad hoc three-person board of conciliation if unable to resolve a dispute on their own, wait for the board to issue a report attempting to reconcile the differences between the parties, and then go through a cooling-off period before a strike or lockout could legally occur. The effectiveness of this Act as a means of reducing strike activity appears, however, to have been limited. Moreover, though the labour movement thought this Act would promote collective bargaining, its effect is uncertain, for it in essence weakened the ability of unions to strike and provided employers a grace period to prepare for a strike (for a discussion of this, see Russell, 1990: 98–103). But whatever the case, the IDIA is important because it required conciliation prior to a strike — a requirement that has continued to be widespread in Canadian labour law to the present day, albeit in modified form (see chapter thirteen).

Even more noteworthy than the IDIA were the developments during and immediately after the first world war. Weakened worker purchasing power due to rampant inflation and profiteering, attempts by employers to degrade craft skills, and discontent with government policies towards labour, led to a surge in labour militancy, and the labour movement more than doubled in size between 1916 to 1919. Unhappy with the relative conservatism of the TLC, and buoyed by the Russian Revolution of 1917, dissidents in Western Canada formed the **One Big Union (OBU)** in March 1919, and, with "solid socialist leadership" (to use one author's characterization), the OBU was quickly able to claim most of the western Canadian and northern Ontario labour movement within its ranks.

In May and June of 1919, Winnipeg workers staged perhaps the most famous event in Canadian labour history: the **Winnipeg General Strike**. This strike involved a six week walkout by virtually all workers in the city of Winnipeg, both union and non-union, in support of metal and building trades workers fighting for employer recognition of their unions and for improved wages. It spread to a number of western towns and cities (Kealey, 1986), but was soon crushed when the Royal Northwest Mounted Police, called in by the federal government, began shooting into a crowd of strikers, wounding as many as thirty and killing one (another was to die a few days later). Thousands of workers were subsequently fired, blacklisted, or harassed by the police, and many of the strike leaders were either jailed or deported (Bercusson, 1974).

The formation of the OBU and the Winnipeg General Strike are significant in at least two respects. First, they would appear to represent one of the few times (if not the only time) in Canadian history in which "class" lines became clearly drawn, and workers became conscious of themselves *as* a class. Second, they appear to have represented the beginning of the end of narrow craft unionism, for they involved large numbers of unskilled workers (including women), giving impetus to the resurgence of non-craft or industrial unionism. Yet, the OBU collapsed over the next few years, in part undermined by the refusal of employers to have anything to do with its affiliates, and in part undermined by craft union attempts to retain their dominance.

Accompanying the collapse of the OBU was a substantial decline in union membership, from a high of 378,000 members in 1919 to a low of 261,000 by 1924. Though union membership grew slightly in the remainder of the 1920s, it barely kept up with the growth in the size of the labour force, and remained at only 319,000 in 1930. This may be attributed in part to the continued spread of paternalistic management practices, particularly employer-dominated company unions. Though these provided workers with no legal rights whatsoever, they do appear to have been effective devices for keeping independent unions at bay (Rinehart, 1996: 50). Also important was the lack of legal protections for unions, coupled with the continued use of coercive union avoidance practices. Though craft workers had traditionally been able to overcome employer resistance, the main potential area for growth in the labour movement was among unskilled and semi-skilled workers, who were often readily replaceable and hence more susceptible to employer intimidation. Finally, throughout the 1920s, unemployment levels were high, as waves of immigrant workers continued to enter this country. This made it far more difficult to find work if workers lost their jobs for union activities.

IV. THE INSTITUTIONALIZATION OF CONFLICT: THE 1930s AND 1940s

The year 1929 brought the beginnings of the Great Depression and with it the end of the era of welfare capitalism. Although a few firms were able to continue their welfare capitalist practices, those commitments became too expensive for most. Coupled with the high levels of unemployment, the collapse of welfare capitalism in turn signalled to many workers that they could not rely on or trust their employers for basic rights and benefits. A new wave of union organizing began, one which saw the emergence of industrial unionism as a major force in both the U.S. and Canadian labour movements, and with it, the formation of two new labour federations: the **Congress for Industrial Organization (CIO)** in the United States and the **Canadian Congress of Labour (CCL)** in Canada. The CIO began as a department within the AFL, but jurisdictional disputes with craft unions led to the expulsion of its unions in 1937, and hence its formation as a separate labour federation. A similar process occurred in Canada. CIO affiliates were expelled from the TLC in 1939, resulting in the formation of the CCL the following year.

In both countries, the new industrial unions came to be known for their more activist, socially oriented philosophy, and for the missionary zeal of their organizers. Partly as a result, the percentage of the non-agricultural workforce in unions in the United States almost doubled in the years from 1930 to 1940, increasing from 12.9 percent to 22.5 percent (Troy and Sheflin, 1985). In Canada, union growth was much slower, increasing from 13.1 to 18.2 percent from 1930 to 1937, but dropping back to 16.3 percent by 1940. There are a number of possible reasons for the greater success of industrial unionism in the United States at this time, but one which is commonly thought to be of major importance is the enactment of the **National Labor Relations Act (NLRA)** in the United States in 1935, providing workers with rights and protections that they were not to receive in most Canadian jurisdictions until well into the 1940s.[8]

The National Labor Relations Act

The NLRA formed part of what has come to be referred to as the **New Deal** legislation enacted under Franklin Delanor Roosevelt in order to quell conflict and establish a basis for rebuilding the U.S. economy. Also referred to as the **Wagner Act,** after its primary sponsor in the U.S. Congress, this Act was to become the model for Canadian legislation a decade later, and in many respects laid the foundation for the post-war system of labour relations in both Canada and the United States. In essence, it both provided workers with the legal right to organize a union free from employer intimidation and required employers to recognize the union and bargain with it in good faith once certified.

Properly enforced, the NLRA protected workers against coercive union avoidance practices by employers and hence greatly facilitated

---

[8] The major exception was Nova Scotia, which enacted similar legislation in 1937.

the organization of unions, particularly industrial unions, whose members were more difficult to organize and typically had less labour market and relational power than their more skilled counterparts in the crafts. However, the agency whose mandate it was to enforce the Act (the National Labor Relations Board) suffered from internal turmoil and staffing problems (see Tomlins, 1985: 197ff), and its sanctioning powers were often insufficient to deter employers from continuing with their coercive union avoidance practices (see Harris, 1982: 20ff). Moreover, it was to be steadily weakened by court rulings and legal reforms, especially over the ensuing decade and a half. Yet at minimum, the NLRA legitimated the organizing attempts of industrial unions, while delegitimating the unfair labour practices of employers.[9] Particularly notable in this respect was the widespread public support for the "sit down" strike at the Flint Michigan plant of General Motors in 1937, when workers occupied the plant in an attempt to obtain employer recognition of their union, while their wives and children walked the picket lines outside the plant. Though the success of this strike was mixed, it was widely regarded as a moral victory for the labour movement and was a spur to further organization.

PC 1003: The Canadian Variant

Despite the enactment by some provinces of stronger legislation in support of union organization in the late 1930s, the Canadian labour movement met with little real success in the 1930s. There were some breakthroughs, perhaps the most notable of which was the success of workers in gaining employer recognition and a collective agreement at GM's Oshawa plant after a 15 day strike in 1937 (MacDowell and Sefton, 1993). But the real breakthrough for the Canadian labour movement was not to occur until World War II. An expanded workforce, discontent with the wartime policies of Mackenzie King's Liberal government, joined unions with increasing enthusiasm, and the labour movement almost doubled its number of members between 1940 and 1944, coming to account for 724,000 workers, or 24 percent of the non-agricultural labour force. This, coupled with a dramatic increase in industrial conflict and the growing popularity of the left-wing Co-operative Commonwealth Federation (CCF) (the precursor to the New Democratic Party), induced the government to introduce a

---

[9] For example, then President of the United States, Theodore W. Roosevelt, is said to have publicly declared that, if he was a worker, he would join a union too.

variety of social and economic reforms (see Panitch and Swartz, 1985: 18–19). Of particular relevance, however, was **Order-in-Council PC 1003,** proclaimed in 1944.

Order-in-Council PC 1003 essentially provided workers with the same protections as those enjoyed by U.S. workers under the Wagner Act of 1935. Though the Supreme Court had ruled in 1926 that the British North American (BNA) Act gave primary jurisdiction over labour–management relations to the provinces (see chapter nine), PC 1003 was enacted under the terms of the War Measures Act of 1917, which enabled the federal government to usurp provincial powers in times of war or any other threat to national security. This Act also enabled it to extend the provisions of PC 1003 for two years after the war into the "reconstruction" era (Heron, 1989: 83) enabling the labour movement to maintain its momentum in spite of often intensive employer hostility.

Despite PC 1003, unions continued to face extensive employer resistance after the war. As a result, 1946 witnessed a massive wave of strikes, mostly over employer refusals to recognize and bargain with unions. Yet, in contrast to earlier times, the labour movement now had sufficient legitimacy and momentum to be able to overcome management resistance. By 1948, unions represented 30 percent of the workforce, almost doubling their 1940 level of 16 percent, and significantly exceeding their 1944 level of 24 percent. It became clear that management would be unable to defeat unions as it had after World War I, and so the federal government finally passed the **Industrial Relations and Disputes Investigations Act**, combining the provisions of PC 1003 with those of the IDIA of 1907. By 1950, all provinces had adopted some form of legislation similar to this Act.

In essence, this legislation formed the basis for the post-war system of industrial relations, a system which remains in place to the present day. Yet, whether this legislation can be interpreted as *entirely* favourable to labour unions is debatable. As we shall see in chapter eleven, the post-war system may have institutionalized the right of workers to join unions and to strike, but it did not preclude employers from attempting to undermine this right by hiring replacement workers during a strike, and it also prohibited workers from striking either during the life of a collective agreement or during a dispute over union recognition. Equally important, this system evolved in a way that excluded workers or their representatives from any legal say in the exercise of managerial authority — beyond often minimal constraints negotiated in the collective agreement. In other words, while governments had undoubtedly given improved rights and protections to workers, they would appear to have done so in a way which was directed more at preserving the status quo in the face of widespread industrial unrest than at effecting substantive change in the nature of the employment relation. As such, unions were to remain in a largely reactive position, and the employment relation was to remain a largely authoritarian one at law, under which workers were allowed to negotiate the terms of their subordination, but not its fact.

The Birth of Human Relations

A final development in the 1930s and 1940s was the emergence of what came to be known as the "**human relations**" school. This school is perhaps most closely associated with the now-famous experiments conducted in the late 1920s and early 1930s at the Hawthorne plant of Western Electric, located in Chicago. Headed by Harvard researcher Elton Mayo, these experiments explored the implications of various incentive schemes and work arrangements for worker productivity, concluding that the "problem" in industry was caused more by a failure to adequately recognize and address the social needs of workers than it was by a failure to provide the appropriate economic incentives.[10]

The conclusions of the Hawthorne researchers have been the subject of considerable controversy, with some authors arguing that a close examination of the Hawthorne data suggests that observed changes in worker productivity could in fact be attributed to economic incentives (see Landsberger, 1958; Carey, 1967; Schlaifer, 1980; Jones, 1990). Moreover, the extent to which they had any immediate effect upon the actual practice of industrial relations is unclear. But they are important in at least two respects. First, they provided the basis for a new anti-union ideology, under which it was argued that industrial harmony was readily attainable and that unions were unnecessary if only management would address the social needs of workers (see Mills, 1948; Bendix, 1956). Second, the Hawthorne experiments provided the major impetus for a whole new area of study, initially referred to as "the human relations movement". This movement stressed the

---

[10] Indeed, Elton Mayo published a book entitled *The Human Problems of an Industrial Civilization* (1933), in which he advanced the Durkheimian argument (see chapter two) that industrialization had resulted in the break-up of the traditional community and that this, in turn, had given rise to widespread social anomie, thereby accounting for industrial conflict. According to Mayo, this problem could be solved if management would only recognize the social needs of employees, for it was now the work organization rather than the local community through which these needs could be most effectively served.

importance of good communication and group work, both of which are central to the "high performance" paradigm that was to become increasingly popular in the 1980s and 1990s.

V.   THE MATURATION OF INDUSTRIAL RELATIONS: THE 1950s AND EARLY 1960s

By the early 1950s, Canada had become a fully developed industrial nation. The core of the economy was increasingly characterized by large, bureaucratic corporations engaged in mass production and operating in concentrated and relatively stable product markets. The workplace in these corporations had, by and large, become rationalized and bureaucratized, characterized by high levels of mechanization, an extensive division of labour, elaborate rules and procedures governing the exercise of authority, and complex job ladders along which workers progressed as they accumulated seniority (see Baron, Jennings, and Dobbin, 1988). Conflict had become institutionalized in the form of state-supported collective bargaining, and the right to strike had been restricted and contained at the bargaining level. Government involvement had also substantially increased, so much so that it was now government's role to attempt to manage the economy through fiscal and monetary policy and to provide various support services — both economic and social.

Consistent with these developments, the 1950s and early 1960s was an era of relative calm in industrial relations. Unions continued to grow in size, and employer resistance to unions would appear to have been at an all-time low. This was not just because unions appeared to be an almost unavoidable fact of life, but also because they helped to reinforce discipline and stability, negotiating rules and procedures conducive to the rational, bureaucratic exercise of management authority, and providing a system of internal conflict resolution (the grievance-arbitration system) to serve as a check on abuses by line supervisors. Finally, despite two recessions, the 1950s and early 1960s were characterized by rapid economic growth and low unemployment, enabling unions to win substantial gains in collective bargaining without unduly jeopardising their members' job security.

In 1956, the TLC and CCL merged to form the **Canadian Labour Congress (CLC)**, following the merger in the United States of the AFL and CIO into the **AFL-CIO** a year earlier. Ideally, this would provide a better basis for resolving union jurisdictional disputes, and would even foster a number of mergers between hitherto competing unions, thus enabling unions to end internecine squabbling and develop the economies of scale and hence expertise necessary to engage in effective bargaining with employers. The number of mergers was not as great as was hoped, and neither federation accounted for all union members within their respective countries. But their formation *did* signal a decline of traditional craft-industrial hostilities, and it *did* enhance the ability of the labour movement in each country to speak with a single voice. They continue to this day to represent the predominant labour federations in Canada and the United States, respectively, although a number of AFL-CIO unions split to form their own Federation in 2005, taking with them about one-third of all union members in the United States.

Though this was a period of relative calm, it would be mistaken to believe that there was an end to conflict or that employers began to "invite unions in" on a wholesale basis. The years 1952 and 1958 both witnessed sizeable increases in strike activity, and union membership growth was largely stagnant, actually declining from 34 to 29 percent of the labour force between 1958 and 1964. Moreover, the maturation of industrial relations occurred largely in the core of the economy, characterized by large manufacturing firms in steel, autos, rubber, meat-packing, and related industries. Those employed in smaller firms received few, if any, of the benefits enjoyed by those in core sector firms, beyond perhaps somewhat improved income levels. Nonetheless, class conflict had largely disappeared, and the labour movement was well established. Though managers in unionized firms may not have been wildly enthusiastic about their adversaries across the bargaining table, they were able to live with them and accommodate most of their demands — provided they were "reasonable" and did not significantly threaten the authority structure of the organization. In essence, this was the era of what is sometimes referred to as "**mature Fordism**" (Aglietta, 1979; Lipietz, 1987), for it epitomized Henry Ford's philosophy of mass production for mass consumption, made possible by elevated living standards and relative industrial calm.

VI. THE NEW MILITANCY: THE MID-1960s TO LATE 1970s

By the mid-1960s, the post-war consensus began to come to an end. Labour unrest was once more on the upswing, with the percentage of working time lost to strikes increasing by 50 percent in 1965, and then doubling in 1966. Throughout the ensuing decade-and-a-half, it fluctuated around this level, in some years reaching the heights of the strike wave of 1946. Of particular note was a massive general strike of public sector workers in Quebec in 1972, during which the strike leaders were jailed for refusing to obey a government mandated back-to-work order. This in turn induced large groups of private sector unions to strike in sympathy.

Union membership also began to gradually increase, with the number of union members more than doubling (to over three million) by 1978, and union density increasing from 30 to 37 percent of non-agricultural paid workers.[11] Accompanying this growth would appear to have been increased recalcitrance in the workplace itself. Though there was little hard evidence to indicate that recalcitrance had increased, it became increasingly common in both Canada and the United States to read about "the alienated worker" and the "decline of the work ethic" (see Burstein et al., 1975), so much so that the U.S. government commissioned a special task force report on the subject (O'Toole et al., 1974). In addition, there seems to have been growing discontent among union members with the perceived conservativism of their leaders, with workers often refusing to ratify the agreements their leaders negotiated and attempting to challenge their leaders in union elections.

There are a number of possible reasons for these developments (see Heron, 1989: 94–119). First, workers possessed heightened economic expectations, fuelled by two decades of economic expansion and a rampant growth in consumerism. Second, there appears to have been growing discontent with the authoritarian nature of work organizations and the narrow, low discretion nature of work itself. Third, there was a rising consciousness of continued income inequalities, especially between predominantly female occupations and their predominantly male counterparts. Fourth, there was a growing social and political consciousness. In particular, Quebec underwent a "Quiet Revolution", reflecting a cultural and intellectual coming of age, and with it a more radically oriented labour movement. Finally, there was a growing unrest in the public sector and, in response to growing pressure, governments legalized public sector collective bargaining, fuelling the growth of public sector unionism (see Fryer, 1995). Particularly important in this latter respect was the federal government's passage of the

---

[11] The increase in the percentage of the labour force in unions is smaller than the increase in absolute membership because the labour force also grew in size during this period.

Public Service Staff Relations Act (PSSRA) of 1967, covering federal public servants.

These developments may all be seen as worsening the sources of conflict identified in chapter three. But perhaps more important were emergent economic difficulties (see Glyn, 2006: 2–15). In the 1950s and 1960s, employers were willing to "buy" labour peace so that they could take advantage of expanding markets, and coupled with substantial productivity gains, were able to grant workers steadily improving incomes and rights at work. This "post-war accord", as it came to be called, helped to essentially keep the lid on conflict. Yet by the late 1960s, economic conditions had begun to change. Employers found themselves subject to growing competitive pressures and labour costs, declining productivity growth rates and profit levels, and rising inflation.

These developments, combined with a slowing of economic growth and other problems in the world economy, meant that employers were no longer as willing or as able to buy labour peace and that workers were finding their standard of living threatened by rampant inflation. Although the sources of conflict had been intensifying, and higher levels of conflict might have been expected in any case, these developments were associated with massive increases in strike activity and a substantial growth in union density (see Table 4–1). Strike activity was especially widespread in Canada (and the United States and Britain), which lacked the institutional capacity to absorb these pressures and forge a new variant of the post-war accord (Godard, 2009b).

In combination, the developments of the late 1960s and the 1970s not only led to a growth in the militancy and size of the labour movement, they also led to a number of important changes in its nature and composition. Most noticeable was the growth of public sector unions, which by the early 1980s accounted for 40 percent of all union members in Canada (Swimmer, 1989), and now account for half (Statistics Canada, 2003a). Also by the early 1980s, 35 percent of all union members were women, a figure which was double the percentage of the early 1960s (Chaison and Rose, 1989: 130) and which has now climbed to almost 50 percent (Statistics Canada, 2003a). Of particular note, however, was the decline in the dominance of U.S.-based "international" unions. In the early 1960s, over 70 percent of unionized workers in Canada were members of such unions. By the mid-1980s, this figure had declined to almost 40 percent (it is now about one quarter), reflecting both the growth of nationally and provincially based public sector unions and a growing nationalism within the Canadian labour movement, spurred in part by the belief that the policies and orientations of U.S.-based parent unions did not sufficiently take into account the unique characteristics of the Canadian economic and political context (see Chaison and Rose, 1989).

Changes in the nature and composition of the Canadian labour movement meant that by the end of the 1970s the labour movement was not only much larger, it was also far more diverse than ever before. It represented public sector as well as private sector workers and women as well as men. Coupled with its increased autonomy from the U.S. labour movement, it had greater freedom to act and speak on behalf of Canadian working people, and this increasingly came to be reflected in a greater emphasis on social issues germane to non-union as well as union workers (Robinson, 1992).

At the same time, the labour movement continued to face a number of challenges and problems. For example, the federal government introduced a three-year program of wage and price controls in 1975, thus greatly restricting the negotiating ability of unions, and portending a number of attempts by the federal and various provincial governments to restrict collective bargaining and strike activity in the 1980s and 1990s (see Panitch and Swartz, 1985; Sack and Lee, 1989).

VII. "NEW REALITIES": THE 1980s AND 1990s

The 1980s and 1990s brought with them an increasingly hostile economic environment, not only for the Canadian labour movement, but for workers in general. This environment was in part attributable to global developments. But it was substantially worsened by the federal government's shift away from the high employment policies of the 1950s and 1960s to policies directed at reducing inflation through higher interest rates. This policy shift substantially increased government debt-servicing costs and hence deficits, placing considerable pressure on the public sector to reduce spending. It also resulted in consistently double digit unemployment, while putting pressures on employers to cut costs and increase productivity. In addition, the negotiation of the North American Free Trade Agreement (NAFTA) substantially increased the ability of firms in some sectors to pick up and move to the United States or Mexico, enabling business groups to pressure governments and unions into adopting or at least acquiescing to their agenda.

Partly in response to enhanced pressures, and partly because of the weakened position of workers and unions, employers attempted to take advantage of new technologies and management techniques in order restructure their operations. The bureaucratic, mass production model of the post-war years, in which workers had relatively secure employ-ment and various rights and protections in the workplace, was to become a favourite target of critics, who argued that more flexible and adaptive arrangements were essential for competitiveness. In both the public and private sectors, management increasingly sought to cut or freeze wages and benefits, intensify the work process, and, in unionized operations, weaken work rules and other restrictions on management authority.

These efforts were especially strong in the public sector. In Ontario in particular, the conservative government of Mike Harris engaged in an all-out attempt to slash costs and weaken unions. How-ever, both the federal government and most if not all provincial governments had engaged in major public sector cut-backs of some form, often cutting wages and benefits and contracting out jobs to private sector employers in order to weaken unions and avoid paying union wages and benefits. When workers found themselves having to engage in strike activity as a means of resisting these cut-backs, governments often simply passed legislation requiring that they end their strike and go back to work. Although such actions by govern-ments may often be justified as in the public interest, the normal alternative is to order a neutral arbitrator to decide what settle-ment would be fair and impose this on the parties. But in a number of cases, governments simply imposed settlements of their own mak-ing, thus undermining the union altogether. Perhaps most noteworthy in this regard was legislation enacted by the British Columbia govern-ment in May 2004 requiring striking health care workers to go back to work with a 20 percent reduction in pay, retroactive to the date that the contract had expired. Although the threat of a general strike caused the government to withdraw the retroactivity provision, this act reflected a general trend that some argue had been developing through the 1980s and 1990s (Panitch and Swartz, 2003).

This era also saw a weakening in many jurisdictions of laws pro-tecting worker and union rights. Laws advancing worker rights were enacted in a few provinces (Ontario and British Columbia) in the early 1990s, but these were for the most part gutted by subsequent gov-ernments, often in conjunction with other reforms leaving workers and unions worse off than they had been to begin with. In one case (Manitoba in 2000), a newly elected government enacted laws to restore some of these rights. But these laws tended to go only part way, failing to return worker protections to their previous levels (Godard, 2003c).

From the point of view of working people, the 1980s and 1990s represented a truly regressive era (Godard, 1997a). Welfare, unemployment insurance, and other programs designed to protect workers were substantially reduced. It became increasingly difficult for younger workers to find stable, full-time employment, and although there was a tendency for popular accounts to overstate increases in the rate of job loss, the net effect of these developments when coupled with the high unemployment rates was to create a substantially more coercive labour market and employment environment. Incomes remained largely stagnant, increasing somewhat in the 1980s, before falling back to 1979 levels by the mid-1990s. They rebounded in the late 1990s, but much of this increase occurred among those at the top of the income distribution. As of 2001, families in the middle fifth of the income distribution (i.e., the 40th to 60th percentile) still earned almost 3,000 dollars, or 7 percent *less* per year than in 1980, while those in the top fifth earned above $22,000, or 21 percent *more* per year after inflation (CANSIM V1546457-9). A 2001 Leger Marketing survey of 1508 Canadians revealed that, at the end of the 1990s, 40 percent thought they were not as rich as a decade earlier, compared to 33 percent who thought they were richer (Panetta, 2001). This was despite a more than 5 percent increase in the average number of hours worked per working age Canadian (Statistics Canada, 2003b: 6), and an increase in average labour productivity of more that 30 percent from 1981 to 2001 (Dachraoui, Harchaoui, and Tarkhani, 2003: 43). Clearly, the era of the "new realities" (including free trade) was not a good one for the average Canadian, even if it may have been for those at the top.

This era was also not a good one for labour unions. As indicated in Table 4–1, working days lost due to strike activity declined to less than a quarter of what they had been in the early and mid-1970s. The decline in strike activity may not necessarily be seen as "bad" if accompanied by gains for union members. However, it was accompanied by a decline in the estimated union wage premium of from approximately 25 percent in the late 1970s, to about 8 percent in the late 1990s, suggesting a significant decline in union power. During both the 1980s and 1990s, major wage settlements averaged below the rate of inflation (Statistics Canada, 2003a: 55).[12] Union workers thus did not, on average, share in any of the gains in labour productivity of this period.

---

[12] These findings refer to agreements covering 500 or more employees.

This era also witnessed a stagnation and possibly even decline in union density. According to the data source reported in Table 4–1, union density was 35.7 percent as of 1980. It peaked at 37.2 percent in 1984 and, as of 1997, it was 34.1 percent. It then dropped to 31.9 percent by 2000. There may be problems with the reliability of these figures.[13] For present purposes, however, it suffices to note that in the era from 1980 to the early 2000s there was, at minimum, no overall growth in union density, and probably some decline.

Finally, this era witnessed the development of new ideologies and management strategies. First, there was the emergence of what has been referred to as the "new HRM", under which it is argued that HRM can make a critical strategic contribution to competitiveness, provided that worker norms and expectations are aligned with those of management. This is in theory achieved through values-based hiring processes, closer monitoring and appraisal of performance, performance-based pay, and related practices. Second, there was the emergence of the **"high performance" model**. This model tends to focus more on the actual work process, with proponents arguing that there was a need to move away from the rigid, bureaucratic model of the post-war era to a more flexible, team-based one, in which workers are empowered to fully develop, share, and apply their knowledge and skills, with positive implications for the quality of their jobs, as well as for performance.

As is discussed more fully in the next chapter, the extent to which employers adopted either or both of these strategies is not entirely clear. Their effectiveness for employers, and their implications for workers and their unions, are also not entirely clear. Nonetheless, they portended a new era in management thinking, if not always in practice, one that largely rejected the post-war accord and the model on which it was based. In considerable measure, this reflected not just increased pressures on employers to improve competitiveness, but also a weakening of worker and labour union power, thereby lessening the perceived need to accommodate worker norms and expectations and possibly inducing workers to lower these norms and expectations.

---

[13] They are based on union membership reports and may in part reflect errors in data collection. For example, the Statistics Canada Labour Force Survey, which is now considered to provide a more accurate source of density data, shows a decline of only 0.3 percentage points between 1997 (when this data began to be collected) and 2003 (Godard, 2003a; Statistics Canada, 2003a). Issues surrounding union density trends are addressed more fully in chapter sixteen.

VIII. NEW MILLENNIUM, NEW DAWN?

Many of the government policies of the 1980s and 1990s were sold as attempts to return Canada to an era of growth and competitiveness, thereby ultimately enhancing the income levels and well-being of all Canadians. This was especially true of the North American Free Trade Agreement (NAFTA), which was to open U.S. markets for Canadian producers, allowing them to achieve the advantages of greater size and market presence while at the same time inducing them to become more innovative and efficient in the face of increased competition from their U.S. counterparts. It was also true of harsh monetary policies (high interest rates) and cuts in social programs during the 1990s, both of which were justified as generating short-term pain (higher unemployment, weakened social protections) in order to achieve the long-term gains of low inflation and reduced government debt loads. This would in turn lead to stable growth in both the economy and the budgetary capacity of governments.

The case can be made that, by the mid-2000s, some of the promised gains from these policies had begun to be realized. The unemployment rate had declined from 10 percent as of the mid-1990s, to 8 percent as of the late 1990s, to 6 percent as of 2006 (CANSIM table 282-0087). After almost two decades of stagnation, the median earnings of full-year, full-time employees increased by 6 percent between 2000 and 2008 (CANSIM table 202-0101). Unions were again able to win wage gains, with major settlements exceeding the rate of inflation (albeit marginally) in most years after 1998 (Statistics Canada, 2009a). Healthier economic growth rates, beginning in the late 1990s, helped to generate the tax revenues needed to improve social programs, especially health care, without increasing taxes. Finally, the percentage of Canadian families living below the Statistics Canada low income cut-off (LICO), conventionally considered to represent the poverty line, fell to 9 percent by 2007 (Statistics Canada, 2009b) from its high of 16 percent in 1996. Yet the rate of productivity growth remained lacklustre (CANSIM table 383-0008), and (as discussed in chapter three) median earnings were still only 2.5 percent higher in 2008 than they had been in 1980. Union density continued its slow decline, dropping from 31.9 percent in 2000 to 29.9 percent by 2009 (see Table 4–1). Meanwhile, income inequality continued to increase, with the twenty percent of Canadians with the highest income enjoying a much larger percentage increase after taxes than those in any other quintile of the income distribution (as discussed in chapter three).

It is possible that the gains of the early 2000s will continue for some time into the future. Yet western capitalism has seemed increasingly unstable since the mid-1990s, and it is arguable that this reflects deeper and more fundamental problems than many have been aware of. The financial crisis of 2008 is just the most dramatic manifestation of these problems to date, and it appears to have been largely caused by economic policies that had served to paper these problems over, likely worsening them rather than addressing their root causes. Canada was, for a variety of reasons, less immediately affected by this crisis than many other western nations. Yet it was not immune. For example, unemployment returned to almost 9 percent in late 2008, and by mid-2010 it was still hovering around 8 percent. It was also not clear that Canada would be immune from future crises. So although the new millennium could well have represented a new era for Canadians, it could also have represented a "false dawn".

IX. CONCLUSIONS

The purpose of this chapter has been to trace the development of work and industrial relations in Canada. In so doing, it sets the stage for studying contemporary industrial relations in Canada. This is especially true with respect to employer policies, the topic of the next chapter.

Contemporary
Management Practices

5

As should be evident from the preceding chapter, management policies and practices have played a central role in the development of industrial relations over the past century. Managers have on the one hand sought to maximize profit through the technical design and organization of work, yet have on the other hand found themselves subject to various forms of worker resistance arising out of the sources of conflict identified in chapter three. Historically, the predominant managerial response to this problem evolved from one of "coercive drive" in the late 1800s, to one of scientific management and welfare capitalism in the decades immediately before and after World War I, to one of bureaucratic accommodation in the post-World War II era. If recent accounts are to be believed, this response is currently evolving into one of "progressive human resources management" and adoption of what has come to be referred to as "high performance work systems". Yet, historical analysis runs the risk of focusing too much on emergent developments and not enough on the considerable variation that can exist across firms, industries, and regions at any particular time. Nowhere is this more the case than with respect to contemporary managerial policies and practices, which can vary considerably from one firm or establishment to the next.

This chapter thus extends the analysis of the preceding chapter by providing an analytical framework for comparing different types of managerial policies and practices. Then, drawing on this framework, it identifies and discusses three types of approaches that appear to be most widespread at present: the "autocratic/exploitive", the "bureaucratic/accommodative", and the "autonomic/consociative". Focus is placed on the third of these approaches, especially when embodied in the high performance model. This model is not only the most developed, it has been widely heralded as a "best practice" and hence as the wave of the future.

At the outset, it should be cautioned that this chapter is concerned primarily with describing and assessing contemporary managerial policies and practices, not with addressing why they vary. The latter is left to chapter six.

I. TOWARDS A DESCRIPTIVE ANALYSIS

One problem confronting any discussion of managerial policies and practices is that they can be complex and multi-faceted. Any attempt to discuss them is thus by necessity likely to be somewhat oversimplified, at best providing only a crude representation of a more complex reality. But for present purposes, it is useful to consider managerial policies and practices as varying primarily along two dimensions: (1) workplace structure, and (2) managerial orientation towards employees.[1]

Workplace structure essentially embodies the methods by which managerial authority is institutionalized within the workplace, and is directed primarily at the organization and control of the way work is performed. A variety of these methods can exist in any particular workplace, and, perhaps of greater importance, the extent to which these methods exist in combination can vary considerably. For the present, however, it is useful to distinguish between three predominant types of workplace structure:

1. **Autocratic**, where superordinates personally allocate and direct the work, monitor and evaluate workers, and determine rewards and discipline.

2. **Bureaucratic**, where employees are subject to a lower degree of direct authority but are constrained by the technical design of work and by formally established rules and procedures, conformity to which in turn forms the basis on which workers are monitored, rewarded, and disciplined.

3. **Autonomic**, where employees are given a high degree of autonomy, and performance forms the primary basis on which workers are monitored, rewarded, and disciplined.

Managerial orientation towards employees refers to the values and objectives that underlie and hence come to be reflected in the

---

[1] A number of alternative schemes have been proposed, particularly in the United Kingdom. See chapter two of Legge (1995) for an excellent overview of these.

exercise of managerial authority. Three types of orientation can be identified:

1. **Exploitive**, where managers display virtually no interest in employee goals and expectations, seeking only to get the most work out of them for the lowest possible wage.

2. **Accommodative**, where managers recognize that employees have their own legitimate goals and expectations and accommodate these to the extent that they are deemed reasonable.

3. **Consociative**, where managers seek to align employee goals and expectations with their own and adopt extensive programs to ensure their identification with and loyalty to the organization.

As indicated in Figure 5–1, it is possible, by drawing on these distinctions, to identify at least nine types of managerial policies and practices, most of which have been widespread at some point in history and continue to be predominant in some firms and industries today. For example, the welfare capitalism which was widespread in the 1920s could probably be located in the bureaucratic/consociative region, while early scientific management, which also continues to predominate in some firms (e.g., small, low-skill assembly operations), could probably be located in the bureaucratic/exploitive region.

Figure 5–1 provides a useful analytical scheme for thinking about and characterizing managerial policies and practices. There are, however, three regions on this figure that are of particular importance: (1) Autocratic/Exploitive, (2) Bureaucratic/Accommodative, and (3) Autonomic/Consociative. These regions are arguably most representative of managerial policies and practices at present, with each representing a distinctive managerial **paradigm**, or set of values, beliefs, and assumptions that guide managerial decisions. Accordingly, the remainder of the chapter will consider policies and practices associated with each in greater depth, characterizing them in general and then addressing their specifics with respect to unions and collective bargaining.

Before proceeding, it should be cautioned that, though the discussion will proceed as if employers can be neatly characterized in accordance with a particular type, they may (and often do) adhere to policies and practices that are consistent with more than one type. Thus, for example, a firm may adopt a number of autonomic/consociative policies and practices with respect to the way it treats workers in general, yet it may also adhere to highly coercive policies and practices (autocratic/exploitive) with respect to attempts by workers

FIGURE 5-1 Categorizing Managerial Policies and Practices

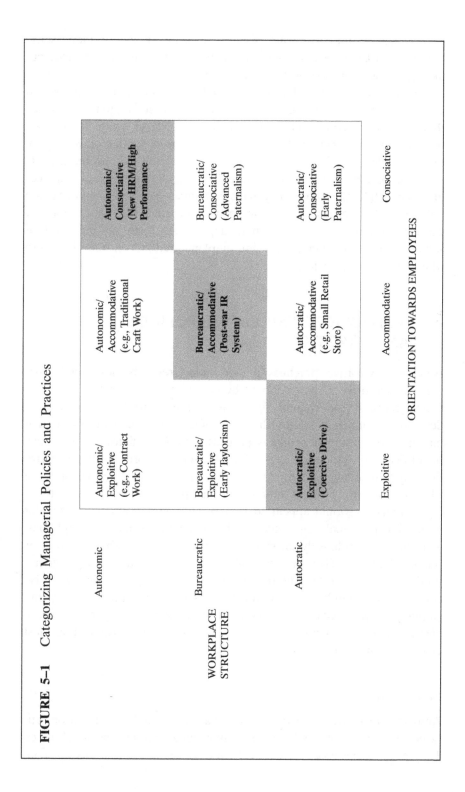

	Exploitive	Accommodative	Consociative
Autonomic	Autonomic/ Exploitive (e.g., Contract Work)	Autonomic/ Accommodative (e.g., Traditional Craft Work)	**Autonomic/ Consociative (New HRM/High Performance**
Bureaucratic	Bureaucratic/ Exploitive (Early Taylorism)	**Bureaucratic/ Accommodative (Post-war IR System)**	Bureaucratic/ Consociative (Advanced Paternalism)
Autocratic	**Autocratic/ Exploitive (Coercive Drive)**	Autocratic/ Accommodative (e.g., Small Retail Store)	Autocratic/ Consociative (Early Paternalism)

WORKPLACE STRUCTURE

ORIENTATION TOWARDS EMPLOYEES

to organize a union. In this respect, it probably makes more sense not to ask *whether* a particular firm conforms to a particular type, but instead to ask the *extent* to which it does.

In addition, it should also be noted that managerial policies and practices can vary not only in accordance with the region with which they are most consistent, but also in accordance with their level of sophistication compared to other employers within this region. For example, two firms may conform most closely to the autonomic/ consociative type, but one may have few formal policies and practices in place, while the other may have a number of highly sophisticated policies and practices. This is important, because the implications of various policies and practices may depend as much on the level of sophistication with which they are implemented as on the type with which they are associated.

II. AUTOCRATIC/EXPLOITIVE POLICIES AND PRACTICES

Autocratic/exploitive practices are in many respects descended from the coercive drive system adopted by many employers in the late nineteenth century (see chapter four) and continue to be widespread in developing countries, where they are often found in workplaces that manufacture consumer products purchased by Canadians. While it may be difficult to find employers who precisely conform to the coercive drive system today (at least in Canada), there is no shortage of those who continue to adopt a number of the practices associated with it. These practices would appear to be most frequently adopted in smaller establishments, operating under highly competitive market conditions, and employing relatively unskilled workers, with little labour market or relational power. They are probably most predominant in the agricultural, retail, and restaurant sectors of the economy, but they are also common in a number of manufacturing sectors, including textiles and clothing. Anyone who has worked in these sectors may have experienced them first hand. An example of them, in perhaps the most extreme form, appears in Box 5–1.

In General

Autocratic/exploitive practices are relatively simple and unsophisticated, for they essentially involve managing through personal edict. They are not necessarily coercive in the sense that employees are con-

BOX 5-1 Formosa Textiles, San Bartolo FTZ, El Salvador

My name is Julia Esmeralda Pleites. I am from El Salvador. I worked in the Formosa Textiles factory in the San Bartolo free trade Zone.

We entered the factory at 6:55 in the morning and we worked supposedly until 5:00 p.m., but almost every day we had to stay working until 6:30 or 7:00 p.m. They didn't let us out until we completed the production goal. Nor did they pay us the time we worked after 5:00 p.m. You had to stay because they took away your badge, your ID card — so you couldn't punch out. If you left you would lose the entire day's pay.

In the factory, we made Nike, Adidas and a USA soccer shirt — but I never saw that label.

I was a sewing operator and my job was to sew both seams on 160 shirts every 2 hours. On this Nike shirt, I worked attaching the lining to the collar front.

Sometimes we have to work on Saturday, but they don't pay us overtime. We get the minimum wage. This always happens before holidays or vacations. They make us make up the vacation time.

The factory is very hot. You are constantly sweating and get dehydrated from the heat. The ventilation is poor. There is a lot of dust and your nose is always stuffed up and you have a constant cold.

There are 30 people to a production line, divided between 6 modules. We sit on hard wooden benches without backs. It is not permitted to have a cushion to sit on, so your back and backside hurt.

Everything is by piece rate. The supervisors scream at you to go faster. At times, they have thrown the garments in the faces of compañeras. If they think you are working too slowly, they come up to you and smash your table with their hand, yelling at you to work faster.

The supervisors are from Bangladesh, and they treat us very hard. They make some of the workers cry.

You need permission to drink water and to go to the bathroom. You need a badge, and there are police who check the badge at the bathroom and the drinking faucet. There are five private police guards in the factory. Almost never can you use the bathroom more than twice a day, usually only once. The police and even the Chief of Personnel scream at you to go faster.

Continued....

BOX 5-1 (continued)

Sometimes the Chief of Personnel, Mr. Castillo, even goes into the women's bathroom, screaming at us to get us out quickly. There is no toilet paper and the bathrooms are very dirty. The drinking water is not purified. It comes from a cistern.

They don't allow you to wear lipstick into the factory. If they see you with lipstick, they punish you. They think you will stain the shirts. You can't bring candy or clean drinking water into the factory. They don't allow you to talk. They give a warning or punish you for that.

Leaving the factory is humiliating, because they search you physically. They make the men drop their pants. The women police search us women. They touch you everywhere.

You have to pay for a pregnancy test when you enter and at the end of your trial period. If you are pregnant, they fire you immediately. During your trial period, they pay you only 50% of the minimum wage.

We pay for Social Security, but they don't give us permission to go to the health clinic. You work sick. If you go to the clinic, you lose 1 or 2 day's pay. They never give permission to be absent, no matter what the crisis.

At Formosa, they won't permit a union and everyone knows it. The minute they find out you belong to a union, they would fire you. Everyone is afraid. There is nothing you can do.

Source: Excerpts from Testimony of Julia Esmeralda Pleites by Formosa Textiles, San Bartolo FTZ, El Salvador. Reproduced by permission of National Labour Committee, New York.

stantly motivated by fear, but they generally entail low tolerance for "misconduct", whether it involves slacking on the job, absenteeism, or insubordination. They can also entail rather arbitrary treatment, with supervisors appearing to favour some employees over others, and providing little explanation or rationale for their actions. Discipline is "summary": that is, employees do not enjoy anything approaching due process, but are instead disciplined on the spot, often with little opportunity to defend themselves or state their case. Finally, management often exhibits low trust for subordinates, minimizing their discretion on the job through close supervision and the imposition of strict rules. Thus, the term "autocratic".

Workers may develop some sense of loyalty towards their employer, especially if they become subject to favouritism. But this is generally not the case. Workers often remain with the employer almost entirely because they cannot find a better job elsewhere, thereby taking a purely economic orientation to their work and "getting away with" whatever they can. The employer, in turn, views employees largely as commodities, to be paid as little as possible (usually around the minimum wage), with few if any benefits (except as required by law). As much labour is extracted as is possible, and employers exhibit little concern for working conditions. Thus, the term "exploitive".

Unions

As might be expected, autocratic/exploitive practices tend to be associated with an aggressively anti-union philosophy, with employers going to considerable lengths to keep unions out, even if this entails circumventing or breaking the law (see Freeman and Kleiner, 1990). Both the intensity and sophistication of these attempts can vary considerably, though it is not unheard of for firms to hire expensive "consulting" firms to advise them on the most effective means of frustrating a union organizing drive. As discussed more fully in chapter eleven, these means can entail a number of illegal acts, such as threatening workers, employing spies, firing union organizers, or even instigating violence in order to discredit the union.

Where a union has become established, employers may engage in a number of tactics to weaken and ultimately undermine it. Four such tactics can be identified as of particular importance (Anderson, 1989b):

1. Introducing workplace changes that lower skill requirements so that, if there is a strike, workers can be easily replaced.

2. Eliminating more skilled work by "contracting out", or paying other, non-union firms to have this work done for the employer, thus further weakening the union.

3. Forcing the union into a lengthy strike or lockout and then hiring new workers to replace those on strike, effectively undermining the strike and ultimately support for the union.

4. Either shutting down, relocating operations, or gradually shifting work to a non-union site.

It is difficult to establish just how widely these practices are used as means of undermining a union, especially because employers seldom admit that this is their purpose. Instead, they contend that the practices are motivated by purely economic considerations having to do with the health of the firm.[2]

III. BUREAUCRATIC/ACCOMMODATIVE POLICIES AND PRACTICES

Bureaucratic/accommodative practices began to emerge with the rise of the personnel function in the 1920s (Kochan and Cappelli, 1983; Jacoby, 1985; Baron, Dobbin, and Jennings, 1986), though they did not become fully developed until the post-World War II era. Generally, these practices were developed in response to a variety of factors, of which the most important ones were the growth in employer size, the adoption of more capital intensive and sophisticated production technologies, and the growth in labour union strength. They have traditionally been most characteristic of large manufacturing firms, including those in the North American steel, automobile, rubber, and railway industries, and of large public sector employers. An example of these practices appears in Box 5–2.

In General

Bureaucratic/accommodative practices are characterized by a high degree of "functional specialization" (i.e., separate departments which specialize on the basis of function) within management, including a separate human resources (HR) and/or industrial relations (IR) function. The HR/IR function is, in turn, typically responsible for a number of activities that might otherwise be handled by line managers. Though the level of sophistication with which these functions are carried out can vary, they typically include:

1. The establishment of employee selection criteria, job classifications and pay differentials;
2. Employee training and development programs;
3. The handling of discipline and rewards;
4. The processing of grievances; and
5. Preparation for and conduct of collective bargaining (if there is a union).

---

[2] For example, see Zeytinoglu (1991, 1992) for the results of a survey of employer explanations for the use of part-time workers.

BOX 5–2   Stelco Inc. and Its Unions (1988)

Stelco Inc. is the largest steel company in Canada, accounting for about 30–35 percent of production. The company operates two integrated plants, two mini-mills and several finishing plants. Its primary union antagonist is Local 1005 of the United Steelworkers of America (USWA). Local 1005 organises most manual workers in Stelco's flagship plant the Hilton Works. Manual employees at other sites are organised primarily in other locals of the USWA. When government certification procedures were introduced in the mid-1940s, 1005 was certified as the bargaining agent for most manual workers at the Hilton Works. During the first formal bargaining round, the company took a hard stand. When the union struck, strike-breakers were hired to continue production. The result was a long and rancorous work stoppage, out of which an accord was reached.

The accord is not a written document, but is instead an informal understanding regarding acceptable behaviour by each side. The prominent features of the accord are these:

1. Management recognises the exclusive and legitimate right of the union to represent the interest of those in the bargaining unit. This stipulation is required by law, and it is fully accepted by management. Stelco makes no attempt to undermine the union or to escape from its responsibility to negotiate with it. If new plants are opened, there is a general understanding that management will voluntarily recognise the USWA as the bargaining agent. For example, when the company opened up a second integrated mill in the late 1970s, it voluntarily recognised a new local of the USWA. For the most part, the other unions with which Stelco negotiates were already established at the time when the company purchased the plants from other organisations.

2. The union recognises the right of management to organise and direct work and to take strategic decisions unilaterally, regarding products, prices and the form of technology, etc. Neither Local 1005 nor any of the other local unions have made any overtures to the company to get involved in strategic decisions. Nor has the company ever seriously considered attempting to restructure its relationship with the union. Stelco considers it to be not only management's right, but also management's duty to manage. The function of the employees is to follow instructions and plans designed by management. It is not their function to co-manage. Consistent with this philosophy, Stelco has not in-

Continued....

BOX 5-2 (continued)

troduced quality circles, zero defects groups, or other forms of shop-floor worker participation.

3. Both sides recognise that, within the bounds noted above, each will vigorously pursue the interests of its constituency. The union is expected to seek high pay, job security and industrial justice, and the company is expected to defend its prerogatives, seek labour costs consistent with competitiveness and maintain discipline. Each side is expected to treat the other with respect, not love. Behind the civility of their relationship lies the knowledge that each has the capacity to do the other considerable harm.

Institutions of Interaction and Their Results

Terms and conditions of employment at Stelco's Hilton Works are decided by negotiations which have taken place every three years for the past several decades. The result is a written collective agreement which has become increasingly complex over the years. Other Steelworker locals have traditionally bargained simultaneously but separately from Local 1005. In the 1980s, however, the bargaining has become more formally centralised, in contrast to a decentralising trend in Canada and other countries.

There can be no doubt that, at Stelco, the unionised employees have had substantial impact on the personnel policy of the firm through collective bargaining. The collective agreement at the Hilton Works regulates not only wages and hours, but also the process of job classification, decision rules for promotions, transfers and lay-offs, training plans, procedures and standards for ensuring health and safety, procedures for involving employee representatives in the introduction of technological change, limitations on management's right to contract out, and restrictions on management's capacity to discipline. Vigilance in regard to the application of these stipulations is maintained via an extensive and active shop steward and safety representative network. There are over 300 shop stewards for the approximately 8,500 members and another 350 health and safety representatives, although some individuals fill both roles.

As required by law, there is a formal grievance procedure which ends in binding arbitration. At the Hilton Works, this procedure is very actively used by the union. Each year, approximately 1,000 to 1,250 written grievances are filed. Of those, the company typically "concedes" 80 to 90 and another 10–20 are settled at arbitration. The remainder are either dropped or become the subject of bargaining. At each bargaining round, there is an attempt

Continued....

BOX 5–2 (continued)

to resolve all outstanding grievances. Recently, the company agreed to implement an enriched pension scheme, permitting some employees to retire early, thereby preserving jobs for others if the union would agree to settle a backlog of pending grievances.

From the workers' point of view, the results of the system have been quite positive. Manual employees at Stelco are among the highest paid in Canada, and the pension, insurance and benefit schemes are excellent. Moreover, the individual employee at Stelco has a high degree of assurance that he-she will not be victimised as the result of capricious and emotional decisions by supervisors. Job security is dependent on fluctuations in the demand for steel. However, USWA members may be certain that if lay-offs are necessary, they will proceed on the basis of the objective standards negotiated by their union.

Whether or not the institutions of job regulation have had a positive or negative effect on the company over the past four decades is hard to say. One may note, however, that Stelco Inc. is considered to be among the most efficient steel companies in the world. It has continually upgraded its steel-making technology, unlike its counterparts in the United States. From its inception in 1910 up to the Great Recession of 1981–1982, it continually operated in the black.

Implications of the Stelco Experience

The Stelco experience suggests that one should be sceptical about some of the implications of the "new IR". Must companies flee from unions and collective bargaining in order to adjust effectively to product market developments, or is the non-union strategy simply opportunistic behaviour in an environment where unions are very weak? Is co-operativism really a superior step up from adversarialism, or is it a trendy fad? Is institutional restructuring the key to heightened competitiveness, or is it a ploy by management seeking to recapture lost ground on the frontier of control?

Source: Excerpted from Roy Adams, "The 'Old Industrial Relations' and Corporate Competitiveness", *Employee Relations Journal* 10 (1988): 3–7. © Emerald Group Publishing Limited, all rights reserved. Reproduced by permission of Emerald Group Publishing Limited, Bradford, U.K.

All of these activities are typically carried out in accordance with well-established rules and procedures, either as implemented by HR/IR specialists, or as negotiated with a union. Employees are typically selected on the basis of objective qualifications (education, experience, and training), expected to perform their work in accordance with objective rules and procedures, and subject to fixed hourly rates of pay, based on objective job classifications and evaluations.

The actual structure of the workplace is designed by industrial engineers or experts versed in principles of management science. As a result, jobs are clearly defined and highly specialized. Of particular importance are well-structured **"internal labour markets"**, consisting of a number of job levels which workers can hope to advance through as they accumulate seniority. Sometimes these involve specific **"job ladders"**, with workers starting at the bottom and working their way up through specific positions or *rungs* on the ladder. Other times, advancement occurs on a department-wide basis (e.g., the shipping department). In still others, it occurs on a plant- or establishment-wide basis. However, seniority as well as ability is an important criterion for advancement, and workers can generally look forward to some form of progression into "better jobs" if they remain with the employer, thereby increasing both their pay and their status over the course of their working life.

Workers may again develop a sense of loyalty towards their employer, but their orientation is largely an instrumental one, under which they do not display a great deal of attachment to their task but are prepared to perform a "fair day's work" if treated fairly by their employer and by their immediate supervisors. Rather than relying solely on coercion, the employer and the immediate supervisor also attempt to win the consent of workers, so that they will choose to obey various rules and directives out of a belief in their legitimacy. The worker-supervisory relationship is generally an accommodative one, often involving considerable "give-and-take". In this respect, the "negotiation of order", as discussed in chapter three, is likely to be most pervasive in organizations with these practices, with workers keeping their side of the "bargain" as long as management keeps its.

Unions

As might be expected, bureaucratic/accommodative practices generally engender a recognition of the right of workers to join unions and a willingness to accommodate "legitimate" union demands. The relationship between union and management officials is primarily an arm's-length one, with the former serving as advocate for union members at the bargaining table and in the grievance/arbitration process. Unions and management tend to be adversaries in the sense that each is aware that there are important conflicts between the interests of their constituents and those of the "other side". (This is similar, for example, to the relationship between two lawyers representing different sides in a court case.) As a result, to the outsider, the union-management relationship may appear to be highly contentious, especially during grievance arbitrations or collective bargaining. Yet, the day-to-day relationship between the two parties is often a professional one, in which there is considerable cooperation. Unions may even serve a number of positive functions for employers, such as communicating worker concerns and problems and helping to keep line supervisors "honest" by filing grievances if they abuse their authority. They may even help to improve productivity, for reasons discussed in chapter seven.

Unions still, of course, create a number of costs for management, not the least of which are higher wages and benefits. Yet management is often able to absorb these or pass them on to customers and consumers for one of the following reasons: (i) competitors can be counted on to pay similar wages and benefits, (ii) the employer faces limited (if any) price competition, (iii) labour costs are a relatively small share of overall costs (as for example, in workplaces with high levels of capital investment per worker employed), or (iv) productivity gains or some source of competitive advantage enjoyed by the employer.

Equally important, many union non-wage demands involve the establishment of rules and procedures governing the performance of work, discipline, and promotion. Though these rules and procedures can entail a number of restrictions on management authority and hence are by no means welcomed by management, they are largely conducive to the bureaucratic structure of the employer and in many respects serve to both reinforce and legitimate this structure. As a result, management is far more likely than might otherwise be the case to accommodate union demands for these rules and restrictions, provided that they are not unduly restrictive or harmful to efficiency. Thus, for example, management may be willing to concede a provision which states that seniority is the primary basis for promotion provided that workers have adequate ability, for such a provision may be consistent with practices adopted by management in the absence of a union, as discussed more fully in chapter fifteen. However, management may be highly resistant to a provision which states that seniority should be the sole basis for promotion, *regardless* of ability, for such a provision could unduly impair efficiency.

Where a union is not established, employers may follow a "**union substitution**" approach, where they adopt many of the practices associated with union settings and provide wages and benefits that are comparable to those offered by union employers in the same industry or region. They may also establish some form of non-union grievance system, though such systems are often referred to as "**internal justice systems**" because this term has more positive connotations. These systems typically fall far short of their counterparts in the unionized sector. For example, they often do not allow employees to take their grievances to an impartial outside arbitrator, thus providing the employer or an employer-established committee with the final say. But they at least, in theory, provide employees with some opportunity to seek redress if they believe themselves to have been unfairly treated.

Even though the bureaucratic/accommodative approach applies to non-union as well as union employers, it essentially epitomizes the "mature" approach to employee relations emergent in the post-World War II years. The developments of the past few decades or so may have rendered the "pure" form of this approach increasingly rare. Indeed, the employer in Box 5–2 was pushed into bankruptcy and eventually taken over by U.S. Steel in the mid-2000s (Waxman, 2009) (although it does not appear that the employer's industrial relations practices could be blamed for this). Many employers would appear, however, to have retained the essential features of the bureaucratic/ accommodative approach. For example, in the 2003–4 PRA survey discussed in chapter 3, two-thirds of workers reported that promotion was based primarily on seniority in their workplace. Over half reported a complex system for classifying jobs. Half reported that job security protections made it unlikely that permanent employees would ever be laid off. These are all consistent with the bureaucratic/accommodative approach.

IV. AUTONOMIC/CONSOCIATIVE PRACTICES, THE NEW HRM, AND THE HIGH PERFORMANCE PARADIGM

Autonomic/consociative practices are most consistent with (in fact they embody) the managerialist perspective on industrial relations. They have a long history, originating in the "welfare capitalism" or "paternalistic management" practices emergent in the early decades of this century (see Jacoby, 2000). As discussed in chapter four, these practices included employee pension schemes, company housing, company unionism, suggestion systems, company supported recreational activities, profit sharing schemes, and other practices. These practices proliferated rapidly with the emergence of the personnel function in the 1920s, and although they were largely abandoned during the Great Depression of the 1930s, they began to grow again in the post-war period. For example, a 1981 survey of 147 large Canadian employers found four in ten to have suggestion systems, seven in ten to have company sponsored sports teams or events for employees, four in ten to have suggestion systems, eight in ten to have special recognition for lengthy service, and almost nine in ten to have human skills training for supervisors (Godard, 1991).

The post-war period also, however, witnessed the proliferation of theories of motivation and commitment emerging out of the human relations school of the 1930s and 1940s and the field of organizational behaviour (its successor) in the 1950s and 1960s. These theories generally suggest that if management communicates effectively with workers and adopts the appropriate HRM practices, high levels of commitment will follow. Workers will therefore act in accordance with employer interests, not because they are coerced to do so (as in the case of autocratic/exploitive practices) or because they are keeping their side of the "bargain" (as in the case of bureaucratic/accommodative practices), but rather because they feel a moral commitment to their employer, even adopting employer goals and priorities as their own.

Traditionally, these practices have been most prevalent in workplaces where workers have a high degree of relational power, either because the technology is highly sophisticated and capital intensive or because product quality and reliability are of critical importance to the firm's success. Thus, they seem initially to have been most adopted by firms in the oil refining, steel, chemicals, aerospace, and automobile industries. However, they received only limited attention until the 1980s. At this time, pundits began to argue that competitive forces associated with a global economy, coupled with new technologies, mandated a much more flexible and committed workforce and hence a transformation away from the bureaucratic/accommodative model towards an autonomic/consociative one.

It came to be argued that human resources and the way they are managed can represent a key source of strategic advantage (Beer and Spector, 1985; Pfeffer, 1994). Not only are organizations, at base, little more than their human resources, thus rendering the effectiveness with which these resources are managed the key to organizational effectiveness, the effective development of human resources is relatively difficult for competitors to copy, making it a source of sustained advantage. Associated with this thesis were two approaches, both of which were mentioned in chapter four: the new HRM, and the high performance model. These approaches have come to be closely related to each other. Workplaces with many new HRM practices may also have a number of high performance practices, while workplaces with many high performance practices may also have a number of new HRM practices. However while the new HRM primarily entails practices within the HRM department or function, the high performance model focuses more on "new" practices within the workplace itself and that are often not strictly considered to be part of the HRM function (Godard, 2009a; 2010). In addition, the latter in particular forms a distinctive model or paradigm and, as such, has been the subject of considerable attention.

The New HRM in General

In its purest form, the new HRM essentially entails a rejection of the assumptions associated with the bureaucratic/accommodative model. Where the latter accommodates worker norms and expectations, and may be seen to be largely consistent with the orthodox-pluralist perspective (see chapter one), the new HRM adopts a more managerialist perspective, one that assumes that worker norms and expectations can be aligned with those of management (Godard, 2009a; Mahoney and Decktop, 1986; Legge, 1989; 1995: 75; Whitener, 2001). Where the focus of the bureaucratic/accommodative model tends to be on maintaining morale and on the orderly administration of internal labour markets, the focus of the new HRM is on the development of a "high commitment" culture, in the belief that HRM can make a critical strategic contribution to competitiveness (Beer and Spector, 1985).

The practices specifically associated with the new HRM are rarely spelled out in their entirety. But they may generally be equated with those advocated in strategic HRM books. Indeed, the very term human resource management was developed to describe these practices and came to replace "personnel management", which was the term most commonly used prior to the 1980s to describe what is now referred to as the HRM function. Some of the practices promoted in the new HRM literature include:

1. sophisticated selection processes that emphasize employee values, attitudes, and preferences to determine whether they "fit" with employer interests;

2. performance management systems, under which individuals are subject to continuous performance measurement and to regular performance appraisals;

3. career planning, under which employees discuss their long-term advancement and career prospects with their employer;

4. substantial training in "soft" skills, including communications, team working, and problem solving;

5. engagement in continuous learning and long-term "talent development" programs;

6. performance-based pay and promotion systems.

These practices generally go beyond, and in a number of respects may conflict with, those of the bureaucratic/accommodative model. As noted earlier, under the bureaucratic/accommodative model, employees are selected largely on the basis of their education and training, expected to perform their work in accordance with objective rules and procedures, subject to fixed hourly rates of pay, and promoted largely on the basis of their seniority. Thus, little attention is paid to values, "soft skills", continuous learning, or career planning, and there are neither performance appraisals nor performance-based pay and promotion systems. Such practices are generally considered to be unnecessary and impractical in workplaces that lend themselves to the bureaucratic/accommodative model.

The High Performance Model in General

As note earlier, some new HRM practices are associated with the high performance model, and some high performance practices are often adopted in conjunction with new HRM practices. But the high performance model goes further than the new HRM by specifically addressing workplace practices. The practices it has become associated with have been alternatively referred to as "workplace innovations", "workplace reforms", "high commitment practices", "alternative workplace practices", "new work practices", and "high performance work practices" (HPWPs). For present purposes, high performance work practices will be used. An illustration of these practices appears in Box 5–3. They essentially entail two main components: job redesign reforms and participatory reforms. However, their effectiveness is considered to depend in part on a third component: complementary HRM practices. Thus, although "high performance work practices" refers to the former two components, the latter also forms part of the high performance model *as* a model.

Below, each of these three components is discussed at some length. The focus is on how the practices associated with each work *in theory*. Debates over how they work in practice are left to the next section.

(1) Job Design Reforms (Autonomic Workplace Design). Job redesign has traditionally entailed some combination of[3] (1) **job enlargement**, under which tasks are broadened in order to provide workers with greater variety and more meaningful units of work; (2) **job rotation**, under which workers are rotated among different jobs, enabling them to develop a better understanding of the entire operation, providing them with greater variety, and introducing the challenge of learning different tasks, while at the same time providing employers with greater flexibility in tasks to which they can assign individual employee; and (3) **job enrichment**, under which employees are given increased challenge, discretion, and responsibility, and hence more opportunity for personal growth and fulfilment.

Beginning in the 1980s, the organization of work into **teams** came to be central to job redesign programs and, in fact, may be seen as forming the *core* element of the high performance model (see Box 5–3). Though the nature of these teams can vary considerably, workers in theory work interdependently, in small groups with from (roughly) six to twenty members. In the ideal, these teams are **self-directed** or **autonomous**, meaning they are given considerable autonomy over the pace at which they work, decide how tasks are allocated among members, and are not subject to direct supervision, instead selecting their own "team leader" and taking joint responsibility for each other's performance. Where possible, they are also given responsibility for an identifiable service, component, or product, and often make their own decisions about how this is to be provided or produced. In theory, this provides workers with substantial autonomy and control over their work, while increasing the opportunity for social interaction. It also tends to engender job enlargement, job rotation, and job enrichment, because jobs are defined more broadly, workers can rotate tasks among themselves, and there is much greater scope for challenge, discretion, and responsibility.

---

[3]   See chapter five of Robbins, 1992, for a representative discussion of these concepts.

BOX 5-3 Self-directed Work Teams at NCR

--- ◆ *Gordon DiGiacomo*

Consultant in Human Resources Management and Labour Relations

Each team consists of six to eighteen members. There are no team leaders but each team does have a coordinator, a position that rotates weekly, and a production scheduler who works with team members on scheduling issues. The production schedule is determined by the team after receiving a general target from the Director of Manufacturing (referred to in the plant as the Coach of Manufacturing).

The teams produce eighteen Automatic Teller Machines and thirty-five Item Processing Machines per day. Each team is responsible for the assembly and testing of a machine and getting it ready for shipment.

The teams meet daily to address parts problems, scheduling and other production-related issues. Team members are guided in their work by the ground rules that they have established. Some of those rules include the following:

At our team meeting, there will be only one conversation at a time.

We will give specific and timely feedback to team members.

We will identify daily production status and see what we as a team can do to help one another to meet linearity.

We will put our name sticker on all the work we do, whether it be sub-assembly or module assembly.

Members of the teams have the authority to shut down production if necessary.

Once a week, each team meets in a problem-solving session to address issues related to plant efficiency. The meeting is facilitated by a manufacturing engineer or a production scheduler.

According to one interviewee, the pursuit of greater efficiency does not mean working harder, it means working smarter. The philosophy that management seeks to impart to associates is summed up in this question: What are the things that are causing problems which, if they are eliminated, will enable us to achieve more?

To be employed in the facility, a prospective associate must have at least Grade 12 equivalency and must pass an extensive screening process. New hires receive about fifteen days of training, including training in team effectiveness and in the necessary technical subjects. Regular employees receive about ten days of in-class training annually.

In hiring new employees (and the plant is presently doing a lot of hiring), plant officials look, among other things, for flexibility

Continued....

BOX 5–3 (continued)

and the ability to work in a group setting. Associates from the team to which the new hire is likely to go participate in the interviewing and in the decision on whether or not to hire the person.

New hires are considered temporary employees for up to one year, after which they are let go, re-hired as temporary employees or made permanent.

Job rotation is practised at the plant. Each team member is trained to do eight or nine different jobs. Theoretically, an associate could assemble a machine on her/his own, with a few exceptions.

Teams are supervised by production coaches each of whom may have accountability for thirty to seventy people. Production coaches report directly to the Director of Manufacturing who reports to the General Manager of the facility. Previously, the line managers, the Manufacturing Manager and the Vice-President of operations came between the associates and the General Manager.

The Director of Manufacturing plays mostly a teaching and coordinating function. Among other things, he/she makes sure the teams have the necessary resources to do what they are supposed to do. To solve production-related problems, associates can deal directly with the facility's engineers and whoever else should be involved and need not go through the Director of Manufacturing.

There is a Director of Quality Assurance but the jobs of quality inspectors were eliminated. Each team is now responsible for quality assurance.

Initially, the performance appraisal for each associate consisted of reviews from five "feedback partners" chosen by the employee with input from the Director of Manufacturing. The partners completed a questionnaire on how well the associate met the expectations of the feedback partners and the objectives of the plant.

This performance appraisal system had been tried four years ago but was discontinued because associates felt uncomfortable discussing other employee's performance. Some associates used the system to "get back" at other employees. It is thought that the greater maturity of the groups will enable the system to work more effectively this time around.

Interpersonal conflicts were cited by an associate as one of the major problems that the teams encounter. For the most part, they are resolved by the team. As the Director of Manufacturing explained, "They have learned **not** to come to me."

Continued....

BOX 5–3 (continued)

Another problem cited by a team member is the stress that comes from interruptions in the work process due, for example, to parts shortages.

The wages and benefits of NCR Waterloo employees are based upon annual industry surveys. In keeping with the philosophy of "shared accountability", a large part of each person's annual increase is determined by the performance of the teams on which he/she participates. In addition, all NCR Waterloo associates participate in bonus plans that are targeted at four per cent of pay. Receipt of a bonus is dependent on whether or not the facility meets certain operational or customer satisfaction goals. These are set annually by management.

The NCR corporate office recently announced its decision to implement a profit-sharing plan for all employees.

Source: From the *Collective Bargaining Review*, February 1997, pp. 61–66, Workplace Information Directorate, Labour Branch, HDRC. Source of Information: Human Resources and Skills Development Canada. Reproduced with the permission of the Minister of Public Works and Government Services Canada, 2010.

(2) Participatory Reforms. Employee participation programs are also associated with the high performance model. This is especially true with respect to so-called **quality circles**. Now often referred to as "**problem solving groups**", quality circles have been widespread in Japan since the 1950s. But they did not come into vogue in North America until the early 1980s, when Japanese firms began to make significant inroads into North American markets, and pundits came to believe that this reflected the superiority of Japanese management practices. Though the exact nature and functions of quality circles can vary considerably, they generally entail meetings held on company time anywhere from once a day to once a month, in which groups of workers discuss any problems or ideas they have with respect to the work process and advance suggestions addressing how this process can be improved. In theory, these circles not only provide a forum for addressing work-related problems and improving both productivity and quality, they enable workers to develop a greater sense of ownership over the work process, given that they have had input into its design. This, in turn, facilitates a greater sense of involvement in, and hence commitment to, their work.

More generally, employee participation schemes can entail various mechanisms for joint labour–management problem solving and decision making. Typically, these entail establishment-wide **labour–management committees**, comprising an equal number of worker and management representatives. Perhaps the most prevalent form of committee is the health and safety committee, which is required by law across Canada for workplaces above a given size (see chapter nine). However, labour–management committees can be formed to address a variety of other issues, including the introduction of new technology, worker training and development, substance abuse, disciplinary problems, and productivity (see Bluestone and Bluestone, 1992: 155–64). In theory, such committees enable workers and their representatives to play a pro-active role in decisions affecting their well-being, instead of having these decisions imposed on them unilaterally and reacting after the fact. Not only does this in theory result in a higher likelihood of finding "win-win" solutions, or solutions which benefit *both* labour and management, workers are more likely to buy into decisions in which they have had an input, thus ensuring their commitment. Because of this, some organizations also have **joint steering committees**, where employee representatives meet with management personnel to discuss broad developments in the workplace and upcoming workplace changes. These committees are also sometimes referred to as **continuous improvement committees** or **re-engineering committees**, in reflection of established workplace change programs (see below).

Finally, growing attention has been paid to the importance of information-sharing processes, especially through **team briefings** and **town hall meetings**. While the former typically involve regularly scheduled meetings through which work teams or groups are informed about developments relevant to their work and subsequent plans which may affect them, town hall meetings tend to be broader, involving meetings with the entire workforce at a particular workplace. In addition, a number of more traditional information-sharing practices which remain popular include sending regular **newsletters** to employees, establishing **suggestion systems** through which employees can hope to receive some form of award if they contribute a suggestion that enhances performance, and conducting internal **attitude surveys** of employee opinions and concerns, sometimes followed up by group interviews.

(3) Complementary HRM Practices. According to pundits, a number of employment policies and practices must be in place if high performance work practices are to realize their full potential (see Pfeffer, 1998: 64–98).

Particularly important is the provision of long-term job security. According to proponents, employees are unlikely to develop high levels of commitment if employers are unwilling to reciprocate with a similar level of commitment. Job security is in theory also important if employees are to adopt a long-run view towards their employment, thereby reducing turnover and hence employer hiring and training costs — both of which can be substantial under the high performance model. Finally, layoffs are contrary to the underlying philosophy of the **high performance paradigm**, which is that employees are to be viewed as strategic resources critical to the employer's long-run survival and growth. For these reasons, employee cutbacks occur only if absolutely necessary, and, where possible, employers rely on normal attrition, redeployment to other jobs, and the use of voluntary retirement incentives. Where actual layoffs do take place, employees are provided with generous severance packages, assistance in looking for a new job, and in some cases even financial aid should they enter a training program to make themselves more marketable. Doing so can be viewed as an exercise in social responsibility, but it also conveys to surviving employees that the employer is doing everything possible for those who have been laid off, and will do the same for them if further layoffs should become necessary.

Intensive training is also believed to be essential if workers are to be able to perform at the level necessary for real performance gains, especially because high performance systems, in theory, rely on employee skill and initiative to solve problems, to initiate changes in work methods, and to take responsibility for quality (Pfeffer, 1998: 85). Not only does intensive training facilitate these skills, it can also symbolize employer commitment to employees (Pfeffer, 1998: 295). Because high performance work practices often entail considerable team work, this training frequently involves "soft" or interpersonal skills as well as "hard" or technical skills required for the work itself. It is ideally continuous, with employees receiving a set number of days of training per year in order to ensure that their skills are up-to-date and to allow them the opportunity for self development. In this respect, the term "the learning organization" has become popular. In theory, employees in these organizations are able to develop and broaden their knowledge, not only of their work tasks, but of the organization in general. Where job rotation or team work have been implemented, it is also common to hear about **multi-skilling** or **cross-training**, under which employees are trained so that they have a broader variety of skills than that required for their own jobs and/or are able to do different jobs. In theory, this makes employees more interchangeable in addition to providing them with a more thorough understanding of how their work fits into the overall picture.

A third practice considered of major importance is the implementation of a **bonus pay** system, under which pay is linked to performance. **Group bonuses**, under which individuals receive bonuses based on their team's performance, are considered especially important for fostering team effectiveness, because employees have an incentive to help each other rather than focusing on their individual tasks. But a number of workplace and firm level systems may also be established. Of particular note are: **gainsharing**, under which pay is linked to productivity gains; **profit-sharing**, under which pay is linked to profitability; and **employee stock ownership plans**, or **ESOPs**, under which employees are given financial incentives to purchase shares in their employer. Most of these systems are not particularly new, finding their genesis in the welfare capitalist schemes emergent in the early decades of this century. However, they in theory help to ensure that employees identify their interests with the performance of the organization and hence are more likely to accept employer goals as their own.

A fourth practice is the adoption of sophisticated selection and socialization processes. These are designed to ensure that workers have work values and orientations that are conducive to a "high performance culture" within the workplace as well as the necessary skills and abilities. Before workers are hired, they go through extensive psychological testing and personality assessment as well as being assessed for their technical capabilities, in essence to ensure that they have the "right" values. Once hired, they then go through elaborate initial orientation programs, designed in part to ensure that they develop favourable attitudes towards their employer and are inculcated with their employer's culture and values. To ensure success in this endeavour, employers may even locate facilities based in areas characterized by conservative values, and in which they can therefore be sure of an ample supply of employees with the appropriate orientations.

A fifth, largely symbolic practice, is the reduction of traditional status distinctions. Most common in this respect is the provision of workers with a monthly "salary" rather than paying them for the precise number of hours worked in a pay period, although in practice employers still typically require fixed hours of work and provide overtime pay or time off for extra hours worked. In addition to this practice, workers may also be allowed to use the same (rather than separate) eating facilities, entrances, and parking lots as do managers, thus symbolizing that everyone is part of the same overall "team". In theory, this eliminates the "we-them" atmosphere of traditional organizations and facilitates greater identification with, and commitment to, employer goals.

A sixth practice is the reduction of the number of job classifications and pay differentials between workers, in effect eliminating the structured internal labour markets of the bureaucratic/accommodative approach. In place of traditional pay differentials, employers may establish **pay-for-knowledge systems**, where workers are paid bonuses based on the number of tasks they can perform. Reduction in the number of job classifications essentially means a broadening of those classifications which remain, while pay-for-knowledge systems encourage workers to learn as broad an array of tasks as possible. As a result, employers have increased flexibility in the tasks they can assign to individual workers and teams.

Broader Programs Associated with High Performance Practices. In addition to the specific components of the high performance model are broader management programs or strategies which often accompany them. Three such programs/strategies have been most popularized in the management literature. The first is **Total Quality Management** or **TQM**. Although TQM systems can vary considerably, they generally entail an emphasis on the continuous improvement of all aspects of quality, from the actual design and manufacture of a product, to the way in which customers are served. More important, they are based on the idea that quality is something for which *all* employees share responsibility — rather than relegating quality related concerns to specific individuals or departments. Thus, workers themselves, rather than supervisors and inspectors, are responsible for inspecting their output and minimizing defects. In order to accomplish this, workers must be given considerable discretion in the workplace, and they must at the same time be highly committed to employer goals. The second is **just-in-time** system. These systems are designed to minimize stock and work-in-progress inventory levels, while providing maximum flexibility to respond to changes in market demands. Finally, the term **workplace re-engineering** is often used to refer to workplace change programs involving (in theory) radical restructuring of work relations so as to cut costs and improve flexibility.

Autonomic/Consociative Practices and Unions

Autonomic/consociative practices are generally premised on the assumption that employee and management interests are compatible, and that any conflict that occurs is attributable to faulty management policies and practices. As such, they entail an implicit rejection of traditional labour unionism and collective bargaining, which are based on the assumption that the two parties often have conflicting interests and that these interests can only be reconciled through an adversarial system, under which each side seeks to protect and advance its own interests.

This implicit rejection may be especially strong with regard to new HRM practices, because a number of these practices are contrary to the terms and conditions of employment that unions have traditionally sought to achieve on behalf of their members. This is particularly true of performance-based pay and promotion. Because performance is often difficult to measure in any objective, reliable way, any system that uses it to determine pay and performance can be subject to a high degree of favouritism and may even be used coercively as a tool to punish employees who do not have the "right attitude". Performance-based pay and promotion may also pit workers against each other and induce them to cut corners, especially with regard to their health and safety. For these reasons, Canadian unions have always fought for a strong role for seniority (i.e., years of service) in the determination of pay and promotion and have resisted performance-based incentives.

Similar problems can arise with regard to high performance workplace practices. For example, in order to prevent unfair treatment of individual employees or attempts by employers to arbitrarily increase workloads, unions have traditionally fought for strong job classifications and "work rules" limiting what employees can be asked to do. Yet the high performance model calls for a breakdown in job classifications and a broadening of the tasks that workers are expected to perform. In addition, some of the participative practices associated with the high performance model may be seen as managerial substitutes for union representation, designed to control the information workers receive and to ensure that any conflicts or concerns that arise are dealt with on management's terms. Not only may they lower demand for union representation, they may threaten to undermine a union where one is established, thus giving rise to union resistance to them.

Employers adopting autonomic/consociative practices may as a result be strongly opposed to unions. But to convey this to employees risks undermining the positive workplace environment that they seek to create — especially if they were to do so in a way that seemed threatening or coercive. As a result, they tend to adopt a more sophisticated, "velvet glove"[4] approach to union avoidance than other

---

[4] "Velvet glove" comes from the phrase "iron fist in a velvet glove", referring to a person who appears gentle but is determined and often inflexible underneath.

employers. Often, the stated policy is that the employer would prefer to remain non-union, but that management respects the choice of their employees and that, if their employees would like to have a union, they are free to organize one without interference.

Of course, should a union attempt to organize workers, the employer may engage in a number of sophisticated tactics to defeat it, often appealing to legal technicalities (discussed in chapter eleven) and arguing that they only wish to ensure that the "true" desires of workers are realized. In Canada, Wal-Mart is perhaps best-known for these tactics. For example, when the United Food and Commercial Workers (UFCW) attempted to organize a Wal-Mart store in Thompson, Manitoba, Wal-Mart tried to have the representation vote negated on the grounds that CBC reporters interviewed some of the workers in the store parking lot on the day of the ballot and that this may have tainted the results. In a similar case in Saskatchewan, Wal-Mart managed to delay the process for almost four years, until a new government was elected and new laws were passed. It then argued that a secret ballot vote should be required to establish if there was majority support for the union, even though such a vote was not required at the time the union applied for legal representation rights, and even though the union had been able to establish that it had the support of a majority of workers, as required under the law at the time it initially applied. In St. Jonquière, Quebec, it simply shut down a store after the UFCW succeeded in organizing its workers, engaging in a sophisticated legal strategy to ensure that it would not be found to be in violation of the law. Wal-Mart has even attempted to prevent the United Food and Commercial Workers from communicating with their employees by asking the courts to shut down a website established for that purpose.

Not all autonomic/consociative employers are necessarily like Wal-Mart. Instead, these employers may indeed respect the legal right of their employees to organize a union. Doing so is not only consistent with democratic values (see chapter seven), it may also help to avoid the often acrimonious relationship that can result should the employer attempt to undermine or frustrate the ability of employees to exercise their right to a union. Particularly notable in this respect is a recent agreement by Magna International, a mostly non-union automobile parts manufacturer with roughly 45 facilities in Canada, to allow employees in each of its facilities to vote on whether they would like the Canadian Auto Workers (CAW) to represent them. This agreement has been highly controversial, because rather than simply accepting the right of workers to unionize, it contains a number of conditions that appear to weaken the potential effectiveness of the union. It is discussed in Box 5–4.

Autonomic/consociative Employee Relations Practices in Non-union Workplaces. In theory, autonomic/consociative practices might be expected to prevent unions from becoming established in the first place. Not only are these practices designed to ensure that employees identify with employer goals, selection processes are designed to weed out applicants whose values are likely to make them sympathetic to unions. However, autonomic/consociative employers may also establish their own distinctive employee relations systems to handle conflicts as they arise, rather than allowing them to fester and eventually create support for a union.

First, autonomic/consociative employers may establish some form of internal justice or complaints system, as discussed earlier with respect to the bureaucratic/accommodative approach. But in contrast to those associated with the latter approach, employee grievances are treated as "problems" rather than as conflicts, to be resolved as informally as possible and in a non-adversarial way. They also tend to be more elaborate. For example, Magna International has a three-stage system. The employee can first speak informally with line leaders and supervisors, who in theory act as neutral adjudicators. If dissatisfied with the outcome, the employee can then take the problem to a management-appointed "Employee Advocate" who attempts to find a remedy. If still dissatisfied, the employee may go to a "Fairness Committee" composed of managers and employees (Lewchuk and Wells, 2006: 644–45). Unlike a union system, there is no independent third party or "neutral" to whom the employee can turn, and little by way of rules and procedures to which the employee can appeal in order to argue her case.

Second, autonomic/consociative employers may establish an employee representation system, where employee representatives meet periodically with the employer to discuss or consult over matters that concern employees. These systems can vary widely in both design and purpose (see Taras and Kaufman, 2006), but they often address issues that would otherwise be addressed by a union — including wages and benefits. As such, they tend to serve a broader role than the committee structures identified earlier with respect to the high performance model. Because they appear to substitute for a union yet are both creations of, and operate on terms set by, the employer, they are often referred to as "company" unions. Company unions are controversial, and have been illegal in the United States since the 1930s on the grounds that they

BOX 5–4   A New Form of Unionism?

... Employees at Magna International who vote to join the Canadian Auto Workers won't have the right to strike under a historic labour relations deal.

In a dramatic change regarding fundamental labour rights, the CAW confirmed yesterday it has agreed to shelve the key strike provision in efforts to build a new management–union relationship at Magna, the country's biggest auto parts maker.

Under the agreement, about 18,000 workers at 45 Magna plants, predominantly in southern Ontario, will have the opportunity at each operation to decide on union representation by voting in favour or against a tentative three-year contract.

CAW president Buzz Hargrove and Magna chair Frank Stronach signed their "framework of fairness" agreement that sets out a process for major changes in traditional union–management relations on the shop floor, including resolution of disputes.

"It's an innovative approach and an opportunity for us, using this model, to try to show the country and the world that you can deal in labour management relations in a different manner, where you don't start out with a fight over whether or not the workers are entitled to have a union," CAW president Buzz Hargrove said at the company's headquarters in Aurora.

Stronach, who founded Magna five decades ago, initiated the idea more than two years ago in an effort to improve the competitive position of the company and the auto industry, which is losing business and jobs to offshore competition.

He told reporters that companies and unions have to build trust so everyone can prosper.

"We have yet a ways to go to really get the respect of the employees," Stronach acknowledged. "You know we're not afraid of labour organizations. I have disagreed with some of the philosophies of the union. But at the same time we all have to change. Business has to change. Unions have to change."

The CAW said the deal gives the union a major opportunity to gain members in the struggling auto sector where its clout has dropped during the past two decades. Despite organizing attempts, the union represents only about 1,000 workers at three Magna plants.

The agreement contemplates an overhaul of traditional bargaining processes, grievance procedures and representation on the shop floor.

If workers vote in favour of the CAW and the contract at their plant, any subsequent collective bargaining disputes would be resolved through binding arbitration rather than a walkout by the union or a lockout by the company.

BOX 5–4 (continued)

The fundamental right to withdraw labour is a provision that unions have protected vigorously for decades as its only ultimate power against management. ... The CAW decision to give up this right [has] triggered criticism from other labour leaders.

"It's a pretty drastic measure and ultimately is not good for workers because they no longer have the right to withdraw their labour." said Wayne Samuelson, president of the Ontario Federation of Labour.

"It's pretty fundamental to the labour movement and collective bargaining. This is not good, especially if it's exchanged for voluntary recognition of the union. It certainly sets a precedent that working people need to be concerned about."

"Hargrove is creating CAW–employer associations," added Wayne Fraser, Ontario–Atlantic director of the United Steelworkers. "What's to stop other employers, especially Magna competitors, from rightfully asking the CAW for the same no-strike right."

. . . .

[In addition], the deal [provided for] a joint "employee relations review committee" of three Magna representatives and three top CAW officials [to] discuss overall goals and projects and negotiate a national agreement covering wages, shift premiums, benefits and retirement programs. There would be some alterations to the deal reflecting local conditions.

Magna currently pays workers the average of the industry and other plants in the community. It also has a profit-sharing program.

[Finally,] In the new agreement, each plant will have an "employee advocate" to raise concerns. The company and union will screen candidates; workers will ratify the selection.

Critics question whether workers will have real power to elect the advocate and union representatives on the main review committee that negotiates contracts.

The two sides have also agreed to change the traditional grievance procedure with a "concern resolution process". ... It involves an "open door" policy to deal with complaints and issues with superiors and safety officials, use of the Magna central "hotline" and review by the employee relations committee and an arbitrator if necessary.

Source: From Tony Van Alphen, "CAW Shelves Right to Strike", *Toronto Star* October 16, 2007, p. B.1. Reprinted with permission — Torstar Syndication Services.

can serve as barriers to the attainment of the kind of truly independent representation associated with unions. However, they would appear to be relatively widespread in that country, covering as many as one out of four workers (Godard and Frege, 2010). In Canada, they are generally legal provided they are not set up to frustrate a specific union-organizing attempt. There is no recent evidence as to how widespread they may be, although they appear to have covered roughly one in eight workers as of the mid-1990s (Lipset and Meltz, 2000).

These systems may not be intended to specifically keep unions at bay. Although they tend to be most consistent with an autonomic/consociative approach, they may be established simply to ensure a "healthy" employee relations environment and hence may be adopted in conjunction with a more bureaucratic/accommodative approach as well. However, to the extent that they are effectively operated, they may both lower demand for a union and serve as "early warning" systems that enable management to detect and head off worker discontent before there is widespread support for a union. As such, they may still have the effect of preventing workers from seeking union representation. Yet, despite their potential for preventing employees from organizing a union, these systems can also actually have the opposite effect. This can occur if employees are given a "taste" of representation and then find this representation to be insufficient, either because the employer fails to take employee representatives seriously or because there is an issue on which these representatives are unable to achieve an outcome that is satisfactory to workers (Taras and Copping, 1998).

Autonomic/Consociative Employee Relations Practices in Union Workplaces. Although attempting to mix union representation with autonomic/consociative practices might seem to be like attempting to mix oil and water, there are unionized workplaces in which management attempts to pursue an autonomic/consociative approach. Where this is the case, management typically attempts to move beyond the traditional adversarial relation associated with the bureaucratic/accommodative approach to establish a cooperative or "partnership" relation, in which unions are included in various management decisions and are expected in return to develop a largely participative and problem solving function. In particular, management seeks to establish cooperative forms of bargaining such as "interest-based" or "mutual gains" bargaining. These are discussed more fully in chapter twelve, but they generally involve the search for "positive sum" solutions that benefit both parties.

Some have argued that, where a union is established, developing such a relationship can actually have positive implications, especially for the effectiveness of high performance workplace practices. First, they argue that the participation of a union in the design and implementation of high performance practices helps to offset worker insecurity and distrust, because workers can be confident that their own elected and independent representatives have played a role and hence that these practices will not have negative implications for them. Second, proponents argue that a high performance system requires a long-term commitment, yet managers often act in ways that undermine a high performance system or the promises associated with it (e.g., job security) in order to satisfy short-term pressures. A union can help to prevent this by holding management to its word, especially if it has managed to negotiate various promises into the collective agreement.

Proponents also argue that not only can unions be good for the high performance model, this model can be good for unions. Specifically, this model provides unions with an opportunity to discard their traditional adversarial role in favour of a more co-operative one, in which they are able to serve as "partners" in the pursuit of "mutual gains" that derive from the effective implementation of a high performance system. In an era characterized by union stagnation and even decline, the high performance model thus serves as a basis for union renewal, ensuring that unions have a much more positive future than otherwise. Failure to take this opportunity will only mean loss of membership support and continued decline, especially as workers will come to see unions as outmoded and standing in the way of changes that are good for them as well as their employers. It is important to recognize, however, that these tend to be theoretical arguments. As shall be apparent below, whether they hold in practice is uncertain.

V. ASSESSING MANAGERIAL POLICIES AND PRACTICES

As mentioned earlier, in the 1980s and 1990s, both the new HRM and the high performance model approaches came to be viewed in some circles as the key to competitive advantage. Many have viewed them as the "wave of the future", particularly the high performance model, which proponents have considered to be "best practice" for virtually all workplaces. The belief has been that, by giving workers the opportunity to realize their potential on the job and to participate in decisions that affect them, high performance practices foster high employee motivation and commitment, which in turn produces high levels of co-operation and productivity. Proponents have therefore tended to view the high performance model as good not only for employers, but also for employees and, ultimately, for society.

Despite the theoretical promise of the high performance model, it does not appear to have been widely adopted. A sizable majority of employers *do* appear to have adopted at least a few of the practices associated with this model, but only a small minority — perhaps fewer than one in ten, appear to have adopted them to a high degree.[5] It appears that most employers have used these practices to augment more traditional approaches rather than to "transform" the way work is done or the relations between employees and their employers. For example, an analysis of the data from the 2003–4 PRA survey of 750 Canadian workers (discussed in chapter three) found moderate to strong, positive correlations between high performance practices, new HRM practices, and traditional bureaucratic HRM practices.

In addition, there has now been considerable research addressing whether high performance practices have the positive implications claimed for them by their proponents. It is important to consider this research and the debates surrounding it, because all too often there is a tendency for practitioners, policy makers, and academics to buy into particular ideas because these ideas are consistent with what they want to believe rather than because they actually work. Unfortunately, there is reason to believe that this may have been at least partly the case with regard to the high performance paradigm (Godard and Delaney, 2000: 485–86). This section thus provides an overview of some of the more important research findings and the issues surrounding them. It also refers to findings with respect to bureaucratic/accommodative and new HRM practices where applicable.

High Performance Practices and Performance. The evidence as to the implications of high performance practices for performance is somewhat mixed. The general consensus now seems to be that it demonstrates a positive association, but not all studies (including some of the

---

[5] For example, a 2001 Statistics Canada survey of 6,223 establishments with over 10 employees found that, although 4 in 10 reported some form of information-sharing, and a quarter reported problem-solving teams, only 9 percent reported self-directed work groups (Statistics Canada, 2004). These findings also reveal somewhat lower levels of adoption than did a comparable 1999 survey of 3,142 employers (Morisette and Rosa, 2003: 25).

highest quality, e.g., Cappelli and Neumark, 2001) support this conclusion, and there have been potentially serious limitations to much of the research that does (see Godard, 2004a; Kaufman, 2010). For example, it is possible that employers who already enjoy high performance have more resources and are thus more likely to adopt high performance workplace practices. In these cases, it is performance that is "causing" these practices, rather than the other way around. Most studies have been unable to address this possibility. Another possibility that has not been addressed is that high performance practices are adopted primarily in workplaces to which they are most suited, so a finding that such practices are associated with performance in these workplaces does not provide the basis for suggesting that they will be in other workplaces (Kaufman, 2010). In addition, many studies include new HRM practices and even some more traditional bureaucratic/accommodative practices not strictly included in the model. It may be these practices, rather than their high performance counterparts, that explain any association with performance. Finally, some studies suggest that there are diminishing returns to the adoption of these practices. That is, the high levels of adoption that one would expect to find in a truly "high performance" workplace do not yield much higher performance than moderate levels of adoption. Indeed, these studies may not even demonstrate that high performance practices are appreciably more effective than more traditional bureaucratic/accommodative ones (Delaney and Godard, 2001).

If these studies demonstrate anything, it may be that work and HRM practices associated with both the bureaucratic/accommodative and the autonomic/consociative approaches likely have positive implications for performance in most workplaces. But the extent to which this is the case, and the specific combination of practices that is likely to be most effective, probably vary from one workplace to the next, depending on a variety of factors, including market conditions, product characteristics, workplace size, past history, and others. In other words, work and HRM practices matter to performance. But there is no simple formula or "magic bullet". It is quite likely that the sources of conflict underlying the employment relation (chapter three) limit the extent to which high levels of commitment can be achieved for any length of time, while making the implementation of various practices more costly than proponents have assumed to be the case. This may be especially true of the full adoption of the high performance model (Godard, 2004a; 2005: 145–46). Thus, not many employers fully adopt it, and where they do, it may not deliver the performance gains expected.

High Performance Practices and Workers. There are also questions about the implications of high performance practices for workers. Proponents have argued that these should be positive, because workers are able to develop their skills and are provided with input into, and information about, decisions that affect them. Skeptics have argued, however, that high performance workplaces are in essence designed to intensify the work process, requiring workers to perform more tasks, often at a more rapid pace. This may be especially true with regard to teamwork, because workers are expected to fill in for other workers if necessary and may feel greater pressure from their co-workers to perform.

Research findings on the implications of these practices for workers has also been somewhat mixed and suffered from a number of possible limitations (Godard, 2004a; 2010). As for the performance effects of these practices, a particularly important problem is that high performance practices can appear to be associated with positive worker outcomes and attitudes, but this may be because these practices tend to be adopted in conjunction with HRM practices not considered to be part of the high performance model, and it is these practices, rather than their high performance counterparts, that are having the positive implications thought to be caused by high performance work practices.

An analysis of the 2003–4 PRA data referred to above explored this possibility (see Godard, 2010), and is probably the most thorough analysis to date — especially within Canada. It found that, while high performance practices initially appear to have positive implications for worker outcomes and attitudes, this is in large part because high performance practices tend to be adopted in conjunction with traditional bureaucratic/accommodative practices, and that it is these latter practices that have the most positive implications for workers. To the extent that bureaucratic/accommodative practices are in place, workers experience lower levels of fatigue and coercion and higher levels of empowerment, satisfaction, and commitment. Although high performance practices still have some positive implications for workers once bureaucratic practices are controlled for, these implications are attributable almost entirely to participative reforms (especially information sharing), which have strong positive implications for worker outcomes and attitudes. But even these associations apply only in union workplaces, which is consistent with the argument that unions help to ensure the effectiveness of these practices (at least for workers). Finally, this analysis found the implications of new HRM practices to be mixed. Although they were associated with higher levels of job satisfaction, they were also associated with higher levels of stress. In short, this study suggests that bureaucratic/accommodative practices matter most to worker well-being in Canada, although the adoption of participative reforms also matters in the union sector.

High Performance Practices and Unions. Finally, the implications of high performance practices for unions have also been a matter of some concern. As discussed earlier, both new HRM and high performance workplace practices are sometimes thought to be "anti-union" because they deny the importance of interest conflicts and hence the need for traditional union representation. As a result, employers may be more resistant to unions than otherwise. Moreover, where a union is established, union leaders may find themselves under pressure to enter into a partnership relation. If they fail to do so, they may appear to be troublemakers. Yet, if they agree to do so, they may be seen to be compromising their traditional adversarial role of "standing up" for workers, leaving their members to wonder exactly why they are paying union dues. Either way, support for the union may be weakened.

Once again, the research findings have been somewhat mixed and may suffer from important limitations (Godard, 2004a; 2008; 2009a). It is likely that much depends on employer attitudes towards unions and the perceived role and tradition of unions themselves, both of which can vary considerably across countries (Godard, 2008). For Canada, however, a recent analysis of the PRA data again provides perhaps the most thorough analysis to date (see Godard, 2009a).

The analysis of the PRA data revealed that low-to-moderate levels of adoption of high performance practices are positively associated with whether a worker is unionized, but that high levels of adoption are negatively associated. This is likely because unions, where established, resist high levels of these practices, and because, where a union is not established, employers that adopt high levels are more likely to resist attempts to establish one.

The analysis also revealed that non-union workers were less likely to desire a union at low-to-moderate levels of adoption but more likely at high levels, probably because low to moderate levels of adoption generally entail an accommodative approach, while high levels entail a more consociative approach under which distinctive worker interests are not adequately addressed.

A further finding with regard to high performance practices was that, where a union is established, high performance practices have no uniform implications for member support. But high performance practices can increase member support for the union if union leaders are perceived to cooperate with the employer *and* to continue to serve the traditional role of standing up for members, if need be. The available research suggests, however, that this requires a tricky balancing act, which often proves to be untenable (see Godard, 2004a).

In addition to the findings for high performance practices, the analysis of the PRA data revealed that new HRM practices are associated with a higher desire for unionization among non-union workers, likely because these practices do not adequately recognize the distinctive interests and expectations of workers (as is the case for high levels of adoption of high performance workplace practices). These practices bore no association with the likelihood of being in a union, likely because higher employer resistance to a union is offset by higher worker desire for one. They also bore no association with membership support for a union where one was established.

The PRA analysis further revealed, however, that bureaucratic/accommodative practices may have the most important implications for unions. These practices bore a strong association with unionization, likely because unions push employers to adopt bureaucratic practices and also because management may be less resistant to unions in workplaces that are conducive to these practices. They also bore a negative association with the desire for a union among non-union workers, probably because the adoption of these practices in non-union workplaces can lower the perceived need for a union, creating a "union substitution" effect.

Overall. If there is a lesson to be learned, it is that high performance practices, and HRM practices, in general, tend to be complex and do not lend themselves to singular conclusions (see Kaufman, 2010). Indeed, the implications of these practices may vary over time, both within workplaces and in the economy in general, as managers, workers, and unions gain experience with them and adjust accordingly, and as the context within which they interact also changes. A further lesson may, however, be that the implementation of various practices can be difficult and complex, likely because they entail often complex social relations and processes, but also because of the sources of conflict discussed in chapter three. Thus, although the idealized, harmonious outcomes promised in some of the management literature might be great in theory, they may not be readily attainable or economically feasible in practice (Godard, 2010). The reasons for this are discussed further in the next chapter.

Ethical Issues

The workplace and HRM practices adopted by employers can also entail a number of ethical issues. These issues are probably most apparent with regard to the autocratic/exploitive model, especially where it entails employer attempts to avoid or undermine a union. Not only do such attempts often entail illegal actions (see chapter seven), they are also contrary to the right of workers to achieve meaningful independent representation at work, which many would argue should be central in any democratic society. Indeed, the freedom to join a union and engage in collective bargaining is widely recognized as a fundamental human right, as discussed in chapter seven.

Ethical issues have also been raised, however, about the high performance model. These issues go beyond more obvious concerns about the implications of high performance practices for the nature of work and the effectiveness of unions to more philosophical issues having to do with democratic rights and freedoms (see Ackroyd and Thompson, 1999: 150–55). According to some critics (e.g., McKinlay and Taylor, 1996; Sennett, 1998), the high performance model can be highly oppressive, because workers are required to accept employer goals and values as their own. In addition, workers are subject to strong peer pressures to be good "team players" and as a result may not feel free to express otherwise legitimate concerns and complaints. From an employer's perspective, this may not be a bad thing. But for critics, high performance practices represent little more than a social engineering technology that stifles freedom of thought as well as expression, both of which are not only associated with a truly free and democratic society, but which are essential to the survival of such a society.

It is possible that these concerns are ill-founded, reflecting a tendency for some authors to under-estimate the ability of workers to think for themselves and to resist these sorts of pressures if, indeed, they exist in the first place (see Ackroyd and Thompson, 1999: 155–62). Yet to the extent that such concerns are valid, it suggests that, from an ethical standpoint, some variant of the bureaucratic/ accommodative approach, perhaps combined with those high performance practices that allow workers more discretion and autonomy, may be preferred. Under this approach, workers are not expected to adopt employer goals and values as their own. Rather, it is recognized that there may be legitimate differences between employer and worker goals, and that there is need for employers to accommodate such differences rather than to attempt to impose their goals onto workers.

Not only may this be more ethically desirable, it may also be more realistic in view of available research findings.

VI. CONCLUSIONS

This chapter has gone beyond the historical analysis of chapter four to address contemporary management policies and practices in labour relations. Though these policies and practices are often complex and inconsistent, it has been possible to identify three general approaches which appear to be most predominant: (1) autocratic/exploitive, (2) bureaucratic/accommodative, and (3) autonomic/consociative. The first of these is most reminiscent of the coercive drive approach emergent at the end of the nineteenth century, and the second of the post-war status quo as it developed in the 1950s and 1960s. The third is born of both the welfare capitalist tradition of the 1920s and the human relations school emergent in the 1930s, but has grown to be increasingly sophisticated over the past few decades, and is now engendered in both the "new HRM" and the high performance model, the latter of which has been touted by many as the wave of the future. Because of this, considerable emphasis has been placed on this model. But a number of issues are associated with it, and the available research suggests that it may not hold the promise for employers, workers, or unions that many of its proponents have assumed.

Understanding and Explaining Management

6

Management can, by virtue of its position of authority in work organizations, be viewed as the dominant actor in industrial relations. As such, if one is to develop a full understanding of industrial relations, it is necessary to move beyond the description and analysis of managerial policies and practices to develop a more in-depth comprehension of the nature of management itself, the factors which influence managerial policies and practices, and the rationale underlying the adoption of these policies and practices. Doing so is a somewhat messy task, for myriad theories of management have been developed over the years. Although these theories often appear to conflict with one another, many offer useful insights into understanding management.[1] This chapter first discusses these theories as they apply to industrial relations, and then draws on this discussion to provide a more developed foundation for understanding and explaining management.

I. THEORIES OF MANAGEMENT AND INDUSTRIAL RELATIONS

A considerable amount has been written over the years, both about what managers *actually* do, and about what they *should* do. The former involves theories *of* management, while the latter involves theories *for* management. Theories of management are primarily **analytical**,

---

[1] The term "theory" is used loosely in the field of organization theory, for most of this literature does not generate the sorts of predictions often associated with the term (see Godard. 1993b). This literature does, however, generate useful explanations of organizational phenomena and it can in this sense be viewed as theoretical.

directed at *understanding* managerial processes and practices and *explaining* why they vary. Theories *for* management are primarily **normative**, directed at providing prescriptions for and hence *influencing* managerial processes and practices.[2] Because this chapter is concerned with understanding and explaining management, focus is on the former.

This section begins by briefly considering the traditional neoclassical theory of the firm, which is typically adhered to by neoliberals. Then, using this as a foil, a number of alternative theories are considered, each of which embodies one or more criticisms of the neoclassical school. These theories will, in turn, form the foundation for the explanatory model of management developed in the subsequent section. In this respect, it shall become clear that the neoclassical school may not be wrong so much as it is oversimplified. As such, it is of limited value, in and of itself, for understanding management, yet it provides a useful starting point for building a more complex picture, which is of value.

Neoclassical Economic Theory

The conventional view of management, especially as advanced by neoclassical economists, has been that managers serve as agents of owners and investors (if they are not themselves the owners), and that, as agents, they continually strive to enhance the efficiency and competitive position of the firm, thereby maximizing profits and ownership wealth. To do so they acquire that mix of factor inputs (e.g., labour, equipment, materials) which enables them to minimize per unit production costs given the relative costs of these factors in the market place. In labour relations, this requires that management provide the minimum terms and conditions of employment necessary to attract qualified workers, and that it employ these workers in a way that maximizes their productivity. Though over the short run they may stray from this objective, market pressures over the long run force them to rationalize their operations or risk economic failure.

Neoclassical economic theory underscores the importance of efficiency and productivity to managerial decision-making, but it has been criticized in a number of respects. Five criticisms are of particular relevance to the present discussion.

---

[2] Traditionally, the field of organization theory and industrial relations in general have been primarily analytical, while the field of management theory — as taught in management schools — has been primarily prescriptive.

1. It presents no model of the internal workings of the firm through which efficiency is maximized.
2. It incorrectly equates efficiency with profitability and in so doing ignores the "political" side of labour–management relations.
3. It proceeds from an oversimplified view of management, viewing managers simply as agents of ownership interests.
4. It does not recognize the limits to managerial rationality.
5. It does not account for the role of managerial values and choice processes.

The first of these criticisms is largely addressed by "contingency theory", the second by "labour process theory", the third by "stakeholder theory", the fourth by "management process theory", and the fifth by "strategic choice theory". In the remainder of this section these bodies of theory are discussed, focusing upon the implications of each for understanding and explaining management in industrial relations.

Contingency Theory

While neoclassical theory concerns itself more with the costs of factor inputs, contingency theory concerns itself more with the internal authority structure of organizations and typically proceeds from a more managerial orientation (see Donaldson, 1995).[3] At risk of oversimplification, this theory essentially argues that bureaucracy is the most effective form of organization when management is subject to low uncertainty and little variability or change in its environment — as is typically the case for large organizations characterized by mass production technologies and operating in stable product markets. As such, management can be expected to adopt a bureaucratic form of organization to the extent that these conditions hold. But to the extent that they do not, and management is subject to high uncertainty and con-

---

[3] Contingency theory is closely aligned with the emergence of the "markets and hierarchies" approach in economics. In essence, this approach argues that firms or hierarchies have increasingly come to supplant markets in order to reduce various costs associated with market transactions. With respect to the employment relation, it also argues that these costs are a primary reason for hiring workers rather than contracting work out. More recently, it has been adapted to distinguish between the conditions under which an organic structure is more efficient than a bureaucratic one (Williamson and Ouchi, 1981), and it is in this sense that it is consistent with contingency theory. However, while this approach is not without its implications for industrial relations, its inclusion in this chapter would add little beyond unnecessarily complicating discussion. For a debate over its contribution to the study of management, see Donaldson, 1990 and Hesterly, Liebeskind, and Zenger, 1990.

siderable variability, bureaucracy becomes unwieldy and inefficient, and so there is need of a much more flexible and "organic" form of organization. In the terminology of chapter five, this can either entail a more autocratic form, characterized by close supervision, or it can entail a more autonomic form consistent with the high performance paradigm. However, contingency theorists typically view the latter as the most likely to be adopted, as it is in theory more flexible and conducive to high employee motivation.[4] This form of organization is the antithesis to bureaucracy, characterized by low specialization, few rules and procedures, and reliance upon teamwork and employee commitment instead of hierarchy to ensure that the work is carried out in accordance with managerial objectives.

Contingency theory is of value because it provides a basis for explaining variation in workplace authority structures and, ultimately, managerial policies and practices in industrial relations. Of note, it is also, by and large, consistent with the argument that we are in a "new" economic era of flexible technology and unstable markets, rendering the bureaucratic/accommodative approach obsolete and requiring a more "organic", autonomic/consociative approach or risk failure. But it focuses primarily on the "technical side" of management, stressing the importance of various contingency factors for attaining the most technically efficient form of work organization. As such, it fails to adequately address how the conflicts underlying the labour–management relation are manifest in what management does.

The Political Side: Labour Process Theory

While both neoclassical and contingency theory focus on the technical side of management, labour process theory focuses upon the political side, and is closely associated with the radical perspective on industrial relations. In its simplest form, it proceeds from the assumption that profit is achieved not so much through the attainment of efficiency in the technical sense, but rather by extracting a maximum of output from workers at a minimum cost. This, in turn, generates resistance from workers and hence gives rise to a "problem" (from man-

---

[4] Contingency theorists have alternatively referred to this as either a "clan" (Williamson and Ouchi, 1981) or an "organic" (Burns and Stalker, 1961) form of organization. Neither term fits the classification system developed in chapter five. In addition, the term organic can be confusing, for contingency theorists use this term somewhat differently than does Durkheim, who considers organic solidarity as resulting from higher rather than lower specialization (see chapter two).

agement's point of view) of control in the workplace. It is this problem which largely drives managerial policies and practices in industrial relations.

This argument has been most inspired by Harry Braverman's 1974 book, *Labor and Monopoly Capital*. In essence, Braverman argued that the emergence and continued popularity of industrial engineering and scientific management in the twentieth century reflected managerial attempts to fragment work and "externalize" the knowledge traditionally held by skilled workers. The intended consequences were twofold, both of which were alluded to in chapter four. The first was to "**de-skill**" the labour process, reducing management's dependence on skilled workers and making it possible to rely upon lower paid unskilled and semi-skilled workers, who tend to have lower labour market and relational power. The second was to gain greater control over the methods and the pace by which workers perform their tasks, thus overcoming recalcitrance in the workplace and ultimately ensuring a higher level of output. In short, then, Braverman's argument is that industrial engineering and scientific management meant more work for lower pay.

This is hardly "efficient" from the point of view of the worker. It may even be inefficient from a technical point of view (see Gordon, 1976; Godard, 1998a) for management may implement a technically less efficient technology if doing so means lower skill requirements and greater managerial control (and hence lower costs and higher effort). But whether this is the case or not, Braverman's argument suggests that managerial decisions about the implementation of new technologies and the design of the workplace are not technically neutral, but rather reflect a bias towards de-skilling and control. This, rather than a misplaced conception of worker needs and motives (which managerialists argue is characteristic of Taylorism), explains the highly fragmented tasks and lack of worker discretion that became increasingly characteristic of the workplace in the twentieth century.

Though it is likely that a major purpose of scientific management may initially have been to de-skill and control workers, Braverman's overall thesis has been subject to considerable criticism (see Littler, 1990). This is especially true with respect to de-skilling. While it *may* be in management's interests to implement new technologies in a way that minimizes skill requirements and maximizes control, these more "political" considerations may be outweighed by "technical" ones having to do with "pure" efficiency gains, in which case new technologies or work reorganizations can result in skill upgrades (Wood, 1982). Moreover, the implications of new technologies and the technical design of the workplace are often complex, and so the most rational (from management's point of view) design may not always be obvious, especially if, as is often the case, decisions are made by technical "experts" who are more likely to emphasize "pure" efficiency considerations (Hyman, 1987: 33; Batstone, Ferner, and Terry, 1984; Burawoy, 1979). It is thus not surprising to find that there is little evidence that overall skill levels have declined throughout this century or that new technologies are associated with lower skills, as noted in chapter three.

In addition to criticisms of his de-skilling thesis, Braverman has been taken to task for his limited conception of control. In essence Braverman concerns himself only with "**direct**", structural methods of control, methods which focus on the design of work and which for Braverman are ultimately based upon management coercion. Yet, as discussed in chapters four and five, this century has witnessed the emergence of more bureaucratic/accommodative management practices and, more recently, more progressive employment practices associated with the high performance paradigm. It would be mistaken to think that these practices do not include direct methods of control and/or various forms of economic coercion. But they also attempt to meet the equity and fairness expectations of workers and, in the case of the high performance paradigm, to induce workers to identify with managerial goals. In this sense, they can also be said to entail "**indirect control**", involving social psychological considerations and directed more towards obtaining the willing cooperation or "consent" of workers (Friedman, 1977; Burawoy, 1979). Note that this entails a broader conception of control than commonly adopted in the debate over the high performance model (see chapter five), so that the commitment approach is viewed as representing an alternative way of exerting control over workers.

In defence of Braverman, it seems quite plausible to expect that, *all else being equal*, management will choose those technologies that require lower skill levels, as doing so typically reduces the labour market and relational power of workers (see chapter one), and this, in turn, translates into lower wage costs (among other things). Thus, there may be a low skill bias in managerial choices. The question, of course, is just how strong this bias is. This question could only be answered if we could compare the way in which technologies have developed against the way in which they *would* have developed if this bias did not exist. Because the latter is largely hypothetical, such a comparison is not feasible.

The issue of de-skilling aside, Braverman's work in the labour process tradition underscores a critical point: control (direct or indirect) is a central problem for management in industrial relations. This problem arises out of the various sources of conflict identified in chapter three, and it can be manifest not just in the form of recalcitrance in the workplace, but also in the form of exit and strike activity (see Godard, 1993a, 1998a). Each of these forms of behaviour can have substantial costs for management, and although these costs can vary considerably, their minimization can be expected to play an important role in managerial decisions and practices in industrial relations.

It follows that, in addition to the "technical" function, management can also be thought of as having a "political" function, reflecting the essentially political problem of control. Managerial attempts to address this problem go beyond the design of the workplace per se to decisions about the terms and conditions of employment, and more generally, the treatment to be afforded workers. In this respect, the labour process literature provides an important basis for understanding managerial policies and practices and will be central to the model presented in the second section of this chapter. Yet, the labour process literature does not provide much insight as to why managerial control strategies vary (Godard, 1998a). Moreover, there has been a tendency to portray managers as simple agents of owners and to neglect the processes by which decisions are made,[5] criticisms that may also be levelled against traditional neoclassical theory. This problem is addressed by stakeholder theory.

Stakeholder Theory

According to stakeholder theory, organizations should be viewed as coalitions of stakeholder groups, each of which contributes resources to the firm in return for various inducements, and each of which can hence be said to have a "stake" in the firm (see Cyert and March, 1963; Mitroff, 1983; Evans, 1993: 335–48). For example, investors contribute financial resources in return for stock dividends and/or increased share value; consumers contribute operating capital in return for the good or service produced; and, most relevant, workers contribute their labour in return for agreed upon terms and conditions of employment. In turn, the role of management is to ensure that the

---

[5] This is especially true with respect to its early proponents, including Braverman himself. There have been increasingly sophisticated attempts by radicals to come to terms with the complexities of management and managerial motives (see especially Hyman, 1987). However, focus has remained upon managerial strategies of control, perhaps because it is these strategies with which radicals are primarily concerned.

various stakeholder groups continue to provide a stable supply of necessary resources by satisfying the often competing demands of these groups. This is accomplished not only by ensuring that the firm operates as efficiently as possible so that these groups can be provided with sufficient material inducements, but also by internalizing their interests and concerns into the goal and policy structure of the firm through policy "side payments". Thus, the policy structure of a firm might include such considerations as seeking to enhance the earnings potential of the firm, providing consumers with a safe, high quality product, and providing workers with good pay and working conditions. To the extent that this policy structure adequately incorporates the interests of the various stakeholder groups and the expectations of these groups are satisfied, organizational "effectiveness" is attained, and organizational survival and growth are assured, thus serving the interests of all stakeholders. But if the expectations of these groups are not adequately satisfied, they may withdraw their resources, thereby threatening organizational survival and growth.

As should be apparent, stakeholder theory is largely consistent with the orthodox-pluralist perspective on industrial relations, which essentially argues that managerial attempts to pursue efficiency and effectiveness can conflict with the expectations workers have with respect to equity and fairness, and that collective bargaining serves as a mechanism for reconciling this conflict. For present purposes, however, it is important because it suggests that employer behaviour is to a considerable extent a reflection of the particular pressures to which management is subject. Thus, to understand employer practices in industrial relations, it is important to be aware of these pressures, not just as imposed by workers and their representatives, but by other stakeholder groups as well. For example, customers concerned about quality may expect the employer to adopt a quality management program and even to achieve some sort of quality accreditation. As discussed in chapter five, this may, in turn, require the adoption of high performance practices, which have come to be associated with these practices. On the other hand, customers may become increasingly concerned with cost reduction, pressuring management to engage in substantial downsizing and work intensification. Either way, understanding these pressures may be critical to understanding what management does.

A problem with stakeholder theory has been a tendency to assume that management is itself largely neutral, and that the interests of no one stakeholder group necessarily take priority over any other. This problem is perhaps most evident for privately owned and managed firms, where management has a clear interest in seeking to maximize long-run profit. In publicly held firms, matters may be somewhat more complex, because there can be thousands of shareholders, most of whom do not own enough share capital to really have much influence on management. This argument is at the heart of the managerial revolution thesis discussed in chapters two and three, and it is this thesis which in many respects forms the basis of the stakeholder model. But most would now agree that the most immediate stakeholder pressure on management is to maximize returns to investors. More often than not, there are at least a few shareholders with a large enough portion of shares that they can have senior management dismissed if unhappy with a firm's performance. In addition, the incomes of top management are often closely tied to profitability, through profit bonuses, stock options, and so forth. As also discussed in chapter three, changes to financial markets over the past few decades may have placed growing pressure on management to maximize profits over the short run, especially in countries such as Canada, the United States, and the United Kingdom.

The intensity with which profits are pursued may vary, depending on the extent to which management is subject to investor pressures and upon management values and beliefs. This may be especially so in privately controlled firms, where owners may even decide that they have some moral obligation to treat employees benevolently, even if this entails some sacrifice in profits. It may also be the case in countries where firms are less susceptible to investor pressures, such as Germany and Japan. As discussed in chapter three, firms in these countries appear to act more in accordance with a stakeholder model. But in countries such as Canada, the United States, and the United Kingdom, it would be mistaken to discount the importance of profit maximization as the primary motivation underlying the exercise of employer authority.

To argue that profit maximization is the primary purpose underlying the exercise of management authority is not to say that stakeholder theory is entirely wrong. Management can still be expected to respond to pressures from all of the stakeholder groups, and these pressures may, in turn, be key to understanding management policies and practices in industrial relations. The difference, however, is that management can generally be expected to respond to these pressures only to the extent it is believed to be consistent with the maximization of profit. Much may therefore depend on the power of various stakeholders (including workers and their representatives) to impose costs on management if their interests and expectations are not met.

The Limits to Rationality: Decision Process Theory

As presented to this point, the various schools of management theory have all by and large been characterized as proceeding from the general assumption that management acts rationally. That assumption has been taken to task in the organization theory literature for almost half of a century. In this literature, management is viewed as an ongoing process, in which managers are continually having to react to various problems, opportunities, and crises. Managers as a result simply lack the time or resources needed to search out all available information, carefully weigh all alternatives, and arrive at the "best" decision. They are also faced with considerable ambiguity and uncertainty, if only because the results of any given decision are often difficult to predict and available information is imperfect. In addition, decision making can be complex, and so there can be a number of difficulties involved in fully weighing and processing all of the information available (see March and Simon, 1958; Cohen, March, and Olsen, 1972; March and Olsen, 1976).

As a result of these limitations, there can be substantial limits to managerial rationality. These may be heightened by internal management politics. Different decisions can have important implications for the distribution of power, status, and resources within management itself. In addition, managers from different areas may come from different backgrounds, have different values, and be evaluated on the basis of different criteria. Thus, management decisions may reflect highly political processes, especially because the "best" decision is not always obvious, allowing different factions to argue for a decision which most suits their particular interests and priorities.

In addition, the limits to rationality may render managers susceptible to various fads and fashions associated with "best practice". Thus, for example, management may decide to adopt some variant of the high performance model, not because it is necessarily best for their firm, but rather because they do not know what is best, and as a result are susceptible to the "flavour of the moment". In doing so, they are able to reassure themselves — and their external stakeholders — that they are adhering to "best practice", even if it may not turn out to be suited to their particular firm.

These arguments help to underscore the complexity of managerial decision processes and of management itself. If nothing else, they help to move us away from the more simplistic, mechanistic view often assumed in economics textbooks. Yet when all is said and done, one is left asking whether management *really* is as irrational as suggested. There are a number of reasons to argue that, in general, it is not.

First, through formal education and training and informal "learning by doing", managers develop practical competencies and informal decision "programs" or "routines" which enable them to act rationally without having to rely on formally rational procedures and methods[6] (see Nelson and Winter, 1982; Byrman, 1984). Indeed, a common refrain in much of the popular management literature has been that these procedures and methods are irrational in their consequences, for they stifle initiative and flexibility (see Godard, 1999b).

It would also be a mistake to forget that the management process takes place subject to relations of authority. As such, senior managers are in a position to establish norms, policies, rules, and various control systems that guide the actions of subordinate managers. In addition, they are able to monitor the performance of subordinate managers through the establishment of performance criteria throughout the organization. As a result, there may only be limited room for politics.

Finally, the limits to rationality may vary by the type of decision involved (see M. Reed, 1989). While less important decisions made on a day-to-day basis may conform in some degree with decision process theory, more important decisions are likely to be made at senior levels within the managerial hierarchy and to involve formally rational planning and calculation. Thus, for example, a decision about a minor disciplinary matter may be made on the spot by a low-level manager, while a decision about whether to refuse the union's "final offer" in negotiations and thereby risk a lengthy strike is likely to be made after careful deliberation by senior managers.[7]

---

[6] This is well recognized by less extreme proponents of decision process theory, who, instead of claiming that decisions are not rational, argue that it is "boundedly rational", or rational subject to certain bounds. See March and Simon (1958); Thompson (1967); March, 1981.

[7] Other criticisms might also be identified. For example, research on group decision processes indicates that an organization lacking in intra-managerial conflict and politics may, in fact, be a less, rather than more, rational one, for intra-managerial dissension and politics can give rise to creative tensions and problem solving, with different managers arguing different points of view. Moreover, conflict between different departments may help to ensure that competing pressures within management are balanced off against one another. For example, conflict between line managers and industrial relations managers can be viewed as a balancing off of the "technical" with the "political" side of management. In other words, industrial relations managers and line managers may serve as a "check" for each other.

In short, there is ample reason to believe that management is far more rational than decision process theory might at first lead one to believe. This is by no means to suggest that we should return to the simple assumption of "pure" rationality. Because management is a highly complex task, there is considerable room for error and misjudgment, and managers may, in general, display considerable variation in their level of competency. Moreover, even though the position of authority enjoyed by senior managers enables them to exert considerable control over subordinate managers, this control is by no means perfect, especially as subordinate managers may disagree with, and attempt to circumvent, the edicts of their superordinates.

Decision process theory is thus by no means without merit. Though it may not pay sufficient attention to the sources of rationality, it does provide us with considerable insight into the nature of management as a day-to-day practice. It also alerts us to the complex nature of managerial decision-making and enables us to move beyond the simple assumption of "pure" rationality to one in which we recognize that rationality is in essence "bounded" by such things as imperfect information, limited time and cognitive capacity, and intra-managerial politics. Indeed, in recognition of this, less extreme proponents of decision process theory have coined the term "bounded rationality" to describe managerial decision-making (March and Simon, 1958; Thompson, 1967).

Perhaps the main problem with decision process theory is that it provides little real explanation as to why managerial policies and practices appear to vary across organizations, instead implying that this variation occurs almost by chance (e.g., Cohen, March, and Olsen, 1972). In this respect, the strategic choice model is of some value.

Strategic Choice Theory

Although the term strategic choice has become especially popular over the past few decades, it is often used to refer to a type of decision rather than to explain why management decisions vary. A major exception, however, is the "strategic choice model" of industrial relations developed by Thomas Kochan and his colleagues at the Massachusetts Institute of Technology in the mid-1980s (Kochan, McKersie, and Cappelli, 1984; Kochan, Katz, and McKersie, 1986). Though this model was intended to have application to both union and government as well as management strategy (e.g., see Kochan, 1991), it is primarily with respect to the latter that it was initially developed.

Kochan, Katz, and McKersie (1986: 12) argue that "the range of feasible options available at any given time is partially constrained by the outcomes of previous organizational decisions and the current distribution of power within the firm and between it and any unions, government agencies or other external organizations it deals with." Given these realities, however, "the range of options considered are filtered and constrained so as to be consistent with the values, beliefs, or philosophies engrained in the minds of key decision-makers, or, in some organizations, to reflect the norms that have diffused from founders or senior executives to lower levels and succeeding generations of managers" (1986: 12). Thus, managerial values, beliefs, and philosophies play a key role, independent of context variables, in accounting for managerial policies and practices in industrial relations. In this respect, Kochan, Katz, and McKersie argue that these values, beliefs, and philosophies tend to be resistant to change, and so do the policies and practices which embody them. In essence, they become institutionalized over time. Change does occur, but only once "environmental pressures" have become sufficiently strong that the survival and growth of the firm is threatened. Under these conditions, management is more likely to rethink its values and beliefs and adapt its strategy accordingly. Thus, though managerial policies and practices typically go through long periods of relative stability, these periods are interrupted periodically by major transformations.

The strategic choice model is of value for two reasons. First, it highlights the importance of managerial values and beliefs for explaining variation in management policies and practices. Second, it suggests that, because managerial values and beliefs can become deeply ingrained in management policies and practices, and because these values and beliefs are resistant to change, major changes in managerial policies and practices occur only under special conditions.

Strategic choice theory was developed to explain what the authors considered to be a major transformation in the U.S. industrial relations system toward the high performance model. Underlying Kochan, Katz, and McKersie's analysis was the belief that the high performance model is superior to more traditional approaches, but that it had not been widely adopted in the post-war era because employers were wedded to these approaches and were under little pressure to change. With the growing competitive pressures of the 1980s, more and more employers were changing their values and beliefs, and the high performance model was becoming widespread.

As discussed in the preceding chapter (and again in chapter sixteen), the predicted transformation does not appear to have taken place, and it is not at all clear that this is simply a problem of managerial values and beliefs. Rather, it may be that the high performance model is of limited effectiveness and hence applicability for a sizeable number of workplaces. In other words, the extent to which it is rational (from management's point of view) to adopt this model may vary considerably in accordance with various context variables, such as workplace size, technology, and market conditions.

This is not to suggest that values and beliefs are unimportant, only that they may provide only one explanation for managerial policies and practices. Perhaps the major question is *the extent to which* these values actually play a role independently of context variables. For example, it may be that managers choose those strategies, policies, and practices which are most rational, and then attempt to reconcile these choices with their values, altering their values accordingly. Research findings suggest that values do play some independent role, but that they also tend to vary in accordance with context variables (Godard, 1996). It also suggests that the latter variables are just as important, if not more so, than managerial values and beliefs in explaining variation (Godard, 1997b). Thus, any attempt to understand employer practices and why they vary must allow a role for context variables.

II. ACCOUNTING FOR MANAGERIAL POLICIES AND PRACTICES

To this point, all of the criticisms levelled at neoclassical economic theory have been addressed, drawing upon a number of competing theories — each of which can contribute relevant insight to the analysis of managerial decisions, policies, and practices in industrial relations. Yet, each of these theories suffers from important limitations. As such, the discussion thus far falls far short of providing a coherent understanding of managerial decisions, policies, and practices and why they vary. The task of this section, therefore, is to draw upon and extend the discussion to this point in order to propose a model which, to the extent possible, does so. This model is depicted in Figure 6–1. Though a simplified representation of a complex and dynamic set of processes and relationships, this figure provides a point of reference for the discussion to follow.

To begin, it should be apparent that management is a complex process, involving considerable amounts of uncertainty and internal dissension, as different managers attempt to pursue their own goals and objectives and to impose their own particular viewpoints, subject to varying degrees of pressure and constraint from external stakeholder groups. As such, it is often difficult for the observer (including workers and union officials) to make sense of what managers are doing and why, so much so that the management process can indeed take on the appearance of chaos and disorganization. To reflect this, managerial decision processes are depicted by a jagged circle in Figure 6–1, inside of which are a number of random arrows.

At the same time, appearances can be deceiving, and there is reason to believe that managerial processes may be far more rational in substance than they are in form. Because of the often complex nature of managerial work, it is necessary for managers to develop practical competencies and tacit skills that enable them to act with some level of rationality, relying not just upon principles of rational calculation, but also upon judgement and intuition developed through formal education and past experience. This does not mean that all managers are highly effective at what they do, for errors are easy to make, and the level of managerial competence can vary considerably. But it does mean that managerial decisions and actions are on the whole much more rational than they may at first appear.

In addition, the process of management occurs within a hierarchy of authority, so that incompetent or overtly political managers are unlikely to fare particularly well. More important, senior managers are generally responsible for strategic decisions and policies, and this enables them to impose rationality downward throughout management. The extent to which the edicts of senior managers actually come to be enacted in the day-to-day practices may vary, especially as they can be subject to tensions between various levels of management (see Child, 1985). Yet senior managers are generally able to exert a considerable amount of dominance within the managerial hierarchy, not just directly, through specific directives, but also indirectly, through norms and values propagated over time.

It follows that, if we are to actually understand managerial policies and practices in industrial relations, it is necessary to dig beneath the surface and identify those considerations which underlie the processes of management and hence come to be reflected in managerial policies and practices over time. In other words, in addition to concerning ourselves with the "how" of management, it is also important to come to terms with the "what" and "why" of management (in other words, what management does and why it does it). To do so, the more rational models associated with neoclassical and radical theorists are of considerable value.

FIGURE 6–1 Management Decision Making

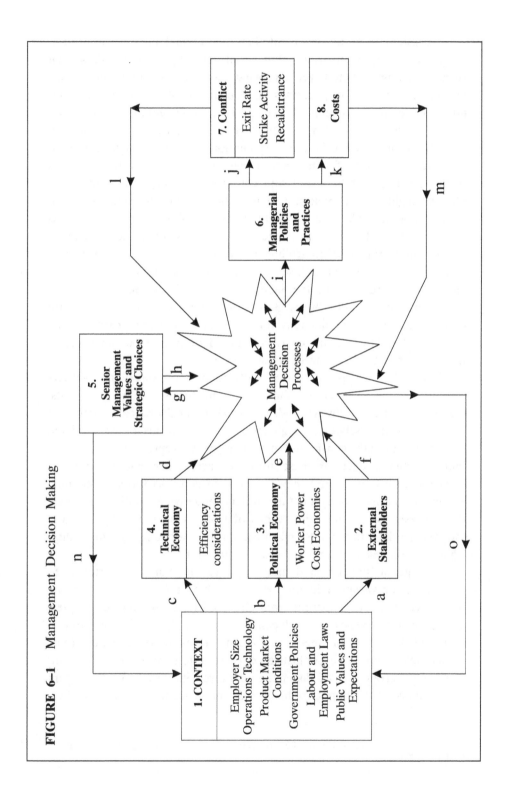

Consistent with the argument that the rational pursuit of profit is the primary purpose to which managerial authority is exercised, we can suggest that two related, yet somewhat contradictory, functions underlie managerial decision processes in industrial relations: **technical economy**, and **political economy**.[8] Technical economy entails minimization of the costs associated with the technical requirements of production. It encompasses efficiency explanations for the design, coordination, and direction of work, and is largely consistent with the focus of the neoclassical school and with contingency theory. Thus, for example, we might expect management to adopt a more "organic" or autonomic approach where uncertainty is high. Political economy entails minimization of the costs associated with the essentially political problem of motivating and controlling workers. It is central to explaining variation in managerial policies and practices in industrial relations, and follows largely from the labour process school. Both are represented in Figure 6–1 (boxes 3 and 4). However, though both are depicted as having implications for managerial decision processes, the function of political economy is considered of primary importance, as illustrated by the bold-faced arrow.

Generally the "problem" of motivating and controlling workers can be manifest in one of three different forms: (1) worker quits; (2) worker strike activity; and (3) worker recalcitrance, whether it involves slacking, sabotage, negligence, or other forms of work-related behaviour normally considered by managers as representing a behavioural problem. Each of these forms of action can entail significant costs for management, and they can be considered as forms of conflict, especially because they generally reflect underlying conflicts between the interests, goals, and expectations of workers on the one hand, and the managerial attempts to maximize profit rationality on the other. They are represented in box 7 of Figure 6–1.

Managerial policies and practices are of major importance to accounting for variation in the extent to which these forms of conflict occur. As should be apparent from chapter five, these can be complex, and their effectiveness can depend on a variety of factors. But it is useful to think of them as ranging from unsophisticated (e.g., autocratic/exploitive) to sophisticated (e.g., autonomic/consociative, but with some recognition of distinctive employee interests). To the extent that management adopts sophisticated employment practices, workers

---

[8] This distinction, and much of the argument to follow, is developed more fully in Godard (1998a).

can be expected to develop higher levels of trust and commitment, and this should be reflected not only in less recalcitrance in the workplace, but also in a lower propensity of workers to engage in strike activity (if there is a union) and/or to quit.

Closely associated with the adoption of sophisticated policies and practices, and of considerable importance for their effectiveness, are the terms of employment. Generally the more favourable these are relative to what workers would receive if they were to quit and look for another job, the more likely their fairness expectations are to be met or exceeded, and the higher the anticipated costs of quitting, being dismissed, or being laid off. As such, workers are less likely to view exit, strike, activity, or recalcitrance as either justifiable or rational.

It should be made clear that the effectiveness of specific managerial policies and practices may vary considerably, depending upon a number of factors, including the past history of the labour–management relationship and the preferences, expectations, and values workers bring into the workplace with them. Thus, we might observe two firms adopting very similar policies and practices but with quite dissimilar results. However, we would expect management to adopt that combination that is most conducive to efficiency. For example, if contingency theorists are correct, management could generally be expected to adopt a more bureaucratic workplace authority structure if uncertainty and variability are low and a more consociative one to the extent that they are high. In addition, we can generally expect to observe lower exit, strike activity, and recalcitrance to the extent that *some* combination of more sophisticated policies and practices is adopted. These means are identified in box 6 of Figure 6–1.

The problem is that more sophisticated policies and practices can be quite costly. For example, new HRM and high performance practices (see chapter five) may require a cadre of specialists to administer various programs and policies, high training expenditures, and even some sacrifice in efficiency (in the technical sense), by designing jobs that are intended to enhance motivation, holding participatory meetings and forums during normal working hours, adhering to a no-layoff policy, and so forth. These costs are expressed in box 8 of Figure 6–1.

It follows that it makes economic sense for management to expend resources on these policies and practices only to the extent that the benefits of doing so outweigh the costs. Of course, management has little way of precisely determining the benefits of particular policies and practices. Moreover, they may not be able to precisely anticipate the costs. Yet, we can generally expect some form of cost-benefit calculation to underlie the management decision process, and while the costs and benefits of enacting various policies and practices may not be readily apparent prior to making initial "strategic" decisions about these matters, they are likely to become clearer over time, if only through processes of trial and error.

Even if no conscious cost-benefit calculation were to take place, it is intuitive to expect management to be more concerned with worker attitudes and behaviour to the extent that worker relational power (i.e., the costs of exit, strike activity, and recalcitrance) is high, and this should be reflected in higher expenditures on policies and practices. As earlier noted, it is also intuitive to expect managers to take into account the costs of various policies and practices. In this respect, some firms may enjoy a number of "cost economies" relative to other firms, and we can generally expect management to adopt more sophisticated policies to the extent that these cost economies apply.

In short, we can generally expect management to adopt more sophisticated policies and practices, to the extent that (1) the relational power of workers is high, and (2) the costs of doing so are low (i.e., cost economies are high).

In turn, we could generally expect worker power, and cost economies to be greatest to the extent that an employer is large in size, employs sophisticated, capital-intensive technologies requiring high levels of skill and training, and operates under favourable market conditions. In large firms, management is likely to enjoy various cost economies with respect to the administration of benefits and the adoption of progressive HRM practices. In turn, sophisticated, capital-intensive technology requiring high levels of skill training generally gives rise to high levels of worker power, for it is costly to replace workers who quit, it is difficult to find replacement workers in the event of a strike, and recalcitrance in the workplace can be extremely costly.

To the extent these conditions hold, we could thus generally expect to observe more sophisticated policies and practices. Thus, highly skilled workers in a large oil refinery can be expected to fare much better and be subject to more sophisticated practices than unskilled workers in a small garment manufacturer. In the oil refinery, management enjoys cost economies and is able to afford the costs of these policies and practices. It also finds it very much in its interests to adopt them, since exit, strike activity, and recalcitrance (especially negligence or sabotage) can be extremely costly. In the garment factory, the opposite is the case: management enjoys few if any cost economies; and the costs of exit, strike activity, and recalcitrance are likely to be minimal, with employers able to replace workers on short notice, at little cost. Thus, we would expect to observe more autocratic/ exploitive policies and practices.

In essence, then, the argument is that these structural variables are central to explaining variation, an argument that is by and large consistent with existing research findings (see Godard, 1998a: 44–46). Accordingly, these variables are represented in box 1 of Figure 6–1. At the same time, however, it is one thing to argue that the extent to which managers adopt sophisticated policies and practices, and quite another to argue that this variation is pre-determined. In this respect, managerial values and strategic choices can play an important role, as indicated in box 5 of Figure 6–1. Not only would we expect managerial values and beliefs to affect the extent to which sophisticated policies are adopted, we can also expect them to have important implications for the specific combination of practices chosen. For example, two employers might adopt autonomic/consociative practices associated with the high performance model (see chapter five), but one may choose to work with unions, while the other may attempt to remain union-free. These decisions are largely a matter of strategic choice, although decisions that turn out to be significantly less effective are less likely to survive or be emulated by other employers over time. Where this is the case, we might also expect the values underlying these decisions to change accordingly.

As discussed in chapter one, it should also be clear that, in addition to the policies and practices it adopts, management is responsible for strategic choices about firm size and structure, production technology, product design, marketing strategy, and a whole host of other factors. In themselves, these can have major implications for worker power and for cost economies, and though the extent to which these implications are actually taken into account in managerial decision-making is unclear, they are represented by arrow *n* of Figure 6–1.

Finally, "external stakeholder" pressures can be expected to have a number of implications for managerial decisions. Labour and employment law play an important role in this respect, as does the extent to which important investors, creditors, and customers associate various policies and practices with "effective management". Also important are product market considerations having to do with costs, quality, and reliability of supply, for where costs are less important relative to quality and reliability, it may be more possible for management to pass on the costs of more progressive practices and more favourable terms of employment to customers, in return for higher quality and reliability of supply. But whether this is the case or not, external stakeholder pressures are clearly important, and are represented in box 2 of Figure 6–1, along with the structural variables identified above.

The model developed in this section is intended to provide a basis for understanding and analyzing variation in managerial policies and practices. However, it is clearly oversimplified, and as such, only provides a basis or starting point. To really understand this variation, it is important to recognize that managerial policies typically develop and change over time. More important, managerial decisions about these policies are not made in a vacuum, but reflect the actions and reactions of workers. They are also subject to conditions and constraints imposed by unions and governments. Thus, we turn to these actors in the following chapters.

III. CONCLUSIONS

This chapter has attempted to provide a basis for understanding both the processes of management and the reasons that managerial policies and practices vary from one firm to the next. In order to do so, the chapter has drawn extensively from the field of organization theory as well as from labour process and strategic choice theory in the industrial relations literature. Throughout, it has emphasized the complexities associated with the management process, on the one hand, while attempting to identify those considerations which account for systematic variation in managerial policies and practices on the other. To do so, a simplified model has been developed, emphasizing the importance of industrial relations context variables and managerial attempts to attain "political economy", while at the same time allowing for the importance of managerial values and "strategic choices". However, only limited attention has been paid to the role of workers and their unions in shaping managerial decisions or to the broader environment within which these decisions are made. The task of the following chapter is to help remedy this imbalance.

Labour Unions as Institutions

7

Labour unions have a long history in North America, dating as far back as the late 1700s.[1] Initially, they were primarily associations of skilled trades and craft workers, and appear to have had two main functions: a regulatory function, under which they attempted to set and enforce uniform wage rates and craft standards; and a "mutual benefit" function, under which they provided financial support to members and/or their dependents in the case of mishap or death (Russell, 1990: 33–36). However, with the emergence of the modern labour movement in the second half of the nineteenth century, the "business unionism" philosophy associated with the American Federation of Labor (AFL) came to be predominant — especially in the United States, but also in Canada. This philosophy was essentially a conservative one, for it was directed primarily at protecting and advancing the immediate economic interests of union members rather than seeking broader economic or social reforms (as did the Knights of Labour and the One Big Union), and it sought to serve this function primarily through collective bargaining at the level of the firm rather than through political activities at the level of the state.

Today, collective bargaining remains central to the activities of the Canadian labour movement. Yet labour unions (and, for that matter, collective bargaining itself) serve a variety of functions beyond the purely economic one, and their activities extend far beyond the

---

[1] In the United States, the first modern **trade union** is normally considered to have been the Philadelphia Shoemakers, formed in 1792. In Canada, 1827 is sometimes considered to be the date when a modern union was first formed (a printer's union in Quebec City), though some research suggests that unions may have been in existence as early as 1798 (see Palmer, 1992: 56).

negotiation of collective agreements. This is especially true in Canada, where the labour movement is said to entail **social unionism**, because it defines its role to include the pursuit of social democratic reforms which serve all working people, whether they are union members or not (see Robinson, 1992).

Despite the broader functions of the labour movement, many continue to view unions as narrow, interest group organizations, seeking only to advance the economic well-being of their members. To view unions only in these terms is at best superficial. Accordingly, the purpose of this chapter is to provide a more in-depth understanding of unions. It proceeds in three stages. First, it addresses why we have unions, examining the conditions under which workers as individuals join unions, theoretical explanations for why we have unions, and the normative case for unions. Then, it turns to the various functions that are or can be served by unions. Finally, it addresses issues having to do with the effects and effectiveness of unions within the contemporary Canadian context.

I.   WHY UNIONS?

It is common to hear that unions may have had an important role to play at one point in time, but that they are now obsolete, and represent little more than dinosaurs from the past. Yet, one in three employed Canadians is still a union member or subject to a collective agreement. Unions are especially prevalent in medium- and large-sized employers. Fifty-six percent of workers in workplaces with over 500 workers are covered by a collective agreement, as are 45 percent of workers in workplaces with between 100 and 500 workers (Statistics Canada, 2010a). Because most of these employers can contain a significant portion of workers who are non-union (e.g., managers), this suggests that most medium- to large-size employers can be expected to have a union somewhere. The question is, why?

This question can be answered on at least two levels: the empirical and the theoretical. While the empirical level entails specific and directly identifiable (through research) reasons for why workers join unions and the conditions under which they are most likely to do so, the theoretical level entails the underlying rationale for why we have unions in general. In this section, each is considered in turn. Then, the issue of whether we *should* have unions is addressed.

The Empirical Level

It is almost a truism to suggest that unions would not exist if workers did not join them. Thus, any attempt to establish why unions exist necessarily asks the question, "Why do workers join unions?" In answer to that, there has been a considerable amount of research exploring the relationship between the attitudes and beliefs of non-union workers and whether these workers report that they would vote in favour of a union if a certification election were held in their workplace (see Godard, 2008). Unfortunately, only three such studies seem to have been attempted in Canada (Krahn and Lowe, 1984; Godard, 2011; Gomez et al., 2002) and the nature and findings of the research conducted in other countries have varied considerably. However, there would appear to be a general consensus that workers are more prone to vote in favour of a union when one or a combination of the following holds:

1. They are discontent with the terms and conditions of their employment and the treatment afforded them by management.
2. They perceive unionization as an effective means of addressing the sources of their discontent.
3. They have a positive general image of the labour movement.

In many respects, identifying these three factors is as obvious as is the question that they answer. A more relevant question, one that also applies at the empirical level, is, "What are the *conditions* that give rise to unionization?" Unfortunately, the answer to this question is not a simple one, as a variety of considerations can be identified. For the present, however, these considerations can be categorized into three groups, as depicted in Figure 7–1.

The first group includes considerations that are directly associated with the initial predisposition to join a union. As might be expected, workers in low-pay, low-quality (e.g., high-stress, low-discretion) jobs are more likely to desire a union if they do not already have one (Godard, 2011). As discussed in chapter five, management practices are also important, with bureaucratic/accommodative practices lowering discontent and, hence, the desire for a union (Godard, 2011). In addition, favourable product-market conditions and, hence, profits can foster a belief that a union will be able to win concessions from management (Hirsch and Berger, 1984). Finally, coming from a "lower" socio-economic background can foster a positive general image of unions (Wheeler and McClendon, 1991).

The second group includes considerations associated with the union organizing process (e.g., Bronfenbrenner, 1992, 1997; Fiorito, Jarley,

FIGURE 7-1 The Empirical Level: Conditions Giving Rise to Unionization†

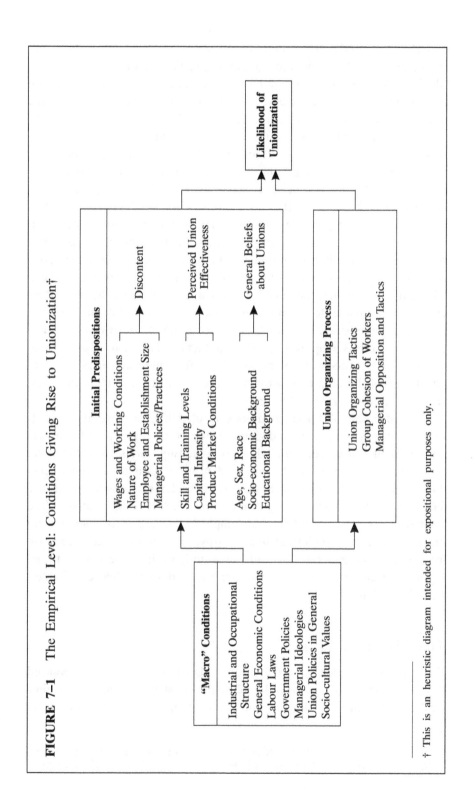

† This is an heuristic diagram intended for expositional purposes only.

and Delaney, 1995). A number of considerations have been identified, including the effectiveness of union organizing tactics, the extent to which workers are cohesive and hence perceive common interests, and the extent to which management opposes and attempts to undermine union certification (see Godard, 2008: 387–91).

The third group includes more "macro" conditions. Their implications are largely indirect, felt primarily through their implications for the first two sets of conditions. Perhaps as a result, it is often difficult to establish their precise effects (see Chaison and Rose, 1991a). One example, however, is that an economy with low levels of manufacturing employment may have lower levels of union density, because it is in manufacturing that workers are more likely to be discontent with their working conditions and hence to join a union. Similarly, poor economic conditions may make workers more grateful just to have a job, and a union may be unable to do much for them, because their employer is unable to afford concessions. However, labour laws are particularly important, because they can substantially restrict the opportunity for various employer opposition tactics. They can also help to ensure that workers will not be penalized for union activities and that the union will be able to represent workers effectively if it becomes established (see Godard, 2008: 390–92).

Identification of these conditions is of value, because it helps us to explain not only why individual workers and groups of workers decide to unionize, but also why union density varies over time and across nations. For example, union density in Canada is more than double that of the United States, in considerable measure because labour laws are much stronger and more effective in Canada (see chapter nine). Yet identifying the empirical correlates of membership provides little real understanding of why, in a more basic sense, we have unions in general. To gain such insight, it is necessary to go beyond the empirical level to consider the underlying theoretical rationale for unions.

The Theoretical Level

Over the past century, a number of explanations have been advanced for the existence of unions.[2] But although most have some value, they tend to point more to the functions that unions can or have served (to

---

[2] These include: (1) a desire of early craft workers to prevent expanded market competition from eroding their income and trade standards (Commons, 1909); (2) attempts by

be discussed later) than they do to the underlying rationale for unions. If we are to understand why unions exist, perhaps the best place to begin is with the orthodox-pluralist perspective.

Under the orthodox-pluralist perspective, it has generally been argued that whatever the sources of variation in the propensity of individual workers to join unions, workers as individuals have historically found themselves at a disadvantage vis-à-vis their employers. They have also found themselves ultimately subject to the uncertainties of competitive market forces, forces which propel management to often make decisions contrary to worker interests and which reinforce employer power. Unions help to remedy this situation, enabling workers to confront their employers as equals and to negotiate terms and conditions of employment which buffer them from market uncertainties.

There has been considerable debate over the extent to which workers do indeed find themselves at a disadvantage vis-à-vis their employers and the extent to which unionization, in fact, equalizes the worker-employer power relation (see Reynolds, 1991, and Kaufman, 1991). This debate is important, as it has implications both for the way in which members of the public view unions and for the decisions of public policy makers concerning unions. But as far as the existence of unions is concerned, it may miss the point. Regardless of whether workers are strictly at a power disadvantage in the labour market, as individuals they find themselves in positions of subordination to management once within an employment relation. Not only can management unilaterally determine the terms and conditions of employment, it can also virtually dictate how the work is to be performed and determine how individual workers are treated. Unionization in effect represents a collective response to these conditions, for when workers join a union, they cease to be the isolated individuals of conventional economic theory and instead become members of an organization through which they can collectively exert influence over the position in which they find themselves. Thus, unions can be viewed as a natural and justifiable response of workers to the powerlessness that they can otherwise experience in industrialized capitalist economies.

---

workers to protect their jobs in the face of a scarcity of alternative employment opportunities (Perlman, 1949); (3) attempts by workers to protect themselves from changes in the nature of work and ensure stability in their lives (Tannenbaum, 1921); and (4) attempts by workers to exert greater control over the conditions of their employment through "job regulation" (Clegg, 1976).

BOX 7-1   Why Organise?

———————————————————— ♦ *IAM Northwest News/CALM*

Organizing the unorganized has always been a driving force within the labour movement. In early years, workers who tried to form unions were beaten by company thugs or shot by government troops. Union organizers risked, and sometimes lost, their lives to win dignity and justice on the job. It is because of these heroic men and women that Canadian workers enjoy the standard of living we have today.

As we near the end of the century, organizing continues to be the labour movement's vital mission. Anti-union attacks take different forms, but they are just as intense and brutal as in the early days of the labour movement. Union-busters now carry briefcases instead of brass knuckles, but their goal is the same: to divide and demoralize workers and to prevent them from having a voice on the job and in society.

Despite the setbacks, trade unionists today are no more willing to give up the struggle than were our predecessors. Workers know that hazards on the job maim and kill thousands every year. Workers know that discrimination and favouritism rob people of opportunities for advancement. Workers know about inadequate health benefits that threaten the well-being of their families. Workers know about the lack of dignity that exists when people are denied a voice in their working lives. And trade unionists understand that everything we have achieved can be taken away if we don't continue to organize. Employers pit one group against another, demanding concessions in order to be "competitive."

For unions, there is strength in numbers. And to be strong, we must remain united. Organizing is the job of every single union member. It is the responsibility of all of us to educate our friends and neighbours about what a union really is. A union is more than a collective bargaining agreement. It is more than improved wages and benefits that come with a union contract. A union is more than its leaders and staff, the stewards, representatives and negotiators, who assist us. It is every one of us, together, working towards the same goals.

Source: From *Labour Studies Bulletin*, University of Manitoba, 1999, p. 5. Reproduced by permission of Canadian Association of Labour Media (CALM).

As far as it goes, this explanation is an accurate one. But there is need to go even further and recognize that unions do not just arise because of a sense of powerlessness. Rather, they also arise because of underlying conflicts between the interests and values of workers and those of management in its capacity as agents of owners — as discussed in chapter three. Thus, the issue is not just that workers as individuals are subordinate to and have no legal say in the exercise of management authority, but also that this authority is exercised in ways that may be contrary to their interests and well-being. Arguably, this conflict extends to the labour market and to government policies in general, with employers and their representatives often opposing the provision of various rights and protections for workers on the grounds that they are too costly, and workers feeling powerless as individuals to do anything about it. Thus, unions arise primarily as a means through which workers can collectively protect and advance their interests and values given their position within industrial capitalist economies *and* the rather fundamental conflicts underlying this position. *This* is the primary reason why we have unions, even though *the extent* to which we have them can vary considerably, in accordance with the empirical considerations identified earlier.

Should We Have Unions?

A further question is whether we *should* have unions. This question is especially germane because, although Canadian labour laws support the right to join a union and engage in collective bargaining, neoliberals have traditionally argued that unions have negative effects on the economy. The implication is that unions are, in effect, "bad", and that there is a need to weaken or even eliminate them through labour law reforms. Accompanying this implication are arguments by some that unions are morally unacceptable, because they restrict the exercise of employer authority and in so doing undermine the property rights of owners and investors. These same critics also tend to argue that unions engage in a form of extortion, using their power to extract wages and benefits which exceed the fair market value of their members' labour. Finally, they maintain that unions restrict the freedom of individual members, imposing restrictions on what they can do in the employment relation and, in particular, preventing them from negotiating their own terms and conditions with the employer.

If one reads some Canadian newspapers, one might get the impression that this view is the dominant one. It is not. For example, a 1996 Angus Reid poll found that roughly two in three Canadians support unions. In the 2003–4 PRA survey (discussed in chapter three), 5 in 10 agreed with the statement that unions are needed to look out for workers (4 in 10 disagreed, 1 in 10 were neutral). In a 2003 Vector Research survey of 2,000 Canadians, 2 in 3 (63 percent) stated that belonging to a union was worthwhile *even if it doesn't get employees higher pay* (CLC, 2003). This support for unions may be explained in a number of ways. Perhaps most fundamentally, unions provide workers with a basic level of collective representation vis-à-vis their employer and more generally, within society as a whole. This view follows from the theoretical rationale for unions (i.e., that workers as individuals often feel powerless and unable to protect themselves against the unfair or exploitive exercise of employer authority). But when considered normatively, it is widely believed that workers *should* have a right to meaningful collective representation by a union.

There is even reason to believe that a healthy, independent labour movement is essential to democracy in general (see Peirce, 2000: 214–16). Weak or non-existent labour movements appear to go hand-in-hand with authoritarian governments, as evidenced by the number of Asian countries in which democracy exists at best in name only, and in which union (and worker) rights are suppressed. They also go hand-in-hand with communist regimes, as evidenced in particular by the former Soviet Union, where unions were largely controlled by the state. Closer to home, it may be no coincidence that Mexico has both a history of government corruption *and* a labour movement that has been largely state controlled.

Largely for these (and other) reasons, there is a growing international recognition of the right to freely associate in unions and to engage in collective bargaining as a *fundamental human right* (see Adams, 1998; Human Rights Watch, 2000: 40–50; Compa, 2001). For example, the 1995 Vienna Declaration of the United Nations, signed by 171 countries, reaffirmed the right "of everyone to form trade unions and join the trade union of his choice [and] ... the right to strike, provided that it is exercised in conformity with the laws of the particular country." In 1998, member nations of the International Labour Organization (ILO) voted 273 to 0, with 48 abstentions, in favour of a solemn Declaration of Fundamental Principles and Rights at Work, reaffirming its long-held principle that its members have "an obligation arising from the very fact of membership ... to respect, promote and to realize in good faith ... the effective recognition of the right to collective bargaining." In 1996, the World Trade Organization (WTO) reaffirmed its commitment to core labour rights, and, in 2000, the Organisation for Economic Co-operation and Development

(OECD) adopted a code of conduct for multinational corporations that contains strong support for the observance of the right to join a union and engage in collective bargaining. Finally, the European Convention on Human Rights includes the ability to form a union and engage in collective bargaining as basic human right.

Recognition by these bodies of the right to join a union and engage in collective bargaining typically does not include sanctions against countries that do not respect this right. But it does reflect a growing consensus that such behaviour is morally wrong. Consistent with this consensus has been a series of rulings by the Supreme Court of Canada finding that the right to join a union and engage in collective activities is protected under the Canadian Charter of Rights and Freedoms. In particular, in *Dunmore v. Ontario* (2001), the Supreme Court ruled that the clause in the Charter guaranteeing freedom of association not only included the right to join a union but also the right to make representations to an employer and to participate in lawful union activities. In *Health Services v. British Columbia* (2007), it extended this ruling to specifically include collective bargaining. Some of the wording in this ruling is especially noteworthy, as reproduced in Box 7–2.

Recognition that the right to union representation and collective bargaining are increasingly viewed as basic human rights also does not mean that either unions or collective bargaining are always as effective as one would like, or that some of the concerns of critics are without any foundation. But supporters of unions argue that, where there is a problem, the solution is not to eliminate or weaken unions, but rather to create the conditions to ensure that unions function effectively, in accordance with both the theoretical and the normative rationales for their existence. In Canada, a number of functions grow out of these rationales.

II.   THE FUNCTIONS OF LABOUR UNIONS

Over the years, a number of theories of labour unionism have been advanced, most of which emphasize one or more different functions of unions (see Ross Martin, 1989; Poole, 1981). It would serve little purpose to consider all of these theories here, but, by drawing upon them it is possible to distinguish five general functions, each of which roughly corresponds to one of five perspectives on labour relations identified in chapter one. These are: (1) the economic function (neoliberal perspective), (2) the democratization func-

BOX 7–2   Unions and Human Rights

Per **McLachlin C.J.** and Bastarache, Binnie, **LeBel**, Fish and Abella JJ.:

Freedom of association guaranteed by s. 2(d) of the *Charter* includes a procedural right to collective bargaining. ... The general purpose of the *Charter* guarantees and the broad language of s. 2(d) are consistent with a measure of protection for collective bargaining.

Further, the ... history of collective bargaining in Canada reveals that long before the present statutory labour regimes were put in place, collective bargaining was recognized as **a fundamental aspect of Canadian society**, emerging as the most significant collective activity through which freedom of association is expressed in the labour context.

Association for purposes of collective bargaining has long been recognized as **a fundamental Canadian right** which predated the *Charter*. The protection enshrined in s. 2(d) of the *Charter* may properly be seen as the culmination of a historical movement towards the recognition of a procedural right to collective bargaining.

Canada's adherence to international documents recognizing a right to collective bargaining also supports recognition of that right in s. 2(d). **The *Charter* should be presumed to provide at least as great a level of protection as is found in the international human rights documents** that Canada has ratified.

Recognizing that workers have the right to bargain collectively as part of their freedom to associate **reaffirms the values of dignity, personal autonomy, equality and democracy that are inherent in the *Charter***. [22] [39-41] [66] [68] [70] [86]

Source: Excerpts from *Health Services and Support — Facilities Subsector Bargaining Assn. v. British Columbia*, 2007 SCC 27 (emphasis added).

tion (orthodox-pluralist perspective), (3) the integrative function (managerial perspective), (4) the social democratic function (liberal reformist perspective), and (5) the class conflict/revolutionary function (radical perspective). Though there has been considerable debate, both over the relative importance of each function and over how well unions have served them, it is useful to proceed from the assumption that all five are of some importance and can contribute to our understanding of unions as institutions in contemporary Canada.

The Economic Function

Most students of industrial relations would agree that the negotiation of favourable wages and benefits for workers has always been a primary function of unions in North America, at least since the modern labour movement began to emerge over a century ago. This function has received the greatest attention in neoclassical economics, which is closely associated with the neoliberal perspective. While it is common to view unions as simply wanting "more" for their members, these economists have typically argued for a somewhat more complex view of their economic goals, arguing that, in raising the wages and benefits of individual members, unions concern themselves with possible **"disemployment effects"** and a resulting decrease in membership.

Disemployment effects can occur for one of two reasons. First, higher wages and benefits can mean that employers are compelled to raise their prices. This can translate into a lower demand for their output, either resulting in layoffs or slowing the employer's rate of growth. Second, higher wages and benefits mean that workers become more "expensive" relative to labour-saving machines or equipment. When this occurs, employers are induced to adopt more capital intensive technologies, thereby making greater use of capital equipment and hence either laying some workers off or hiring fewer workers in the future. In both cases, the number of workers employed is adversely affected.

The extent to which unions take disemployment effects into account has long been a matter of debate (Simons, 1948: 131–32; Dunlop, 1944). However, there is little doubt that unions often take measures to lessen these effects. These measures may include accepting lower wages, lobbying governments for trade restrictions so that lower cost imports are kept out, "taking wages out of competition" by organizing and negotiating uniform wages throughout a particular industry (see chapter eight), public campaigns encouraging consumers to buy union-made products, negotiating restrictions on management's ability to implement technological change, and others (see Ehrenberg and Smith, 1985: 376–81). Thus, whatever the exact nature of the "wage-employment" trade-off, the neoclassical literature suggests that the economic function of unions may go far beyond merely seeking improved wages and benefits. It also includes attempts to allow for and minimize potential disemployment effects.

By pointing to these effects and the strategies upon which unions embark in order to avoid them, neoclassicists illustrate an often neglected aspect of the economic function: ensuring membership job and income security. But a role which they typically overlook that can also be considered part of the economic function is ensuring *fairness*. Although it may be true that union leaders would prefer to maximize economic returns, their ability to do so depends on the willingness of members to strike. This in turn depends at least in part on worker expectations and fairness perceptions. Workers are less likely to vote for a strike if management's latest offer meets these expectations and perceptions. In turn, union leaders have little need to seek economic returns above those that are perceived to be fair, because workers are likely to be satisfied with union negotiators once fairness perceptions are met. Thus, an important aspect of the economic function is to ensure that member fairness perceptions are met. Doing so may go beyond issues having to do with wages and benefits to include a whole host of issues having to do with fair treatment in the employment relation, including work loads, promotion and layoff rules, and others (see chapter fifteen). All of these represent part of the overall package or "wage-effort" bargain and so they tend to involve trade-offs against wages and benefits in negotiations.

A further area, one which can also be associated with the economic function of unions because of its implications for earnings capacity, is workplace health and safety. Although health and safety laws apply to non-union workplaces as well, unions typically possess the resources and expertise needed to ensure that health and safety standards are satisfied and that workers are able to obtain compensation in the event of work-related injuries or health problems. Thus, unions can play an important role in this respect — one which is not available in non-union workplaces.

The Democratization Function

The democratization function is most emphasized by orthodox pluralists, who view the role of unions more as one of providing workers with various forms of representation vis-à-vis management, thereby introducing an element of democracy into the employment relation (Leiserson, 1973). There are at least five ways in which unions are thought to provide this function.

First, unions provide workers as individuals with quasi-legal representation in the event that the terms of employment have been violated or they have been subject to the arbitrary or pernicious exercise of management authority. This is accomplished through the grievance/ arbitration process, which in effect serves as a system of industrial jurisprudence (Slichter, 1941: 1; Chamberlain and Kuhn, 1965), providing the worker with independent representation (i.e., by the union) and neutral third party adjudication. Though the grievance/arbitration process is discussed at greater length in chapter fourteen, the important point to be made here is that it introduces an element of democracy into the workplace by providing individuals with rights and protections similar to those enjoyed under civil law in most democratic states.

Second, and most fundamental (as discussed earlier), unions provide workers with collective representation vis-à-vis employers, thereby enabling them to have a voice in decisions that affect them collectively, whether these pertain to the terms and conditions of employment or to more job-related decisions having to do with technological change, health and safety, or related matters. This is accomplished primarily through the process of collective bargaining, though it is also accomplished during the term of an agreement, as union officials meet with managers to address problems and issues not addressed in the agreement — much as elected politicians represent their local constituents to the executive branch of government (see Chamberlain and Kuhn, 1965: 122).

Third, unions help to provide workers with "concrete freedom on the job" (Perlman, 1949), negotiating rules and procedures governing the pace of work, crew sizes, skill requirements, job classifications and responsibilities, overtime rights and requirements, and other considerations associated with the day-to-day exercise of management authority. In doing so, unions regulate the exercise of managerial authority in much the same way that laws establishing citizenship rights and freedoms limit the exercise of government authority in a democratic state.

A fourth, less direct aspect of the democratization function, has to do with the political nature of unions. In contrast to work organizations, where authority is top-down and a single overall objective (i.e., profit maximization) can be established, unions are democratic organizations in which authority runs from the bottom to the top. While union democracy is sometimes not all that it should be (as is discussed in the next chapter), union officials must generally be responsive to pressures and constraints imposed by various membership factions. Thus, the democratization function of unions goes beyond representing a single set of worker concerns and preferences to encompass a more complex political process, in which union leaders attempt to reconcile or at least balance off competing concerns and preferences within their membership — much as political leaders do in a democratic state (at least in theory). Only to the extent that they succeed are they able to effectively represent their members collectively. And to the extent that they do, the terms and conditions negotiated are likely to be more reflective of union member preferences in general. This is in contrast to non-union settings, where there is little by way of a mechanism to address competing concerns and preferences (see Freeman and Medoff, 1979).

A fifth and related aspect of the democratization function is the provision of opportunities for members to *participate* in democratic processes that they would otherwise not have at their place of work. As formally democratic organizations, unions have their own constitutions, elected officers, and meetings (see chapter eight). This is in sharp contrast to conventional work organizations (especially in North America), where workers have no say in the election of top management, and top management has no legal accountability to them. While it is true that employers sometimes implement participatory reforms which allow workers or their representatives some say in workplace decision processes, these reforms typically fall far short of providing equivalent opportunities, if only because they do not entail independent organizations and normally exist on management's terms and at management's behest. Participatory management techniques should thus not be confused in any way with democracy.

The Integrative Function

The integrative function is probably the most difficult to characterize, for pluralists, radicals, and managerialists have all, in one form or another, argued that unions can, should, or do serve to integrate workers within the status quo. However, the notion that unions arose primarily to serve an integrative function and that they *should* serve such a function is most consistent with the managerialist perspective.

Perhaps the most notable theorist arguing this within the managerial tradition is Frank Tannenbaum, who viewed labour unions by-and-large as a response to the process of industrialization. According to Tannenbaum, union membership helps to restore the sense of community and the stability characteristic of pre-industrial times, providing workers with a sense of identity and belongingness (Tannenbaum, 1951: 10). It also provides workers with a sense of belongingness in, and identification with, the workplace itself (1951: 199).

A closely related argument is that unions provide workers with a vehicle for personal status and advancement, through attainment of a position in the union (Bakke, 1945). In this sense, unions can serve as alternative mechanisms through which workers are able satisfy needs and aspirations that have been frustrated within the employment relation itself.

A third aspect of the integrative function applies specifically to the effectiveness of high performance practices. As discussed in chapter five, unions can in theory help to overcome distrust of employer motives by assuring workers that these practices will not be used to intensify their work or "downsize" the workforce. They can also help to ensure that workers have greater input into the design of these practices, and that employers are less able to renege on various promises associated with them in order to address short-term pressures. Thus, unions may ensure that the conditions are in place for fostering the trust and commitment levels advocated by proponents of these practices.

A fourth argument, one which has been advanced largely by orthodox pluralists, is that the democratic function of unions can also have integrative consequences. Under this argument, unions can have positive productivity effects even where high performance practices are not established. This is because they provide employees with "voice" (Freeman, 1976). In the absence of a union, employees are likely to quit if they have a number of concerns or complaints which remain unaddressed. Where it is not feasible for them to quit, these concerns and complaints translate into poor morale, with negative performance implications. In a union setting, however, employees are able to voice these concerns and complaints and ideally have them addressed, either through the filing of grievances or through the collective bargaining process. Indeed, these processes not only allow employees to voice their concerns, they serve as mechanisms for the resolution of conflict, ultimately resulting in higher levels of performance.

Finally, it is logical to expect workers to value the democratic rights and protections provided by unions in and of themselves. Because they have these rights and protections, they are likely to feel more secure in their employment and to view the terms and conditions of employment as more satisfactory. Thus, they are likely to view their jobs more favourably, again reducing the likelihood of quitting and enhancing their morale, with further positive implications for performance.

The Social Democratic Function

The social democratic function essentially involves attempts by labour unions to encourage social democratic reforms both within the economy and in society in general. The precise nature of these reforms can vary considerably, from an improved workers' compensation system, to reduced wage inequality within and across firms, to support for human rights campaigns in the developing countries. Though in some cases these reforms may directly serve the interests of union members, they are often more altruistic than this, based more upon a common identity with working people and the disadvantaged in general. As noted earlier in this chapter, the Canadian labour movement has become especially known for this broader focus, and hence is associated with the term "social unionism". There are a number of ways in which unions can serve the social democratic function.

First, union organizing is of central importance to the social democratic function of unions. It tends to be emphasised by social unionists, who view collective bargaining more as a means of improving the wages and working conditions of working people in general than as a means for furthering the narrow self-interests of particular groups.

Second, unions engage in political activities, seeking legal reforms designed to strengthen the effectiveness of collective bargaining and broader economic and social reforms designed to reduce inequality and protect the disadvantaged. To this end, they attempt to influence governments directly, through lobbying and presenting briefs to government officials, and indirectly, through affiliation with political parties and organizations. In Canada, for example, the labour movement is closely linked to the New Democratic Party (NDP) and is allotted a number of delegates at NDP conventions.

A third means by which unions pursue a social democratic function is through participation in various economic and social causes, and the formation of coalitions and alliances with groups representing these causes. In recent years, for example, unions have become increasingly involved with women's organizations, environmental groups, food banks, and church groups. Some have even established special funds for these purposes. A prominent example (see Box 7–3) is the **"social justice fund"** negotiated by the Canadian Auto Workers, under which participating employers are required to donate one cent for each straight time hour worked by each worker in the bargaining unit to a designated charity, food bank, or international relief effort.

Finally, the social democratic function typically entails the education of members and their workplace representatives about social issues. Indeed, a number of unions sponsor educational programs for local level union leaders, and these programs typically address broader social democratic issues as well as technical issues pertaining to collective bargaining and grievance handling.

BOX 7–3   CAW's Social Justice Fund Educates, Politicizes Workers

—————————————————————————— • *Asad Ismi*

"We are about solidarity, not charity," explains Carol Phillips, who is in charge of the Social Justice Fund as director of educational development and the international department at the Canadian Auto Workers.

"The purpose behind the CAW's contributions to different projects, nationally and internationally," she explains, "is to create a fairer, more humane world. We want to educate and politicize our members and help them to see that people everywhere have a right to a decent standard of living, with health care, education and basic needs fulfilled.

"This is not a matter of charity. I don't ever want our members to take a holiday in a Third World country without thinking, 'What kind of social system does this place have? Are its people's essential needs being addressed by their government?'"

The CAW created its Social Justice Fund in 1990. According to a collective agreement between the union and companies that employ CAW members, the corporations pay one cent per hour per workers (in the form of deferred wages) into a fund administered by the union. Phillips cites the CAW's mine removal project in Mozambique as a good example of solidarity.

"This is our biggest project. We're giving $1.25 million for de-mining in Mozambique (in Nampula and Inhambane provinces), one of the most severely mine-affected countries in the world with up to million mines. The Canadian government has matched this, so the total amount being spent is $2.5 million."

"But we're not going to help remove mines and then just leave," she added. "For us, de-mining is a way of facilitating long-term development. It completes the anti-apartheid work that we've been involved in since 1980 during which we developed strong links with the trade union movement in Southern Africa."

"The mines in Mozambique cause daily casualties and deny land to rural communities, which hinders development. Our work focuses not only on land mine removal but also on victim assistance and microeconomic projects for communities affected by mines."

According to Phillips, "In this, our purpose is to break down the isolation of workers from one another. So we arrange exchanges with progressive Third World unions. It then becomes more difficult for workers to consider each other faceless competitors in a world market controlled by and for capital. Once they

Continued....

> **Box 7–3 (continued)**
>
> have visited each other's workplaces and met each other's families, they can never go back to that narrow view."
>
> She emphasized that CAW "wants to contribute to a humanist analysis by creating a new Canadian worker who is educated for responsibility on an international level. We want to inform our members about international human rights issues and encourage a global perspective so they understand the difference between charity and solidarity."
>
> **Source:** From *Labour and Workplace Studies Newsletter W-2000*, p. 9. University of Manitoba, Department of Labour Studies. Reproduced by permission of Canadian Association of Labour Media (CALM).

The Class Conflict/Revolutionary Function

The class conflict/revolutionary function has a long history, both within the labour movement and among theorists of the labour movement (see R. Martin, 1989). Radicals have viewed unions as of central importance to the revolutionary overthrow of employer capitalism and its replacement by a new economic order. Of course, few if any contemporary labour leaders would seriously advocate a revolution in the conventional sense of this term. But Canadian unions still very much represent a working class *movement* and continue to serve as a basis for mass protests and political actions. Perhaps the most recent example was the Ontario "Days of Action" protests mounted in 1995 and 1996 to protest against the Ontario Government of Mike Harris. Although these protests were of questionable success and included other groups as well (e.g., environmentalists), they entailed attempts to shut down selected cities through a series of one- or two-day general strikes (see Reshef and Rastin, 2003), and were in many respects protests not just against the Harris government, but also against the broader class interests it was perceived to represent.

In addition to their role as vehicles for class mobilization, unions can also be seen as vehicles for "class conflict" at the workplace level. As argued in chapter three, many of the forms of conflict behaviour engaged in by workers in part reflect their reactions to the

BOX 7–4 The Gainers Strike: A Class Conflict?

In Edmonton the Alberta class battles of the mid- to late-1980s raged most dramatically. Peter Pocklington, fresh from his failed attempt to take over the federal Tory leadership with a crass combination of big dollars and blunt New Right ideology, struck a pose of defiant determination. He wanted to drive unionism from Gainers, his Edmonton meat-packing plant. With meat consumption declining in the face of new trends in health and diet, Pocklington demanded that 1,000 workers accept a five-year wage freeze, a two-tiered payment system — with new employees going for the abysmal rate of $6.99 an hour — and other insulting givebacks....

For much of the summer the Gainers UFCW picket line was the focus of national media attention. As strikebreakers were bused in to the plant, violence erupted and local police spent most of their waking hours patrolling the struck work site, protecting the scabs. Eventually police outnumbered strikers by a two-to-one ratio. The entire annual overtime budget of the Edmonton police force was eaten up in a few days. Huge rallies of 10,000 were organized against the provincial labour laws and the actions of the police; one day 3,500 marched on the plant. As the buses were smashed and battered, pelted with rocks and sticks, mass arrests took place. A fifteen-year-old boy and a seventy-five-year-old woman both ended up in jail one week, the arrest figure climbing to 252 for one busy seven-day period. In one sweep 125 picketers were charged. The police superintendent walked through the crowd pointing out individuals and saying, "Take that one and take that one." Some of the pro-strike protestors were arrested 500 metres from the plant gate. One of the first taken into custody was Alberta Federation of Labor president Dave Werlin, a Communist who would later challenge Shirley Carr for president of the CLC. All told some 600 went to jail during the conflict, clogging the courts for weeks....

From across the country came moral and material support, as the Gainers strike symbolized a new combativity within Canadian working-class circles. The CLC asked its 8,000 affiliated union locals to contribute $100 weekly to "adopt a Gainers striker," and organized labour promoted a national boycott of the company's products. The ongoing "Battle of 66th Street" was shaping up as one of the most protracted and militant class struggles of the 1980s.

Source: Excerpts from Bryan D. Palmer, *Working Class Experience: Rethinking the History of Canadian Labour, 1800–1991*, Second Edition, pp. 394–95 (Toronto: McClelland & Stewart, 1992). Reproduced by permission of Bryan D. Palmer.

sources of conflict embodied in the employment relation and to the broader context within which workers find themselves. This is especially true with respect to strike activity, but it can also be reflected through other union associated behaviours, such as the grievance process, refusal to work for health and safety reasons, and so forth. *If* one views these forms of conflict as reflections of broader, class-based conflicts between capitalists and workers, then they can also be viewed as forms of class conflict, in which unions play an important role.

In short, unions cannot in any sense be viewed as "instruments of revolution", at least in contemporary Canada. But one of their functions continues to be that of class mobilization at the political and even the workplace level. Thus, even though the class conflict/ revolutionary function as traditionally understood may seem both undesirable and outmoded, to dismiss it out of hand would be mistaken.

III. THE EFFECTS AND EFFECTIVENESS OF UNIONS

Identification of the various functions served by unions suggests a largely positive picture of the Canadian labour movement. But the effectiveness with which unions actually serve these functions may be another matter. There has also been considerable debate over the economic effects of unions, with critics arguing that they harm efficiency and are detrimental to Canada's competitive position. It is therefore of some value to briefly consider the available evidence addressing these two questions, beginning with the research into the economic effects of unions.

The Economic Effects of Unions

Debate over the economic effects of unions has been primarily between neoliberals and orthodox pluralists. Neoliberals have tended to view unions as artificially raising wage and benefit costs and interfering with the exercise of managerial authority, with negative implications for productivity. The result is, in theory, lower profit levels, less investment in unionized workplaces, higher prices, and ultimately lower rates of economic growth. In contrast, orthodox pluralists have argued that, because unions serve a number of positive functions identified earlier, they are associated with lower turnover, an ability to attract "better" workers, and ultimately higher productivity. These effects may, in turn, offset any negative effects unions have on employer labour cost structures.[3]

A problem with attempting to resolve this debate is that the effects of unions can vary considerably from one workplace, industry, or sector to the next, depending on such things as union strike power, employer values and beliefs about unions, and market conditions. They may also vary substantially across nations and over time, depending on macroeconomic conditions, government social policies, labour and employment laws, and a host of other factors. Thus, to speak of union "effects" as if they are invariant can be highly misleading. We can only attempt to establish what these effects appear to be *on average* at a *particular time* in a *particular country*. This creates difficulties for any attempt to consider the economic effects of unions in contemporary Canada, because much of the research into these effects has been conducted in the United States. It may not generalize to Canada, where the context of collective bargaining differs in a number of respects.[4] In addition, both U.S. and Canadian research is often based on data that are a decade or more old and may be dated, especially in view of economic and policy changes that have occurred over the past number of years.

Even in the absence of these limitations, there are a great number of methodological difficulties involved in reliably estimating the average effects of unions. These are much the same as is the case for high performance practices, as discussed in chapter five. Not only is it difficult to control for possible alternative explanations that could account for observed associations between unions and various outcomes, there is always the problem of cause and effect. For example, although we may find union wages to be higher than non-union wages, this may be in part because workers with high wages are more likely to join a union rather than quit when dissatisfied with their employer. Thus, high wages may "cause" unions as much as vice versa. Although

---

[3] This debate became especially heated in the United States after the election of President Obama in 2008, because he had promised to support labour law reforms that would make it more difficult for employers to undermine union organizing drives. A report by a management consultant (Farrar, 2009) sought to weaken the case for these reforms by arguing that unions have a number of serious negative effects. For critical analyses of this report and why some of the estimates in it cannot be trusted (and why they are not reported in this chapter), see Johnson (2009), and Sran and Stanford (2009).

[4] This is an even greater problem with respect to other countries where union effects research has been conducted, such as the United Kingdom and Australia. This research is thus not reviewed here.

researchers have devised a number of sophisticated ways of addressing these sorts of problems, the extent to which they have been successful is uncertain.

In view of these and other limitations, available research findings should be interpreted with caution. However, they generally suggest the following:

Wage Costs. The most recent Canadian research has generally suggested that, on average, unions raise wages by between 8 and 12 percent after allowing for possible alternative explanations for union/non-union wage differences (Fang and Verma, 2002; Godard, 2007). This compares to about 15 percent in the United States and 5 percent (or even less) in Britain (Blanchflower and Bryson, 2003; Godard, 2007).

Benefit Costs. There is only one Canadian study to date assessing the magnitude of union effects on benefits (Renaud, 1998). It found that unions raise benefits by about 45 percent. But because benefits represent a relatively small portion of compensation in Canada, this amounts to only a 2 percent increase in total compensation per worker. In other words, if the effects of unions on wages alone is 8 percent on average, their effects on wages and benefit costs combined would be 10 percent on average.

Turnover and Labour Quality. Studies in the United States have found union employers to have lower turnover and higher labour "quality" (e.g., better educated workers) than their non-union counterparts (see Addison and Belfied, 2004: 581). The finding for turnover holds even after allowing for the higher wages paid by union employers (Freeman, 1986: 191–92; Blanchflower and Freeman, 1992), suggesting that workers value unions for their non-economic functions. There appear to have been no comparable studies in Canada.

Productivity. There has also been little research on union productivity effects in Canada. However, research in the United States suggests that these can vary considerably by industry and sector (e.g., Bronars, Deere and Tracy, 1994), yet *on average* tend to be negligible (see Doucouliagos and Laroche, 2003, for a review and analysis). It would appear that much depends on management's willingness to work with and accommodate the union (Blanchflower and Freeman, 1992). Where management is successful in doing so, productivity effects tend to be positive. Where it is not, they tend to be negative (see Bemmels, 1987).

Profitability and Investment. In the United States, research studies find that unionized workplaces tend to have lower profitability than their non-union counterparts (Doucouliagos and Laroche, 2009), largely as a result of higher wage and benefit costs (Becker and Olson, 1992: 414). They also tend to have slower employment growth (Leonard, 1992) and less new investment (e.g., Hirsch, 1992; Cavanaugh, 1998). However, these findings are based on data from the early 1980s and before, so whether they still apply is uncertain. A somewhat more recent study, using data from 1983 to 1990, found that unions do not appear to have any effect on the likelihood of a firm becoming insolvent (Freeman and Kleiner, 1999). This suggests that the union profit effect largely involves a transfer of wealth from shareholders, and that unions generally do not obtain gains beyond an employer's ability to pay. U.S. studies directly exploring whether union profit effects are associated with ability to pay have, however, yielded mixed results (Freeman and Kleiner, 1999: 511, fn. 1).

In Canada, there would appear to have been only a few relevant studies. One, of manufacturing industries (Laporta and Jenkins, 1996), found that, as of 1987, unions appeared to have negative effects on profitability, but only in industries dominated by one or a few firms and characterized by low levels of competition. It found that they may actually have slightly positive effects on profitability in industries where competition is high. This is probably explained by a tendency for union wage and benefit effects to be higher in the former, reflecting a greater ability of employers in these sectors to grant wage concessions without becoming insolvent. In the latter, it may reflect the ability of unions to take wages out of competition.

Another Canadian study using data from 1967–1987 (Ogders and Betts, 1997) found that, as the percentage of firms with unions increases in a given industry, there is a negative effect on investment levels, but only until this reaches about 50 percent. Beyond this, there is a slight positive effect on investment. It is possible that this reflects a tendency for non-union firms to match the wages and benefits of their union counterparts as an industry begins to become unionized, thus reducing the capital available for investment. Once density exceeds 50 percent, all firms are already providing equivalent wages and benefits, so this effect diminishes.

Finally, there have been a few studies of the implications of unionization on employment growth. The most recent such study finds growth in union workplaces to be from 1 to 2 percent lower per year than is the case for their non-union counterparts (Walsworth, 2010) — a relatively small effect.

Strike Costs. Canada has one of the highest levels of strike activity of the developed (and probably the undeveloped) world. Between 1997 and 2006, an average of 186 days of work were lost per year for each one thousand workers, compared to 54 in the United States, 21 in Britain, and an overall average of 37 days for all developed (OECD) nations (Hale, 2008). But although the Canadian strike rate is *comparatively* high, it still works out to the equivalent of less than .1 percent of working time (see Table 4–1), or roughly one day per worker every five years. If only union workers are considered, it works out to less than two-thirds of a day per year. Of note, these figures are much less than what they were in the 1970s, when .4 to .5 percent of working time was lost in a number of years due to strikes.

Inflation. In the 1960s and 1970s, there was considerable debate as to whether union wage gains were to blame for inflation, or whether inflation was caused by over-heated demand in product markets, enabling firms to increase prices. But as discussed in chapter four, union wage gains have, on average, not even kept up with the rate of inflation since the early 1980s, despite an increase of close to 50 percent in productivity per hour worked. Although unions did make some gains from 1998–2009, these gains were, on average, less than 0.5 percent above the rate of inflation (Statistics Canada, 2009a), which was still below the rate of productivity growth. Thus, unions do not appear to have been a source of inflation, beyond perhaps helping their members to keep up with increase to the cost-of-living.

Overall. It would seem that, overall, the implications of unions for the economy are murky. If they do have negative effects, these would appear to be relatively small. The main exception appears to be with respect to profitability. But one would expect unionized workplaces to have lower profits if unions have been serving their economic function, because this function is essentially one of ensuring that workers obtain a reasonable share of "economic rents", or earnings above those which are needed to sustain viability. Thus, whether this effect is "good" or "bad" largely depends on one's point of view. It is also important to be mindful that, although the economic effects of unions are no doubt important, at least equally important is their effectiveness in serving their members on each of the five functions identified earlier.

The Effectiveness of Unions

There has been surprisingly little research directly addressing union effectiveness in serving the five functions identified earlier. However, it is useful to consider that research which has been conducted.[5]

The Economic Function. The finding that unions tend to increase wages by 8 to 12 percent is consistent with the economic function. There is also some evidence that unions in Canada are associated with higher satisfaction with pay, even after controlling for union/non-union wage differences (Evans and Ondrack, 1990). This suggests that unions enhance the perceived fairness of pay, which is also consistent with the economic function. Again, consistent with this function, U.S. studies have found that mandated health and safety committees are considerably more effective in union than in non-union workplaces (Weil, 1999) and that workers in union workplaces are far more likely to receive workers' compensation benefits (Hirsch, MacPherson, and Dumond, 1997).

The perceptions of Canadian workers reinforce these findings. In the 2003 Vector Research poll of 2,000 Canadians (CLC, 2003: 6) referred to earlier, four in ten participants stated that, with a union, workers do "a lot better" with regard to health and safety conditions, job security, and health-related benefits, and another four in ten stated that they do "a little better". With regard to pay, however, only slightly more than a quarter thought that workers do a lot better, while half thought that they do a little better.

The Democratization Function. There has been little research directly addressing activities associated with the democratization function. However, an analysis of data from a 2009 telephone survey of 1,000 U.S. workers reveals that union representation is positively associated with worker perceptions of security, fairness, and justice (Godard and Frege, 2010), which is consistent with the democratization function. In addition, a number of U.S. surveys have asked union members about internal union democracy. They have typically found that, depending on the question asked, from 70 to 80 percent of union members are satis-

---

[5]   Only one study, the 1995 telephone survey of 341 randomly selected Canadian labour market participants referred to in chapter one, has attempted to do so systematically (Godard, 1997c). In this study, participants were asked their beliefs as to how much effort unions put into activities associated with each of the five functions, and then asked how successful they believed unions to be on each. Because the sample was relatively small and may now be somewhat dated, it is not reported here.

fied with the amount of say they have in their union (Freeman and Rogers, 1999: 78). In addition, one U.S. study (Bronfenbrenner, 1997) underscores the importance of the democratization function, finding that union organizing attempts are more likely to be successful if unions place an emphasis on union democracy and on the attainment of dignity, justice, and fairness.

The Integrative Function. If unions serve an integrative function, then we might expect union members to express higher levels of job satisfaction, other things being equal. Initial studies, all in the United States, found the opposite: that unionized workers tend to be less satisfied with their jobs. More recent U.S. studies, using better data sets, have found that this is attributable to factors associated with the presence of a union, and that unionization per se has no effect one way or the other (Bender and Sloane, 1998; Gordon and DeNisi, 1995). Canadian research suggests similar results (Evans and Ondrack, 1990; Renaud, 2002). Thus, while the job satisfaction research does not indicate that unions serve an integrative function, it also does not support the argument that they have *dis*integrative effects. This conclusion is reinforced by the studies examining the effects of unions on productivity, as discussed earlier. The finding that unions *can* have positive productivity effects suggests that unions have at least an integrative *potential*, and that this potential is realized *if* management decides to work with, rather than against, union officials. It is likely that this is also the case for job satisfaction.

The Social Democratic Function. The reduction of inequality is central to the social democratic function of unions. Contrary to this function, the research suggests that unions increase the disparity *between* the earnings of union and non-union workers (e.g., Form, 1985: 134). But this is as would be expected, given the effects of unions on wages in the union sector. More important is whether unions reduce disparity *among* union workers, for which there is support (Freeman, 1982; Meng, 1990). Unions also appear to reduce disparity *between* union workers and their managerial/professional counterparts (Freeman, 1980; Quan, 1984). In addition, research indicates there has been more rapid growth in income inequality in the United States than in Canada and that much of this difference can be explained by the substantial decline in union density in that country (Asher and DeFina, 1997; DiNardo and Lemieux, 1997). This would appear to be especially so for earnings inequality among males (DiNardo and Lemieux, 1997) and young workers (Bratsberg and Ragan, 1997). Finally, one Canadian study found that unions not only reduce inequality, they do so in large part by raising the income of the disadvantaged and working poor (Chaykowski and Slatsue, 2002).

The Conflict Function. There have been few studies directly addressing the success with which unions serve the conflict function. However, in a 1995 Canadian survey (Godard, 1997c), backing workers if they strike received the highest ratings of a wide range of activities asked about, with four-fifths rating union effort as high on this activity, and half reporting their success as high. Other activities associated with this function also received relatively high effort ratings. Notably, however, "fighting against big business" received by far the lowest success rating of all the activities in the study. Only 12 percent rated union success as high on this activity, and only half rated it as at least moderate. It seems that unions are viewed as particularly disadvantaged in this respect.

Overall. Though unions can and do serve a number of functions, it would be mistaken to view all unions as serving each of these functions equally. It would also be mistaken to suggest that they should do so. But overall, the research suggests that unions have a number of effects that are consistent with each of the five functions. It is also worth noting that, in the 1995 survey referred to above, there was a tendency for unions to be perceived as trying hard but achieving only moderate success on many of the activities that unions engage in. This finding may be too dated, but it suggests that unions are viewed either as incompetent or as lacking the power and resources to achieve higher levels of success. In view of the relatively positive attitudes Canadians hold about unions, it is likely that the latter is the case. Either way, perceptions as to the limited effectiveness of unions in a number of areas do not appear to be attributed to a lack of perceived effort.

IV. CONCLUSIONS

This chapter has addressed the reasons that we have unions, their functions as institutions, their effects on the economy, and their effectiveness in serving the various functions associated with them. A major purpose in doing so has been to move beyond the narrow view of unions as existing purely to serve the economic interests of their members. To this end, this chapter has established that workers join unions for a number of reasons, ultimately reflecting their position of subordination and the conflicts which underlie the employment relation. It has also established that, in addition to any economic effects they may have, unions can serve a number of functions other than simply negotiating improved wages and benefits. These include a democratization function, an integrative function, a social democratic function, and a class conflict function. The following chapter picks up where the present chapter leaves off, moving beyond the general discussion of unions as institutions to a more specific discussion of unions as organizations.

Labour Unions as Organizations

All a union *necessarily* consists of is a local organization of workers who select one or a few of their peers to represent them collectively to their employer. However, most unions consist of far more than this, with staffs of full-time and sometimes highly specialized employees engaged in a variety of activities and servicing affiliated locals across a multitude of locations and even occupations. Thus, most unions are not just organizations of workers, they also entail work organizations in their own right, characterized by their own employees and their own rules and procedures. Unions also tend to be associated with one another in a variety of ways, most notably through membership in a labour federation. It follows that, in order to understand unions, it is important not only to have a sense of *why* they exist and *what* functions they serve as institutions, but also to be familiar with *how* they are structured and *how* they function. The present chapter is intended to serve this purpose. It begins by providing an overview of the structure and functioning of unions: first at the local level, then at the parent level. Next, the chapter turns to a discussion of the structure and functioning of the Canadian labour movement in general. Finally, it addresses the nature of unions as political organizations, focusing in particular on the issue of union democracy.

I.   THE LOCAL LEVEL

As discussed in chapter one, a local union can either be independent or it can be affiliated with and subject to the authority of a **provincial**, **national**, or "international" (U.S.-based) parent union. In the former circumstance, the local level *is* the union, while in the latter, it serves as the basic unit *of* the union. But whichever is the case, union locals (or simply locals, as they are referred to) are typically established on the basis of geographical proximity. In manufacturing and most service industries, locals typically represent eligible workers at a single location, though in the case of so-called "**amalgamated**" locals, where two locals have joined together, they may represent workers at a number of locations within a geographical area (e.g., a city). This is also the case in construction, where workers often have no fixed employer, and hence become members of the same local regardless of their employer or whether they are in fact employed. In trucking, locals can be based upon specific branches of the industry in a given locality, such as transport drivers, local delivery drivers, garbage truck drivers, and so forth. Finally, public sector locals can cover all employees in a municipal region or even a province.

The Role of Union Locals

Whatever the exact scope of the union local, it is generally the local that represents workers on a day-to-day basis, and it is at the local level that most union members have the greatest opportunity for participation in union affairs. Though turnout is often small (around 10 or 15 percent of membership), members have the right to take part in local meetings and to vote on local level issues having to do with such things as the collective agreement, dues increases, major expenditures, the election of local officers, and the selection of delegates to parent union conventions. They also have the right to run for union office themselves, and, if they wish, to volunteer to serve on local committees.

Probably the primary day-to-day role of the local union is ensuring that the collective agreement is adhered to, and, where called for, grievances are filed and pursued. However, local unions also represent their members in collective bargaining, either through the actual conduct of negotiations (if these are at the local level), or through some form of representation on the union bargaining committee (if negotiations cover several locals). In addition, local officials or their appointees may become involved in the processing of workers' compensation claims, in the representation of the union in local area social and political activities, in various consultative processes with management, and in formally established labour–management committees.

Local Union Structure

Locals generally elect their own officers in order to oversee union affairs, including a president, one or more vice-presidents, a financial officer (treasurer, secretary treasurer, or financial secretary), and a recording or corresponding secretary. With the exception of larger locals, these positions are typically part-time, often on a voluntary basis. Larger locals also often have paid staff. This can include a full-time "**business agent**" to assist in the handling of day-to-day union functions, especially in locals where membership is dispersed across a number of small workplaces, as is often the case in craft, retail sector, and professional employee locals. Most locals also have union **stewards** or "**reps**" elected or appointed to represent workers in specific departments or areas. These stewards may, in turn, be members of a stewards' committee, presided over by a general steward. In contrast to business agents, stewards remain in their regular job, performing their duties as steward on a part-time, unpaid basis. However, because their primary role is grievance handling, much of their work as steward is done during regular work hours, on company time.

II. THE PARENT LEVEL

A **parent** union can generally be said to exist when a number of locals are affiliated under the same name and are subject to a common overarching constitution and structure, both of which supersede the constitution and structure of the locals themselves. Virtually all national and international unions, and many provincial unions, are comprised of a number of locals and thus can be thought of as parent unions. There are 270 such unions, accounting for 95 percent of union membership in Canada. A mere 15 of them, each with a membership of 50,000 or more, account for roughly 70 percent of all union members (Workplace Information Directorate, 2003). These unions are identified in Table 8–1.

The Role of Parent Unions

As just noted, the overwhelming majority of local unions in Canada are affiliated with a parent. This union not only collects a sizeable portion of dues from the local, it also places various restrictions on what that local can do. Why, then, do local unions remain affiliated with a parent? Part of the reason is that they are often organized by a parent and automatically become affiliated with it. But parent unions serve a number of roles that are of value to local union members. Five such roles are of particular importance: (1) taking wages out of competition, (2) organizing the unorganized, (3) the provision of expertise in negotiations and grievance handling, (4) the provision of strike support, and (5) representation of membership interests both inside and outside the labour movement. Each of these roles will be discussed below.

Taking Wages Out of Competition. As discussed in the preceding chapter, taking wages out of competition helps to ensure that the provision of favourable wages and benefits does not place individual employers at a labour cost disadvantage relative to their competitors.

TABLE 8–1   Unions with Largest Membership, 2009

	Membership (000s)
Canadian Union of Public Employees	570
National Union of Public and General Employees	340
United Food and Commercial Workers International	280
United Steelworkers of America	245
National Automobile, Aerospace, Transportation, and General Workers of Canada (the CAW)	225
Public Service Alliance of Canada	182
Communications, Energy, and Paperworkers Union	128
Federation de la santé et des services sociaux	122
International Brotherhood of Teamsters	108
Service Employees International Union	92
Alberta Union of Provincial Employees	75
Elementary Teachers' Federation Ontario	74
FTQ Construction	70
Laborers International Union of North America	69
Ontario Secondary School Teacher Federation	63

Source: Published in *Union Membership in Canada* — 2009, URL: <http://www.hrsdc.gc.ca/eng/labour/labour_relations/info_anlaysis/union_membership/index2009.shtml>. Human Resources and Skills Development Canada, 2009. Reproduced with the permission of the Minister of Public Works and Government Services Canada, 2010.

Not only does this help to minimize any disemployment effects associated with union wage premiums, it also makes employers more able and willing to grant wage and benefit increases. Parent unions help to facilitate this by negotiating equivalent wages and benefits for all unionized operations in a particular industry or product market. In some cases, this can entail "multi-employer" bargaining, where the union negotiates a common agreement with a number of employers, as discussed in chapter twelve. Where this is not the case, parent unions attempt to coordinate settlements across establishments and employers to ensure that similar wage and benefit packages are agreed upon.

Organizing the Unorganized. A second and related role of parent unions is that of organizing the unorganized.[1] An organizing drive can originate either because union officials have been contacted by disgruntled workers or because the union has targeted the employer as strategically important, or both. After a preliminary investigation to determine the chances of success, an "organizing committee" is formed, consisting of one or more paid union organizers and a small number of highly committed workers (see Box 8–1). The next step is to attempt to obtain or develop a list of workers who are likely to be considered by the labour board as within the election unit (see chapter eleven), and to persuade as many of these as possible to sign a union membership application or "card". In Canada, it is illegal to do so on company time, and unions have no right of access to company premises. This can therefore be an arduous process, involving direct mail, telephone calls, and even visits to individual homes. But if a sizeable majority of workers signs up, the union can, in a number of Canadian jurisdictions, apply to the labour board for automatic certification. Otherwise, it can apply for a "certification vote", conducted by the labour board to establish if a majority are in favour of unionization.[2]

Union organizing drives can be expensive, and the likelihood of success is often quite uncertain. Why, then, do unions commit to organizing drives? One reason is that successful organizing drives enhance total union membership which, in turn, increases the resources at the parent's disposal and the power and influence of union leaders.

---

[1] For an excellent discussion of the organizing process, see Peach and Bergman, 1991: 36–53.

[2] The legal framework for union organizing is discussed more fully in chapter ten.

BOX 8–1   The Organizing Committee

An organizing committee generally consists of the most committed and most active supporters of the union drive, and in many respects it is the main actor in the process of unionization. The union organizer is essential in building the committee and giving it direction and guidance, and the workers as a whole must vote in the election and maintain the life of the union once it is established, but the union organizing committee plays the most critical role in the formation of the union and, from a sociological standpoint, provides an interesting model of emergent social organization. The organizing committee embodies the practice of unionism, exemplifying its values and sensibilities during a period when these are taking root and are subject to challenge, skepticism, and attack.

The members of the organizing committee carry out the daily tasks of union education, attempting to convince others in a systematic way of the power of collective interest and organization. This is a formidable task in most workplaces. Employers maintain considerable resource structures to control employees. Organizing committee members not only must develop the fortitude to withstand the intense pressures brought to bear by the employer, but also must illustrate to others the possibilities and benefits of solidarity through their own activities and values. The committee must provide an area of social space within the employer-dominated workplace where an alternative definition of social relations and power can be provided and maintained.

Leadership ability is forged largely in the work of the committee, with the union drive becoming a critical training ground for activists. One key role of the union organizer is to identify potential members of the committee and to cultivate certain leadership qualities. One union organizer noted the elements he sought in forming the committee:

> What we have to do is to identify the leaders, or the potential leaders, in every work area and on every shift. But it's not necessarily the person who promotes himself or herself as a leader, not somebody who stands up on a soapbox and engages in long speeches. They may turn out to be leaders, but there are other kinds of people who are leaders the person who others clearly respect, who is paid attention to when they have something to say. That person is able to express and articulate feelings and sentiments that other people have but aren't able to [express]. The person who, in a very quiet way, has a dignity that not only the co-workers respect, but even the management does those are the people you're looking for, who are the "natural" if unrecognized leaders.

Source: From Rick Fantasia (1988), *Cultures of Solidarity: Consciousness, Action and Contemporary American Workers*. The Regents of the University of California, University of California Press. Reproduced by permission.

A second reason, one that follows from the social democratic function discussed in the preceding chapter, is that parent officials are genuinely committed to and believe in the rights and protections gained by workers under collective bargaining. As such, they believe it is their mission to organize the unorganized. Third, organizing the unorganized makes it easier to take wages out of competition. If a sizeable number of employers in an industry is not unionized, or if non-union employers perceive little threat of unionization, then the union is less likely to achieve wage and benefit gains for their members without placing the employer at a competitive disadvantage. Thus, it makes sense for the union to attempt to organize as many employers as possible in a particular product market and to ensure that the threat of union organization is sufficiently high that non-union employers find it necessary to match union wages and benefits or find themselves unionized.

Collective Bargaining and Grievance Handling. A third role of parent unions is to assist local unions in collective bargaining and grievance handling. Over the years, collective bargaining has become an increasingly complex process, often requiring extensive background research, sophisticated bargaining skills, and specialized technical expertise in the development and analysis of various wage and benefit proposals. Similar complexities arise in the grievance/arbitration process. This process can be highly bureaucratic and legalistic, and therefore requires highly experienced union (and management) representatives and, at the arbitration stage, legal representation. As noted earlier, a great many locals do not even have full-time officials, not to mention specialists needed for collective bargaining and grievance handling. Without these specialists, they can find themselves at a severe disadvantage vis-à-vis the employer.

One option is for a local to hire an outside professional (sometimes referred to as a "hired gun") to represent it in negotiations and a local labour lawyer to handle grievances and arbitrations when they arise. But doing so can be expensive, and the person hired typically cannot be expected to have a thorough knowledge of the industry, the firm, or the personalities involved. In contrast, parent unions generally have the resources to hire specialists on a full-time basis, making them available to local unions as required. In some cases, parent unions may also rely on outside experts with extensive experience in and knowledge of the industry, but these experts are normally kept on retainer.

Strike Assistance. Parent unions can also provide locals with assistance in the event of a strike or lockout. This can involve legal advice and representation in the event that the employer appears to be engaged in illegal practices, strikers are arrested, or the employer seeks a court injunction restricting the right of workers to picket (see chapter eleven). Perhaps most important, however, is the accumulation and administration of strike funds. During a strike, these funds are used to assist individual strikers, often on the condition that they put in a specified amount of time on the picket line. Though strike pay is only a fraction of the striker's normal wage, it can go a long way towards cushioning the economic impact of a strike. In its absence, therefore, the strike option becomes much less viable for workers and, aware of this, management is under much less pressure to grant meaningful concessions in negotiations. Indeed, management is in a better position to force the union into a strike that it (the union) is likely to lose, thereby undermining its credibility with its members and potentially resulting in a decertification vote.

Of course, strike funds ultimately come out of membership dues, and so it is quite feasible for an **independent local union** to generate its own fund. The problem is that the establishment of an adequate strike fund can take some time, and local unions which have just been organized or have recently undergone a lengthy strike are unlikely to have sufficient strike reserves. It is in this respect that affiliation with a parent union can be of critical importance, for the availability of strike pay can mean the difference between "life" and "death", especially for a recently organized local union.

Representation of Membership Interests. The fifth role of a parent union is that of representation of membership interests and concerns to third parties. Particularly important in this respect is the representation of membership interests to government. Government policies, practices, and decisions can have critical implications not only for the economy in general, but also for specific industries and/or firms. For example, an employer may require some form of government assistance in order to remain viable. Depending on the political party in power, a union may be able to exert considerable influence in this respect. But also important are government policies on tariffs and import quotas in specific industries. To the extent that firms from low-wage, developing countries are able to export their goods to Canada on an unrestricted basis, it may be extremely difficult for Canadian employers to compete at all, let alone to provide reasonable terms and conditions of employment to their workers. Conversely, to the extent that foreign governments enact barriers to trade within their countries, Canadian firms may find themselves at a competitive disadvantage in those countries. Where either of these problems arise, both employers and unions may "team up" to lobby the government on trade and related issues. In so doing, they may also seek to mobilize public opinion in their favour, placing added pressure on government to conform to their concerns and requests.

There are also "**sector councils**" involving unions and employers within the same industry (Chaykowski, 1998). Though these councils can potentially serve a number of purposes, their primary activity has been to establish joint, industry-wide training and education initiatives. They also engage in labour adjustment activities, designed to minimize layoffs or at least cushion their effects. Parent unions represent their member locals in these councils.

In addition, parent unions represent union members within the labour movement, through membership in a labour federation. As noted in chapter one, labour federations are associations of unions formed at the national (e.g., the Canadian Labour Congress or CLC) and provincial levels (e.g., the Ontario Federation of Labour, or OFL). As is discussed later in this chapter with respect to the CLC, labour federations can serve a number of functions, including representation of the labour movement in general to governments and the public, coordinating the activities of member unions and reconciling disputes between them, providing various support services, and others.

Finally, parent unions represent workers within society in general, primarily through the pursuit of broader social democratic reforms. This was covered in chapter seven.

The Structure of Parent Unions

As is the case at the local level, parent unions have a number of elected officers, including a president, a number of vice-presidents, and a secretary-treasurer (or a secretary *and* a treasurer). Yet as should now be apparent, the role and responsibilities of the parent can be quite extensive. For this reason, the president and a number of the vice-presidents are full-time, paid employees in most unions. In addition, most unions also employ a sizeable cadre of full-time staff specialists and office staff, divided into a number of departments on the basis of function. Thus, most large parent unions have departments for organizing new members, for conducting research and preparing briefs for government, for educating and training local level union officials, for researching and providing advice on health and safety issues, for handling union finances, and so forth. Indeed, because parent unions are employers in their own right, they sometimes have to face an organizing drive by their own workers, negotiating a contract with these workers if this drive is successful!

Many national and international unions are also divided into regions, often referred to as "**districts**" or "**councils**". These coordinate union activities and provide services in different geographical regions, bringing the parent union closer to the local level and enabling it to address the needs and problems specific to a particular area. Each district typically has offices staffed by union officials, and in many cases administered by and represented at the parent level by a vice-president elected from within the district. In recognition of the distinct nature and needs of labour unions in Canada, many large international unions have established separate Canadian districts and have granted these districts considerable autonomy. However, on the whole, districts remain the creation of the parent union, and with the exception of those Canadian districts, their autonomy is generally limited.

Finally, unions typically have an **executive council** made up of elected officers and some senior staff specialists. These councils meet periodically (e.g., once a month) to map out strategy and make policy decisions concerning the day-to-day operation of the union, organizing activities, bargaining strategies, and so forth.

Administratively at least, a parent union may appear at first blush to have many of the characteristics of a conventional work organization. However, there is an important difference. As Arthur Ross pointed out a half century ago (1948), conventional work organizations operate essentially as economic organizations controlled by investors, while unions operate essentially as political ones, much like political parties. As in a political party, senior union officers are elected, either directly, in a vote of union members or, indirectly, by a vote of membership elected delegates. In addition, officer authority is constrained by a duly established constitution specifying disciplinary procedures within the union, the duties and power of officers, restrictions on the tenure of officers, and so forth. Finally, as is the case for political parties, unions hold major conventions every one to five years, during which delegates from each local nominate and elect officers, make any constitutional amendments deemed necessary, and decide upon major policy and strategy issues. In essence the convention is the supreme governing body of the union, for it establishes policies and guidelines for the ongoing conduct of union business.

III. THE ORGANIZATION OF THE CANADIAN LABOUR MOVEMENT

To this point in the chapter, focus has been upon the structure and functioning of unions as organizations in and of themselves. Yet, in addition to their status as independent organizations, unions are also part of a broader labour movement, and as such they are interdependent with one another. Thus, any attempt to consider unions as organizations is incomplete without a discussion of the relationships between them and the organization of the Canadian labour movement in general. Particularly important in this respect are labour federations, which are associations of unions formed at the national and provincial levels. As discussed in chapter one, a number of federations exist in Canada, but by far the largest is the Canadian Labour Congress (CLC); its member unions account for roughly seven out of every ten of all unionized workers in Canada.

The Role and Functions of the CLC

The Canadian Labour Congress serves five primary functions for its affiliated unions. First, and perhaps most important, it represents member unions to the federal government. As is discussed in the next chapter, government legislation and policies can have implications for industrial relations in a variety of ways, including the actions of governments as employers, the enactment and administration of legislation with a direct bearing upon the practice of industrial relations, and the formulation of broader policies and laws that have implications for the economic and social context within which industrial relations take place. As such, the ability of the CLC to influence the formulation and administration of government laws and policies can have critical implications for the effectiveness and future of member unions and, indeed, the labour movement in general.

Though individual unions also attempt to exert influence, these attempts are typically targeted at laws and policies with implications for their members alone. When it comes to broader laws and policies, it makes far more sense for the labour movement to speak with a unified voice, establishing a general position and presenting this position on behalf of the labour movement and working people in general. Of course, this is not always easy, for member unions often have different interests and philosophies. Complicating matters is the lack of any formal authority over affiliates, with the result that those opposed to CLC policy can speak out against it with little fear of reprisal.

While doing so is consistent with democracy, it can greatly weaken the CLC's political effectiveness.

The second function of the CLC is the coordination of relations between member unions. As should be evident from the discussion in chapter four, this coordination has historically been important in attempting to reconcile jurisdictional disputes between unions, as craft unions and industrial unions have often claimed workers in the same workplace. These sorts of disputes have diminished over the years, but it is still not unheard of for more than one union to attempt to organize the same group of workers — an activity which represents a waste of organizing resources and can undermine the likelihood of any union becoming certified. Even more important is the problem of union "**raiding**", where one union persuades workers who are already members of a union to change their affiliation. Though this provides disgruntled workers with an opportunity to get rid of a union which they consider to be ineffective, it can also cause considerable internecine warfare, sapping the resources and the effectiveness of both the unions involved. To avoid this, the CLC has a policy which generally outlaws raiding. Again, however, it has little actual authority to prevent raiding from occurring, other than reprimanding the guilty party and possibly trying to either suspend or expel it from the CLC.

The third and related function of the CLC is to attempt to maintain ethical standards within its membership. To this end, the CLC has a code of ethics set out in its constitution prohibiting corrupt leadership practices and stating (among other things) that union members have a right to honest elections, to run for union office, and to receive fair treatment from union officials. If this code appears to have been violated, it is up to the executive of the CLC to attempt to persuade the union involved to change its behaviour, though yet again, it has no legal authority to require such a change.

The fourth function of the CLC is to provide member unions with services they might not otherwise be able to afford. These services are especially useful for independent locals and smaller national and provincial unions that lack the membership base necessary to afford the services and expertise characteristic of their larger counterparts. The services provided can include extensive labour education programs for union officials and staff, assistance in and research for collective bargaining, and even participation in organizing activities.

The final function of the CLC is the representation of the Canadian labour movement internationally. Particularly relevant in this respect is the **International Labour Organization** (ILO) of the United Nations. This tripartite agency, located in Geneva, Switzerland, is made up of governments, trade union federations, and employer organizations. It collects and disseminates information pertaining to the conditions of employment and the rights afforded workers throughout the world (see Zeytinoglu, 1989). As part of this function, it sets international standards, referred to as "**conventions**", which serve as guidelines for member countries. If a party believes these guidelines have been violated, they may bring their case before the ILO and ask it for a ruling. However, the ILO lacks real power to enforce them (Panitch and Swartz, 1985).

The Structure of the Canadian Labour Movement and the CLC

As is the case for most national and international unions, the CLC consists of a president, a secretary-treasurer, and over thirty vice-presidents, including presidents of major affiliated unions and of provincial and territorial labour federations. Combined, these officers comprise the executive council, which is responsible for policy decisions between conventions. However, the supreme governing body of the CLC is the convention, held biennially and attended by roughly 3,000 delegates from affiliated unions. It is this convention that establishes the constitution and major policies of the CLC, elects its officers, and votes upon the admission or expulsion of individual unions.

As is also the case with most parent unions, the CLC consists of subordinate bodies, including provincial and territorial federations and over 100 local labour councils. In addition, the CLC has a number of internal departments, each with its own director. These include accounting, educational services, political action, and research and legislation, among others.

Perhaps more important, however, is the structure of the CLC as it pertains to the Canadian labour movement in general, for as already noted, the CLC consists of affiliate unions over which it has little direct authority beyond admonishment, suspension, or expulsion. The CLC consists of over 100 member unions, which in combination comprise over 10,000 locals. Of the more than three million members of its affiliated unions, little more than a third are in U.S.-based, international unions, while almost two-thirds are in Canadian-based, national, provincial, or independent local unions.

IV. UNION DEMOCRACY

Union democracy represents an important issue, because any organization which is supposed to provide workers with democratic rights and protections in the workplace should also provide such rights and protections internally. But it is also important because concerns having to do with union democracy have been used by anti-union groups and governments as pretexts for discrediting unions and ultimately implementing laws that undermine their effectiveness.[3] This section thus addresses the various issues that have been raised about democracy in unions, beginning with commonly identified limits to union democracy.[4]

The Limits to Union Democracy

In the ideal, it would be preferable for unions to operate like "town hall democracies", holding frequent meetings in which all members participate equally, allowing and even encouraging internal debate and disagreement, and establishing an electoral system in which members feel free to run for election and are able to mount a credible challenge to incumbent officers. In practice, however, most unions fall far short of this ideal. At the parent level, few union presidents are ever voted out of office, and when they retire, they are typically able to ensure that their hand-picked successor is elected to take their place. When there *are* challenges to incumbents, challengers often have few resources available to them, and there is rarely (if ever) an institutionalized opposition party through which they can mobilize support. In contrast, incumbents have the resources of virtually the entire union at their disposal. For example, in most unions incumbents can effectively control union periodicals (most unions produce and distribute newsletters or magazines to members on a regular basis) and hence the information received by rank-and-file members.

---

[3] For example, the Landrum-Griffin Act, and to a lesser extent the Taft-Hartley Act, implemented in the United States in 1959 and 1947, respectively, were justified as enhancing union democracy, even though they had the effect of making it more difficult for unions to organize and bargain successfully. In Britain, the Thatcher/Major governments followed a similar strategy in the 1980s and early 1990s. This strategy has, in turn, been picked up by some Canadian governments. For example, the Manitoba Conservative government of Gary Filmon also followed this strategy in the early and mid-1990s.

[4] One of the best discussions of union democracy available remains that of Lipset, 1960: 357–99. For a more recent discussion and review of the literature on union democracy, see Strauss (1991).

They also exert considerable control over the appointments and salaries of union staff members, enabling them to reward loyalty and to ensure that their "people" are in key positions of influence within the union.

Moreover, while conventions are in theory highly democratic, with members from different locals throughout Canada (and, in the case of international unions, the United States) sending duly elected delegates to represent them, much of what goes on during the convention can depend on an agenda which is established in advance and on various policy positions formulated by union officials. In addition, while a number of delegates may participate on various committees that report to the membership, senior officers are often able to determine who is appointed to these committees and the types of issues they are allowed to address. Finally, on the floor of the convention, dissidents may find themselves ignored by the chair, and if they become unruly, may face eviction.

At the local level, things often do not appear to be much better. Locals are often run by small groups of activists and it is not uncommon to hear rank-and-file members express frustration and disenchantment as a result. Moreover, rather than the full turnout we might expect of a town hall democracy, it is often the case (as noted earlier) that only 10 to 15 percent of local members attend union meetings. Making matters worse, these meetings are often dull and routine, with the agenda controlled by the local president and little opportunity or reason for debate and disagreement.

A further complaint is that the process of collective bargaining is itself often highly secretive. Members are often kept in the dark about what is going on and, indeed, even local union representatives are often provided with only limited information. Even where negotiations are conducted entirely at the local level, proposed settlements often require the approval of senior officials at the national/international levels. Moreover, these officials often must give their approval before a strike is called, and may decide to withhold strike funds if a strike goes ahead without their approval.

Explaining the Limits to Union Democracy

Why is it that unions in general do not conform to the ideal of a town hall democracy? At least four related explanations can be advanced. The first and perhaps most famous is "**the iron law of oligarchy**" thesis first proposed by Robert Michels to account for similar problems in established political parties (Michels, 1959 [1911]). A student and colleague of Max Weber (see chapter two), Michels argued that, as political parties become established and begin to accomplish their initial objectives, members gradually become apathetic, believing that their concerns are being attended to. In addition, as the party develops and matures as an institution, it establishes an elaborate administrative bureaucracy and comes to be increasingly dominated by experts with specialized knowledge, with the result that individual members come to feel both powerless within the party and lacking sufficient competence to question the decisions of party officials. Finally, leaders themselves come to enjoy the status, salary, and power that they have acquired, and develop a strong vested interest in suppressing opposition. As such, they actively control information and communication channels so as to ensure membership support, and they do everything possible to make themselves irreplaceable. The result, according to Michels, is a state of oligarchy, in which a small elite is able to entrench itself and, in fact, undermine democratic processes which could threaten its tenure.

Though developed with respect to political parties, these arguments would appear, at least at first blush, to be especially applicable to unions. Once workers have succeeded in organizing a union, and the union has established a stable relationship with management, their major concerns are likely to have been addressed and they are likely to begin to take their union for granted, provided that it continues to "deliver the goods". Moreover, in view of the sophistication of collective bargaining and the grievance/arbitration process, it becomes extremely difficult for members to question the decisions of their leaders, especially when they involve inputs from staff experts. Perhaps most applicable, however, is the argument about status, salary, and power (see Lipset, 1960: 367–72). While politicians in the larger society are likely to have well-paid occupations (e.g., in law or business) to which they can turn if voted out of office, most union leaders typically have few if any alternatives other than returning to their old job, if, in fact, they still have a job to return to. As such, being voted out of office can be catastrophic for union leaders, especially if they have been in a leadership position for some period of time and have come to take their power, status, and living standards for granted.

The second explanation is that democracy can, in fact, seriously impair a union's effectiveness. Under this explanation, only experienced union officials possess the knowledge, experience, and skills necessary to make effective decisions (Ross, 1948: 39). These officials require a fairly free hand to decide what is in the interests of their members, and cannot be continually consulting with or attempting to placate all of their members all of the time. Particularly important in this respect is the process of collective bargaining. As discussed earlier, this process can be highly complex, requiring a considerable amount of sophistication and expertise. To keep members fully informed, or to constantly seek membership input, might therefore undermine the effectiveness of union negotiators. Similarly, to allow individual locals to negotiate settlements that are out of line with those negotiated by other locals could substantially weaken union solidarity and therefore strength. More generally, there is always a risk of factionalism and internal divisiveness if democracy is allowed to flourish, and this can also seriously undermine the union's ability to serve its members, especially if employers seek to exploit this divisiveness in bargaining or in the grievance/arbitration process (see Taft, 1956: 240). Finally, if leaders are constantly subject to membership pressures, their decisions are much more likely to be purely political ones, designed to appease various factions within the union rather than to enhance the long-term effectiveness of the union.

The third explanation has to do with the contradictory position in which workers find themselves in capitalist economies. As discussed in chapter three, there are a number of quite fundamental sources of conflict underlying the employment relation. Yet, there are also a number of sources of cooperation, not the least of which are various limitations to union power and the dependence of both workers and union leaders on the survival of their employer. Often, dissident movements which arise in unions essentially reflect the underlying sources of conflict and are much more idealistic and radical than the established leadership. That leadership views these movements as a threat not just to its own tenure but also to the future of the union, for (from the point of view of the leadership) these dissidents do not understand the limitations to union power or the broader "realities" of capitalism (Hyman, 1975: 88–93). Thus, they suppress dissidents and place constraints on the democratic process to ensure that dissidents do not pose a serious threat within the union (for an example, see Lichtenstein, 1985).

A fourth explanation goes a step further, suggesting union leaders themselves have become co-opted and serve as a further source of cooperation in the system. In other words, union leaders not only come to enjoy their status, salary, and power, they also lose touch with the realities of the workplace and come to identify with the "status quo", developing conservative ideologies, and thinking more like managers than workers. As a result, union leaders can become little more than "managers of discontent", seeking to limit membership aspirations and concerning themselves primarily with ensuring discipline and control in the workplace. In the words of one author, "in the evolution of the labor contract, the union becomes part of the control system of management.... The union often takes over the task of disciplining [workers] when management cannot" (Bell, 1967: 214–15). Democracy runs the risk of enabling more aggressive members to upset this status quo, and is suppressed for this reason.

These four explanations are clearly consistent with one another, and combined, they suggest that there are a number of quite strong pressures against the realization of the democratic ideal in unions. Yet, when all is said and done, to say that there are a number of limits to and pressures against the attainment of this ideal is *not* to say that unions are inherently undemocratic. In this respect, it is also possible to identify a number of sources of democracy.

Sources of Democracy

There are a number of sources of union democracy (see Strauss, 1991), but five are perhaps most important. First, union officials *are* elected by their membership, and if a sizeable enough portion of the membership is unhappy with the way things are going, they can cause a number of problems for the leadership, if not through a direct leadership challenge then through the defeat of various motions and policies advanced by the leadership at meetings and conventions. Thus, union officials can find themselves under considerable pressure to be responsive to member concerns.

Second, a union's reputation can have important implications for its ability to organize new locals (Maranto and Fiorito, 1987) and where the membership of an established local or region is sufficiently discontent, it may decertify (become non-union), disaffiliate (remain unionized, but without a parent), or switch affiliations (change to a different parent union). Thus, unions which are not sufficiently democratic may find themselves subject to a decline in membership and hence in both the power and the resources available to union leaders.

Third, though members often do not attend meetings, they always have the *right* to do so if unhappy or if important issues are to be decided upon. Thus, the local union meeting *can* serve as an important source of democracy even if attendance is normally low. Indeed, low attendance may reflect not a lack of democracy or disenchantment with the union but rather a satisfaction with the responsiveness and functioning of the union and a belief that there is no need to attend meetings. In fact, it is not unheard of for local leaders to go to considerable lengths to improve attendance, sometimes by offering door prizes or arranging a social event after the meeting. They may do so for a number of reasons, though clearly the more active workers are in the union, the more committed they are likely to be and the greater the support union leaders are likely to enjoy at negotiating time.

Fourth, and equally important, the rank-and-file is able to reject the settlement negotiated by their leadership if dissatisfied with it, and this can place considerable pressure on union leaders. Notably, member attendance at union meetings often increases sharply at negotiating time, and turnout for the ratification vote on a proposed settlement regularly exceeds 75 percent. Thus, though members may be kept in the dark during negotiations, officials usually go to considerable lengths to ensure that their bargaining positions are responsive to the concerns of local members and that the settlement will meet their concerns.

Finally, it would be mistaken to think that union officials are by nature autocrats who can be expected to suppress democracy at every opportunity. Though union leaders (like everyone else) are no doubt concerned with maintaining their jobs, many also espouse social democratic values and justify their actions, to themselves as well as others, in terms of these values. Their commitment to democracy may not extend as far as to encourage challenges to their positions, but many view themselves as members of a *social* movement, the ultimate purpose of which is to further the rights of working people. While the extent to which this view translates into a genuine effort to strengthen democracy probably varies considerably and is at best probably somewhat limited, to ignore it out of hand would be a mistake.

In essence, therefore, it is probably more accurate to recognize that, while unions rarely appear to function as town hall democracies, they also rarely function as repressive autocracies (at least in Canada). Indeed, while there may be considerable room for improvement in the labour movement in general, unions are far more democratic than are contemporary work organizations, where workers have no legal right to elect their rulers or to participate in managerial decision processes. Thus, the question may not be so much *whether* unions are democratic, but rather *the extent to which* they are. This may vary considerably in accordance with the size, the traditions and the constitution of the union, leadership values, membership diversity, and membership priorities and expectations (see Strauss, 1991: 226–233). Recall from the preceding chapter, however, that between 70 and 80 percent of union members participating in a 1994 U.S. survey expressed satisfaction with their say in union affairs, depending on the issue they were asked about. Moreover, two-thirds of participants in the 1996 survey of 341 Canadian labour market participants discussed in that chapter indicated that unions put high effort into ensuring members had a say in union affairs, and an additional 20 percent indicated that they put moderate effort into doing so. Although these statistics may be dated, they seem to suggest that unions do quite well in view of the various barriers to full democracy.

The real problem may not be that of union democracy per se but rather the fact that, because leadership authority in unions ultimately derives from the rank-and-file, unions can be highly political. Union leaders find themselves almost invariably having to balance the often competing priorities of various membership groups, while at the same time having to perform the multitude of roles and functions identified earlier in this and the preceding chapter. As in any political system, coalitions are likely to be formed, and certain individuals and groups may find themselves on the "outside", with limited influence. Whether this reflects a problem of union democracy or of democracy in general can be debated. But it is important to attempt to distinguish between disgruntlement which may follow from the political nature of unions and the consequent impossibility of "pleasing all of the people all of the time", and disgruntlement which may occur due to genuine attempts by leaders to stifle democracy. Though the former may well lead to the latter, this need not be the case. It is important not to confuse the two.

None of this is to suggest that the issue of union democracy is not an important one. Arguably, union democracy is over the long run essential for the internal vitality and perhaps even the very future of the labour movement, as insufficiently democratic unions are likely to be characterized both by apathetic members and by a poor public image, which, in turn, weakens membership resolve and impairs organizing effectiveness (Strauss, 1991). But even if this was not the case, democracy constitutes a valued end in and of itself, and should be encouraged if only for this reason alone.

V.   CONCLUSIONS

This chapter has presented a profile of unions as organizations and of the Canadian labour movement in general. As should be apparent, unions are typically much more than local organizations of workers, under which one or a few volunteers are selected to represent members collectively to their employer. While such unions do exist, most local unions are affiliated with a national or international parent, consisting of full-time officers and staff experts and engaged in a variety of activities, from organizing workers, to providing negotiation and arbitration assistance to local affiliates, to representing workers to the public and to governments. The result is that unions are formal and often complex organizations, under which members often feel a distance from their leaders, and within which complex political problems can become widespread. As a result, complaints about union democracy are almost inevitable, even though there is little to indicate that these complaints are particularly well-founded.

Further complicating matters, most parent unions are affiliated with a labour federation, whose primary functions include coordination and dispute resolution between member unions, the provision of various services to member unions, international representation of the Canadian labour movement, setting and monitoring ethical standards within the labour movement, and representing member unions to provincial and national governments. The last function is perhaps most important and has become increasingly so over the past decade, as the role of government in industrial relations has become more and more apparent. This has been so not only with respect to labour law, but also with respect to broader economic and social policies and with respect to government's role as an employer in its own right. This role is addressed in the following chapter.

The Role of the State

9

In chapter one, the relationship between labour and management was identified as forming the core subject matter of industrial relations. Yet, it should also be apparent by this point that a critical role is played by governments and their agencies, or what is more simply referred to as **"the state"**. Not only does the state enact and enforce laws that comprise the legal context of labour–management relations, it also serves as an employer in its own right. In addition, states can attempt to shape the values and beliefs of the parties and provide various forms of support in order to facilitate "positive" labour relations. Perhaps even more important, the state is responsible for broader economic and social policies that structure the economic context within which labour and management interact. In many respects, the state shapes the employment relation itself. The purpose of this chapter is to address these roles. For the present, they can be referred to as: (1) the regulative role, (2) the employer role, (3) the facilitative role, (4) the structural role, and (5) the constitutive role (see Godard, 2002).[1]

I. THE REGULATIVE ROLE

The state plays a major role in regulating the relations between employers and employees and their unions through law. Usually, a distinction is made between labour laws and employment laws. **Labour laws** are those pertaining to the right of workers to join a union and engage in collective bargaining. Ideally, these laws enable workers to

---

[1] Much of this chapter is drawn from Godard (2002).

confront their employers as equals and hence to negotiate decent terms and conditions of work. Yet, two-thirds of all Canadian workers are not covered by union agreements and, even where they are, these agreements may not provide adequate protection. Partly in recognition of this, each jurisdiction also has a system of **employment law**, which is the term used to describe all laws in Canada dealing with individual (as opposed to collective) rights.

With the exception of federal government employees and a select number of industries (e.g., banking, interprovincial transportation), labour and employment law in Canada is a matter of provincial and territorial jurisdiction. Thus, there are in actuality fourteen jurisdictions: ten provincial jurisdictions, three territorial jurisdictions (Nunavut, the Yukon, and Northwest Territories), and the federal jurisdiction.[2] In addition, though each jurisdiction has one system of laws to cover all (or most) private sector workers, most have separate acts to cover different groups of workers in the public sector. Thus, there is considerable diversity within Canada.[3] Nonetheless, there are important similarities within and across jurisdictions.

Labour Law

As discussed more fully in chapter eleven, labour law in Canada (and in the United States) is characterized by an **administrative approach** to unions and collective bargaining. That is, workers have no automatic right to collective bargaining under the law. Rather, they must first apply to a **labour board**, which is an independent, government-appointed agency in charge of administering labour law. The labour board must then decide which workers should and should not be eligible to be represented by the union, determining what is referred to as the **bargaining unit**. Although this unit can vary depending on the workers in question, it most often includes all workers in broadly similar occupations (e.g., blue-collar work) within a single workplace. Once this unit is decided, the board must also determine whether a majority of workers eligible for coverage are in favour of union representation. Where a majority of workers vote in favour of union representation or (in a number of Canadian jurisdictions) the union can establish that a clear majority (the exact percent depends

---

[2] However, the three territories rely on federal labour laws, as of this writing.

[3] Existing labour and employment laws, broken down by jurisdiction, are available at <http://hrmanagement.gc.ca/gol/hrmanagement/interface.nsf/engdocBasic/3.html>.

on the jurisdiction) have already signed up with the union, the board will grant it legal **certification**, giving it the right to represent workers as their exclusive agent in collective bargaining. In turn, the employer is required to **recognize** this union as such and enter into "**good faith**" or serious negotiations with its representatives.

Throughout this process, employers are generally prohibited from unduly interfering with the union organizing drive or from disciplining or dismissing workers because of their union activities. If they do either, they are said to have committed an **unfair labour practice**, and the labour board may impose a number of "remedies" intended to prevent further violations and to repair any damage already done. These can include, for example, immediately holding a ballot, reinstating unjustly dismissed workers with back pay, and (in most jurisdictions) even imposing certification regardless of whether a majority supports the union or not.

In the private sector, workers also have the right to go on strike without fear of employer retribution against them as individuals (unless they engage in illegal tactics), provided the collective agreement has expired, a good faith attempt has been made to negotiate a new one, a majority has voted in favour of striking, and various other conditions have been met. Alternatively, the employer has the right to "**lock out**" these workers, or refuse them access to their jobs, again provided that these conditions have been met. In the public sector, the right to strike is often more restricted, as discussed in the next section. But in both sectors, the parties sign a **collective agreement** outlining the terms and conditions of employment and the rights of each party once these have been agreed on. This agreement is usually of a fixed duration (most often from one to three years). If a dispute over adherence to this agreement arises during this period, the aggrieved party files a **grievance**, which is normally a written complaint stating the issue in dispute. If, in turn, union and management officials are unable to satisfactorily resolve the grievance on their own, they are required to appoint a **grievance arbitrator**, who is an outside "neutral" paid to adjudicate the issue in dispute.

The Canadian system of labour law would appear to be an effective one for ensuring that, where a majority of workers is in favour of union representation, they stand a reasonable chance of obtaining it (Godard, 2003a; 2004b). This would appear to be different than the United States. Although the Canadian system was initially modelled after the U.S. system, the latter has become notorious for the ease with which employers can undermine a union, either during the certification process or after a union has been certified (Wood and Godard, 1999).

In the United States, a vote is required in all cases, and employers have substantial opportunity to delay union recognition votes so that they have time to "persuade" workers that a union is not "in their best interests". Although employers cannot legally threaten workers during this period or dismiss them for engaging in legal union activities, they can engage in a number of forms of implicit intimidation, including requiring workers to attend meetings in which anti-union lies and propaganda are presented. They can also question individual workers about their voting intentions. If a union does become certified, the employer may appeal the decision, introducing a further delay of as long as two or three years. In the event that the employer does commence bargaining with the union, it can readily push the union into a strike position with little fear of being found guilty of bad faith bargaining. In turn, once workers are on strike, it can hire replacement workers on a permanent basis. Thus, employees may find themselves permanently out of work simply because they attempted to exercise their right to collective representation under the law.

In Canada, the legal system generally precludes employers from engaging in these sorts of tactics. For example, employers are much more restricted in what they can say about the union. In addition, where votes are required, they are typically held within a week after a union has applied for certification. There is little scope for an employer to appeal the board's final decision, and if a settlement is not reached within a reasonable time due to employer recalcitrance, the union can normally ask the government to appoint an arbitrator who, in turn, imposes one. Finally, an employer cannot hire permanent replacement workers in the event of a strike. In a few jurisdictions, the employer cannot even hire replacement workers on a temporary basis.

The results are rather dramatic (e.g., Wood and Godard, 1999: 215; Godard, 2003a). Only one in eight working Americans is now a union member, compared to three in ten working Canadians, even though the level of general support for unions has traditionally been about the same in both countries (Lipset and Meltz, 1998: 18). As of the mid-2000s, half of all U.S. workers without a union said they would vote in favour of union representation if they had the chance (Freeman, 2007). In comparison, the Canadian figure was one in three (CLC, 2004), largely because Canadians who would like to be represented by a union are more likely to already have one. Finally, almost all newly certified unions are able to achieve a first collective agreement in Canada, while only slightly more than half are successful in doing so in the United States (Ferguson, 2008).

Despite its effectiveness relative to the United States, the Canadian system has been criticized on a number of grounds. One in particular is that it creates an unnecessarily adversarial relationship between unions and employers. According to Roy Adams (1993b, 1995), a well-known expert on alternative industrial relations systems, any attempt by workers to form a union tends to be viewed as an attack on management rather than the legitimate exercise of a positive human right. Not only does this generate a negative response from management, it also means that employees are more likely to view the exercise of this right as being disloyal to their employer. Because of this, workers are more likely to exercise it only as a last resort, if they are discontent with the employer and see little viable alternative to doing so. The result is not only that workers are less likely to exercise their right to representation, but also that, when they do, the union-management relationship starts off on a negative footing. Adams believes that this is a major reason why, even though union density is high in Canada compared to the United States, only three in ten employed Canadians is currently in a union. He maintains that, if workers were given an automatic right to be represented by a union, without having this right administered through a labour board, this problem would be avoided, not only lowering the degree of adversariness in the system, but also increasing density considerably.

Although there is a lack of research as to whether the nature of the certification process is to blame, there is evidence that non-union workers fear employer reprisals and that this matters to whether they are likely to vote for a union. In the 2003–4 PRA survey of 750 employed Canadians referred to in chapter three (Godard, 2004d), half of the non-union participants (there were 488) reported that it was likely that management would respond negatively if it found out that they were actively engaged in a union certification drive. Another one in four stated that they were unsure. Of 49 non-union workers who had participated in a union certification vote in their workplace and voted against a union, a quarter admitted that part of the reason was fear that co-workers or managers would be upset with them if they voted in favour. This latter statistic is based on too small a sample to draw strong conclusions, but it does suggest that the hostile environment surrounding union certification votes is a factor in reducing union density levels. The 2004 Vector poll of 2000 Canadians (CLC, 2004), also referred to in chapter three, supports this conclusion. It found that when eligible non-union workers were asked what they would do if they did not have to fear employer reprisals, the percentage responding that they would vote for a union increased by 10 percentage points (from 33 to 43 percent).

A further problem with the Canadian system derives from **"residual rights doctrine"**. Under this doctrine, all decision making remains within the exclusive prerogative of management unless the union is successful in negotiating provisions to the contrary into a collective agreement. As a result, the union is in a reactive position, having to fight an up-hill battle in order to win rights and protections for its members. In this battle, much can depend on its ability to impose costs on the employer through a strike. If a union's ability to do so is low, the employer may have little reason to grant meaningful concessions. Where this is the case, there may be little that a union can really do for its members. Where it is able to win concessions, the result can be a highly bureaucratic and unwieldy collective agreement. Overall, therefore, the residual rights doctrine may further increase the level of adversariness and provide an additional explanation for why a large portion of the labour force is not in a union.

Finally, and as noted above, one of every three working Canadians who do not have a union would vote for one if they had a chance. Although this is substantially lower than in the United States, it is a sizeable number nonetheless. In view of the apparent effectiveness of the Canadian system in protecting the right to join a union, this statistic would appear to be explained by the majority requirement. That is, a great many workers may wish to have union representation, but are denied it because they are in the minority in their workplace.

In sum, it would appear that the Canadian system of labour law may be reasonably effective in ensuring that workers have a good chance of obtaining union representation when a majority is in favour, but that it may also foster undue adversariness, place unions in a reactive, disadvantaged position, and deny representation to a significant portion of the labour force. If so, there may be substantial room for improvement, as discussed more fully in subsequent chapters.

Employment Law

There are five main components to employment law: (1) minimum standards legislation, (2) human rights legislation, (3) employment equity legislation, (4) health and safety legislation, and (5) unjust dismissal law.[4]

---

[4] Much of the ensuing discussion of employment law is drawn from Peirce (2000) and from England, 2005. More detailed information is available at <http://www.hrsdc.gc.ca/en/gateways/nav/top_nav/program/labour.shtml>.

Minimum Standards Legislation. There has been a growing emphasis on minimum standards legislation over the past few decades. One reason has been the limited coverage of unions, which has meant that a majority of labour force participants are left to rely on legislated standards. Others, however, have included increased concerns about the effects of job loss, an increasingly diverse labour force, and a growth in the number of women in the workforce.

The areas covered by minimum standards laws generally include minimum wage levels, hours of work and overtime pay, statutory holidays, annual vacation entitlements, parental leave, and the minimum notice period employees are entitled to in the event of termination. As for labour law, this legislation varies by jurisdiction. In addition, minimum standards laws may not apply to all employees. For example, part-timers, subcontractors, and temporary workers are often not covered. In some jurisdictions, entire industries such as farming, fishing, and domestic employment are also excluded. Finally, managers are excluded from some provisions (e.g., overtime pay). However, the main components of minimum standards legislation in Canada include the following:

1. *Minimum wages.* As of November 2010, the general minimum wage ranged from $8.00 per hour in British Columbia to $10.25 per hour in Ontario. Four jurisdictions had special, lower rates for certain categories of workers (e.g., those who receive gratuities, those with limited experience, and those under 18).

2. *Hours worked.* Although a number of jurisdictions have no limit on the maximum number of hours an employee can be asked to work, all have provisions for "standard" hours worked. This varies from 8 to 16 hours per day, and 40 to 48 hours per week. Where these amounts are exceeded, workers are normally entitled to an overtime pay rate of time-and-a-half their regular wage.

3. *Statutory holidays.* Statutory holidays, required by law and for which employees must normally be paid, range from five to ten days per year.

4. *Paid Vacations.* Annual vacation entitlements entail a minimum of two weeks paid vacation per year in all but one jurisdiction (it is three in Saskatchewan), though in six jurisdictions this increases to three weeks after an employee has been with the employer for a specified number of years (anywhere from 5 to

15, depending on the jurisdiction), and in one (Saskatchewan), it increases to four weeks after ten years of service.

5. *Pregnancy and parental leave.* Pregnancy leave entails the right to take time off in the period surrounding birth. Parental leave represents an additional period either taken off by one parent or shared by both. The former is typically 17 weeks in duration, and the latter 37 weeks. A majority of jurisdictions permit both parents to take full parental leave. Both leaves are unpaid and as such only ensure an employee's right to get her job back (or a similar one) provided certain requirements have been met. However, between them, new parents may be eligible to collect up to 52 weeks of employment insurance, at 55 percent of regular pay to a maximum of $457 per week (as of June 2010).

6. *Compassionate Care Leave.* Employees in all jurisdictions are entitled to leave in order to care for a family member in need. The maximum duration of this leave ranges from 8 to 16 weeks, although in some jurisdictions an employee may be entitled to an extension of this time if certain conditions are met.

7. *Termination.* Notice of termination is typically one or two weeks at minimum for an individual employee, although in most jurisdictions this period varies with the length of time an employee has been with the employer, extending up to eight weeks for employees with, for example, ten or more years of service. In the case of group termination (e.g., due to a permanent lay-off), this period may be extended to as long as eighteen weeks, although this often depends on the number of workers being laid off (larger layoffs can require longer periods).

Human Rights Legislation. Human rights legislation is intended to prevent discrimination against individuals on the basis of personal characteristics (e.g., race, gender, age, sexual orientation), beliefs (e.g., religion), affiliations (e.g., political party), or either physical or mental disability, unless it can be shown that doing so can be justified for performance reasons. Though there is some variation by jurisdiction in the specific grounds for discrimination, employers cannot discriminate on these bases in hiring, promotion practices, pay, or the conditions of employment, and they have a duty to do everything in their power to ensure that employees are not discriminated against or harassed by other employees. In most jurisdictions, there are exemptions from human rights law for religious and philanthropic organizations. For example, religious schools may be able to require their teaching staff to be of the same faith.

Human rights legislation is normally administered by a government-appointed commission or council, which hears and rules on individual complaints.[5] Where discrimination is found to have occurred, the remedy is usually to make employees "whole" by restoring them to the circumstance they would have been in had discrimination not occurred. For example, discrimination against an employee in the promotion process may mean that the employer is required to offer an equivalent position to the employee within a reasonable time period and to compensate the employee for any lost pay, expenses (e.g., hiring a lawyer), and mental duress.

In some cases, employers may discriminate indirectly or inadvertently by establishing job requirements that place a particular group at a disadvantage. Unless the employer can establish that there was a bona fide reason for these requirements, the employer may be held liable. That is, the employer must be able to establish that these requirements are directly necessary in order to satisfactorily perform the work. For example, airlines have traditionally required flight attendants to be women, to be within a certain weight limit, and to be below a certain age. Yet, although passengers may have come to expect these requirements, they have little to do with the actual tasks required of flight attendants. As such, they have been ruled to be in violation of human rights. Similarly, firefighters have traditionally been required to meet certain strength and height requirements, making it more difficult for women to qualify. The strength requirement is not a human rights violation if the employer can show that applicants who cannot meet this requirement cannot adequately do the job, but the height requirement is likely to be, especially if it is based on the assumption that shorter individuals are unlikely to be strong enough, which need not necessarily be the case.

There has also been a growing tendency to require employers to accommodate those employees who cannot fully comply with employer requirements or perform their duties under the same terms or conditions as others because of their gender, religion, or some related characteristic. In general, employers must do so if a failure to accommodate would constitute an undue hardship for the employee and any performance implications of failing to comply are not sufficient to justify this hardship. For example, if an employee has a physical disability

---

[5] See Peirce (2000: 235–39), for a lengthier discussion of this legislation.

and as a result needs special equipment to do her work, the employer may be required to provide this equipment, depending on its cost. This requirement is referred to as the **duty to accommodate**.

As suggested earlier, human rights law pertains not just to whether individuals are provided with the same opportunities as others, but also to the way they are treated on a day-to-day basis by others within their workplace. An employer may be found in violation of human rights law if an employee is harassed due to personal characteristics or beliefs that are protected under the law, regardless of whether this harassment is by superordinates, co-workers, customers, or others who the employee may come into contact in the course of doing her job. Sexual harassment has in this respect tended to attract the greatest attention in recent years. Two forms have been identified:

1. Exercising, or promising to exercise authority, either explicitly or implicitly, in a way that is either beneficial or harmful to an employee if the employee provides or fails to provide a sexual favour.
2. Allowing a "poisoned" work environment to exist, in which the employee is subject to insults, humour, or other behaviour likely to cause the employee psychological distress.

As may be apparent, it can be difficult to establish specifically whether either of these forms of harassment has occurred. Much may depend on the specific actions involved and the context within which they have taken place. As may also be apparent, the second form in particular can impose a substantial burden on the employer, who may have difficulty altering the work environment, especially if the behaviour is deeply ingrained (e.g., as in traditional all-male or all-female occupations) or extends to customers, suppliers, or others outside of its scope of authority. However, only the employer has the authority to ensure a harassment-free environment. If the employer does not exercise its authority accordingly, an individual employee may otherwise have little alternative but to quit, which most would agree is not a fair solution.

Normally, the employee who is subject to harassment must notify the employer and allow the employer an opportunity to rectify matters prior to taking the matter to a human rights tribunal. But if the employer fails to act accordingly, it may ultimately be found in violation of the law, regardless of whether its own employees are the cause of the problem. To avoid such a finding, the employer must be able to establish that it responded seriously and rapidly to the employee's complaint and that it introduced a sexual harassment policy into the workplace, identifying inappropriate forms of conduct and outlining the process by which employees can issue complaints should such conduct occur. Where the employer has been able to establish that other employees have engaged in such conduct, it is expected to have disciplined these employees accordingly.

Pay and Employment Equity Legislation. Pay and employment equity legislation is intended to eliminate established inequalities in the pay received by women and members of minority groups working for a given employer. These inequalities may not reflect attempts to explicitly discriminate, but may have developed over time, with women or minority groups tending to be clustered into lower paying occupations and positions. If it can be established that employees in these groups are paid less than other employees, yet perform work with equivalent skill, effort, and responsibility levels, then an employer may be required to improve their pay accordingly. If it can be established that these jobs indeed have lower skill, effort, and responsibility requirements, the employer may be required to identify and eliminate (to the extent reasonable) any barriers preventing these groups from qualifying for better jobs and to engage in positive hiring and training practices in an attempt to ensure that they are fairly represented. However, the nature and extent of pay and employment equity legislation varies considerably across jurisdictions. For example, in some jurisdictions, pay equity laws may only apply in the public sector, while in others they may include the private sector as well.

Health and Safety Legislation. Health and safety legislation requires employers both to meet specific health and safety standards *and* to promote health and safety at work in general. While the former can entail elaborate and often highly detailed regulations, the latter means that employers have a general duty to ensure a safe working environment. This includes ensuring that its employees and supervisors are properly trained on matters of health and safety, that equipment is properly maintained, that protective equipment is being properly used, and that it cooperates with health and safety officials (England, 2005: 251). In addition, individual workers have the right to refuse unsafe work without fear of reprisal, and employers are required to give workers notification of and access to information about health and safety risks. This latter requirement is especially stringent for hazardous materials, due to a nationally agreed system requiring elaborate labelling, handling, and risk assessment procedures (the Workplace Hazardous Materials Information System). Finally, all jurisdictions require the establishment of joint labour–management health and safety committees in workplaces above a certain size (usually 20 employees). These committees are to contain an equal number of employee and employer representatives, and must meet on a regular basis (e.g., at least once every three months) to address health and safety issues, including worker complaints, health and safety training, any new government standards or reports of relevance, and other matters. However, they exist largely in an advisory and informational capacity, and as such lack the power to require an actual change in employer practices.

Unjust Dismissal Law. Under Canadian law, an employee is said to enter into an employment contract with his/her employer at such time as he/she is hired, regardless of whether this contract is in writing. Under this contract, the employer is obliged to provide workers with the type of work for which they have been hired or have become accustomed to once in the employment relation, in accordance with the terms and conditions agreed to or understood by the parties. The employee is in turn expected to perform his or her job honestly and competently and to obey the orders of the employer, provided they are legal, reasonable, and within the scope of the employee's normal duties.

If an employee has been meeting these criteria, yet the employer still wishes to terminate the employment contract, the employee must be given a reasonable period of time in which to find new employment, referred to as **reasonable notice**. If such notice is not given, the employee is entitled to be paid the amount he or she would have earned during the period. The minimum notice period is established under employment standards law, as discussed earlier in this chapter. However, the employee may have an agreement with the employer specifying a longer period of time. If not, the employer may still be obliged to provide a longer period if it can be established that the employee is likely to require such a period due to the state of the labour market or the employee's personal skills and qualifications, length of service, experience, age, or occupation. For most lower level, unskilled occupations, this period may be no longer than the minimum termination notice specified under employment standards legislation. But for higher level professional and managerial occupations, this period may be deemed to be as long as 24 months or even longer.

If an employee has not been performing his/her job honestly and competently, there may be grounds for dismissal without notice. However, unless the employee has engaged in serious misconduct, such as dishonesty, flagrant insubordination, or gross incompetence, the employer must first give the employee reasonable warnings and opportunities to correct his/her behaviour. Otherwise, the employer will be said to have engaged in **unjust dismissal**. The criteria involved are outlined in Box 9–1.

One tactic sometimes used by employers is to engage in **constructive dismissal**. Constructive dismissal is said to have occurred if, rather than dismissing an employee outright, the employer unilaterally alters the type of work the employee performs or the terms and conditions

---

BOX 9–1   When Can You Fire Someone with Just Cause?

♦ *Randall Scott Echlin*

To allege or not to allege just cause? That's the question facing many employers in terminating staff members after workplace misconduct.

Recent cases show that Canadian courts increasingly take a dim view of companies that allege just cause for tactical reasons, and then abandon the allegations either shortly before or at trial.

Several decisions have showed that additional damages against the employer are appropriate in such circumstances.

So how does an employer decide whether there is serious enough misconduct to sustain the legal finding of just cause? And even if there is just cause, is it always the best business decision to allege it in the circumstances?

To answer these questions, professional advice is needed in assessing the evidence. Can the case be proven to the satisfaction of a court?

It is also important to review matters from a business standpoint. How much time and money will be consumed in dealing with the expected litigation?

Aside from out-of-pocket expenses, there is the management time involved.

Also, litigating with a former employee will have a negative effect on the "survivors" in the work place. The litigation will attract unwanted publicity and may affect suppliers and customers.

Continued....

BOX 9-1 (continued)

Before making a business decision, the likelihood of succeeding with a just cause should not be asserted if:

- The decision to dismiss the employee has been made quickly and without reflection.
- The employer is acting out of anger or frustration. A cooling-off period is always advisable before a decision is made.
- A level of substandard performance or misconduct has been knowingly accepted for a period of time.
- This is an isolated, out-of-character incident. Is a second chance appropriate?

If the misconduct is serious enough, before dismissing a worker for just cause an employer should properly investigate the incident. The company should interview all witnesses and ensure they will testify.

The employer should decide whether the misconduct is of such a nature that the company wants to send a message to others in the work place that it does not tolerate such actions.

Aside from reviewing all the factual circumstances and making a dispassionate determination, companies should be particularly careful dealing with long-service employees.

Recent case law has indicated that they are expected to give more leeway to a veteran worker than to a recent hire.

An isolated incident of poor judgment might not be found to be just cause because the employee is owed "more than the benefit of the doubt." Courts have held that loyalty and additional support come into play with long-service staff. In this way, employment contracts are viewed in a different light than standard commercial contracts.

If a company intends to allege just cause, it must be careful it does not knowingly "condone" the misconduct upon which it is relying. An employer cannot knowingly decide to continue the employment of someone who has committed serious misconduct and then later try to dismiss the employee for the same wrongdoing.

Alleging just cause also requires a great deal of time and labour. A short-service, low-level employee may simply not merit the expense and resources involved. If the employee's entitlement is minimal, it may be preferable, from a business standpoint, to simply make a severance offer and call it a day.

Before dismissing for just cause, employers should investigate thoroughly and afford the individual his or her "day in court." A company should confront the person with the allegations of

Continued....

> ## BOX 9–1 (continued)
>
> wrongdoing and call for and receive answers. By acting in this fashion, an employer will avoid jumping to conclusions and hanging people for crimes they might not have committed.
>
> The vast majority of dismissals in Canada do not involve employee misconduct sufficient to stand as just cause. Most partings of the way arise from corporate reorganizations, downsizings, or more trifling dissatisfactions.
>
> There are high risks in making a just-cause allegation, proceeding to fire an employee without notice or severance pay, and then entering into one or two years of litigation.
>
> There is much riding on who wins and who loses. The result is usually black or white, because the Supreme Court of Canada has indicated that near cause (misconduct that falls short of just cause) does not exist. There is no halfway house. At trial, there is no room for compromise.
>
> Depriving individuals of their livelihood while making serious allegations of misconduct is a highstakes game. It may be appropriate in certain instances, such as provable theft or sexual harassment. However, in many cases involving lesser transgressions, discipline short of outright dismissal, including warnings, may be more appropriate.
>
> The law requires employment decisions be taken carefully. Similarly, common decency and business efficacy demand no less.
>
> If employers approach such matters with care and thoughtfulness after a proper investigation, having given the individual an opportunity to respond, the right result will be achieved.
>
> **Source:** From *The Globe and Mail* (February 21, 2000), p. M-1. Courtesy of The Honourable Mr. Justice Randall Scott Echlin, Superior Court of Justice (Ontario).

associated with it so that they are no longer consistent with what the employee has become accustomed to and the employee therefore perceives little option but to quit. Where this is the case, the employer's actions are deemed to have had the same consequence as an outright dismissal and hence have the same status as unjust dismissal. An example would be where a high level manager has been demoted to a low level support staff position. The loss of pay and status, coupled with the requirement that the employee perform duties that do not use his or her skills and expertise, would make continued employment untenable to the employee, and hence would have the same ultimate effect as outright dismissal.

If the employee in question is covered by a union contract, he or she may seek redress through the grievance procedure, subject to the terms of the collective agreement (see chapter fourteen). In a few jurisdictions, there is also a legally mandated adjudication process to which non-union employees may apply, provided they were in a non-managerial position and meet length-of-service requirements (e.g., one year in the federal jurisdiction). But otherwise, the employee has only two alternatives, both of which may prove unsatisfactory.

The first alternative is to turn to the relevant government employment standards agency. However, this agency can only at best require the employer to pay the employee the amount owed for failing to meet the minimum notice period established under employment standards legislation, and cannot order the employer to reinstate the employee.

The second alternative is to take the employer to court on the grounds that the notice period should be longer than the legal minimum. Normally, the appropriate period is established in accordance with the criteria referred to above for reasonable notice. But if it can be established that the employer has acted unprofessionally or in bad faith in handling the dismissal, it may be extended by as much as eight months. The courts may also extend this period if it can be established that the employee had recently left a secure, well-paid job in order to work for the employer, in the expectation that the employer would provide similar security.

Although this second alternative can yield more compensation for the employee, it also suffers from problems. First, as in the first alternative, it does not allow the employee to win reinstatement. Second, and more important, it can entail an uncertain, stressful, and expensive process. For most lower and middle level employees, it is not likely to yield enough by way of additional compensation to make this worthwhile. Except under unique circumstances, the only employees likely to find it so are those in managerial and professional occupations, as they are typically considered to require a substantially longer notice period than established under employment standards law, and their pay levels are substantially higher to begin with, thus increasing the amount of money involved. Yet, even here, employers are often able to effectively bribe employees into accepting substantially less than they might otherwise be entitled to in return for not having to go through the court process.

Overall. As may be apparent, there is much that can be criticized about employment standards legislation. For example, the possibility that someone could work for an employer for a lengthy period of time and then be summarily dismissed without due process and with only a few weeks or months notice or pay in lieu of notice seems out of place in a society with any pretence to democratic values. It also seems difficult to understand how minimum wages could be so low: even employees working full-time, 40-hour weeks year-round are likely to find themselves living below the poverty line (before any government transfers), especially if they have any children to support. Two weeks also seems to be a remarkably short vacation period in a country as economically advanced as Canada. In turn, maternity and parental leaves in combination typically allow a new mother a year prior to returning to work. Yet, at a maximum of $457 per week, this can mean a substantial economic sacrifice, especially where the mother is the primary household income earner. Complicating matters, enforcement of many of the employment laws on the books is notoriously weak. This is especially true of health and safety legislation, as evidenced by the discussion in chapter three. But it also applies to much of employment law, as many who have worked in part-time, temporary, or some other form of marginal employment can attest to.

An even more fundamental shortcoming is the absence of any a priori right for employees to have some form of *legal* representation or rights of participation in the workplace. In a democratic society, one would expect that workers would have substantial say in what happens to them at work — especially given that, for many, their job is a central life activity. It seems difficult to justify why those with perhaps *the* major stake in organization decisions have so little input. To an extent, the right to be represented by a union addresses this. But as discussed above, under the current system of labour law, only a third of all working Canadians are so represented. Moreover, the residual rights doctrine sharply limits the ability to obtain participatory rights, even though these may be in high demand. For example, a 1994 U.S. survey found that over eight out of ten workers would prefer their organization to be run jointly by employees and management. Nine out of ten workers had a preference for some form of elected representation (Freeman and Rogers, 1999: 142, 147). There is little reason to believe this is any different in Canada.

These shortcomings are typically justified on the grounds that stronger employment laws would impose an undue economic burden on employers, and ultimately result in job losses. But the extent to which this is the case is unclear. For example, considerable research has now been conducted into the effects of minimum wage increases, and this research reveals that moderate increases have few negative effects, especially where there is a lower minimum for vulnerable groups, such as teens (e.g., Neumark and Wascher, 2004).

In addition, one need not look hard to find examples of countries that do far better. For example, in Germany, everyone is entitled to a minimum of six weeks holidays. In addition, workers in firms with over five employees also have an a priori right to form a **works council**, consisting of elected representatives with extensive say in most, if not all, decisions directly affecting employees. In Britain, employees have the right to representation and due process prior to dismissal whether a union is recognized or not, and may take their case to an industrial tribunal for adjudication if they have one year or more of service. They also have information-sharing and consultation rights on a variety of issues, including employer strategy and workplace change. Finally, in Sweden, maternity leave is 16 months, the first 13 of which are at 80 percent of pay, up to about $750 per week (as of 2009).

Even if such laws do impose economic burdens on employers, it is difficult to believe that these burdens are so great as to deny Canadian citizens (or anybody else) what would seem to be such basic rights and protections. At minimum, there is need to pay much greater attention to how any such burdens can be minimized (Godard, 2003b).

II. THE EMPLOYER ROLE

The role of the state as an employer extends beyond the employment of civil servants to include that of teachers, university professors, hospital workers, nurses, police, firefighters, social workers, postal employees, and any number of additional groups at the municipal, provincial, and federal levels. Combined, public sector employment accounts for close to a quarter of all jobs in Canada. Three-quarters of the workers in these jobs are covered by a collective agreement, compared to one-fifth in the private sector (Statistics Canada, 2010). This may in part reflect the preponderance of large workplaces and employers in the public sector, as large workplaces are far more likely to be unionized. Nonetheless, it means that roughly half of all union members are public sector employees. In fact, the two largest unions in Canada are the Canadian Union of Public Employees, and the National Union of Public and General Employees. Together, they have well over three-quarters of a million members (see Table 8–1).

A major problem that arises in the public sector, however, is that governments are responsible for making the laws which regulate labour–management relations in their sector as well as the private sector. Thus, while neutrality can be maintained in the private sector, in the public sector the government has a clear interest in enacting laws and setting policies which are biassed in its favour. This problem is especially serious when governments are responsible for laws governing their own employees, which is generally the case at the provincial and federal levels (municipalities are generally subject to provincial laws).

This problem is also complicated by the fact that public sector work often involves the provision of "essential services" and occurs outside of the "discipline" of the market system. As such, government not only has an interest in enacting policies and laws which give it the upper hand, it also has a ready-made justification for doing so. Thus, for example, when postal workers go on strike, the federal government can (and has done on more than one occasion) order them back to work on the grounds that the postal service is an essential one. When government wants to impose wage controls upon civil servants and hence circumvent the bargaining process, as the federal and a number of provincial governments did in 1982–83, or when it wishes to unilaterally freeze wages so that unions cannot bargain over them, as the federal and the Ontario governments did in the early 1990s (Panitch and Swartz, 2003: 173, 186), it can claim that this is justified by the insulation of these workers from market forces. When concerned about the ability of a group of public sector employees to impose costs on them through a strike, governments can simply eliminate or restrict their right to strike on the grounds that all or a portion of the workers in question provide an essential service.

This is not to suggest that restrictions are unjustified in the public sector. It is to suggest, however, that because of their vested interests, governments are likely to err on the side of imposing more, rather than fewer, restrictions on public sector unions than may be necessary. The *extent* to which they do so is in part constrained by public opinion, though the public often also has a vested interest in these restrictions and, it would seem, has over the past few decades been less and less sympathetic towards public sector workers. This, coupled with the election of increasingly conservative governments at the federal and a number of provincial levels since the early 1980s, has meant an increase in government restrictions on public sector workers and their unions, and a markedly increased willingness to order striking public sector employees back to work (see Panitch and Swartz, 2003).

Although some of these actions may have been justified, it seems clear that there is a need of some mechanism for ensuring that the rights of public sector workers are not abrogated for reasons of political expediency. Presently, however, there appears to be little appetite for such a mechanism amongst Canada's political leaders.

III. THE FACILITATIVE ROLE

In addition to its role as regulator and as employer, states can — by intention or otherwise — shape the beliefs and values adhered to by the parties. They can also provide support services which assist the parties in various ways.

State policies toward unions in general may be particularly important. It has historically been argued that the state serves as an exemplar both in the way it treats its own employees and in the policies it adopts towards the regulation of unions and employment relations in general. For example, if the state adopts positive policies towards unions, employees may feel more encouraged to join a union while employers may feel more obligated to respect or even encourage employees to exercise their right to unionize. It has been argued, for example, that government normative support and pressures on employers rather than labour law per se represents the main explanation for union growth in the United States during the 1940s (Adams and Markey, 1997). It has also been argued that, in the U.K., government normative support for collective bargaining can be credited for union density levels of approximately 57 percent by the late 1970s, despite a lack of effective labour law protection (see Adams, 1994). Conversely, it has also been argued that hostile government actions help to account for the decline of unions in both of these countries during the 1980s and 1990s.[6]

In addition to policies towards unions, states have actively attempted to facilitate diffusion of high performance work practices, in the belief that these are consistent with employer interests, but that employers either lack the expertise and support necessary to implement

---

[6] In the United States, Ronald Reagan's hiring of replacement workers when air traffic controllers went on strike in the early 1980s is viewed by many as helping to create a normative environment condoning and perpetuating anti-union employer practices (e.g., Dubofsky, 1994: 228–29). In the United Kingdom, Margaret Thatcher's government succeeded in breaking the miner's union in the mid-1980s. Coupled with other policies and legal reforms implemented by this government, this appears to have signalled an end to state support for collective bargaining, and a new era in which unions were to be discour-

them on their own (Kochan and Osterman, 1994: 210–12) or need to be educated as to the advantages of these practices. For example, in the United States the Office for the American Workplace was established within the Department of Labor in 1993 to provide assistance in the implementation of new forms of work organization, although it became a victim of cutbacks three years later. The Baldrige Award was established in 1988, to create a normative environment in which employers adopting these practices could receive national recognition.

This approach need not be restricted to high performance practices per se. In Britain, there has been a long history of government agencies promulgating "codes of practice" (most notably with respect to appropriate disciplinary procedures) and diffusing these through seminars and training sessions (Gennard and Judge, 1997: 175–79). The government also grants an "Investors in People" certification, along the lines of an ISO (International Standards Organization) quality accreditation, to employers meeting certain training standards (see Pfeffer, 1998: 286). Both of these are intended to induce employers to adopt "good practice" through a combination of education and exhortation.

There are fewer explicit examples in Canada. However, Human Resources and Skills Development Canada (HRSDC) has adopted a number of strategies to attempt to promote high performance work organizations, including the 1998 launch of a new periodical, *The Workplace Gazette*, to disseminate information as to developments in labour–management relations in general, and the diffusion of high performance work practices in particular. This would also appear to be a major mission of the Workplace Information Directorate, a department within HRSDC. Its Web page[7] is a treasure trove of information as to labour and employment law, relevant statistics, and other considerations. In addition, Canadian governments (as do their U.S. and U.K. counterparts) offer mediation and conciliation services to help the parties resolve disputes. In the case of the federal government, this service also offers a number of programs to promote more harmonious labour–management relationships.

The effectiveness of these programs is uncertain, and they seem to be poor substitutes for the provision of meaningful rights and

---

aged rather than encouraged. In both countries, union density was to plummet. Although a number of other factors were undoubtedly involved, it would be a mistake to think that actions did not help to create a less favourable normative environment for unions.

[7] The address is <http://www.hrsdc.gc.ca/en/lp/wid/contact/contact_us.shtml>.

protections to workers. Often, there may be a disjuncture between what the "experts" believe to be in the best interests of the parties and what the parties themselves believe to be in their interests. Nonetheless, where this is not the case, and where these programs are used as complements to, rather than substitutes for, meaningful rights and protections, they may play an important role.

IV. THE STRUCTURAL ROLE

The state also structures the industrial relations context in ways that have important implications for the parties. It may do this in a number of ways, but two would appear to be most important: (1) shaping the economic and financial constraints to which employers are subject, and (2) shaping labour market conditions.

Economic and Financial Constraints

State policies may shape the economic pressures and opportunities to which employers are subject. Most notable in this respect are trade policies, which affect both the intensity of competition and opportunity for market expansion. But policies altering the level of economic activity can affect the level of competitive pressure to which employers are subject, particularly with respect to whether they are in growing or contracting markets. For example, state **monetary policies,** as enacted by the Bank of Canada, determine the rate of interest at which chartered banks are able to borrow money from the federal government. At risk of oversimplification, higher bank rates increase the costs of borrowing within the economy in general and reduce the level of consumer spending. As a result, employers can find themselves subject to contracting markets and hence higher levels of competitive pressure.

Also important are government **fiscal policies**, especially the structure of taxation laws and the level of government spending. For example, a government may increase its level of expenditure so that it exceeds revenues, thus stimulating the economy and hence reducing the competitive pressures to which employers are subject.

In turn, competitive pressures are generally believed to have a "disciplinary" function, limiting both worker wage and benefit expectations and employer willingness to grant more favourable terms and conditions of employment. In theory, they also induce employers to engage in a continuous search for productivity enhancing technologies and innovative work methods. Yet if too severe, these pressures may also be manifest through "short-termism", as discussed in chapter three. In other words, competitive pressures may induce employers to attempt to enhance productivity through short-term cost-cutting and work intensification, forsaking the kind of long-term policy commitments associated with a well-trained, experienced, and loyal workforce (e.g., Soskice, 1990a; Hutton, 1995). The result is a "low cost" approach to industrial relations, involving regressive "low skill, low wage, low quality" policies, rather than the "high commitment" approach involving more progressive "high skill, high wage, high quality" policies advocated by proponents of the high performance model (discussed in chapter five).

State policies may further heighten the problem of short-termism if they foster risk and uncertainty (Corry, 1997). For example, flexible exchange rates, deregulation of domestic markets, and promotion of new technologies may all enhance risk and uncertainty, inducing employers to turn to more flexible or precarious employment policies (see chapter five), where they hire employees on a part-time and temporary basis rather than a full-time, permanent basis (Mitchell and Zaidi, 1996: 18). They may also induce employers to adopt a short-term view towards their regular employees, investing less in training and providing lower job security.

Policies shaping financial markets and the relation between managers and owners may be even more important (Porter, 1992; Roe, 1994; Hutton, 1995; Gospel and Pendleton, 2003). To the extent that these pressure management to maximize shareholder value over the short-term, they can also be expected to give rise to short-termism, having effects similar to intensified competitive pressures identified above. To the extent that any such pressures are long-term, this may be less likely to be the case, with possible implications for the effects of economic policies discussed above. Over the past decade, there has been a growing concern that North American and British employers have increasingly come to fit in the former category, especially with the growth of mutual funds that place them under continuous pressure to demonstrate high returns over the short run. As noted in chapter three, the opposite is reputed to have been the case in, for example, Japan and Germany (Berglof, 1990; Porter, 1992), where interlocking ownership (Japan) and extensive bank financing (Germany) have meant that direct shareholder control is limited, thereby reducing the pressures for short-term results. Though these differences can only be partially attributed to state policies, it would appear that these policies have played an important role (see Doremus et al., 1998; Vitols, 2001).

Labour Market Conditions

State policies also operate through their implications for labour markets. Tight monetary policies, as embodied in high interest rates, not only enhance competitive pressures, they also increase unemployment, affecting the ease with which employers can attract and retain qualified employees, with unemployment, in turn, serving as a further disciplinary device. That is, unemployment may render employees more compliant than otherwise, because they have fewer alternatives and are more fearful of job loss (Kalecki, 1971 [1943]). In turn, where employees are easy to replace, have low mobility, and are fearful of job loss, employers may have far less incentive to adopt a high commitment approach, because employee loyalty is already at a satisfactory level, and various behavioural problems (including quits) are minimal. Under these conditions, employers may also find more casual, low-cost policies effective, because employees have little alternative but to accept what is offered them, and little expectation of the employer.

These effects may be especially strong where the state has failed to enact or has cut back on social and labour market programs designed to minimize the costs of job loss (Burawoy, 1985: 126). In effect, the creation of coercive labour markets, through a combination of high unemployment and weak support programs effectively helps to reduce the problems of motivation and control for employers, rendering more expensive high commitment policies less necessary. This appears to have been the case in Canada and the United Kingdom during the 1980s and early 1990s (Godard, 1997a). Conversely, low unemployment and strong labour market programs (e.g., high unemployment benefits, generous training and relocation programs) render employee motivation and control more difficult, making high commitment practices necessary (Berggren, 1992: 19).

Trade agreements also play an important role. In addition to heightening the economic pressures to which employers are subject, relaxed trade restrictions essentially render employers more mobile and the workplace more readily "disposable" (Drago, 1996). As discussed in chapter five, employees are as a result effectively coerced to cooperate in workplace change programs for fear of job loss, again enabling employers to rely on a lower cost control approach rather than a higher cost commitment approach. This appears to have been the case in the auto industry, explaining the number of studies indicating that new forms of work organization in this industry often entail little more than an intensification of the labour process (see Landsbergis, Cahill, and Schnall, 1999). There is also concern that employers can use this mobility to extract concessions from unions with regard to collective agreement provisions, and from states with regard to labour law and employment standards (see Gunderson, 1998, for a review of the relevant literature). This possibility has been a major concern with respect to the North American Free Trade Agreement (NAFTA) involving Canada, the United States, and Mexico, although the long-term effects of this agreement have been difficult to establish.

There may be important interactions between labour market conditions and the degree of regulation of the employment relation. For example, in the early 1980s, conservative governments were elected in both the United States and Canada. Both sought to curb what they considered to be unacceptable levels of union militancy and inflationary wage gains. But in Canada, limited federal government jurisdiction over labour law meant that it had to rely on monetary policies to do so. In contrast, the federal government in the United States was able to rely directly on weakened labour laws and labour law enforcement, rendering harsh monetary policies less "necessary" (Godard, 1997a: 414–20).

As a further example, Michael Burawoy (1985: 126) argues not only that improved state social insurance programs and legislation have historically resulted in a shift from "despotic" (i.e., based on coercion) to "hegemonic" (i.e., based on consent) workplace "regimes", and that the degree and form of state regulation has played an important role in explaining differences in the form of hegemonic regime to emerge. Comparing Britain to the United States, he argues that, in Britain a lack of state regulation of industrial relations helped give rise to a system of informal or "fractional" bargaining in the workplace, while in the United States the Wagner Act and related legislation helped give rise to a more bureaucratic one (1985: 138–48). Burawoy also explicitly incorporates a role for trade policy, arguing that, coupled with a lack of state control over the movement of capital, free trade policies are giving rise to a new type of regime, which he labels "hegemonic despotism", because although it entails consent, this consent is coerced by the fear of job loss (1985: 148–52).

Finally, labour market conditions may even have implications for training and skill levels. Glynn and Gospel (1993) have argued that low skill levels in an economy may reflect a demand rather than a supply side problem. Drawing on the U.K. experience, they establish that low unemployment has historically been associated with improvements in workforce quality and productivity in the U.K., because employers have a greater incentive to efficiently utilize labour and to reward investments in education and training workers.

V.   THE CONSTITUTIVE ROLE

States also play an important role in shaping and enforcing rules and rights which form the basis for economic activity in general (see Fligstein, 1996: 660–65). As such, the state plays an important role in how modern economies are constituted. Most important in the present analysis, however, is the role of the state in constituting the employment relation itself. To illustrate this role, it is useful to distinguish between predominantly "liberal market economies" and predominantly "co-ordinated market economies" (see Hall and Soskice, 2001). Both entail extensive state involvement in order to function (see Klare, 1988: 17–24; Polanyi, 1944). But in the former, established institutions primarily facilitate *rather than* constrain markets, while in the latter, established institutions constrain, *as well as* facilitate, markets.

In predominantly liberal market economies, such as the United States and Canada, the employment relation is treated by the state as a contract of service rather than of partnership or cooperation (Arthurs et al., 1993: 131). As such, it is considered distinct from ordinary contracts under property law (see Hepple, 1986: 11). Unlike a contract between two legal equals, in which legal rights and obligations not explicitly agreed on by the parties derive from implicit understandings and norms that have developed over time, the employment contract is interpreted as providing employers with broad residual authority over virtually all matters not specified in contractual form (see Block, 1994: 701–702; Godard, 1998a; Hepple, 1986). As discussed in chapter three, employees are generally deemed to be in positions of subordination to managerial authority, with little, if any, say over how this authority is exercised.

Not only does the employment relation become an asymmetrical one once entered into, managers are generally under a fiduciary obligation to owners (if they are not themselves owners). The result is that capital-labour interest conflicts become internalized within the employment relation, as managers seek to manage the firm in accordance with ownership interests, with little direct accountability to employees. This fundamentally shapes both how employers conceive of their rights and obligations with respect to the exercise of authority and how employees react to this exercise. This, in turn, has critical implications for the actions of both parties and the relations between them, as discussed throughout this book (especially chapter three).

In more co-ordinated market economies, such as Germany and the Netherlands, employees are also in positions of subordination. However, they may be granted a number of rights which bring the employment relation closer to a common law conception of contractual relations. In Germany, for example, workers have legal "co-determination" rights which appear to substantially alter the legal relation between management and workers and ultimately the goals which underlie managerial decisions. These rights include extensive worker representation on boards of directors (referred to as "supervisory boards") as well as "works councils" (discussed earlier). One of the results is that labour–management relations are far less adversarial. Another appears to be that employers are more likely to forgo the "low cost" route in favour of one that entails high skill and wage levels (Streeck, 1997).

Overall, therefore, it may be the constitutive role of the state which is its most important one, because it effectively determines the nature of the employment relation, with implications for the problems and concerns which the state is required to address in its other roles.

VI. CONCLUSIONS

This chapter has addressed five roles of the state: the regulative role, the state as employer role, the facilitative role, the structural role, and the constitutive role. When these roles are considered in combination, it becomes apparent that the state really is a key actor in industrial relations even if its role is often indirect and hence not immediately obvious. For this reason, it is important to discuss variation in how these roles are served and why this variation occurs. This is the task of the following chapter.

Understanding
the State

10

In chapter four it was argued that governments in Canada have faced a basic dilemma. On the one hand, they have historically sought to maintain the institutional status quo. Yet, in part because of conflicts underlying the labour–management relationship, they have often been faced with considerable economic unrest and industrial conflict. Thus, in order to maintain the order and stability necessary to attain this outcome, they have found it necessary to provide workers with increased rights and protections, and these have in turn had the effect of altering the status quo. In short, they have had to alter the status quo in order to maintain it. This chapter first provides a brief historical overview of the development of state labour relations policies in Canada, going beyond the discussion in chapter four. Then, it turns to various theories as to why these policies evolve as they do and who they serve.

I. THE DEVELOPMENT OF STATE POLICIES IN CANADA: A BRIEF REVIEW

The argument that Canadian government policies are driven by a desire to maintain order and stability is undoubtedly oversimplified, for these policies are shaped by a variety of considerations — as we shall see in the next section. Moreover, the extent to which the status quo has been substantively altered as a result of these policies can be debated, especially as the underlying nature of the employment relation remains largely unchanged. Yet, this basic argument provides a useful frame of reference for analyzing the development of state policies and actions in industrial relations. For now, it is useful to distinguish five phases in the development of state policy:

(1) repression, (2) containment, (3) paternalism, (4) accommodation, and (5) retrenchment.[1]

Repression (pre-1870s). Until the 1870s, state policies in industrial relations were largely repressive. It was illegal both for workers to form unions for the purpose of raising wages and for them to strike against their employers. As such, workers not only had no rights or protections vis-à-vis their employers, they were subject to possible legal sanctions if they sought such rights and protections through collective action. These sanctions did not completely preclude workers from organizing. Nor did they prevent them from striking: for example, Canada's first strike wave occurred during the 1850s, despite a number prosecutions during this decade (Russell, 1990: 45–46). Yet, they did mean that these actions had no legitimacy under the law, and at minimum served to dampen union activities.

Containment (1870s–1900s). The early 1870s saw the constraints on unions relaxed. In an attempt to reduce the length of the working day, organizations associated with the Nine-Hour Movement developed a coordinated strategy that foresaw a series of strikes if employers resisted their demands. This strategy was upset and the momentum of the movement broken when the Toronto printers struck ahead of time and its leaders were taken to court by the newspaper publishers. Yet the Nine-Hour Movement did demonstrate the ability of worker organizations to challenge the status quo. It also made it clear that laws repressing unions and strike activity were not only not effective, but could give rise to broader class-wide unrest — unrest that could ultimately threaten the status quo. As such, it served as a major impetus to the enactment by Parliament of the Trade Union Act of 1872, which recognized the right of workers to form unions and exempted them from conspiracy charges for engaging in collective activities. However, it was also accompanied by legislation making it illegal to picket one's employer (Russell, 1990: 47). Thus, although it may have provided political legitimacy for unions, the 1872 Act can be viewed, in large part, as an attempt to contain unrest and the growth of working class organizations. For the next three decades, workers were to remain subject to coercive employer practices, which were often reinforced by government actions ordering workers back to work or even providing police assistance to put down strikes.

---

[1] See Sack and Lee (1989), for a similar breakdown and analysis.

Paternalism (1900s–1940s). Though the Trade Union Act may have helped to head off widespread class conflict in the late nineteenth century, strike activity became increasingly predominant with the growth of industry, especially after the turn of the century. Thus, the state began to develop a more paternalistic role, providing for conciliation in order to avoid industrial unrest. Of particular note was the Industrial Disputes Investigation Act (IDIA) of 1907, enacted largely in response to the western Canada coal strike of autumn 1906 and requiring the parties to undergo conciliation after a cooling off period. As was the case for the Trade Union Act, this Act was also something of a mixed blessing, because it interfered with the right of workers to strike. Its overall implications for the labour movement have thus been a matter for some debate. Yet, it *did* have the effect of further enhancing the legitimacy of labour unions, and in this sense can be seen as a precursor to the accommodation of labour unions within the status quo.

The adoption of a more paternalistic role did not, of course, mean an outlawing of coercive management practices; these remained widespread. It also did not mean an end to coercive state practices, as witnessed by the state's role in putting down the Winnipeg General Strike of 1919. Moreover, state policies appear to have played a key role in retarding the growth of labour unions throughout the 1920s and 1930s. Of particular note were open immigration policies which helped keep unemployment rates high and provided a sure source of replacement workers in the event of a strike. In short, state polices and laws continued for the most part to create a hostile environment for both workers and their unions.

Accommodation (1940s–1970s). It was only with the rapid growth of the labour movement, coupled with widespread unrest both during and after the second world war, that the governments in Canada were induced to accommodate unions within the status quo, passing laws which protected the right to organize unions free from intimidation and requiring employers to bargain in "good faith". Again, however, the state appears to have been motivated, in large part, by the objective of maintaining order and stability. Particularly important were strikes over employer refusals to recognize and bargain with unions, which became especially widespread after World War II. In the absence of a legislative framework compelling employers to accept collective bargaining, a continuation of these strikes would, at minimum, have jeopardized the post-war economic recovery, and, at maximum, created the conditions for a more direct challenge to the status quo. Similar problems arose in the public sector in the 1960s and these, in turn, were a major impetus to the enactment of legislation legalizing collective bargaining in this sector during this decade, most notably the Public Service Staff Relations Act (PSSRA) of 1967.

Despite the state's accommodation of the labour movement, unions remained at best "junior partners" in the status quo throughout the 1950s and 1960s. Indeed, there was a quid pro quo for this accommodation: the right to strike was limited only to disputes over the negotiation of collective agreements. This was even more the case in the public than in the private sector, where the right to strike was (and still is) often highly circumscribed. In essence, a guiding belief underlying the enactment of much post-war labour legislation was that conflict is a fact of life and that rather than attempting to repress it, order and stability are better preserved by establishing institutions which enable it to be resolved in an orderly fashion. Thus, emergent labour laws appear to have been designed more to foster order and stability than to provide workers with rights and protections per se.

In addition to accommodating the labour movement, the early post-war era was one in which high and stable levels of unemployment became a central concern of the federal government, and in which a variety of social programs were introduced or greatly expanded — including Unemployment Insurance, Family Allowances, the Canada Pension Plan, and, by the early 1960s, universal medicare. These policies were implemented partly for humanitarian reasons, and to foster stable economic growth (Campbell, 1991: 4). But as was the case for labour law, it would appear that they were also motivated in large part by an attempt to pre-empt more radical change (Campbell, 1991). After the hardships of the 1930s, there was considerable concern within federal government circles (and elsewhere) that a failure to provide opportunities for employment and relative security could mean widespread unrest, with the country even, in Mackenzie King's words, "falling into the hands of inexperienced men who might head its affairs in the directions of a socialistic state" (cited in Campbell, 1991: 2). These and related policies and programs not only meant an increased role for the state in the economy, they also meant a considerable growth in the size of the public sector as an employer.

Retrenchment (1970s–2000s). By the late 1960s and early 1970s, industrial unrest had once again increased and inflation had begun to rise, introducing considerable instability into the economy. The federal government's response, especially after the election of Brian

Mulroney's Conservatives in 1982, was to discard the high employment objective in favour of monetary and fiscal policies designed to eliminate inflation (see Campbell, 1991). As discussed in the preceding chapter and in chapter four, there was also an increase in the willingness of governments to restrict the right to strike and to impose wage and price constraints, and continual cutbacks in government programs and services. At least part of the motivation for these changes in direction has been the belief that order and stability could be restored not by further incorporating labour into the status quo (though there was some experimentation with this alternative) or providing workers with further rights and protections, but rather by weakening the power of the labour movement and reducing these rights and protections. In the terms of chapter three, while the historic trend in Canada has been to seek order and stability less and less through coercion and more and more through consent, this trend appears to have been reversed in the 1980s (also see Panitch and Swartz, 2003). It largely continued to be so throughout the 1990s and 2000s.

It follows from this brief sketch that the quest for order and stability can indeed provide a useful frame of reference for analyzing the development of state policies and actions in industrial relations. Not only has major legislation, from the Trade Union Act of 1872, to the IDIA of 1907, to the PSSRA of 1967, developed largely in response to the quest for order and stability, it has been reinforced by state economic and social policies which appear to have been largely motivated by this objective.[2] Yet, this explanation is limited in at least two respects. First, it paints history with too broad a brush. While it is useful as a *primary* explanation for addressing *broad* patterns of development, it would be wrong to attribute all government policies and actions solely or even primarily to this objective. Second, it does not adequately address the question, "order and stability for whom?" In other words, it fails to address why Canadian governments seek order and stability, and, more generally, why specific policies and actions are chosen. This is an important question, for the answer to it is critical to understanding the actions of governments in the present as well as the past. Thus, there is need to go beyond this general explanation and consider more specific theories of the state.

---

[2] This argument is largely consistent with "French regulation theory", which informs the analysis in this section.

II. WHY STATES DO WHAT THEY DO

A number of theories of the state have been advanced over the years, and though these have seldom received much attention from industrial relations scholars (for two exceptions, see Giles, 1989, and Adams, 1992a), proponents of different perspectives in industrial relations have typically proceeded from assumptions about the state that largely conform to one or more of these theories. Thus, this section discusses the assumptions adhered to under the various perspectives and classifies existing theories of the state according to these perspectives. As we shall see, all have something to contribute to our understanding of how the state functions.

The Neoliberal Perspective

Traditionally, the neoliberal perspective on the state has been an essentially normative and prescriptive one, advocating a minimal role for the state beyond that of maintaining law and order, providing for national defence, and facilitating the operation of "free" markets.[3] Because of this, neoliberals have traditionally opposed most labour and employment laws, arguing that they distort the operation of market forces and impair efficiency, and that unions are little more than "monopoly institutions" which seek to obtain economic rents (wage premiums) at the expense of everyone else.

Though essentially normative, the neoliberal perspective is closely aligned with something referred to as "public choice theory" (see Downs, 1957; Buchanan and Tullock, 1962; Mueller, 1989). As is the case in neoclassical economic theory, public choice theory views both voters and politicians as rational, self-interested utility maximizers. Government officials are concerned primarily with maintaining their status and power, and this generally requires weighing the preferences of voters and choosing those policies which, in view of these preferences, will be most conducive to re-election. The problem, however, is that, in this process, governments are unduly influenced by interest groups. Not only can interest groups significantly affect public opinion in general, they are also able to buy influence through campaign contributions, thus affecting the ability of politicians to market themselves to the public.

---

[3] See Waligorski, 1990, for a useful discussion of the normative political ideas of neo-classical economists.

Though not all of its proponents necessarily adhere to the neo-liberal ideal, public choice theory does provide a normative basis for this ideal (see Borins, 1988). In effect, it suggests that interest groups both distort public policy and result in the proliferation of "big government", rife with programs designed to serve special interests rather than the public interest in general. The only answer is to sharply restrict both interest group activities and government spending (Colander, 1984). In this respect, unions are often singled out as an unduly powerful interest group, one that has been able to distort public policy in a way which is contrary to the free play of market forces and ultimately to the broad public interest (see Coughlin, 1985). Thus, there is a need to curb the political influence of unions, particularly their ability to use membership dues for political purposes.

The Managerialist Perspective

Proponents of the managerialist perspective in industrial relations have traditionally focused entirely on management policies and practices within work organizations and as such have generally not concerned themselves with the workings of the state. Yet as is discussed in chapter ten, a managerialist perspective on the state has emerged in recent years, advocating government policies that facilitate greater labour–management cooperation and which enhance competitiveness through greater support for the private sector in areas such as education and training, research and development, and transportation and communications (see Porter, 1990: 617–82). As should be evident, this perspective is also largely prescriptive, as is the case for its neoclassical counterpart. However, it views the state as having a somewhat more positive, benevolent role, one which is aimed at fostering prosperity and, with it, stability and cooperation, both in industrial relations and in the economy in general. The assumption here seems to be that, rather than public opinion shaping state laws and policies, the state's effectiveness in fulfilling its role will shape public opinion and hence the government's re-election chances. In this respect, little attention is paid to the various pressures and constraints which shape state choices at any particular point in time.

Beginning in the 1980s, a number of political sociologists began to argue for a "state centred" approach (see Skocpol, 1985), an approach which would also appear to be largely consistent with the managerialist perspective. However, this approach entails a somewhat less naive conception of the state, viewing state choices as in part reflecting the agendas of policy makers, past policy commitments, the balance of power within the state itself, and the relations between the state and other states (e.g., the United States and Canada). Under this approach, for example, order and stability are sought in industrial relations primarily because unrest jeopardises state economic policy and ultimately the ability of the state to rule, not necessarily because it serves the public interest per se (see Zeitlin, 1985).

State centred theorists also emphasize the importance of history in explaining state structures and policies (Pierson and Skocpol, 2002). In essence, they maintain that these structures and policies become deeply ingrained or "institutionalized" over time, through both formal and informal rules and understandings, and that this has major implications for the kinds of structures and policies that are subsequently adopted and the likely success of these structures and policies. Thus, for example, it has been argued that Canada has a stronger tradition of state intervention in the economy than does the United States, because in Canada the state played a much greater role in national development. As a result, labour boards, which play a central role in administering labour laws, have been able to acquire more power than in the United States, rendering them more effective (Taras, 1997a).

Orthodox-Pluralist Perspective

Orthodox pluralists have historically been much more concerned than their managerialist counterparts with state policies and actions (see Kochan, 1980: vii–viii). For them, the state's role is a critical one, aimed primarily at balancing off the competing interests of labour and management without unduly interfering in the economy or injuring third parties (e.g., consumers). Indeed, orthodox pluralists have traditionally considered one of their primary roles to be that of providing policy prescriptions that enhance the state's effectiveness at fulfilling this role.

Though pluralist assumptions about the functioning of the state are rarely articulated (for exceptions, see Clegg, 1975; Kochan and Katz, 1988), they are by and large consistent with the pluralist conception of the state that was dominant in political science throughout much of the 1950s and 1960s (see Dahl, 1961; Polsby, 1980; Rose, 1967). Under this conception, the claims of different interest groups often involve a competition for scarce resources and can reflect conflicting interests. But they do not involve irreconcilable conflicts, for all groups generally have a stake in preserving the status quo and adhere to common values as to the status quo's legitimacy. Moreover, in contrast to public choice theory, the existence of these groups is viewed positively rather than negatively, for they in theory provide a linkage between individuals and the government, both informing their members and representing their members to the state. As such, they strengthen democracy rather than undermine it.

Traditionally, an underlying assumption of most orthodox pluralists (see Dahl, 1961) has been that different interest groups have an approximately equal amount of power with which to influence government policies and laws, and that an important function of government is to ensure that this balance is maintained. However, in recent years, there has been a growing recognition that how this balance is to be defined is itself likely to reflect the existing distribution of power and prevailing public ideologies (e.g., Kochan and Katz, 1988: 80).

It follows that the state's role is viewed as one of maintaining a balance of power between labour and management, yet specific policies and laws affecting labour relations are viewed as responses by the state to the often conflicting pressures imposed by labour and by management, subject to the broader dictates of public opinion and shifts in the balance of power. In the ideal, however, the state plays a largely neutral, adjudicative role in industrial relations, allowing the parties to pursue their interests subject to broader institutional constraints which enable them to confront one another on equal terms and reconcile their differences with a minimum of conflict.

The Liberal-Reformist Perspective

Liberal reformists have generally proceeded from a more critical view of the state than have their orthodox pluralist counterparts, typically adhering to a contemporary version of elite theory (see Mills, 1956; Dye, 1986).[4] Contemporary elite theory views society as hierarchically stratified, with elites at the top of this hierarchy exerting undue power and influence over state policies. Business leaders, government officials, and political leaders generally constitute the most powerful elites, but depending on the circumstances, the elite structure can also include senior clergy, academics, top military officers, and even union leaders

---

[4] Traditional elite theory (Pareto, 1935 [1915–1919]; Mosca, 1939 [1896]) is largely conservative in nature, based upon the argument that the domination of society by a ruling elite of one form or another is a natural condition, and that those in the ruling elite are typically superior to the masses over whom they rule. Indeed, the masses are generally incapable of ruling themselves, and so elite dominance is not only inevitable, it is also desirable. This is especially so where there is competition among elites, thus allowing for elite circulation over time. See MacPherson, 1973.

— most of whom derive their power from large bureaucratic organizations over which they preside.

There can be considerable disagreement and competition both within and between elites, and in this sense elite theory is similar to the orthodox pluralist model of the state. However, elite theory differs in four important respects. First, though members of an elite may actually claim to represent particular constituents (e.g., shareholders in the case of the business elite, workers in the case of the labour elite) or the public interest in general, the extent to which they actually do so is another matter. Instead, they often attempt to control and manipulate their constituents, and the public in general, in a way which furthers their own agenda and protects their own interests — an argument which is largely consistent with Michel's iron law of oligarchy (see chapter eight). Second, there can be substantial variation in the power and influence of elites, so much so that the term "dominant" elite is sometimes employed to distinguish between those in primary positions of power and those in secondary positions.

Third, because the state is dominated by elites, the types of policies and laws which come to be established reflect the overall elite power structure, not a balancing of interest group claims per se. Issues which do not conform to elite interests, and groups that are not part of this power structure, generally receive short shrift, at least until such time that they are able to muster sufficient public support and organizational resources to gain access to the "political arena".

Fourth, because of their privileged position, elite members have a vested interest in maintaining the status quo, and this comes to be reflected in shared values and beliefs as to what issues and alternatives are to be considered legitimate at any point in time. Thus, while voters may perceive that important choices are made by the state and that they have a role in determining these choices through the electoral process, the actual range of choices presented to them is usually limited, with most real decisions made behind the scenes.

There are two main elite-based interpretations of state policies and laws in industrial relations (Giles, 1989: 140). One views labour leaders as incorporated within the elite structure. Where this is the case, state policies typically protect the organizational base of labour unions without significantly threatening the interests of the business elite. The result is a system of laws which largely excludes from consideration the interests of the non-union labour force and does little to substantially alter the nature of the employment relation. The second interpretation views labour leaders as largely excluded, and argues labour and employment laws are enacted to buy off discontent without altering the elite structure or significantly sacrificing elite interests (see Piven and Cloward, 1979). The former interpretation was especially predominant among elite theorists in the United States during the 1950s and 1960s, with these theorists tending to argue that the leadership of the AFL-CIO had been co-opted into the power elite, and as a result was more concerned with maintaining the status quo than with responding to membership concerns or with seeking broader economic and political reforms (see Mills, 1948, 1956). The latter has tended to be more predominant in Canada, where, except when NDP governments have been elected, labour leaders have generally been excluded from policy formation processes.[5]

The Radical Perspective

Of the five perspectives on industrial relations, proponents of the radical perspective have displayed the greatest interest in the functioning of the state (e.g., Hyman, 1975). Indeed, much of the radical industrial relations literature is closely linked to the radical literature on the state (e.g., see Russell, 1990: 12–19), for this literature often concerns itself directly with the implications of more fundamental conflicts between "labour" and "capital" for the operation of the state.

Traditionally, radicals have tended to adopt an **instrumentalist** view of the state, considering it as little more than an instrument of the capitalist class (Miliband, 1969; Domhoff, 1983). According to this view, capitalists possess a variety of means with which to control the state, not the least of which are political contributions, close personal and professional ties between senior corporate and senior government officials, and the domination of the media, thereby controlling public opinion. Because of these sources of control, government policies and actions are ultimately directed at protecting and enhancing the interests of capitalists, and most "progressive" legislation (e.g., labour laws, social programs) is enacted primarily to placate the working class and hence to forestall more fundamental challenges to the status quo. This view is similar to elite theory, except that political leaders are viewed as stooges of the capitalist class rather than as forming an elite with interests of its own.

---

[5] There *has* been considerable interest in some circles in establishing national level structures which incorporate both business *and* labour within the policy process, something which has been widespread in Europe and is commonly referred to as **corporatism**. But while there have been some initiatives along these lines over the past few decades, these have largely failed.

Beginning in the 1970s, this rather simple view of the state began to give way to a more complex, **structuralist** view (see Poulantzas, 1978; Offe, 1984). Under this view, radicals argue that there are important conflicts within the capitalist class (e.g., large corporations versus small business), and this can result in considerable disagreement over which state policies and actions are most consistent with the interests of this class. This, coupled with various limits to capitalist control over the state, means that the state has a certain amount of freedom to manoeuvre, finding itself in a position of "relative autonomy" from the capitalist class (Poulantzas, 1978). In other words, governments can exercise a certain amount of independent choice over the formulation and direction of economic and social policies, thereby enabling different governments to pursue different strategies and to proceed from different political philosophies. Thus, for example, a conservative government may cut back on social programs, while a social democratic government may expand them (e.g., see Offe, 1984). Complementing this view is the more recent argument that conflicts between different employer groups (e.g., large vs. small employers) lead some of these groups to form cross-class alliances with labour, resulting in policies that serve their particular interests and those of labour but not those of competing employer groups (see Thelen, 2002).

A third theory that can be associated with the radical perspective is **power resource theory** (see Olsen, 2002: 125–37). Although this theory allows for cross-class alliances and state choices, it argues that the ability of labour to mobilize its resources politically and put pressure on governments is critical to explaining variation in what states do. To the extent that labour is able to do so, class conflict shifts from the workplace to the political arena, as the government attempts to enact policies favourable to labour in the face of resistance from the private sector (see Shalev, 1980; Korpi, 1983).

At the same time, radicals tend to argue that government choices are limited over the long run. One reason for this is that the capitalist class is capable of overcoming internal conflicts and engaging in concerted action, especially where the various factions consider their combined interests to be threatened. According to radicals, this, for example, happened in many western countries in the late 1970s and in the 1980s, as capitalists mounted a "class offensive" against labour and other social groups (see Akard, 1992). But under the structuralist view, the more important limitation is an indirect one having to do with the very structure of capitalist economies in general: the need to maintain a favourable investment climate. If such a climate is not maintained, and the interests of the capitalist class are not well served, they will invest their money elsewhere (i.e., in other provinces or countries) — either as a way of putting pressure on the state or, more simply, because doing so yields higher returns. An unhealthy economy results, and this, in turn, means fewer jobs and fewer resources (i.e., taxes) with which to support social programs. Ultimately, the government finds itself voted out of office. Thus, though the state may not be an instrument of the capitalist class per se, it is held hostage to the interests of this class, having to ensure that these interests receive priority over those of the working class.

The concerns of radicals have become especially serious over the past few decades, as international markets have grown. The problem, they argue, is not so much that there has been a growth in trade. Rather, it lies more in the internationalization of financial markets, a process which has greatly enhanced capital mobility and hence further increased the power of capital relative to labour, consumers, and other groups. As a consequence, nation states have become increasingly held hostage to the interests of capital, and hence placed under substantial pressure to conform to a neoliberal model, reducing (or eliminating) corporate taxes, weakening labour and employment laws, and cutting social programs. Radicals tend to be divided over the ability of states to resist these pressures. Many argue that globalization claims are overstated, serving largely as part of an ideology for legitimating what states have been doing and that states retain considerable discretion over what they do. Others have argued that there is urgent need of supranational institutions which regulate and control state actions so that they cannot be held hostage to the interests of capital. But most view working class mobilization as critical.

Analyzing State Policies

As stated at the outset, all five of these perspectives on the state can be of value in analyzing state policies and laws, for each focuses on a different explanation of how these policies and laws come about. For example, it is difficult (as public choice theorists suggest) to deny that various interest groups can have undue influence on state policies, in effect buying influence from public officials. Yet to argue that state officials act solely in accordance with their self-interests (as public choice theorists also suggest) and are incapable of acting autonomously of interest group pressures would seem to be at best unduly cynical. To the contrary, there can be little doubt that government policies can be largely driven by "state centred" imperatives (as state centred theorists argue) or that these imperatives can be directed at serving the public interest (as managerialists often assume). Ideally, politicians enter politics out of a desire to serve the public, and even though this ideal may be less than fully realized in practice, to dismiss it out of hand as one plausible explanation for state action would be mistaken.

A major problem with such a conception, however, would appear to be that the "public interest" is not easily defined. As pluralists argue, there exists a diversity of actors and groups, each of which attempts to convince politicians to adopt their own often self-serving conception of the public interest, and each of which attempts to mobilize their membership and the public in general to pressure policy makers accordingly. Though these groups can undoubtedly act to distort state policy, they can also serve a positive function, for they *do* help ensure that various "issues" are addressed and they serve to represent otherwise anonymous individuals to the state. The difficulty, as elite theorists argue, is that different actors and interest groups often do have different amounts of power and influence, and their leaders often do appear to develop their own vested interests. It is thus necessary to examine the elite power structure, for it reflects the main distribution of influence over state policies and laws, explaining why it is that certain issues and interests appear to be given primacy over others. But even this may not go far enough, for, as radicals argue, state decisions and actions are ultimately constrained by the economic realities of capitalism — realities which have become increasingly harsh over the past few decades. While the state may have considerable autonomy, the need to ensure a favourable investment climate limits the extent to which, and ways in which, public opinion, political convictions, interest group pressures, and various elite influences can shape decisions.

Perhaps the real question lies with the relative value of each of the competing theories for understanding state policies in industrial relations. This question is not easily answered. For example, all are more or less consistent with the argument that major policy initiatives in industrial relations in Canada have been motivated by a desire to maintain order and stability. Under public choice theory, for example, order and stability are achieved by responding to the pressures imposed by a particular interest group: the labour movement. Under both managerialist and state centred theory, order and stability are sought because they maintain the system and enable the state to pursue its established policy agenda. For pluralists, unrest reflects shifts in public opinion and the power of various interest groups, and state attempts to achieve order and stability essentially reflect attempts to bring policy in line with these shifts. Elite theorists would be somewhat more cynical, arguing that order and stability are sought in order to preserve the status quo and protect the positions of dominant elites. Finally, radicals would interpret state polices directed to this end as ultimately designed to maintain a favourable investment climate and prevent unrest from developing into a full-blown "class" conflict.

A growing consensus in the literature on the state would appear to be that the value of each of the competing theories depends upon specific historical circumstances and upon the issues and policies at hand (see C.J. Martin, 1989; Vogel, 1989; Prechel, 1990; Hooks, 1993). For example, over the past decade, it would appear that governments have been under the sorts of pressures identified by both instrumentalist and structuralist versions of the radical perspective. As a result, they have had limited autonomy with respect to social and economic policy, and many of the social policies developed in the 1950s through to the 1970s have come under threat. Yet three decades ago, when the economy was expanding, there was far more room to manoeuvre, and politicians were able to adopt a number of "progressive" reforms, in reflection of public opinion, political convictions, various interest group pressures, and even (perhaps) a "liberal" dominant elite.

Moreover, the extent to which the state is currently driven by the sorts of factors identified by instrumentalist and structuralist explanations may vary. For example, state cut-backs in the public sector may be explained by direct pressures from corporate interests in general, while the movement away from Keynesianism (where states intentionally run a deficit so as to stimulate the economy) may be accounted for by structural factors. Yet, it could be argued that labour boards have for the most part remained autonomous from government policy, continuing with an agenda which attempts to ensure that the right of workers to collective bargaining is protected. Although there has been some weakening of labour laws, the basic system has remained relatively stable (see chapter sixteen).

This approach is useful, but it leaves us without any underlying understanding of the state. To develop that, it seems necessary to recognize that, at the very least, the state has had to ensure a **relatively** favourable investment climate, for reasons advanced by both instrumentalists and structuralists. To the extent that it succeeds, it has increased autonomy with which to deviate from this requirement and pursue alternative agendas. In turn, the policies adopted to ensure a favourable investment climate, and the extent to which it pursues alternative agendas, will depend upon two factors: (1) the political feasibility of doing so, as reflected in the ability of various groups and classes to either mobilize popular support or to threaten order and stability and hence the investment climate, and (2) the personal agendas of key decision-makers within the state (e.g., the prime minister and senior cabinet ministers).

This is clearly an oversimplified view, but it *is* useful for understanding the historical development of state policies in industrial relations. The state has historically sought to maintain a favourable investment climate by protecting a status quo which has largely served the interests of the wealthy and powerful (for both instrumentalist and structuralist reasons). Yet, for a variety of reasons ultimately attributable to the sources of conflict identified in chapter three, order and stability have been a recurring problem, and so it has had to cede various rights and protections to workers and their organizations over the past century or more. This has been especially true when repression has not been politically feasible and has been inconsistent with the values of key decision-makers in the state. Though these rights and protections have often been quite limited, workers and their organizations have seen significant improvements over the development of industrial capitalism within Canada. During the 1980s and 1990s, however, the investment climate in Canada became relatively *un*favourable and economic conditions worsened. This, coupled with both a changing political climate and the election of neoliberal political leaders, gave rise to a retrenchment.

III. CONCLUSIONS

This chapter has proceeded to briefly review the historical development of the state's role in industrial relations. It then addressed the debate over the functioning of the state, drawing upon the five perspectives identified in chapter one. The next chapter moves to a more specific topic: the structure and administration of labour laws pertaining to labour unionism, collective bargaining, and the right to strike. Though briefly discussed in chapter nine, these laws are in many respects at the heart of the Canadian system of industrial relations. Thus, they require more thorough consideration.

Labour Law
The Regulation of Labour–Management Relations

11

Although chapter nine included a brief discussion of labour law, it did not address the content and administration of this law in any depth. Yet, labour law plays a critical role in shaping the structure and functioning of the Canadian industrial relations system. This is so in two main respects. First, it recognizes and protects the rights of workers to join unions and to bargain collectively with management over the terms and conditions of their employment. As such, it has important a priori implications for the relationships between labour and management and for the outcomes of these two parties. Second, in recognizing and protecting the right of workers to join unions and engage in collective bargaining, labour law helps to maintain and protect the organizational basis and hence the strength of the labour movement in Canada. As such, it also has broader political and ultimately social implications. Thus, this chapter builds on the brief discussion in chapter nine, expanding on the content, rationale, and problems of labour law in Canada.

Any discussion of Canadian labour law necessarily suffers from two limitations. First, and as noted in chapter nine, even though the overall system of labour law is generally the same throughout the country, the specifics vary from one jurisdiction to the next and, within most jurisdictions, between the private sector and the public sector (and various segments thereof). Second, labour law is susceptible to frequent change. Particularly important in this respect are legislative reforms introduced by governments. Also important, however, are decisions made by labour boards and the courts, both of which can affect the interpretation of the law.

Because of these difficulties, to attempt a full-blown discussion of Canadian labour law in all of its specifics would not only be quite tedious, it would also in all likelihood quickly become out of date.

Instead, therefore, this chapter concerns itself more with the general system of labour law, noting the existence of specific differences where appropriate, but not delving into these differences in detail.[1] It proceeds in six stages: (1) a brief introduction to labour law; (2) the certification process; (3) the duty to bargain in good faith; (4) the right to strike and strike tactics; (5) union authority, security, and obligations; and (6) management authority and rights under collective bargaining. All of these topics involve often controversial issues and are important to understanding both the rationale for, and a number of problems often associated with the contemporary labour law in Canada. These issues will thus be identified and discussed as the chapter proceeds, placing particular emphasis on the effectiveness of labour law in establishing and protecting the right of workers to join unions and engage in collective bargaining.

I. INTRODUCTION TO LABOUR LAW

In 1926, the Supreme Court ruled that, under the British North America Act of 1867, the federal government's jurisdiction over labour relations is limited to employees of the federal government and of employees in those industries which fall specifically under the federal jurisdiction under the terms of the Act (such as banking, communications, interprovincial transportation, defence and defence-related, grain handling, and uranium mining). As a result, the provinces have jurisdiction over roughly 90 percent of private sector employees, as well as over their own employees and those of public sector institutions within their purview (e.g., municipalities, hospitals, and schools). Legislation has also enabled the territories to claim separate jurisdiction, though they have to date chosen to remain subject to federal law (the Canada Labour Code). Thus, there are eleven jurisdictions with their own systems of labour law as of this writing.

For the private sector, labour law in each jurisdiction is administered primarily by an appointed labour board, typically consisting of a neutral chairperson and vice chairs, along with an equal number of labour and management representatives. Though these boards report to

---

[1] Specific legislation for a particular jurisdiction can be obtained from a copy of that jurisdiction's Labour Relations Act. For comparisons of specifics across jurisdictions, see the HRSDC Workplace Information Directorate Web page, at <http://www.hrsdc.gc.ca/en/gateways/topics/lzl-gxr.shtml>. An excellent, lengthier discussion of labour law in general can also be found in Arthurs et al. (1993).

the minister of labour in their respective jurisdictions, they are regarded as having considerable autonomy, serving as neutral bodies charged with administering the law independently of the political party that happens to be in power. Depending on the size of the jurisdiction in question, they can have sizeable support staffs, whose role it is to provide relevant information, make inquiries about and receive information relevant to the board's mandate, and investigate and receive complaints having to do with the laws for which the board is responsible.

The actions of these boards are framed by legislation, referred to in most jurisdictions as the Labour Relations Act. However, labour boards have considerable scope for interpreting legislation, and as such their decisions also serve as an important source of law. The labour relations Act (or its equivalent) for a particular jurisdiction may also cover a majority of local public sector workers, in which case these workers are also within the purview of labour boards. However, a majority of jurisdictions in Canada have separate acts to cover public sector employees, and in some cases they have acts to cover specific groups thereof.

While both the content of labour legislation and the way in which it is interpreted and administered by labour boards varies by jurisdiction, it is possible to identify three general purposes which underlie labour law in Canada. The first is to foster democracy (Sims, Blouin, and Knopf, 1995: 33). As discussed in chapter seven, the ability to form unions, bargain collectively, and go on strike is considered a basic right of workers in any democratic society. It is also closely associated with the principle of freedom of association, which is viewed as fundamental to the effective functioning of a democracy.

The second major purpose of labour law is to establish a working balance of power between workers and management within the employment relationship (see Adell, 1988: 116; Sims, Blouin, and Knopf, 1995: 36). Thus, it allows workers to enhance their power by organizing a union, but it also entails restrictions upon union activities, especially the right to strike, so that management does not find itself at a disadvantage (Woods, 1973: 64–70, 86–93; Sims, Blouin, and Knopf, 1995: 35).

The third and final major purpose underlying the contemporary system of labour law is to institutionalize and provide a means for the orderly resolution of conflict, thereby ensuring that stability and efficiency are maintained in the economy (Woods, 1973: 119–25; Sims, Blouin, and Knopf, 1995: 33) and that more radical challenges to the status quo are forestalled.

In addition to these three purposes are three principles that in theory underlie contemporary labour law: (1) **majoritarianism**, or the notion that the majority should rule with respect to worker decisions about joining a union, accepting a collective agreement, or going on strike; (2) **exclusivity**, or the notion that a single union should represent all workers in a given work situation, serving as their exclusive "agent"; and (3) **voluntarism**, or the notion that unionized workers and their employer should be encouraged to resolve disputes and disagreements voluntarily and to the mutual satisfaction of both sides, through a process of **"free collective bargaining"**, under which there is a minimum of government intervention (Sims, Blouin, and Knopf, 1995: 36).

These purposes and principles are closely associated with the orthodox-pluralist perspective on labour relations, which has formed the primary basis for the labour law in both Canada and the United States for more than half a century. According to orthodox pluralists, in the absence of a system of collective bargaining, workers all too often find themselves (a) subject to authoritarian management practices, (b) at a power disadvantage relative to management, and (c) having to engage in both collective and individual forms of conflict in order to "fight back". Thus, the three purposes of labour law: the introduction of democracy, the balancing of power, and the resolution of conflict. In turn, orthodox pluralists (at least in North America) have traditionally believed that the most effective system of labour relations is one in which: (a) workers are encouraged to decide issues democratically, (b) a single agreement covers all workers within a bargaining unit, and (c) parties are free to negotiate that settlement which best suits their particular preferences and circumstances. Hence the three principles underlying labour law: majoritarianism, exclusivity, and voluntarism.

II.   CERTIFICATION

The certification process determines the ease with which a union can become formally **"certified"**, or recognized under the law as the legal bargaining agent for a group of workers. As such, it is in many respects the cornerstone of labour law, with critical implications for the percentage of Canadian workers who are union members and who are covered by collective agreements (see Godard, 2004b, 2008). Indeed, differences in certification processes are considered by some as providing the primary explanation for differences in the fate of the Canadian and U.S. labour movements, as discussed in chapter nine.

The certification process normally begins when union organizers file an application for certification with the labour board. When this application is received, the labour board first seeks to establish whether all of the workers covered by the application are indeed eligible for union representation under the law and whether the bargaining unit proposed for election purposes is acceptable. If either is not clear cut, it may hold a hearing at which the parties can present their points of view, prior to making a final determination.

Eligibility

Though there is some variation across provinces, workers are generally deemed eligible under most Canadian legislation *unless* they are: (1) managerial employees, defined as employees in positions of substantive authority,[2] or (2) employees in positions of confidentiality by virtue of their access to information deemed to be relevant to negotiations (e.g., the employer's cost structure). In a few jurisdictions, some groups of professional employees are also excluded, including doctors, dentists, lawyers, architects, and engineers. Finally, a few jurisdictions exclude domestics, and a few also exclude agricultural workers.

The exclusion of various groups from eligibility for legal representation has been a matter of some concern (see Beatty, 1983: 306–308), even though the criteria employed in Canada are substantially narrower than in the United States (Wood and Godard, 1999: 216). With respect to managerial employees, for example, the conventional rationale is that managers are in a position of trust and must remain loyal to their employer. Yet they are also in a position of subordination, and are just as subject to arbitrary treatment as are non-managerial workers. Moreover, all union certification entails is the right to negotiate collectively and to "grieve" if unfairly treated. As such, it need not engender any less trust or loyalty than would otherwise be the case. To the contrary, it could enhance trust and loyalty by serving as a means of communication and conflict resolution (i.e., integrative function).

As for professional employees, it can be argued that workers in the professions are members of professional associations that already represent their members adequately. Yet studies have found that professional workers in an employment relation often find themselves

---

[2] Because supervisors often do little more than monitor workers, they are eligible under some Acts (B.C., the federal jurisdiction, and some provincial public sector jurisdictions), provided they form a separate election unit and bargain separately.

under pressure from their employer to violate professional ethics and standards. Arguably, this pressure would be lessened if these workers could join a union and hence protect themselves.

Perhaps most troubling, however, is the exclusion of agricultural workers and domestics in some jurisdictions (e.g., see Stultz, 1987; Beatty, 1983). These workers are typically among the most disadvantaged in the labour market, and arguably have the greatest need for protection under labour law. There may be a number of reasons for these exclusions, from issues having to do with the requirement of fealty in the case of domestics, to those having to do with the temporary nature of work and the costs of a strike at harvest time in the case of agricultural workers. But none would seem sufficient to deny these workers the basic rights and protections associated with collective bargaining. At most, they may justify some restrictions on these rights (e.g., restrictions on striking).[3]

The Bargaining Unit

The determination of the bargaining unit can be of considerable importance and hence, a source of contention. For example, although there may be strong support for a union in one of an employer's departments or establishments, support may be lower in others. If the labour board defines the unit broadly, to include the latter, the likelihood of union success may be substantially lessened.[4] In addition, if the resulting unit includes a highly diverse group of employees (e.g., professors and maintenance staff), defining the unit broadly may also result in considerable internal instability and hence reduce the ease with which a settlement can be reached. Yet, if an employer operates

---

[3] The Supreme Court went part way to recognizing this in its 2001 *Dunmore v. Ontario (Attorney General)* ruling. The Ontario government of Mike Harris had passed legislation that, among other things, excluded agricultural workers from coverage under the law, reversing a provision enacted by its NDP predecessor. The court held that, under the Canadian Charter of Rights and Freedoms, agricultural workers have a right to collective representation, and that, given their position of vulnerability in the economy, this right warrants state protection under the law. However, it did not rule that the right to such protection extends to bargaining or going on strike. The Ontario government thus subsequently enacted a law protecting the right of agricultural workers to legal representation to an employer, but not granting them the right to engage in formal collective bargaining or to strike (see Panitch and Swartz, 2003: 212–14). This law was held to be illegal by the Ontario Court of Appeal in 2008, but this decision was appealed to the Supreme Court and has yet (as of this writing) to be resolved.

[4] This happened, for example, in Nova Scotia, where in order to attract the Michelin Corporation to the province the government enacted the famed "Michelin Bill" of 1979, stipulating that the election unit must cover all plants of the same employer if these plants are interdependent with one another.

a number of establishments in the same general vicinity and the election unit is declared to be the individual establishment, a union may find it easier to become certified, and there may be greater internal stability, but the employer may be able to continue to supply customers from other establishments in the event of a strike,[5] so the union is likely to have little bargaining power.

In addressing these (and other issues), labour boards in Canada have tended to rely on the following criteria: (1) the wishes of the parties; (2) traditional methods of organizing in the industry or trade which is involved; and (3) whether there is a "community of interest" between workers within an establishment or across a number of establishments, including whether the work done and/or required skills are similar, workers are in geographical proximity (e.g., the same city), and operations are closely linked. Though there is thus some variation, the result is (as seen in chapter nine) that the bargaining unit is typically defined as all employees within a broad occupational category (e.g., all manual workers, all clerical workers, all technicians) or profession (e.g., professors), employed in a single establishment by a single employer. However, the parties may subsequently agree to merge two or more units, so the eventual bargaining unit may be broader.

The Certification Vote

Once eligibility is decided and the bargaining unit established, the board determines if certification is warranted. Doing so can involve up to three stages. In the first stage, the labour board establishes whether the employer wishes to contest the union's application for certification. If not, and the employer voluntarily chooses to recognize the union, then certification is automatic. However, this would appear to be a rare occurrence. Far more often, it is necessary for the board to proceed to the second stage, which entails determining the percentage of eligible workers who have signed a union "card". If a "clear" majority has done so (the exact percent varies by jurisdiction, from 50 percent plus one to 65 percent), and there is no reason to call this majority into question (e.g., there is no evidence of coercion to sign a union card), then certification follows in a number of jurisdictions.

---

[5] This problem has been especially serious in the banking industry, where customers can simply carry out their business at a nearby branch if the one they normally deal with is on strike (see Lennin, 1976). In part because of this, and in part because management's willingness to violate the law with impunity, a sustained drive to organize the banks in Canada in the 1970s largely failed (see Warskett, 1988).

If a clear majority cannot be established but a sizeable minority can (a minimum of from 35 to 45 percent, depending on the jurisdiction), or if a ballot is required by law, the labour board proceeds to the third stage, under which it arranges for and holds a formal ballot, usually within a one- or two-week period. In some jurisdictions, 50 percent plus one of the total *eligible* workers must vote in favour of the union before certification is granted, while in others the requirement is 50 percent plus one of those who actually vote, provided that the voter turnout exceeds a given level (e.g., 70 percent of those eligible). Also of note, a number of jurisdictions require a vote regardless of whether a clear majority has already signed union cards. Where this is the case, there is usually provision for a ballot within five to ten days (depending on the jurisdiction).

Provision for "card certification", where established, coupled with the expeditious holding of a ballot, are seen as strengths of the Canadian system, credited with helping to explain its effectiveness compared to its U.S. counterpart (see Godard, 2003a; 2004b). In the United States, card certification is not allowed, and a considerable amount of time can elapse before a ballot is held — especially as employers are able to delay the process by appealing labour board decisions on the bargaining unit, something which is generally not an option in Canada. In addition, a number of Canadian jurisdictions allow labour boards to hold a **quickie** or pre-hearing vote within a day or two of a union application if there is reason to be concerned about employer behaviour. The United States does not. As a result, there is considerably less opportunity for employer interference in Canada than in the United States. Nonetheless, there is still some concern that requiring a vote when a union can already demonstrate a clear majority unnecessarily opens the door for employer interference. This may be so even when the vote is expedited. There has now been a considerable amount of sophisticated research in support of this argument (e.g., Campolieti et al., 2007; Riddell, 2010).

The majority requirement has also been a cause of some concern (see Adell, 1986). As discussed in chapter nine, it has generally been argued that, if a major purpose of labour law is to foster and protect the right of workers to bargain collectively with their employer, then workers wishing to join a union and engage in collective bargaining should be able to do so regardless of whether a majority of their counterparts also wish to be collectively represented. Some have therefore argued in favour of **minority unions,** in which unions are provided bargaining rights even if they represent a minority of workers. Giving minority unions the right to strike could be unduly disruptive, especially if a strike could be expected to shut down all operations. But the right of workers in a minority union to strike could always be restricted.

Conversely, it has been argued that, if a minority of workers do *not* wish to be represented by a union, they should not be required to accept this representation. This issue is especially serious in workplaces where workers are required to join a union as a condition of employment, but even where this is not the case, workers in a unionized workplace are in most jurisdictions effectively required to, at minimum, pay the equivalent of union dues (see Taras and Ponak, 2001: 544). The usual rationale is that many workers would otherwise choose to become **"free riders"**, receiving the benefits of union representation (e.g., higher wages) without undergoing the costs (e.g., paying dues, suffering lost wages during a strike), and that this, in turn, both substantially weakens unions and creates considerable instability in the workplace. More fundamentally, the Canadian system is based on the principle of majoritarianism. If a majority votes against a union, the minority in favour must respect that decision. The same rule should thus apply if a majority is in favour. If it does not apply in the latter case, then failure to also apply it in the former (i.e., allow minority unionism) would be inconsistent and prejudicial against unions.

Unfair Labour Practices

Unfair labour practices occur when one party illegally attempts to undermine the other, either during a union organizing drive or after a union has been established. Though they entail restrictions on both parties, they apply primarily to management behaviour during the certification process. Some of the main prohibitions on management follow (also see Arthurs et al., 1993: 196–204).

First, management cannot dismiss workers for legitimate union activities, even if these appear to form only part of the reason for dismissal. For example, management may have bent over backwards to keep from firing a recalcitrant worker, and then learned that the worker was trying to organize a union. Even though this might be the "last straw", to fire the worker would be declared an unfair labour practice if there was any hint that union activities played a part in management's decision. The reason for this is not difficult to understand. Most simply, if a worker is fired in whole or in part because of union activities, then his or her right to organize free from employer retribution has been violated. Moreover, if even one worker is perceived to have been fired for union activities, this can instill a considerable amount of fear in other workers, intimidating them in a way which can substantially "chill" an organizing drive.

Second, the employer cannot, during the course of an organizing drive, unilaterally alter the terms and conditions of employment *unless* it can be established that to do so is consistent with its past practices and is therefore not related to the organizing drive. For example, if it is normal for management to adjust employee wages for inflation every six months, and it does so in accordance with past practice during an organizing drive, it will probably not be deemed to have committed an unfair labour practice. But if it is not normal for management to do so, or if management gives an increase which is substantially greater than the increase in the cost of living, then it may be deemed to have committed an unfair labour practice. Even though management may alter the terms of employment because the organizing drive has taught it "the error of its ways", doing so may also be little more than a ploy to "buy off" discontent until the organizing drive is over. Not only is it difficult to ascertain management's true intent, allowing management to alter the terms of employment would greatly enhance the difficulty of organizing workers in general and the willingness of parent unions to contribute resources to union organizing would be greatly reduced. This would, in turn, make it far more difficult for workers to realize their right to organize under the law.

Third, management is not allowed to issue any threats or promises to workers during the course of an organizing drive. Management *can* make factual information available to workers, but only if doing so cannot be interpreted as implying a threat or promise. Thus, management might make available information to show that the terms and conditions it is providing compare favourably with those offered by comparable employers, or it might "open the books" to workers to demonstrate that it cannot afford to improve upon these terms and conditions. But it cannot claim or even imply, for example, that it will shut down operations if the organizing drive succeeds, or that it will cease to provide various benefits, or even that it will improve the terms of employment if workers vote against the union. As is the case for dismissal, threats can substantially chill an organizing drive, and they entail intimidation of workers for merely exercising their legal rights. In turn, promises may be little more than ploys, and in any case can (again) ultimately reduce parent union organizing success and hence willingness to devote resources to organizing campaigns.

Fourth, and closely related, employers cannot resort to spying on or interrogation of workers, and they cannot attempt to surreptitiously infiltrate the union or influence its activities. While spying and interrogation can entail substantial intimidation, surreptitious acts can clearly impair the organizing process and undermine the union.

Fifth, the employer cannot attempt to alter the employee composition of the election unit. In particular, it normally cannot go out and hire a number of additional employees. New employees are likely to be grateful for being hired and unlikely to have any grievances against their new employer. Moreover, if they are hired on a part-time or a temporary basis, they are less likely to be interested in having a union. The upshot is that they are more likely to vote against unionization, thereby weakening the union's chances.

Sixth, the employer is not allowed to do anything that might compromise the integrity or the autonomy of the union, either before, during, or after an organizing drive. In particular, management cannot attempt to bring in a "sweetheart" union with which it has made a secret "deal". Indeed, management cannot provide *any* form of support to a union during the course of an organizing drive, nor can it attempt to influence the workers' choice of unions if more than one union is attempting to organize them. Otherwise, workers might find themselves signing up for a union which is not fully independent of management and hence cannot be counted upon to serve membership interests. The employer *can* establish a **"company union"**, which is a union set up and effectively controlled by the employer and not legally certified (as discussed in chapter four), but *not* if the intention is to prevent a bona fide independent union from becoming organized (Taras, 1997b).

Seventh, management generally cannot close down and relocate operations in order to avoid unionization or attempt to get rid of an established union, even if this constitutes only one of a number of reasons for doing so. For example, management may have a marginally profitable operation and decide, once a union is established, that it is no longer worth the trouble to keep it open. If it appears that the certification of the union had anything at all to do with this decision, then management is likely to be held guilty of committing an unfair labour practice.[6]

To some, these restrictions may appear one-sided or unduly restrictive. But it must be recognized that, as outsiders, union organizers generally face an uphill battle and that employees are often in a state of considerable dependency on their employer (i.e., for their livelihood) and hence can be very fearful of employer retribution (see

---

[6] Quebec is an exception. If the employer can demonstrate that a closure is permanent and genuine, employees have no legal recourse.

Taras, 1997a). As a result, even the most subtle actions by management can undermine a union organizing drive. This has led some to suggest that any form of employer involvement, including the presentation of factual information, should be illegal (Peirce, 2000: 287).

There are also a number of restrictions on the union's activities. For example, union organizers commit an unfair practice if they resort to any form of coercion to sign workers up. Also "inside" union organizers (i.e., those working for the employer) cannot engage in union-related activities on company time, and "outside" union organizers are not allowed on company premises without management permission. These latter restrictions are considered by some to place unions at an increased disadvantage, because it can be both difficult obtaining the names and addresses of all employees and time-consuming attempting to contact them outside working hours. It may also create the impression among employees that they are somehow doing something wrong if they become involved with the union. Finally, it is illegal for workers to engage in strike activity or any other form of retaliation during an organizing drive.

Remedies for Unfair Labour Practices

Of as much importance as the content of unfair labour practices are the "remedies" relied on by labour boards in the event that the law is held to have been violated. For, if these remedies are not sufficient to ensure employer compliance, labour laws protecting workers from unfair labour practices are at best of limited value. To enforce these laws, labour boards have a number of courses of action at their disposal.

First, if the employer is found to be guilty of unfair labour practices, labour boards may issue an order to cease and desist from these practices. This order is, in turn, registered with the courts, and if not obeyed, the employer can then be charged with contempt of court. As earlier noted, the board may also order an immediate or "quickie" vote.

Second, the labour board may impose a variety of remedies based on the "**make whole**" doctrine of civil law (Arthurs et al., 1993: 207). This means that, rather than seeking to fine or jail a party for contravening the law,[7] this party is merely required to right past wrongs, usu-

---

[7]   One exception is Manitoba, where the law explicitly allows for punitive damages of up to $2,000.00 if the aggrieved party has not undergone a loss of income and is thus ineligible for a "make whole" remedy.

ally by restoring the injured party to the position it would have been in had an offence not been committed. Thus, if an employee has been unfairly dismissed for union activities, the labour board will likely order reinstatement and compensation for lost income — usually determined as the difference between the employee's lost wages and any income she was able to earn elsewhere.

In most jurisdictions, the labour board may, subject to some restrictions, grant a **discretionary certification**, under which they go so far as to ignore the results of a vote and unilaterally certify the union on the grounds that the process has become so badly tainted that these results do not reflect the true wishes of employees. After one year, employees may choose to decertify if they wish. By this time, however, the union has had a chance to become established, and so any such vote is, in theory, less likely to be tainted. A particularly well-known and controversial example of such a certification, involving a Wal-Mart store in Ontario, is discussed in Box 11–1.

Finally, if an employer is deemed to have closed one or more of its establishments in part to eliminate the union, labour boards typically require the employer to make a cash settlement with displaced employees and/or to offer them equivalent jobs in the new or remain-

---

BOX 11–1 Windsor Wal-Mart Wins Right to Union

Firm intimidated staff, board rules

♦ *Paul Waldie and Marina Strauss*

Toronto — A Wal-Mart store in Windsor, Ont., has made history by becoming the first store in the U.S. retailer's 35-year history to be unionized.

In a ruling released yesterday, the Ontario Labour Relations Board certified a union at the store even though workers voted against the union last May.

The board overturned the vote — which was 151 to 43 against the union — saying executives from Wal-Mart Canada Inc. subtly threatened workers who supported the drive by the United Steelworkers.

Even though company officials didn't discipline, harass or fire any of the in-house organizers, the board said the threats were

Continued....

BOX 11–1 (continued)

severe enough that a new vote would be inappropriate and that the Steelworkers' local will be certified.

"We have no doubt that the intentionally generated implied threat to job security which occurred in this case had the result of rendering the representation vote taken on May 9, 1996, meaningless," the board said, noting that a week before the vote, the union had issued 91 membership cards. "We are of the view that a second representation vote in this case would be equally meaningless."

The board's decision was three to one. A dissenting opinion said the evidence was not strong enough to overturn such a large vote against the union.

The ruling is a major blow to Wal-Mart, the world's largest retailer. The company has successfully fought off every attempt to unionize since it was founded by Sam Walton in Arkansas in 1962. None of its roughly 3,000 stores worldwide are unionized.

Mary McArthur, a worker at the Windsor store who helped organize the union drive, was stunned by the decision.

"Oh my God, I cannot believe we won," she said when told of the ruling last night. "I just can't believe it. That's incredible."

Ms. McArthur said managers had left the impression with many employees that Wal-Mart would close the store if the union vote was approved.

She said yesterday she is confident that won't happen and she encouraged other Wal-Mart workers to organize.

"I'm sure that a lot of other stores will see this as a door opening for them," she said. Employees elsewhere should "completely stick with it. It's definitely worth it."

Marie Kelly, a lawyer for the Steelworkers, which appealed the vote to the labour board, said the ruling will make it easier to organize other Wal-Mart stores in Canada.

"It's certainly a sign to employees of Wal-Mart that if they want to make a choice to have a union represent them, that is possible contrary to what other people might believe," Ms. Kelly said.

"We are very surprised and disappointed with this decision," said Wal-Mart Canada spokesman Ed Gould. He added there's "a strong possibility" the company will appeal the ruling.

Mr. Gould stressed that the board decision is inconsistent with the wishes of the majority of employees at the Wal-Mart outlet.

"It may be difficult for many of our associates to understand the board decision given the fact that the overwhelming majority voted loud and clear that they did not want a union," Mr. Gould said.

Continued....

BOX 11–1 (continued)

In the meantime, "it will be business as usual. We are in the business to open stores, not to close them."

Ironically, the board used Wal-Mart's culture of openness with employees against the company. The board noted that Wal-Mart describes its employees as family and that all employees have a right "to get answers quickly to whatever they ask."

However, when the Steelworkers began a drive at the Windsor Store last April, the board said managers gave inadequate and misleading answers to questions about the future of the store. In the week before the vote was held, Wal-Mart sent four regional managers — including a vice-president — to the store to talk to employees about the union vote.

Some employees were told benefits would be taken away if the union was successful. However, the board said the managers refused to answer questions about plans to close the store if it was unionized.

Given Wal-Mart's culture of openness, the managers' failure to respond to direct questions about closing the store was tantamount to an overt threat, the board said.

"In our view [Wal-Mart] cannot have it both ways," the board said. "If you adopt the approach of constantly soliciting questions in an environment such as was present in this case, you have to answer them. Either you answer the questions that were asked or you do not circulate amongst employees in the manner in which management did in this case."

The managers' actions were "a subtle but extremely effective threat to the job security of the [employees]."

However, the board stressed that its ruling on Wal-Mart's subtle behaviour was unique because of the company's usually forthcoming treatment toward employees.

But one analyst said the ruling will have widespread repercussions.

"It looks like a hand grenade's gone off," said Richard Talbot of Thomas Consultants International Inc. in Markham, Ont. "It seems to me there are some huge implications for the whole retail industry."

Mr. Talbot said many stores in Canada have tried to cut down their unionized staff to compete against some of the newer U.S. players, especially Wal-Mart.

"If Wal-Mart had to be unionized, that would be a big bonus for Canadian department stores. It would put them back on a level playing field again."

Source: From *The Globe and Mail* (February 12, 1997), pp. A1, A9. Reproduced with permission from The Globe and Mail.

ing establishments. They can also require that the union involved be automatically certified in these establishments, or even that the establishment in question be reopened, though to date no labour board in Canada has ordered that.

These remedies may at first seem somewhat drastic. Yet, overall, it is not clear that they provide much of a disincentive, for employers are seldom substantially worse off for committing and being found guilty of unfair labour practices than if they had obeyed the law (Adell, 1988: 124–27). For example, firing one or two union activists can significantly chill a union organizing drive, for there is little certainty as to how the board will rule, and other workers will fear finding themselves in a similar situation. Yet, the only expense to the employer is likely to be that of compensating the activists for lost income if and when an unfair labour practice is deemed to have occurred. This is a trivial cost if the employer is of any size at all, even though it may be instrumental in breaking an organizing drive.

One possible exception is the ability of most labour boards to ignore the results of a vote and unilaterally certify a union if they believe that employer unfair labour practices have prevented the union from gaining majority support. This option is rarely used, and in practice employers are still able to undermine the union subsequent to certification. This happened, for example, in the Wal-Mart case reported in Box 11–1 and referred to earlier. Yet the mere possibility of the labour board resorting to this option may serve as a disincentive for employers to engage in unfair labour practices, in knowledge that doing so may only increase the likelihood of a union. Unfortunately, the extent to which this is the case is not clear.

An underlying problem would appear to be that, to impose more punitive sanctions (i.e., fines, jail sentences) generally requires criminal prosecution, in which case it is necessary to establish guilt beyond a reasonable doubt. Because it is so often difficult to meet this standard, labour boards instead act under civil law, which enables them to find an employer in violation of the law if "the balance of probabilities" indicates that an unfair labour practice appears to have occurred. Thus, on the one hand, the use of punitive sanctions is generally precluded by the burden of proof this would require. On the other hand, the failure to do so means that there is little to discourage unfair labour practices from occurring.

These problems make the process by which a union is certified especially important. By allowing for card certification or limiting the length of time to the holding of a ballot, the opportunities for employers to engage in unfair labour practices are substantially lessened, so the tendency for remedies to these practices to be weak does not matter as much. It might, in theory, be desirable to require a vote in all cases and to allow for a longer decision period so that employers are given some input. But within the Canadian context, doing so would likely only mean an increase in employer unfair labour practices unless, perhaps, the penalties for such practices were substantially strengthened.

Decertification

Just as a union can become certified, so can it become **"decertified"**. Though relatively rare, this can occur under the following conditions: (a) if the union becomes inactive and ceases to adequately represent its workers, (b) if the employer goes out of business, (c) if employees petition for and vote in favour of decertification, or (d) if workers vote to "displace" the union with a different one. The last of these generally involves the raiding of one union by another, and is legal only at certain times during the life of an existing contract (in most jurisdictions in the last two to three months of an agreement).

III. THE DUTY TO BARGAIN

Where a union is certified, it is the exclusive "agent" for all workers in the election unit, whether they have signed up or not. As such, the employer has a legal duty to bargain with it in "good faith". The doctrine of **good faith bargaining** is somewhat ambiguous, but it generally requires the following (see Bemmels, Fisher, and Nyland, 1986; Arthurs et al., 1993: 259–63):

1. That the parties meet and commence bargaining.

2. That both fully discuss the issues at hand and the rationale for their positions on these issues.

3. That neither party suppress or distort information required by the other party or intentionally mislead the other party.

4. That neither party frustrate the bargaining process by contradicting itself or simply going through the motions with no intention of making meaningful concessions — a strategy commonly referred to as **"surface bargaining"**.

5. That management not attempt to circumvent the union by making an offer directly to union workers, a practice referred to as

"**Boulwarism**", after Lemuel Boulware who, as vice-president of General Electric, first used it in the 1950s.

Clearly, without the requirement that management adhere to these conditions, legal recognition of the union can be virtually meaningless, especially where workers lack much power and hence are unable to use the threat of a strike to induce management to enter into serious negotiations.

If it is determined that the employer has not bargained in good faith, then the labour board may require it to reimburse the union for any costs it has undergone (e.g., the salaries of union negotiators). It may also make the contract retroactive to the date at which, in the board's judgement, it should have been settled. Where this is the case, workers are thus entitled to back pay. A summary of one recent unfair labour practice ruling appears in Box 11–2.

A problem, however, is that it is difficult to establish that an employer is indeed refusing to bargain in good faith. For example, an

BOX 11–2 Duty to Bargain in Good Faith

*Buhler Versatile Inc. — and — National Automobile, Aerospace,
Transportation and General Workers Union of Canada
(CAW — Canada), Local 2224
Case No. 220/01/LRA, Manitoba
July 30, 2001*

The Union testified that, during the bargaining meetings, the Chief Executive Officer (CEO) made many comments such as "You're not going to like my proposal" or "If backed into a corner, I'll padlock the doors." He also made constant threats to sell or to close the plants. He failed to provide supporting material to justify his demands as requested by the Union. At each meeting, he would demand further concessions from the Union. After the sixth meeting, the Union went on strike as it was of the view that the CEO was bargaining it to impasse. After the strike had been on for two months, the Union became aware that the CEO failed to disclose a vital decision to allow a customer to terminate a contract to purchase tractors rather than requesting an extension of the contract. At this point, the Union filed an application alleging that the Employer had failed to bargain in good faith and failed

Continued....

BOX 11-2 (continued)

to make every reasonable effort to conclude a collective agreement.

Held: The Board found that the CEO ought to have known that certain of his demands that would eliminate a number of long-standing provisions in the existing collective agreement, including the health and welfare benefits and seniority, could not have been accepted by the Union and still have them maintain credibility with its members. It was troubled that his strategy was based on his constant threats of plant closure. The CEO consistently displayed an unwillingness to enter into any rational and informed discussions and provide supporting arguments throughout those negotiations. The evidence was clear that each time the Union modified its position, the CEO offered less. [This], in itself, satisfied the Board that he breached the duty to bargain in good faith by purposely avoiding attempts to find some "common ground" to resolving the outstanding issues. The Board decided that the tactics utilized throughout by the CEO were calculated to see how much more he could squeeze out of the Union before it capitulated to his demands. The Board found unequivocally that the Employer's actions caused the strike to take place. It was satisfied that the Employer's conduct during the bargaining sessions, up to the strike were such that they contravened the duty to bargain in good faith and to make every reasonable effort to enter into a collective agreement. In addition, the Board found that the decision to allow the termination of the tractor contract fell within the types of decisions that labour boards have stated must be disclosed to a union in a timely fashion. This issue would have been a major point of discussion during the bargaining sessions, as it would have serious ramifications as to the continued viability of the plant. The law clearly put the onus of this type of disclosure on an employer. This, the Board was satisfied, was not done. Therefore, the Employer committed a further breach of section 63(1) of the Act.

The Board ordered the Employer to cease and desist any action that contravened the requirements to bargain in good faith and the parties were to immediately commence collective bargaining with the view to entering into a collective agreement. The Board stated that the remedies were to be compensatory, and not punitive, as they are intended to bring the employees back to the status that they had enjoyed prior to the strike. The Board, having satisfied itself that the strike was precipitated by the Employer's contravention of the duty to bargain in good faith, ordered the Employer to immediately compensate each employee who was a

Continued....

BOX 11-2 (continued)

member of the bargaining unit and who was employed by the Employer at the time the strike commenced for all lost wages and employment benefits they would have earned had the strike not occurred, less monies earned, exclusive of strike pay. It also ordered that the terms and conditions of the expired collective agreement were, in keeping with the provisions of section 10(4) of *The Labour Relations Act*, deemed to be in full force and effect up to and including the day the strike ended. Further, the Employer was ordered to compensate the Union for the strike expenditures totalling $170,025.00. The Employer was ordered to pay interest at the prime rate on all monies payable. The Board declined to issue compensation to the Union with respect to its legal and expert witness fees, and further declined to issue compensation with respect to severance, as there [had] been no closure of the plant and the Collective Agreement between the parties [had] been made whole.

Source: Manitoba Labour Relations Board, *Summaries of Significant Board Decisions,* 2003.

employer may claim that it is simply not feasible to grant any of the concessions a union is seeking. As long as it does not violate any of the above conditions, the labour board is not likely to find that the employer has failed to bargain in good faith. This has been a major problem in the United States, helping to explain why a collective agreement is never achieved in a third of workplaces in which a union is newly certified. In Canada, however, a majority of jurisdictions actually allow for **first agreement arbitration** if the parties are unable to negotiate an agreement on their own, often regardless of whether bad faith bargaining can be established. This involves the appointment of a neutral arbitrator by either the minister of labour or the labour board. This arbitrator, in turn, awards workers wage and benefit increases commensurate with those received by workers in similar jobs in the local area. Depending on the jurisdiction, it provides for either a one- or two-year contract, after which the parties are again on their own. In theory, the union is by then sufficiently established that employer anti-union tactics are less likely to succeed and initial animosities are more likely to have dissipated.

IV. STRIKE ACTIVITY UNDER THE LAW

The right to strike has long been considered by most observers to be of critical importance in industrial relations. It is viewed as essential to a democratic society, closely linked to the principle of freedom of expression and association. It also serves as the primary means by which workers are able to pressure employers into engaging in serious negotiations, thus helping to ensure a working balance of power. Finally, both the threat and the act of striking are important means of resolving conflict, for they induce the parties to modify their expectations so that a mutually acceptable agreement can be reached. Thus, the right to strike can be viewed as consistent with each of the three purposes underlying labour law, as identified earlier in this chapter.

At the same time, strike activity can have serious consequences, not just for the parties directly involved, but also for third parties who are dependent on the goods or services produced. There has also been concern that the unfettered right to strike can result in imbalances in bargaining power (in favour of the union), especially where it entails the withdrawal of essential services or where a small group of workers is able shut down a much larger employer operation. Drawing on these and related arguments, Canadian governments have therefore imposed a number of restrictions on the right of workers to strike and on the actions of employees during a strike. They have also provided employers with a number of (sometimes controversial) rights during a strike.

Restrictions on the Right to Strike

Perhaps the most notable restrictions are outright prohibitions on the right to strike. Though these sometimes apply in the private sector, they are by far-and-away most prevalent in the public sector. Half of the provinces prohibit their civil servants (those in the direct employ of the government) from striking, instead requiring the parties to undergo arbitration (Ponak and Thompson, 2001: 429). In others, workers designated as providing "essential" services are also denied this right. The essential services designation can apply to all members of a bargaining unit (as is almost always the case for firefighters and police). But if only a portion of workers is so designated, then the remainder are allowed to strike. However, even these workers are subject to "back-to-work" legislation if the government deems this to be expedient, an option which has been relied on with increasing frequency over the past few decades, as noted in chapter nine. Normally, such legislation calls for compulsory arbitration in place of the right to strike, and is "one-shot", applying only to the strike at hand. However, as also noted in chapter nine, some governments have been known to impose their own preferred settlement, thus effectively undermining the right to meaningful collective bargaining.

These prohibitions are clearly controversial. There is always room to debate whether employees designated as essential *are* in fact essential and whether back-to-work legislation is implemented for reasons of political expediency rather than because a strike has caused undue hardship to third parties. As noted in chapter nine, governments are employers as well as legislators, and so they clearly have an interest in enacting laws which are biassed in their favour. Particularly serious are situations where workers have a legal right to strike, but as soon as they exercise this option they are faced with back-to-work legislation. The result is one in which workers are unable to express their discontent, and in which underlying problems may not be adequately resolved to the satisfaction of the parties. Thus, even though the denial of the right to strike may be politically expedient in the short run, it may only make things worse over time — a possibility that appears to be borne out by existing research (Hebdon and Stern, 2003; Hebdon, 2005).

In addition to prohibitions on the right to strike are "**timeliness**" restrictions. Depending on the jurisdiction in question, as many as five conditions must be met before a strike is deemed to be timely and hence legal. First, in all jurisdictions, any previous collective agreement must have expired. Second, again in all jurisdictions, the union must have made a "good faith" attempt to reach a settlement, subject to the same conditions as discussed earlier in this chapter with respect to management. Third, in a number of jurisdictions, the minister of labour must be notified before a strike occurs, and can require that the parties first undergo **conciliation** (this procedure is discussed in chapter thirteen) to see if they can reconcile their differences. If the conciliation process is not successful, a report is filed with the minister, and the union can strike only after a seven to fourteen day period subsequent to the issuance of this report. Fourth, a number of jurisdictions require the union to first hold a strike vote and win majority support from its members, and in some jurisdictions the ministry of labour has the right to order and hold such a vote if so requested by an employer. Finally, in some jurisdictions the union must give management a formal notification of the intent to strike anywhere from two to fourteen days in advance of doing so.

At least two issues can be raised about these restrictions. First, the imposition of conciliation against the will of one or both parties is likely to be ineffective in helping resolve the dispute, and may even worsen matters by introducing a time delay and enabling one or both sides more time to prepare for a lengthy strike. Largely as a result, ministers of labour are hesitant to require conciliation unless a strike is expected to substantially contravene the public interest.

The second issue is the restriction on the right to strike during the term of the agreement. In theory, this helps to ensure a stable relationship, especially as conflict which arises during this period can be resolved through the grievance process. Yet, as Larry Haiven has argued, this process can become overloaded, and management may act in ways which, though contentious, do not violate the contract and hence are not grievable (Haiven, 1995). By the time the next set of negotiations begins, pent-up frustrations, coupled with the number of issues which have built up, can greatly enhance the difficulty of arriving at an agreement. In contrast, Haiven argues, the right to strike during the term of the agreement could provide workers with the leverage to resolve issues as they arise. This could ultimately have positive implications for the labour–management relationship, fostering greater order and stability as well as enhancing the democratic rights of workers.

Employer Rights During a Strike

In addition to issues having to do with the timeliness of strikes are those having to do with employer rights during a strike. Perhaps the most controversial one is the right of employers to continue operations during a strike, either by using employees from "outside" of the bargaining unit (e.g., managerial personnel), or by encouraging striking workers to cross the picket line, or by hiring replacement workers. In the United States, replacement workers can be hired on a permanent basis, with the result that workers can effectively find themselves out of a job merely for exercising their legal right to strike. In Canada, however, workers on strike normally have a right to get their job (or a similar one) back at the end of a strike. In some jurisdictions, the right of employers to even hire temporary replacements is either prohibited or restricted.[8]

---

[8] In Quebec, employers are not only unable to hire temporary replacements or use supervisory employees, they also cannot hire additional, non-union workers prior to a strike and they cannot bring in non-striking workers from other establishments. Similar

There are at least three arguments in favour of allowing management to continue operations.[9] The first is that failure to do so can unduly upset the balance of power in favour of the union. The second is that a complete shut-down may create undue economic hardship for the employer. This may, for example, be especially serious if there are high costs to shutting down, as has traditionally been the case in the steel production sector. The third is that workers are free to work for other employers during a strike, and that the use of replacement workers by employers is an equivalent right.

Against these arguments is the argument that allowing employers to continue operations clearly frustrates the underlying purposes of labour law discussed earlier, especially where replacement workers are involved. Where employers find it expedient to exercise this right, strike power is greatly weakened, in some cases rendering the right to strike meaningless and hence enabling the employer to effectively undermine the right to collective bargaining (e.g., Godard, 1998b; Blouin, 1995). Doing so can also cause irreparable long-term harm to union-management relations and even result in violence. Perhaps the most dramatic case in recent years was the Giant Gold Mine case in the early 1990s, where nine replacement workers were accidentally killed in an explosion set by frustrated strikers attempting to sabotage mine operations.

The right to continue operations can also introduce considerable inequality into the system, especially as the use of replacement workers tends to be most effective and hence most widely employed where jobs require low levels of job-related skill and training, and in establishments that are small relative to the size of the local labour market (and hence able to hire enough replacements). Often, therefore, a strike is least effective for workers who are in the most disadvantaged jobs (where there is low exit and job power), and most in need of an effective union (Beatty, 1983). In contrast, they are most effective for workers in the most advantaged jobs and least in need of an effective union.

---

legislation was passed in both Ontario and British Columbia in the early 1990s, though it was eliminated by the then newly-elected Mike Harris government in Ontario in 1996. Finally, the federal government has passed legislation outlawing the use of replacement workers if the purpose in doing so appears to be to break a union.

[9] See England (1983: 277–86), Godard (1998b), and Sims, Blouin, and Knopf (1995: 138–50) for more extensive analyses of this issue.

Restrictions During a Strike

Restrictions also apply with respect to the right of workers to picket their employer during a strike. Generally, workers must have permission if they wish to picket on any privately owned premises, even if these premises are provided for public use (e.g., a shopping centre parking lot) and are not owned by their employer. They also cannot legally obstruct exit from or entry to such premises, and they cannot harm or intimidate individuals who choose to cross the picket line. Moreover, if there is any indication that picketers are violating these restrictions or reason to believe that they may do so, the employer can apply to the courts (in B.C., to the labour relations board) for an "injunction" to restrict the number of picketers allowed at one time, or even to end picketing altogether.

In addition to restrictions on the right to picket one's employer, are restrictions on **secondary** picketing, where striking workers picket firms that continue to do business with the employer during a strike. Subsequent to a 2002 Supreme Court ruling, secondary picketing is now generally legal in Canada, provided that it is not used for purposes of intimidation. However, each jurisdiction can place restrictions on secondary picketing, provided that they do not unduly clash with the right to free expression enshrined in the Charter of Rights and Freedoms.

A final, closely related, restriction on strike activity has to do with **sympathy strikes** (a strike to show support for workers already on strike) and refusal by workers outside of the bargaining unit to cross picket lines. Generally, both are illegal, though workers can refuse to cross a picket line if they have reason to fear physical harm or to believe that doing so is consistent with their own collective agreement, even though provisions to this effect in collective agreements are also not legally binding on an employer. Workers can also refuse to do work that would normally be performed by striking employees.

It can be argued that restrictions on employee rights during a strike and the prevention of non-striking workers from acting in sympathy are consistent with the policy objective of stability and efficiency. However, when considered in conjunction with employer rights and with timeliness requirements, it becomes clear that the right to strike is by no means an absolute one, and that there are important limitations on the use of a union's strike power. Whether such limitations are justified is, of course, an issue for debate, for the case can be made that these limitations weaken a union's ability to ensure a fair settlement is reached. This is especially likely to be a problem where an employer is in effect attempting to "break" a union and has managed to keep operations open during a strike. To counter these circumstances, the union has to be able to rely upon alternatives to the simple withdrawal of its members' labour. To the extent that it is unable to do so under the law, it is likely to find itself at a major disadvantage. For these reasons, restrictions on secondary picketing have in the past proven especially controversial.

V.   UNION AUTHORITY AND THE DUTY OF FAIR REPRESENTATION

Once a union has been certified, it becomes the exclusive agent for workers in the election unit. Workers within this unit cannot seek out an alternative form of representation, and individual "side-bargains" with employers are illegal unless specifically allowed for in the agreement. Though most jurisdictions require unions to conduct a vote ratifying the collective agreement before it can become legal, the union has the sole authority to negotiate a collective agreement for workers, and it normally acts as their sole representative during the term of this agreement. Workers *may* not be required to join the union, depending on the union security clause negotiated (see chapter fifteen). But in most jurisdictions, they are effectively required to pay the equivalent of union dues, and they are still subject to the terms of the collective agreement.

Moreover, unless there is a contract provision or specific law to the contrary, individuals in most jurisdictions possess no legal a priori right to file or pursue a grievance on their own. Instead, a grievance must be filed by the union (albeit on behalf of the griever) and, once filed, union officials "own" the grievance, having complete say over how it is processed and resolved. This means that, even if the initial griever wants to withdraw the grievance, he or she is unable to do so. Rather, this decision is up to the union. While this helps to prevent frivolous grievances from being filed by discontented workers, this, in combination with union control over the terms of the agreement negotiated, means that union officials can have a considerable amount of authority over workers.

To ensure that union authority is not abused, most jurisdictions in Canada require that unions represent all workers in the election unit equally, even if they are not actually members of the union. This "**duty of fair representation**", as it is referred to, generally requires that a union may not treat any of its members in a way that is arbitrary, discriminatory, or in bad faith. Though this duty applies most often to the processing of grievances, it can also apply to negotiations. In the former case, union officials must process grievances on the basis of merit. In the latter, it cannot arbitrarily neglect or sacrifice the interests of individuals or minority groups of workers.

Unfortunately, the duty of fair representation may not provide individuals with as much protection as might be desirable. In this respect, labour boards generally find themselves caught between concern over individual rights and the more fundamental principle of free collective bargaining. To rule in favour of the individual in effect undermines a union's right to behave authoritatively, in accordance with its understanding of the collective interests of its members and the intended meaning of the collective agreement (Brown, 1983; Arthurs et al., 1993: 190). And, it is often difficult to establish with any certainty whether the duty of fair representation has, in fact, been violated, especially if the union can make a plausible case as to why individual interests were sacrificed. For example, a union may decide to select some grievances to pursue while abandoning others, either because the costs would be too high, given the matter at hand, or because they do not perceive a reasonable chance of winning (McQuarrie, 2010).

A further problem is that, where duty of fair representation complaints *are* filed, it may be for tactical reasons rather than because the complainant has in fact been treated unfairly (Knight, 1987a, 1987b). In other words, the complainant may wish to inflict political damage on or harass an incumbent union official, either for personal or for political reasons. In addition, individuals may file a complaint or threaten to do so as a means of pressuring union officials to pursue a grievance which is lacking in merit, thus negating the rationale for union ownership of grievances. Perhaps as a result, a substantial number of complaints are dismissed by labour boards.[10]

One option to the duty of fair representation is to enable workers to pursue grievances independently of the union, hiring their own lawyer if necessary. This option is specifically provided for in the federal jurisdiction and in some provincial jurisdictions with respect to public sector employees. Some provincial jurisdictions also specify that private sector workers have a right to file written grievances independently

---

[10] In B.C., For example, more than 90 percent were dismissed during the early 2000s (McQuarrie, 2010).

of their union, though they do not provide for the pursuit of these to the arbitration stage without the union's consent. Finally, it is legal for labour and management to negotiate a provision for the independent pursuit of grievances, an option which would appear to have become increasingly popular in recent years. Though allowing individuals to pursue their own grievances can cause problems similar to those created by duty of fair representation cases, it seems that unions have increasingly become sensitive to the frustrations experienced by individuals who feel they have not been fairly represented.

A more drastic option is to allow individuals to reject union representation, act as their own agents, and cease to pay union dues altogether. Under this option, individuals have the "right to work" without coming under the authority of the union or paying union dues. In the United States, a number of states have "**right to work**" laws under which this is the case, but it is generally illegal in Canada, primarily because it creates a circumstance in which individuals may benefit from the existence of a union without paying dues or being required to go on strike (as discussed earlier in this chapter).

VI. MANAGEMENT AUTHORITY AND RIGHTS

One of the primary concerns raised by neoliberals and managerialists about collective bargaining has been that unions negotiate undue restrictions on managerial authority and rights. Unions often negotiate bureaucratic rules and provisions concerning promotion and advancement, crew sizes, work pace, job assignments, job classifications, and so forth. Indeed, a major function of unions in North America has historically been to impose such restrictions, consistent with the democratization function discussed in chapter seven. Thus, there can be little doubt that certification of a union can ultimately result in a number of restrictions on managerial authority.

At the same time, it is important to be aware of various limits to these restrictions. Of particular importance is the doctrine of "**residual rights**" which has come to form the basis for arbitral decisions in grievance arbitrations. As also discussed in chapter nine, this doctrine stipulates that anything that is not specifically included within the collective agreement remains, by default, under the sole authority of management. Thus, the only restrictions on managerial authority (with a few exceptions) are those which management itself has agreed to (even if reluctantly) in the collective bargaining process!

In addition, those restrictions which unions *do* negotiate on managerial authority are typically limited to narrow "personnel"-related decisions. They do not involve broader, "strategic" decisions about such things as new investments, production methods, and plant closings, all of which can have major implications for workers. They also rarely involve an actual sharing of authority, where the consent or agreement of the union is necessary *before* management can act.

It follows that, while unions do negotiate restrictions on managerial authority, and while these restrictions may not be to management's liking, unions remain very much in a "junior" and reactive position during the term of the agreement. Indeed, it could well be argued that it is because of the position that unions find themselves in that it becomes necessary for them to negotiate often complex and bureaucratic rules and procedures into the collective agreement. Otherwise, under the doctrine of residual rights, unions have little way of directly influencing the exercise of managerial authority. Not only may this be counterproductive, it also means that the ability of unions to protect their members from the arbitrary and unfair exercise of authority may depend in large part upon their ability to negotiate these restrictions — an ability which itself varies somewhat arbitrarily, largely in accordance with strike power.

One option is to eliminate many of the restrictions on the right to strike (Godard, 1998b). As discussed earlier, this would enable workers to pressure management to consult union officials during the term of the agreement. In addition to this option, however, scholars have suggested various alternatives to the doctrine of residual rights — alternatives which enable unions to provide greater protection for their members, yet which also reduce the need for bureaucratic restrictions in collective agreements. At least four such options can be identified.

The first such alternative is to replace the doctrine of residual rights with the doctrine of **"fair administration"**, in which workers are entitled to "fair and reasonable" treatment regardless of the provisions of the collective agreement. Thus, for example, a worker who is arbitrarily passed over for advancement may grieve even if there is no specific contract provision dealing with the issue.

A second alternative is to adopt what some authors have referred to as an **"implied obligations doctrine"** (Giles and Jain, 1989: 324), under which management has an implied obligation to consult with and obtain the agreement of union officials before making major changes that are relevant to the collective agreement. For example, if a major technological change is being planned, and this may affect the nature of workers' jobs or may even result in a number of layoffs, then management would be required to first consult with the union.

A third possible alternative is the "**doctrine of shared rights**" (Beatty, 1984). Under this doctrine, an informal or implicit contract is deemed to exist in addition to any formal or implicit contract negotiated at the bargaining table. As discussed in chapters one and three, this contract entails various understandings and customs that have developed over time as to the nature of work and the obligations and duties of each party. Thus, if management has traditionally acted in accordance with various informal rules or procedures, any attempt to deviate from these rules or procedures without the union's consent could provide grounds for a grievance.

A fourth possibility entails the "**doctrine of job rights**". Under this principle, workers accrue certain job rights over time, and these balance off against managerial property rights. Thus, for example, if a worker is laid off, he or she would have a right to some form of compensation and/or assistance in qualifying for and obtaining another job, with the level of compensation depending upon the length of service. This would help to provide income and job security without having to negotiate such provisions into the collective agreement.

All of these alternatives have enjoyed some acceptance in practice. For example, some arbitrators have attempted to take issues of fairness into account when settling grievances. Though their ability to do so has been largely circumscribed by the courts (Haiven, 1991: 97–100), this is consistent with the doctrine of fair administration. Additionally, a number of jurisdictions require management to consult with union officials and even enter into negotiations with the union over major technological changes during the life of an agreement, which is consistent with the implied obligations doctrine. Most jurisdictions also require employers to pay employees extended termination benefits in the event of a group layoff, as discussed in chapter nine. Though these are still relatively limited, they are consistent with the doctrine of job rights. Finally, General Motors and the United Auto Workers (the U.S. counterpart to the Canadian Auto Workers) experimented with the doctrine of shared rights at GM's Saturn plant in Tennessee, adopting what has been referred to as a "**living agreement**". However, this plant was closed in 2009. The principle of residual rights continues to be predominant, and there is little to suggest that this is about to change in the near future (see Haiven, 1991: 92–94). If it did, it could clearly portend quite fundamental implications for the nature of the labour–management relation and the processes of collective bargaining.

VII. CONCLUSIONS

This chapter has discussed the legal framework regulating the relationships between unions, workers, and employers in Canada. Because this framework varies from jurisdiction to jurisdiction and over time, the intention has been not to delve into great detail about the specifics of this framework, but rather to describe the general content of labour law in Canada and to address various issues that can or have been raised about this content. The following four chapters address the processes and outcomes of collective bargaining and contract administration.

Collective Bargaining
Structure, Process, and
Outcomes

12

Collective bargaining forms the heart of the Canadian system of industrial relations, at least in the union sector. Not only does it establish worker pay and benefit levels, it also establishes the formal rules which regulate the labour–management relationship during the term of a collective agreement. These rules are especially important in the Canadian system, because, under the doctrine of residual rights, workers have few rights and protections unless provided for in the collective agreement. Collective bargaining also serves as an important means of conflict resolution, ideally enabling both parties to come to a mutually satisfactory compromise on issues of concern to their constituents and enabling them to work together during the term of an agreement, potentially lowering the incidence of alternative forms of conflict (e.g., quits, sabotage). Thus, this chapter addresses collective bargaining, beginning with the structure of collective bargaining, then the process, and, finally, the outcomes.

I. THE STRUCTURE OF COLLECTIVE BARGAINING

When considering the structure of collective bargaining, it is useful to distinguish between "formal" and "informal" bargaining structures. While the former represents the actual unit designated for purposes of collective bargaining and covered by a collective agreement, the latter represents the relationships between formal bargaining units, particularly the tendency for a settlement in one to have implications for settlements in others.

Formal Bargaining Structures

As discussed in chapter eleven, labour boards normally determine the bargaining unit for purposes of a certification election, based on: (1) the wishes of the parties, (2) traditional arrangements in the occupation or industry, and (3) whether employees in a proposed unit have a "community of interest". More often than not, the unit is defined to cover all employees in broadly similar jobs or occupations within a single workplace. However, the parties may decide that they would like to combine these units into a broader bargaining unit, negotiating agreements which cover more than one group or workplace, more than one employer, and even more than one union. In addition, governments may legislate a broader bargaining unit. This is especially so in the public sector, where bargaining units may cover all employees within a given occupation in a particular jurisdiction (e.g., all hospital nurses, all secondary school teachers). Thus, although Canadian labour boards tend to define bargaining units narrowly, a number of alternative bargaining structures can exist. Six are most often identified:

(1) Single-employer, Single-establishment, Single-union. This is the usual unit defined by a labour board for election purposes and is among the most common in Canada. Note, however, that a number of separate units may coexist within the same establishment, each of which entails a separate negotiation and may involve a different union. For example, in a university there can be separate units for professors, for librarians, for part-time lecturers, for teaching assistants, for secretaries, and for maintenance staff — all of which are represented by a different union.

(2) Single-employer, Multi-establishment, Single-union. This unit is also relatively common. It involves negotiation between a single employer and a single union, but covers more than one workplace. In the private sector, for example, General Motors, Chrysler, and Ford each negotiate a single agreement with the Canadian Auto Workers to cover all of their assembly operations in Canada. In the public sector, a single negotiation may cover all establishments within a particular jurisdiction, as is typically the case for municipal firefighters and, in a number of provinces, for teachers (Peirce, 2000: 356).

(3) Single-employer, Single-establishment, Multi-union. This unit is rare in Canada, largely because labour boards include all employees with broadly similar characteristics in the same bargaining unit for purposes of certification. But in Britain, where employers have traditionally recognized unions voluntarily (often subject to union pressure), bargaining structures have traditionally been far more fragmented, with different groups of workers represented by different unions.[1] As a result, a third of all workplaces in which collective bargaining takes place have "single-table" bargaining, in which all of the unions combine to negotiate a single agreement with the employer (see Cully et al., 1999: 110). In addition, recent labour law reforms in Britain have been designed to increase the incidence of this form of bargaining in workplaces where there is more than one union (ERB, sch. 1: 34). If, as discussed in chapter eleven, some form of minority unionism was to become legalized in Canada, a similar structure might be expected to develop here as well.

(4) Single-employer, Multi-establishment, Multi-union. This type of bargaining unit is also rare in Canada. However, it is most likely to occur in the case of large employers with dispersed operations involving a variety of different craft unions. An example is the railway industry, where craft unions negotiate a single overall agreement with each of the major rail companies (Chaykowski, 1995: 232).

(5) Multi-employer, Multi-establishment, Single-union. This type of bargaining unit typically covers all establishments within a given industry. Where this is the case, it is referred to as **industry** or **sectoral** bargaining. For example, in health care, a single employer association, consisting of all of the hospitals in a region or province may combine to negotiate with the provincial nursing union (Chaykowski, 1995: 232). Though relatively rare in Canada, occurring mostly in health care, trucking, construction, and forestry, industry-level bargaining is the predominant type of bargaining structure in most northern European countries. It is also regularly credited with helping to explain what some consider to be the superior social performance of these countries, for reasons returned to below.

(6) Multi-employer, Multi-establishment, Multi-union. This entails a highly concentrated form of bargaining, occurring on an industry or even multi-industry level. Though perhaps the rarest of the six types

---

[1] Though these groups have in the past tended to be subject to industry-wide agreements, industry bargaining has broken down over the past few decades, leaving a fragmented bargaining structure.

of bargaining structure in Canada, it *has* been used at times in the construction industry, where a strike by one trade can substantially limit the ability of other trades to do their work and hence effectively shut-down all or parts of the industry (Rose, 1992). Of note, it has been used in some countries to cover all workers within a broad category in the economy as a whole. In Sweden, for example, the major private sector labour federation (LO) and employers' association (SAF) used to negotiate a central agreement covering all of Sweden's blue-collar workers. However, the employers' federation pulled out of this arrangement in 1992, and bargaining is now conducted on an industry-wide basis.

There are a number of possible variations and combinations of these bargaining structures. For example, in most countries with industry-level bargaining systems, supplementary negotiations are conducted at the employer or workplace level. Where this is the case, the general wage increase and wage-related issues tend to be negotiated centrally, while issues having to do with incentive payments and with most non-wage considerations are negotiated at either the workplace or the employer level. In Canada, this kind of arrangement tends to be relatively rare, because negotiations occur predominantly at the workplace level. However, in the case of multi-establishment, multi-employer units, it is not uncommon for the parties to negotiate a single, **master agreement** to cover broader issues which apply to all workplaces in a unit, such as wage levels, benefit plans, and job security, and a series of workplace level, **supplemental agreements** to cover issues which vary across workplaces in accordance with the specific nature and requirements of the work being done, such as working hours, crew sizes, and other locally-specific issues. These "two-tier agreements", as they are sometimes called, have been popular in industries such as steel, auto, and forestry (Chaykowski, 1995: 233).

Informal Bargaining Structures

Collective agreements are not negotiated in isolation from one another. Rather, there is a tendency for "informal" structures to exist, with the results from each set of negotiations having implications for other sets. This is perhaps most obvious when multiple agreements are negotiated by the same employer. Unless the employer can provide very good reasons for not doing so, it has little effective choice but to provide a broadly similar settlement to all of its bargaining units if it wants to avoid a strike. Thus, for example, if a university administration has recently negotiated a wage increase and various benefit improvements with its faculty union, it is likely to have a difficult time justifying a less favourable settlement to its support staff.

A similar process often arises across employers, especially within industries. Unless one employer is experiencing economic conditions which differ substantially from others, it is difficult for it to provide a less favourable settlement than the other, at least without considerable union resistance and worker discontent. In some industries, this may even entail something referred to as **coordinated bargaining**, in which separate agreements are negotiated, but on the understanding that all negotiations will reach essentially the same settlement, with only minor modifications at most. For example, although General Motors, Ford, and Chrysler each have a separate agreement with the Canadian Auto Workers (CAW), their negotiations are conducted almost simultaneously (see Kumar and Meltz, 1992). However, the CAW targets one of these three employers for possible strike action. This becomes the key negotiation and hence is settled first, establishing the standard for the remaining two firms.

Is Decentralization a Good Thing?

Although informal bargaining structures can play an important role in Canada, the tendency for most agreements to be negotiated at either the establishment or employer level means that it has one of the most decentralized bargaining systems in the world. This may have important implications.

First, negotiations can require a considerable amount of time, resources, and expertise. Where bargaining is centralized within an industry, the related costs are dispersed across a large number of employers and union members, and negotiations are conducted by experienced experts. But when bargaining is decentralized, the costs can be substantial for both the employer and the local union, while the level of professionalization may be substantially lower. As a result, employers may be more resistant to unions, unions may have to charge significantly higher dues to their members, and strike activity may be substantially higher.

Second, decentralized negotiations can foster distrust and hostility within the workplace. This is especially so if there has been difficulty reaching agreement. But distrust and hostility can result even when this is not the case, as employers attempt to deceive the union as to their ability to grant concessions, and union officials foster membership hostility and hence willingness to strike in order to bolster their position at the bargaining table. When negotiations are decentralized, this distrust and hostility can carry over after an agreement is signed, because the parties involved must deal with each other on a day-to-day basis. But when negotiations are centralized, both the local union and local managers play only a small role in the process and so the likelihood of distrust and hostility carrying over into their day-to-day relations is much lower.

These arguments suggest a strong case for more centralized bargaining. However, it has also been argued that more centralized bargaining can have negative economic effects if it occurs at the industry level (Calmfors and Driffill, 1988). Because wages and working conditions are in effect taken out of competition, the parties have less to worry about if they agree to sizeable union gains, thus resulting in higher labour costs and possible efficiency losses. In contrast, when bargaining is at the employer or workplace level, there is reason to be concerned that such gains will place the employer or workplace at a disadvantage relative to other employers or workplaces.

There are two problems with this argument. First, even when there is industry level bargaining, employers may be able to opt out of agreements, as in many European countries. This can put pressure on negotiators to keep gains relatively low for fear that some employers will otherwise have an incentive to opt out and hence undercut those that do not. Second, increased costs and efficiency losses can mean lower demand than otherwise, as consumers decide to spend their money on other goods and services. They can also mean a loss of market share to foreign competitors. Thus, even where employers cannot opt out, employers have some incentive to keep union gains down under industry bargaining, an incentive that increases to the extent that they are also subject to international competition.

Perhaps the strongest argument for decentralized bargaining is that it provides more flexibility, allowing the parties to reach a settlement that is most suited to their circumstances. However, this can be addressed in considerable measure through supplemental agreements. So whether workplace or employer level bargaining is necessarily better for the economy is not entirely clear. Rather, it likely depends, on the one hand, on the extent to which the laws enable employers to opt out of industry level agreements and demand for the good or service produced is sensitive to price and, on the other hand, on the extent to which the parties are able to negotiate supplemental agreements.

It is also important not to focus on economic issues alone. If one purpose of unions is to improve the wages and working conditions of their members, and this is seen as a positive outcome for society, then a bargaining structure that prevents them from doing so may be seen as counterproductive. The critical question in this respect may not be whether a particular structure has negative economic effects per se, but rather whether it allows workers to achieve fair terms and conditions of employment without *unduly* negative economic consequences. For example, in highly competitive markets, such as in the trade and the food and accommodation sectors, unions are often hotly resisted by employers and unable to win many improvements for their members. This is at least in part because bargaining is at the workplace level and employers fear that they will be placed at a competitive disadvantage if they accept a union and grant any concessions. As a result, unions have been unable to make many gains in these sectors. Yet workers in these sectors tend to be subject to low pay and poor working conditions, and hence may be most in need of such gains (Godard, 2004a: 450–51). If industry level bargaining was established, it might be possible to address this problem, without unduly negative economic effects.

Whatever the pluses and minuses of industry-level bargaining may be, this level of bargaining remains relatively rare in Canada. Moreover, attempts to establish it in more competitive sectors have been hotly contested by employer groups. In addition to the economic concerns of these groups, a great many employers in Canada appear to have a deep-seated emotional opposition to labour unions and are hence unwilling to accept any arrangements that might provide unions with an increased role. Such opposition is not unique to Canada, and may be even stronger in the United States. However, it would appear to be much less deep-seated in other developed countries, especially those in Northern Europe and Scandinavia, where industry bargaining is widespread. Indeed, a number of such countries have even more centralized bargaining, in the form of either highly co-ordinated bargaining across industries (e.g., Sweden) or centralized, economy-wide bargaining (e.g., Ireland, Italy). It is widely believed that, where bargaining is so highly centralized, there is a more direct relationship between what the parties agree to and any resulting economic consequences. Hence, the parties in theory have a greater incentive to take the latter into account, resulting in more moderate settlements (Headley, 1970; Calmfors and Driffill, 1988). However, whether this actually occurs would also appear to depend on a number of factors, especially whether individual employers and unions are willing or legally required to follow the negotiated agreement (Traxler, 2003).

II.   THE NEGOTIATIONS PROCESS

It is commonplace in some university courses to provide students with a mock bargaining case, with "management" on the one side, and "the union" on the other. These cases are useful in at least two respects. First, they provide students with a sense of the *process* of negotiations. Second, they increase the familiarity of students with various collective bargaining issues. Yet, they fail to adequately allow for the pressures and uncertainties faced by negotiators — pressures and uncertainties that arise from sources external to the bargaining process itself. Thus, before considering the actual issues and stages involved in negotiations, it is important to understand these pressures and uncertainties.

Understanding Negotiations

Negotiations can be highly complex. One reason is that the issues themselves are often complex, as will become more apparent in chapter fifteen. But more fundamentally, the negotiating teams on both sides of the bargaining table can often find themselves subject to a variety of pressures and uncertainties throughout the bargaining process. This is especially the case for union negotiators, who can find themselves having to appease various competing factions within the union and/or caught between the expectations of workers and the "realities" of the negotiating process. Thus, for union negotiators, the negotiating process is not just a matter of getting the best deal they can, but making sure that they can sell this deal to the membership of the union and various factions within it.

To complicate matters, negotiators may have considerable difficulty determining just what the best deal is. As we shall see, the negotiation process is one in which each side attempts to disguise its "bottom line". This creates uncertainty for both sides, but especially for union negotiators, who are not privy to confidential financial information and cannot be certain just what management can afford to concede (see Reder and Neumann, 1980). Adding to this uncertainty is further uncertainty as to just what the membership of the union will accept. Often union officials may not be able to determine this until an actual vote is held to ratify the agreement.

Complicating matters even further may be parent union constraints on what constitutes an acceptable settlement. For example, in the 1984 Canadian auto negotiations, union negotiators found themselves subject to pressures to conform to a recent settlement in the United

States, even though they believed that they would be unable to sell these terms to their members. This was a major reason for the secession of the Canadian auto workers union from its U.S. parent in 1985.

Management negotiators can find themselves in a similar situation. First, there can be considerable disagreement within management over the type and level of concessions that should be made. The difference, of course, is that this disagreement can be resolved — by senior executive directives if need be — before negotiations begin or, at the very least, before negotiators have to commit to a position. Yet negotiators may find the directives they receive to be unrealistic or counterproductive in view of the union's position. As a result, they may find themselves as go-betweens, negotiating not only with union officials at the bargaining table, but also with other managers behind the scenes, trying to persuade them to alter their directives.

Moreover, decision-makers within management can find themselves subject to a variety of external pressures and uncertainties from various stakeholder groups in their environment (as discussed in chapter six). This is especially true in the public sector, where managerial decisions can have important political consequences, either because of their implications for government spending or because of public support for the union's position (Kochan, 1973). But it can also be true in the private sector, where customers may threaten to switch suppliers in the event of a strike or a price increase resulting from higher wages, or where consumer boycotts of the employer's product may result if management appears to take an unreasonable position in negotiations.

In addition to these pressures and uncertainties, there are broader uncertainties as to future economic conditions, especially as they pertain to competitive conditions and inflation during the life of the collective agreement (or, in the case of governments, budgetary restrictions). These uncertainties are important not only in and of themselves, but also because they can fuel internal dissension and politics within each side, as different factions attempt to exploit these uncertainties to push for bargaining positions that serve their own, often particularistic ends.

The extent to which negotiators on either side find themselves subject to these sorts of pressures and uncertainties undoubtedly varies, but it is important to be aware of them if one is to understand the negotiation process. For the problem faced by negotiators can be less one of negotiating an agreement between themselves than it is one of negotiating with their constituents to change their expectations — a process referred to as **intra-organizational bargaining** (Walton and

McKersie, 1991). Indeed, in some cases negotiators on both sides may have a good idea of the appropriate settlement long in advance of reaching an agreement, but find themselves having to go through largely ritualistic motions in order to satisfy their constituents and/or to persuade them to alter their expectations (see Sass, 1989). Thus, rather than settle well in advance of the strike deadline, negotiators may wait until the last minute or even go beyond this deadline, in large part for the sake of appearances.

Negotiating Issues

Though it is not always easy to categorize negotiating issues, it is useful to distinguish between: (1) those which are substantive, (2) those which are procedural, and (3) those which are relational.[2] In considering these issues, it is also useful to think of them in accordance with the extent to which they are "**distributive**", in the sense that a gain for one side entails a loss for the other, and the extent to which they are "**integrative**", in the sense that both parties potentially benefit from their resolution.

Substantive Issues. Substantive issues are most associated with the economic function of unions. They are the ones most likely to entail direct conflicts between the interests of the two parties. Most evident in this respect are wages, but additional issues include benefit plans, workloads, job security protections, restrictions on technological change, and others. These issues are generally distributive, but not necessarily so. For example, if an employer is having difficulty attracting and retaining workers, it may be in the employer's interest to grant higher wages whether a union is established or not. Even if the employer is not having difficulty, granting more favourable wages and working conditions may result in a surplus of applicants, allowing it to be more selective and ultimately to hire better "quality" employees. Moreover, employee morale is likely to be higher, especially if more favourable terms and conditions are perceived to result from positive employer policies rather than the threat or act of striking. Thus, there may be some benefit to an employer from providing more favourable terms and conditions than otherwise. This benefit may not equal the costs of doing so, but it may help to offset them.

---

[2] These distinctions are adapted from Walton and McKersie, 1991

Procedural Issues. Procedural issues involve the processes by which the parties interact during the term of the agreement. Most noteworthy in this respect is the grievance process, through which the parties resolve conflicts over adherence to the collective agreement once it has been negotiated. But other procedural issues can include notification of workers in advance of a pending layoff, the processes by which overtime is allocated, and promotion or transfer procedures. Issues having to do with employment equity, harassment, and health and safety procedures may also be considered within this category.

Granting concessions on these issues does not usually entail a direct cost to the employer. Indeed, coming to an agreement on them is often in the interests of both sides, because they ensure that there are processes in place to resolve or avoid disagreements during the term of the agreement. For this reason, these issues tend to be substantially more integrative than are their substantive counterparts. But their negotiation can also engender conflict, especially because many of them entail provision of rights that employees would not otherwise have. These rights can, in turn, entail a diminution of employer authority or the flexibility with which it can be exercised — something which managers often guard zealously even when the economic costs of granting concessions may be low.

Relational Issues. These issues are most closely associated with the integrative function of unions. They can include factors affecting union strength and security, particularly whether employees will be required to join the union or at least to pay dues. But they also include issues having to do with union participation in workplace decision-making processes, the establishment of joint union-management committees, and other matters pertaining to the union's role in the workplace. Despite the managerialist literature on the need for cooperation and participation mechanisms, actual contract provisions implementing such mechanisms appear to be relatively rare. It is likely that, again, such provisions are viewed as restricting the flexibility with which employer authority can be exercised. Nonetheless, where these issues are negotiated, they can be even more integrative than procedural issues, because they are directed at enhancing the level of cooperation between the parties.

The Positions of the Parties

The positions which the parties bring to and develop while at the bargaining table have important implications for the ease with which a settlement is likely to be achieved. To understand how this is the case, it is useful to think of these positions as varying from each party's most preferred settlement to its least acceptable one, or **bottom line**. If the two parties' bottom lines overlap, we can say that there is a **positive settlement zone**. If they do not, there is a **negative settlement zone**. For example, the union may hope that it can achieve a 5 percent wage gain for its members, yet have a bottom line of 2 percent, while management may hope that it can achieve a settlement of 1 percent, yet have a bottom line of 4 percent. Thus, there is a positive settlement zone, because both parties are prepared to accept a settlement between 2 and 4 percent. However, if the union's bottom line is 4 percent and management's 2 percent, then there is a negative zone, because there is no settlement that can be acceptable to both sides.

The ease with which an agreement can be reached will depend in considerable measure not just on *whether* there is a positive settlement zone, but also the *size* of this zone. We can think of this zone as a target: the larger it is, the easier it will be for the parties to find it. If this zone is small, the parties may still reach an agreement without a strike, but negotiations will be more difficult, with much depending on whether each side accurately reads the other and does not make a "mistake", triggering a strike which should not take place. Matters become even more difficult where a positive contract zone does not initially exist, because at least one side must lower its expectations and set a new bottom line if a settlement is to be reached. A strike may be required before negotiators and their constituents will give in. In this regard, we might expect that, the larger the negative zone, the more likely it will be that a strike will occur, and the longer this strike is likely to be.

Although this characterization is useful, it may be a little simplistic, if only because negotiations typically involve a multitude of issues. Issues that are less important to the parties are more likely to have positive contract zones, or at least "softer" bottom lines, because the parties are less willing to risk a strike over them. Thus, only on those issues of high priority to one or both sides is a small positive or a negative zone likely to seriously affect the likelihood of agreement. Yet, even low priority issues are not negotiated in isolation. Usually, the parties are willing to trade off these issues, with one giving in on a particular issue if the other will give in on a different one. Each party may in this sense be seen as having an implicit bottom line in terms of the number of issues it is willing to make concessions on. If the other does not reciprocate, then negotiations can become bogged down, creating a circumstance where the parties do not even begin serious bargaining over the high priority issues until after a strike has begun.

On both high and low priority issues, the likelihood of a positive zone is likely to depend on a number of factors. So is the rate with which the parties are likely to adjust their bottom line in order to achieve such a zone. Two such factors may be the type of relationship between the negotiators and the extent to which negotiators are experienced professionals. But much may also depend on the attitudes and expectations of their constituents. Negotiators may seek to set or change a bottom line so that it is conducive to a settlement, but be unable to do so because their constituents either will not accept the outcome or actually wish a strike to occur. These factors will be discussed more fully in the next chapter. What is important at present, however, is that the ease with which negotiations are likely to proceed, and a settlement reached, can vary considerably. The idea of settlement zones is useful for conceptualizing this.

Preparation For Negotiations

As should already be evident, the negotiation process can be lengthy, beginning shortly after the union gives notice to the employer to bargain for a new agreement, and lasting as long as a year or more. Where an agreement is in place, notice must be given to the employer anywhere from 30 days to four months (depending on the jurisdiction) before the existing agreement expires, and bargaining must commence anywhere from "forthwith" to within 20 days thereafter (HRDC, 2000). Negotiations thus typically begin from three weeks to four months (or longer) prior to the expiration of the collective agreement.

Negotiations are preceded by varying amounts of preparation on both sides. On the union side, local officers may formally or informally canvas workers to establish what their concerns and expectations are, sometimes holding meetings at the local level in order to do so. Then, these officers may meet and discuss member concerns and expectations among themselves, drafting a preliminary bargaining agenda. This may involve input from parent union "staffers", who provide information and advice having to do with other settlements (i.e., outside of the bargaining unit) of relevance to negotiations, with competitive developments in the industry, with company profits and "ability to pay", and so forth. It is also at around this stage that the union negotiating committee is established, usually consisting of an experienced chief negotiator supplied by the parent union, and representatives from various locals and/or factions within the bargaining unit. Though these representatives may not participate in the actual bargaining process, they are in a position to advise the chief negotiator and to help work out proposals and counter-proposals.

Within management, similar processes may also take place, with senior management officials canvassing line managers in an attempt to pinpoint what sorts of problems are occurring in the workplace, and compiling information about industry trends and settlements, developments within the union, and so forth. Often, a senior industrial relations/human resources management official will hold the position of chief negotiator, with the remainder of the management bargaining team consisting of senior line managers and staff experts (if the employer is large enough to have such experts in its employ). The employer may also, however, rely upon a "hired gun", or outside professional who specializes in negotiations.

By the date of the first negotiating session, both sides ideally have a pretty good idea of what it is they hope to achieve in negotiations as well as what their initial positions will be. It is in this respect important to be aware that these initial positions may bear little resemblance to what it is that the parties are ultimately prepared to accept. For example, both sides may be prepared to accept an average wage settlement of between 4 and 6 percent, in which case a positive settlement zone exists. But instead of each initially advancing a proposal within this zone, the union may ask for 10 percent, and the company may claim that it can only afford 2 percent. Over the course of negotiations, each will gradually move closer to the other, though each will conceal its bottom line in the hope of obtaining a more favourable settlement. Thus, while management may be prepared to grant 6 percent, it may seek to convince the union that such a settlement is out of the question, in which case it may be able to get the union to agree to, say, 5 percent.

The Stages of the Negotiating Process

The actual process of negotiations can involve at least four stages: settling in, consolidation, finalization, and mopping up (Fisher and Williams, 1989; Peirce, 2000). Because a major purpose of negotiations is to resolve conflicts involving divergent interests and expectations, each of these stages can be important to the process. If one party attempts to skip or hurry any of them, the other may perceive that the former is not willing to take its position seriously, instead forcing negotiations to move forward before its issues and concerns have been fully voiced. Negotiations involve a process of communication as well as actually bargaining, and either side may view this process as a valuable forum for expressing, and getting the other side to understand, its point of view. Indeed, a negotiator who does not attempt to understand where the other side is "coming from" is unlikely to be particularly effective at resolving potential disagreements as the process progresses.

Settling in usually involves the first few bargaining sessions, during which the two parties exchange initial demands and positions. Because this stage is at the beginning of the process, there is generally little sense of urgency. As a result, it is relatively congenial, with each side often resorting to humour, possibly laced with sarcasm. In an established relationship, each side is confident that the initial position of the other merely represents a starting point, and that, over the course of negotiations, the other side will make a variety of modifications and concessions. Small and less conflictual issues may be addressed at this point, often with each side agreeing to take certain issues "off the table" if the other will reciprocate. At the same time, it is at this point that negotiators get a sense of what the main issues in dispute are likely to be, staking out some of their key positions. In this respect, there can be considerable posturing, as each feels out the other, attempting to determine what the other is likely to agree to and to shape the other's perceptions of its own positions.

The second stage, *consolidation*, is the longest and often the most frustrating. Each side ends its posturing and attempts to get down to serious bargaining. A problem is that, even though each side normally comes to the bargaining table with the expectation that it will have to make concessions and that the other side will reciprocate, there may be a tendency for each to underestimate the concessions the other side will expect them to make, and overestimate the concessions that the other side can be expected to make. Thus, it is easy to become frustrated at this stage, as each side takes positions which the other views as unreasonable. Both sides may still make a series of concessions, often believing that they are acting in good faith, in order to move negotiations along and induce the other side to reciprocate. However, on the main issues they may be less willing to do so, especially on issues which either or both sides (or their constituents) consider as a matter of principle or as representing a major departure from prior agreements. For example, seniority provisions have always played a major role in union contracts, particularly when layoffs are involved. If the employer seeks to eliminate these, a strike is virtually inevitable.

During this process, each side may also go to considerable lengths to convince the other that it is prepared to "dig in" on certain key issues, and in so doing try to get the other to readjust its expectations and ultimately its willingness to make concessions, thus laying the groundwork for a more favourable settlement than it might otherwise be able to attain. As one might expect, this can involve considerable bluffing, adversariness, and outright deception, as each side attempts to convince the other that it is unable or unwilling to make more than minimal concessions.

At the same time, if both parties are at all interested in reaching a settlement, they eventually *do* make concessions on some of the more important issues, usually attending to less controversial ones first. In so doing, the negotiators begin to hammer out the makings of the agreement, with each side initializing or "signing off" on the proposed contract wording for those issues that have been agreed to. They may also alter their bottom lines on various issues, as they come to realize that they are unlikely to get what they initially hoped for. In the process, it is not unusual for either side to return to its constituents and either attempt to get them to modify their expectations or at least "feel them out" to explore their likely response to further concessions.

Because the most controversial issues are left to the last, the *finalization* stage often does not begin until the strike deadline approaches. Ideally, by this point each chief negotiator has a good idea as to both what the other is able and willing to concede and what he can accept and sell to constituents. If it appears that an acceptable settlement is possible, then this stage may simply involve a game of finesse, as each tries to influence the terms of that settlement in its favour. If an acceptable settlement does not appear possible, then this stage may involve further attempts by each party to change the expectations of its own constituents or of the other party's constituents. This can involve considerable "grandstanding", with one or both sides breaking off formal negotiations and claiming that the other side is not bargaining in good faith. Of note, however, both sides may all the while remain in contact informally, discussing any problems they may be experiencing with their constituents and even asking the other's patience and co-operation.

If a positive contract zone exists, and each party correctly "reads" the other, then the parties can be expected to reach an agreement prior to the strike deadline, signing what is commonly referred to as a **"memorandum of agreement"**, which contains everything that has been agreed to. However, this memorandum is often vague, containing the bare outlines of what each side believes to have been agreed on. It is at this point that the mopping up stage ideally begins.

In the *mopping up* stage, union officials take the outlines of the agreement back to their members for a ratification vote and, if ratified, the new contract usually takes effect as of the date of its predecessor's expiry. Often, however, the parties may reach an agreement without having finalized the specific contract language. Doing so also becomes part of the mopping-up stage. It can be extremely important, because each side may find that its understanding of what was agreed to is not entirely consistent with the other's. Moreover, a number of details may arise which were not considered or were taken for granted in the negotiating process. If one side is not vigilant, it may find itself left with contract language which is unacceptable.

Impasses are said to occur when the parties are unable to reach an agreement. Provided that certain conditions have been met (discussed in chapter eleven), the employer may decide to "lock out" workers. But, more frequently, union leaders may decide to call a strike of their members, in some cases after holding a membership vote on the employer's most recent or "final" offer. It is also not unheard of for union leaders to misread their membership, agreeing to a contract that members subsequently vote to reject. In this latter case, the employer may decide to make further concessions in order to avert a strike. Otherwise, a strike is likely to begin within a few days, lasting until one or both sides modifies its expectations and is willing to make further concessions.

The decision to hold a vote on the employer's final offer is normally up to union officials. But, in some jurisdictions, the minister of labour may require a vote at the request of the employer on the grounds that the decision to strike does not represent the will of the majority of union members. The problem with this is that union negotiators may have valid tactical reasons for not putting an offer to a vote, reasons that could be undermined if made public. Union members also may not be privy to, or expert enough to interpret, all of the information relevant to the issues at hand. In addition, members typically have a number of options if union leaders are indeed acting against their wishes. Not only may workers begin to cross the picket line, local leaders are likely to find themselves voted out of office, and workers may subsequently vote either to decertify or to replace the union with a different one. Thus, for a minister of labour to require a vote in all but the very rarest of circumstances can represent an unwarranted and highly partisan intrusion into union affairs.

Finally, the parties may use the services of a conciliator, a mediator, or an arbitrator in an attempt to either avoid or shorten a strike. As discussed more fully in the next chapter, a conciliator attempts to persuade the parties to reconcile their differences, while a mediator gets actively involved in negotiations, serving as a go-between for the parties. An arbitrator decides on and imposes a final settlement, based on similar settlements in the industry and labour market.

III. BARGAINING OUTCOMES

Central to the negotiations process, of course, is the question of the extent to which each side is willing and able to make concessions. Over the years there has been a great deal written about this (see Bacharach and Lawler, 1981). For present purposes, however, it is useful to consider three factors as of importance: (1) the bargaining power of the parties; (2) their interests, values, and expectations; and (3) their negotiating skills. As shall become apparent, many of the considerations identified with each follow from the discussion in this and preceding chapters.

Bargaining Power

Bargaining power is the most important, yet perhaps the messiest, of these three factors. It has been conceptualized in a variety of ways (for a review, see Leap and Grigsby, 1986), most of which assume that, if some aspect of the industrial relations context is associated with the terms of the agreement, it is because of its implications for bargaining power (e.g., Kochan and Block, 1977; Leap and Grigsby, 1986; Mishel, 1986). The problem with doing so is that anything and everything that is associated with bargaining outcomes tends to be considered a source of power, thus rendering the concept virtually meaningless. It thus makes sense to define bargaining power more narrowly. Specifically, we can say that each side has **bargaining power**, and hence is likely to win concessions from the other, to the extent that a strike is likely to have direct and indirect costs for the other side.

In the private sector, the direct costs of a strike for management revolve around losses in profits, both during the strike or after, due to lost sales and market share. Generally, these costs are highest in periods of economic expansion (when demand is high), in firms which are unable to effectively use replacement workers and/or to supply customers from other operations, and in firms which produce a good or service that cannot be stockpiled in advance of a strike. In the public sector, the sources of strike power are somewhat more complex, but they generally revolve around public sympathy for the strikers and losses in public confidence in the government. In both cases, however, they can generally be expected to increase management's willingness to grant concessions, for the higher they are, the more likely the benefits of granting concessions are to outweigh the costs (as discussed in chapter six).

Indirect costs for management include the costs of increased exit and recalcitrance due to worker discontent and adversariness which may linger after a strike. They are typically highest where high levels of skill and training are required to perform the work in question and where highly complex, rigid, and capital intensive technologies are employed (see chapter one).

For the union, the direct costs of a strike revolve around the extent to which members are able to make up for lost income, which is a function of the amount of overtime they are able to work before or after a strike, their ability to find temporary or part-time income elsewhere, and the amount of strike pay the union is able to provide them during the strike. Indirect costs include potential job losses which could result from a strike, as well as any subsequent changes in managerial polices which may translate into more arduous conditions in the workplace (e.g., increased workloads, harsher discipline).

Interests, Values, and Expectations

Interests, values, and expectations are important because they determine the extent to which each party is likely to resist the other's demands and hence risk undergoing the costs of a strike. With respect to management, we would expect three sets of factors to be important. The first is the costs of various concessions — costs which can be expected to vary depending on employer cost-economies. As noted in chapter six, some firms may find it less costly to give in to various union demands, either because they enjoy certain economies of scale, or because their operations are more conducive to the bureaucratic rules and procedures sought by union negotiators, due, for example, to standardized production processes which require little flexibility. The second set of factors is the extent to which management adheres to adversarial, anti-union values and ideologies. To the extent that this is the case, management can be expected to take a tougher stance in negotiations than otherwise. The third set of factors is the extent to which managerial decision-makers believe that it is possible to absorb or pass on the costs of various settlements and hence are prepared to do so. In the private sector, this is likely to depend in part upon the financial health of the employer, and in part upon whether competitors are unionized and have made (or can be expected to make) similar concessions. In the public sector, much may depend upon budgetary conditions and upon the ability to pass the costs on to taxpayers through higher taxes.

With respect to the union, three similar sets of factors are likely to be important. The first is the extent to which workers and/or their negotiators consider the costs of making various concessions to be high. This is especially true with respect to substantive issues such as wages and benefits, but it also applies to many procedural issues, as these have important implications for worker rights and protections during the term of the agreement. The second is the extent to which workers and/or their negotiators are militant, either because of their broader political values or because of pent-up frustrations and discontent with managerial policies and practices. Third, are the fairness perceptions of workers, especially as influenced by perceptions of the employer's ability to grant concessions and by comparisons with the terms and conditions of employment received by similar workers elsewhere.

Negotiating Skills

The negotiating skills of the parties are important in two respects. The first, and most obvious, is each party's skill at getting the other side to alter its expectations and bottom line. The second is the ability of each party to accurately read the other's position. Doing so usually means an analysis of the other's behaviour at the bargaining table, in an attempt to see through the other's posturing and determine how far that party is prepared to move from its initial position. But it can also be less direct, in which case an attempt is made to assess the power of the other or the values and expectations of the other's constituents. Thus, for example, if unemployment is high and if the union strike fund is empty, management is likely to expect a better settlement than otherwise, for the costs of a strike to workers are higher, making them less willing to go out and their negotiators more willing to make concessions. In turn, if worker exit, strike, and job power are high, union negotiators are likely to expect a better settlement, for the costs to management of worker discontent are higher, making management negotiators more willing to grant concessions.

Analyzing Variation

As may already be apparent, these three sets of factors can be quite interrelated. For example, if the bargaining power of the union is low and that of management is high, then we might expect workers to lower their expectations and to become less militant, in the recognition that a strike would be extremely costly. We might also expect management to raise their expectations and adopt a less accommodative, more adversarial approach in negotiations. It is important to recognize that these and other interrelationships may exist, but to attempt to specify exactly what they are would be futile, for much depends on the actors involved and the interactions between them. It is important to be aware that variation in bargaining outcomes ultimately reflects the conscious choices of negotiators and their constituents. While contextual considerations can have important implications for these choices, they can in no sense be thought of as strictly determining them — especially in view of the uncertainties and complexities to which negotiators are subject.

IV. COOPERATIVE BARGAINING

Much of the discussion to this point has assumed an "adversarial" model of collective bargaining. That is, though union and management negotiators may recognize that they have a number of interests in common, they view their role as achieving the best results they can for their "side". Traditionally, it is the union side which makes the most demands, seeking to obtain gains for its members.

Managerialists, in particular, have argued that this model fosters an unnecessarily conflictual relationship, and rather than serving as a basis for resolving conflict, the conventional, adversarial approach too often simply aggravates it. According to this criticism, there is thus a need to discard this approach in favour of what may be referred to as "**cooperative bargaining**".

A number of variants of cooperative bargaining have been advocated over the years, variously referred to as "integrative" bargaining, "single team" bargaining, "principled" bargaining, "mutual gains" bargaining, "interest-based" bargaining, and "target-specific" bargaining (e.g., Walton and McKersie, 1991; Fisher and Ury, 1983; Cohen-Rosenthal and Burton, 1992; Cutcher-Gershenfeld, Power, and McCabe-Power, 1996). But with all of these approaches, areas of conflict are viewed as problems to be solved rather than as positions to be won. Thus, the parties should adopt a problem-solving approach, working together as a single team to determine the most effective resolution to their differences. They should also focus on positives rather than negatives, highlighting the areas in which they can expand the pie and hence both benefit, thus achieving mutual gains.

These approaches tend to assume that adversariness and conflict in negotiations are in large part attributable to the orientations of the parties and their tendency to become fixated on set positions (i.e., bottom lines) rather than objectively evaluating what is in their best interests. Advocates of cooperative bargaining thus argue that there is greater need for the parties to focus on objective rather than subjective criteria when evaluating outcomes and that they need to be able to put themselves in the position of the other party. To achieve these things, advocates typically argue that, prior to negotiations, both sides should undergo extensive joint consultation and preparation. One of these variants, "target-specific" bargaining, actually requires a five-step process of joint training and preparation, most of which involve a neutral facilitator, before negotiations even begin (Cutcher-Gershenfeld, Power, and McCabe-Power, 1996)! These are outlined in Box 12–1.

Cooperative bargaining, in theory, goes hand in hand with high performance practices, as discussed in chapter five. As is the case for these practices, its value can be debated. If one adheres to a managerialist perspective, then it makes immanent sense. But if one believes that there are genuine conflicts of interest between labour and management, and that adversariness typically occurs because one side intentionally seeks to implement changes which will serve its interests at the expense of the other, then the apparent feasibility of this approach will seem limited. Complicating matters is the position of subordination in which workers find themselves in the employment relation and the distrust this can generate. Perhaps for these reasons, it appears that cooperative bargaining often enjoys only limited, if any, success (Hunter and McKersie, 1992; Cutcher-Gershenfeld, Kochan, and Wells, 2001). As for the high performance model, managerialists have identified a variety of reasons for this, all of which they suggest can be readily overcome. But cooperative bargaining approaches have been advocated at least since the 1960s. It may be that, given the structure of the labour–management relation in North America, they are only workable in a limited number of workplaces — those in which workers have high degrees of power, rendering cooperative relations in the employer's interests, or those in which the future of the workplace is threatened, so that workers and their negotiators have little choice but to accept management's agenda.

BOX 12–1 Stages Advocated Under the "Target-Specific" Bargaining Variant

1. The problem seeking stage: each side meets separately with its constituents in order to learn what problems they are experiencing in the workplace.
2. The problem assembly stage: the problems are assembled into lists, with members of each side having access to their side's list only.
3. The joint problem review and explanation stage: each party first presents its list separately to the facilitator, and then both meet to discuss their list with the other.
4. The information needs and format request stage: the parties jointly "brainstorm" to identify the data needed to solve the problems and then break into joint teams, with separate teams working on separate problems.
5. The data gathering stage: all of the information and outcomes of the preceding stages are compiled into a manual for both sides' use in negotiations.
6. The negotiation stage: involves first setting an agenda, grouping the problems into categories, and discussing and solving each problem from each category in sequence, using problem-solving methods.
7. The ratification stage: each side takes the agreed on "solutions" back to their constituents, explains them, and gets them ratified.
8. Follow-up stage: every member of each committee takes full responsibility for the implementation of the agreement, and there are joint meetings every three months or so in order to assess how well each party is living up to its commitments.

Source: Summarized from Joel Cutcher-Gershenfeld, Donald Power, and Maureen McCabe-Power, 1996. "Global Implications of Recent Innovations in U.S. Collective Bargaining", *Relations Industrielles*, 51(2): 281–301.

V.   CONCLUSIONS

This chapter has addressed the structure, processes, and outcomes of collective bargaining within the Canadian context. An assumption has been that the parties actually wish to seek an agreement and that they are able to do so on their own. Neither of these assumptions necessarily holds. The following chapter thus addresses more fully the role of and reasons for strikes, and considers various forms of third party "intervention" in the negotiation process.

Strikes and Dispute Resolution

13

The analysis in the preceding chapter focused on the processes by which the parties achieve settlements, why these settlements vary, and the role of bargaining structures in shaping both. Often, however, negotiations may result in an impasse, resulting either in a strike or in some form of "third party intervention". This chapter begins by providing a more in-depth discussion of strikes and why they occur. It then addresses various forms of third party intervention and their implications for collective bargaining.

I.   STRIKES

As discussed in chapter three, labour–management conflict can be seen in a variety of forms, but strikes are undoubtedly the most dramatic and intense, with both sides typically undergoing considerable expense and stress. Strikes are also the most publicly visible, receiving attention in the media, and often inconveniencing or even harming third parties. This is especially true in Canada. Although days lost due to strike activity are now a quarter of what they were in the 1970s, they are still high in comparison to other countries (see Figure 13–1). This is often seen as a negative, engendering lost productivity and infringing on the ability of employers to manage their operations smoothly and without outside interference. Indeed, as noted in chapter seven, some people view strikes as little more than attempted extortion, in which workers and their union "bosses" shut-down a workplace until the employer agrees to "pay them off" with terms and conditions of employment above those justified by market conditions. Why, then, are strikes permitted? The answer is that, while strikes may indeed involve a number of costs and inconveniences, they may

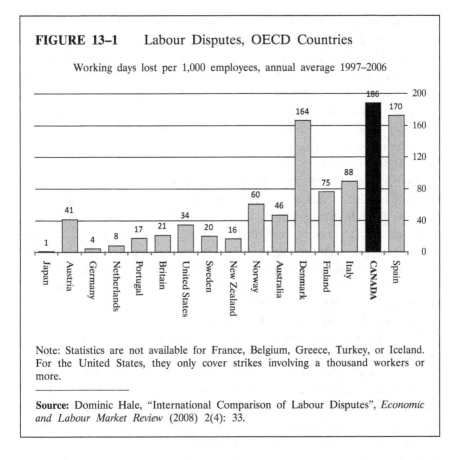

FIGURE 13–1 Labour Disputes, OECD Countries

Working days lost per 1,000 employees, annual average 1997–2006

Note: Statistics are not available for France, Belgium, Greece, Turkey, or Iceland. For the United States, they only cover strikes involving a thousand workers or more.

Source: Dominic Hale, "International Comparison of Labour Disputes", *Economic and Labour Market Review* (2008) 2(4): 33.

also serve a number of positive functions. Thus, before addressing why strikes occur, it is of value to understand what these functions are.

The Functions of Strikes

Perhaps the primary function of strikes is, paradoxically, to resolve conflict. If, for one reason or another, the parties are unable or unwilling to reach a compromise in negotiations, the costs both of them incur in an ensuing strike pressure them to rethink their bottom lines and lower their expectations to the point where a mutually satisfactory compromise is possible. This may occur either before or during a strike. But if a strike is not permitted, then such a compromise may never be reached, because neither side will be under the same pressure. Conflict may thus continue to fester during the term of a collective agreement, as manifest in a number of the less obvious forms discussed in chapter three, from increased quit rates to fractious relations between workers and their supervisors, and even to sabotage. Grievance rates may also be higher. For example, a study of grievance arbitration rates in the Ontario public sector found them to be substantially higher for workers who are not permitted to strike than for those who are (Hebdon and Stern, 1998). A follow-up to this study found similar results in the United States (Hebdon and Stern, 2003; Hebdon, 2005).

In addition, the absence of the right to strike can mean that management has little reason to even respond to union demands. It is one thing to provide workers with the right to union representation, and quite another to ensure that this right is a meaningful one. In the absence of the right to strike, the latter is much less likely to be the case, other things being equal. Indeed, it is not just the right to strike which is important, but the ability of workers to impose costs on management through a strike.

Finally, the ability to strike without fear of reprisal is critical to freedom of expression. When workers are discontent, strike activity is a primary means through which this discontent can be expressed. An outright ban on all strike activity would amount to violation of the right of freedom of expression, and would be considered as such by most international rights forums, including the United Nations and the International Labour Organization (see chapter seven). But again, it is not just the legal right to strike which is important, but also the *ability* to strike without fear of reprisal. For example, workers in the United States have the right to strike, but the employer can hire permanent replacement workers if they do. Thus, workers have reason to fear that they could lose their jobs merely for exercising what is generally considered a human right. Even in Canada, a decision to strike can mean severe costs for workers, especially if the employer decides to make them "pay" by engaging in "hard bargaining" and ensuring the strike is a protracted one. Nonetheless, Canada's relatively high strike rate suggests that the expected costs are not so great as to effectively negate the legal right to strike, as is often the case in the United States.

It follows that some level of strike activity may even be desirable. This may be especially so if strike activity represents the primary means by which workers can pressure employers or express discontent. As discussed in earlier chapters (e.g., chapter eight), a number of European countries allow for works councils which enable worker representatives to have more influence in employer decision processes, so that the outcomes of these processes are more conducive to employee interests and less likely to engender conflict. Moreover, firms tend to be managed as much to serve worker as investor interests, lessening the basis for conflict. Finally, bargaining is often more centralized than in Canada, allowing for more professional and less emotion-ridden negotiations (see chapter twelve). Thus, lower strike rates are to be expected in these countries. But these conditions are not characteristic of Canada. Thus, while it may be argued that Canada's level of strike activity is too high and that there are ways to reduce it without violating workers' rights, Canada's higher level of strike activity may not only be expected, it may also not be entirely unhealthy. Indeed, if one believes that underlying conflicts are fundamental to labour–management relations, then a substantial decline in current levels of strike activity might even be considered a worrying development.

Restrictions on Strike Activity

To argue that the right and ability to strike without reprisal is to be desired is not to suggest that strikes are somehow good. Strikes often *do* entail substantial costs for third parties as well as workers and their employers, and they *can* increase rather than reduce levels of distrust and hostility. In some cases (perhaps many), they may also reflect "mistakes" by one or both sides, as will be discussed more fully below. For these reasons, the right to strike is restricted in a number of ways in Canada.

As discussed in chapter eleven, it is illegal for workers to strike unless they are represented by a certified union in their workplace. They may also not legally strike during the process by which their union is seeking certification or, if their union is already certified, during the term of a collective agreement. Rather they may legally strike only after an existing contract has expired, a "good faith" attempt has been made to negotiate a new one, a majority of workers in the bargaining unit have voted in favour of a strike, and, if the minister of labour so requires, the parties have undergone conciliation or mediation (discussed later in this chapter). In the public sector, the parties also may not be able to legally strike at all if the government has deemed them an essential service. Moreover, governments are likely to introduce legislation to end any strike which they deem to be injurious to the public interest, something which they have increasingly done over the past few decades.

It seems difficult to envision how governments in Canada could place further restrictions on strike activity without virtually banning it altogether. Indeed, there is reason to argue that strikes may already be overly restricted. This may be especially true in the public sector, where governments have a vested interest in unduly restricting the right to strike, for reasons discussed in chapter nine. But it also applies to the private sector. As discussed later in this chapter, restrictions on the right to strike may have a number of negative consequences. First, however, it is important to understand how and why strikes occur.

The "Causes" of Strikes

There is an extensive body of literature on the causes of strike activity, with authors suggesting a wide range of explanations. For present purposes, however, these can be divided into two general approaches: (1) the strikes as mistakes approach, and (2) the strikes as collective voice approach.

Strikes As Mistakes. As discussed in the preceding chapter, negotiations can be extremely complex, and they involve considerable uncertainty and misinformation, as each side seeks to bluff the other into believing that its position is "tougher" than it really is while at the same time attempting to "read" the other's true position. Though each side may have various sources of information as to the other's likely position, it may still misread that position and hence come to believe that the other is prepared to concede more than is actually the case. As a result, either or both parties may fail to modify their position sufficiently over the course of negotiations, with the result that a positive settlement zone is not found. In other words, the parties' negotiating positions may not converge to the point where an agreement can be reached. Where this occurs, it is only once the contract expiry deadline is reached and/or a strike has begun that either or both come to realize that they have misread the other and adjust their position accordingly.

This explanation can be termed the "**strikes as mistakes**" explanation because it suggests that, under ideal conditions, strikes would not occur. It makes considerable sense if both sides are viewed as seeking only to maximize their economic self-interests, for strikes are costly to both sides, and both would rather avoid these costs if at all possible (Hicks, 1932; Siebert and Addison, 1981; Lacroix, 1986). Indeed, if it were not for problems of limited information and complexity, each would be able to anticipate the ability and willingness of the other to grant concessions and what the outcomes of a strike would be in advance, thus enabling the parties to reach a settlement without undergoing the costs of a strike.

It is possible to identify a number of circumstances under which negotiation mistakes are likely to occur.[1] The first involves the "maturity" of the bargaining relationship (Lester, 1958: 41). In an immature relationship, the negotiators may be lacking in skills and experience and, as a result, they are more likely to miscommunicate their own position and misread the position of the other. Moreover, negotiators on one or both sides may harbour a dislike for the other side or a personal ideological agenda, both of which can interfere with their ability to negotiate rationally. Finally, if the negotiators are simply unfamiliar with one another they are unlikely to have developed a bargaining "protocol", or set of implicit rules and understandings for the conduct of negotiations (Reder and Neumann, 1980). As a result, they are more likely to miscommunicate and misread one another.

A second circumstance has to do with changes in the employer's ability to grant concessions, due, for example, to changes in the employer's competitive environment. Under these conditions there is a problem of "information asymmetry", for while management is privy to the relevant product market and financial information, union negotiators are not (see Tracy, 1987; Hayes, 1984; McConnell, 1989). Thus, in order to determine if management is telling the truth about its ability to grant concessions, the union negotiators call management's bluff and go out on strike. If management is indeed bluffing, it will change its position quite quickly. If not, it will continue to refuse concessions and the union will recognize that management is telling the truth. Thus, a strike conveys important information to the union about the financial condition of the employer.[2]

A third circumstance has to do with changes in the expectations or the strike power of either party, which can occur not only if the firm's competitive environment changes, but also if the rate of inflation or the level of unemployment changes. When this happens, there is increased uncertainty as to just what the other side will accept and/or

---

[1] For present purposes, I am defining the strikes as mistakes approach somewhat more broadly than has been the convention in the literature (see Kaufman, 1992), to include all neoclassical economic models of strike activity (as defined in Godard, 1992c; and Cohn and Eaton, 1989).

[2] It can be argued that, because of this, strikes are not a mistake but rather an efficient way for the union to obtain information. But unions always have *some* level of information. If they go on strike, it is because they believe, based on this information, that management can afford to grant better concessions. If their information is wrong, they will have made a mistake. If it is correct, then management will have made a mistake by underestimating the union's militancy.

just what the costs of a strike are likely to be. As a result, one or both parties may miscalculate the other's willingness to give concessions and/or the costs of a strike. When this happens, a strike is more likely to occur (Kaufman, 1981; Gramm, Hendricks, and Kahn, 1988).

A fourth, closely related circumstance entails unrealistic worker expectations. Strikes may occur not because union or management negotiators miscalculate, but rather because workers do. In other words, while union negotiators may have realistic expectations, their constituents may not. The problem is that, unless union negotiators represent the aspirations of workers, workers are unlikely to ratify the agreement and may even vote them out of office in the next election. Thus, strikes may represent mistakes not by union negotiators but rather by workers themselves. Where this is the case, it may be only once a strike has occurred that workers begin to modify their expectations, thus making a settlement more possible (Ashenfelter and Johnson, 1969).

A final circumstance under the strikes as mistakes approach has to do with the complexity of the situation itself (Cousineau and Lacroix, 1986). If, for example, the issues in dispute are complex or if negotiations are complicated by disagreements between internal union or management factions, a breakdown in negotiations is more likely. Generally, we might expect these sorts of difficulties to arise where the bargaining unit is itself complex, covering a number of establishments and/or a diversity of occupations and skill levels.

The strikes as mistakes explanation is a valuable one because it focuses on factors that influence the calculations (and miscalculations) of the parties. It also suggests that strikes are fairly readily avoidable if steps are taken, either by the parties themselves or by government policy makers, to ensure that problems of uncertainty and misinformation are minimized and a "mature" negotiating process, conducted by skilled experts, is encouraged. Yet even with such factors in place, it is unlikely that strikes would go away. There are two reasons for this (Godard, 1992b, 1992d).

First, the strikes as mistakes view proceeds from an unduly narrow conception of the rationale of negotiations and strikes, generally assuming that both parties are concerned only with maximizing their economic well-being, either in a single negotiation or over time. As such, it discounts the "behavioural context" within which negotiations occur and the role of affective and moral considerations which often lie at the heart of the decision to strike. As discussed in chapter three, strikes may indeed appear to be irrational from an economist's point of view. But from the viewpoint of the parties themselves (especially workers and their representatives), the decision to strike often involves a much broader rationality, one which involves competing values, principles, and fairness beliefs, and often reflects underlying sources of discontent in the workplace (Hyman, 1977). Thus, while the parties undoubtedly consider the economic consequences of a strike, these consequences are by no means the only consideration (or even necessarily the primary one) taken into account when they decide to strike. Rather, a great deal depends on the level of discontent among workers, either in general or with management's unwillingness to grant concessions workers believe they are entitled to.

Second, and equally important, is the nature of the employment relation. As also discussed in chapter three, workers are in a position of subordination to management, a position which is not altered substantially by the right to engage in collective bargaining. As is the case in authoritarian states, workers cannot elect or appoint their rulers, and they have little or no legal right to participate in the legal governance of the organization for which they work. This, coupled with the conflicts which underlie labour–management relations, means that distrust and resentment almost always pervade the workplace, albeit in varying degrees. Though manifest in a number of ways, striking serves as the primary mechanism by which workers can voice this distrust and resentment collectively (Godard, 1992c).

It follows that to view strikes only as mistakes in negotiations is too narrow. Although imperfect information or negotiating mistakes can no doubt result in a strike, strikes may ultimately serve as a means to express worker discontent and distrust and, hence, may be viewed as mechanisms for "collective voice". (This approach is developed more fully in Godard, 1992b, 1992c, 1998b.)

Strikes As Collective Voice. With the strikes as collective voice approach, there is always *some* likelihood of a strike occurring, if only because *some* level of distrust and discontent almost always pervades the labour–management relationship. Yet, this does not mean that the likelihood of a strike, or its duration, is necessarily high. In this respect a number of factors are important.

First, much may depend on the extent of worker discontent. Of particular importance in this respect may be managerial policies and practices and the nature of work. To the extent that management provides workers with job autonomy, good working conditions, and some say in decisions which affect them, we might generally expect worker discontent to be low, as discussed in chapter five. We would also expect discontent to be lower in smaller firms, where work is typically less routine and where workers are less likely to develop a sense of themselves as a distinctive "class". In both these circumstances, union negotiators are likely to have far less support for a strike and, therefore, are far less likely to call for one. Moreover, where a strike *is* called, they are likely to seek as early a solution as possible, for fear that members will begin to cross picket lines.

A second and related factor may be management's willingness to accommodate worker expectations and to buy off discontent. To the extent that management is willing to make concessions, workers are far less likely to view a strike as justified, and it is far easier for union negotiators to get a settlement that is satisfactory to their membership.

A third consideration is the relative viability of alternative means of expressing discontent, especially exiting (Gunderson, Kervin, and Reid, 1986). To the extent that exit (or some other alternative) is viable, discontented workers are more likely to choose this option, hence reducing the likelihood of a strike. In this regard, unemployment can play an important role, for workers are likely to have more employment alternatives to the extent that it is low. However, these alternatives may not be particularly viable if the employee has accumulated various seniority benefits or has managed to progress to a higher paying job because of skills and abilities she has developed while working for the employer, because the employee may be forced to start at the bottom with a new employer. Thus, for many workers, quitting may not be much of an option regardless of the level of unemployment.

Also important, however, is the viability of striking itself. As suggested earlier, strikes are most likely to occur where union strike power is high (Rees, 1952; Shorter and Tilly, 1974). Not only does high strike power mean (other things being equal) that management will be more likely to give in to union demands,[3] it also means that the strike is a more effective device for expressing discontent and getting back at management without fear of retribution, and that it is likely to be more cathartic for workers (Kerr and Siegel, 1954).

A fourth consideration has to do with more purely social influences (Fantasia, 1988). Two of these can be identified. The first involves the ability of union leaders and activists to mobilize discontent. Often, discontent may remain latent or hidden, largely because workers see little way of expressing it. During negotiations, however, union leaders may attempt to bring this discontent to the surface, thus

---

[3] If power is high, management is likely to be more accommodative in negotiations, in part offsetting the higher propensity of workers to strike. Yet we would still expect a positive association, for the simple reason that, when union power is low, a strike can be virtually suicidal. Thus, power is a virtual precondition for striking. See Korpi (1974).

ensuring that workers will back them up in the event that negotiations break down. Because their success in doing so enhances the viability of the strike option, it not only enhances their credibility at the bargaining table, but also the likelihood and duration of strikes occurring (Batstone, Boraston, and Frenkel, 1978). The second social influence involves socio-cultural factors. Particularly important is the extent to which the local community is cohesive and views strike activity as legitimate (see Kerr and Siegel, 1954; Stern, 1976; Gilson, Spencer, and Granville, 1989). Where this is the case, not only are workers themselves likely to be more strike-prone, members of the community can also be expected to provide moral and even financial support to workers if they strike. They can also be expected to place a variety of pressures on the employer, especially in the public sector, where an unpopular strike can undermine the re-election chances of politicians (see Kochan and Wheeler, 1975). As such, the effectiveness of striking as an option is enhanced.

A number of additional factors can also be identified, including internal union politics (Godard, 1993b), the values and ideologies of union leaders (Taft, 1956), and the ability of unions and workers to have their concerns addressed through the political arena, thus reducing the need to strike (see Korpi and Shalev, 1980). Yet the point should be clear: the likelihood of a strike depends not just on the activities of negotiators but on the "behavioural context" within which negotiations occur. It also reflects underlying sources of conflict arising from the nature and structure of the labour–management relationship in the Canadian economy: in the absence of these sources, strikes might be far less likely to occur in general.[4]

This is not to suggest that the activities of negotiators are unimportant. But the strikes-as-collective voice approach suggests that, where the behavioural context of negotiations is not conducive to striking, union negotiators are far more likely to attempt to avoid a "mistake". Moreover, if a "mistake" does occur, they are far more likely to seek a quick solution, in the knowledge that support for a strike is weak. In this respect, at least one study has concluded that the strikes as mistakes approach may be more useful in accounting for variation in the likelihood of strike activity than it is in accounting for the duration of strikes (Godard, 1992b).

---

[4] Elsewhere, I have proposed a three-tier model of strike activity that explicitly recognizes the importance of broader institutional and political factors for these underlying conflicts (Godard, 1992c).

As discussed earlier, a relatively high level of strike activity may not be an unhealthy sign in view of the conflicts underlying labour–management relations and the way in which the Canadian system is structured. Yet this is not to say that strikes are necessarily a "good thing". To the contrary, they can entail substantial costs not only for the parties involved, but for third parties as well. It is thus in everyone's interests to seek ways of minimizing strike activity provided that these ways do not unduly infringe on the right or ability of workers to strike if they believe it necessary to do so. The two approaches to explaining strikes suggest somewhat different ways of doing so.

The strikes as mistakes approach suggests that it would be possible to do so by reducing negotiation mistakes. As already suggested, one such measure would be to adopt more centralized bargaining structures, thus ensuring higher levels of expertise and professionalism. Another would be to adopt some of the cooperative bargaining methods discussed in the preceding chapter, although the effectiveness of these is uncertain. Yet a third is to adopt some form of third party assistance, such as conciliation or mediation, as discussed below.

The strikes as collective voice approach suggests a need to reduce the sources of distrust and discontent that give rise to strikes. One option is to encourage employers to adopt progressive practices, particularly as embodied in the "high commitment" approach associated with the high performance model. But as discussed in chapter five, these practices often may not be in employer interests, and the extent to which governments can create conditions more conducive to their adoption seems uncertain at best. A more fundamental alternative is to make institutional changes which enhance worker decision-making rights and induce employers to give higher priority to the well-being of workers. As discussed above with respect to some European countries, such changes would conceivably reduce the degree of conflict and provide alternative measures for dealing with it, reducing strike activity accordingly. A further, complementary alternative, is to reduce levels of insecurity and discontent which give rise to strike activity (and conflict in general) by enacting stronger employment laws ensuring satisfactory wages and benefits, safe working conditions, and fair treatment in employment relations

Most of these options suggest the need for reforms to the Canadian system. As such, they are left to the concluding chapter. The one exception, however, is third party dispute resolution. Because third party dispute resolution procedures are already well established in Canada, they deserve attention at this point.

II.   THIRD PARTY DISPUTE RESOLUTION

There are two types of third party intervention in negotiations: facilitative and adjudicative. While the former attempts to facilitate a voluntary settlement by the parties and does not prevent them from ultimately going to a strike or lockout, the latter entails the imposition of a settlement upon the parties and typically involves a prohibition on strike activity. The former can vary considerably in the process it entails, and usually involves some form of "conciliation", "mediation", or "fact-finding". The latter can also vary, but usually involves some form of "interest arbitration". Below, each will be considered in turn.

Conciliation, Mediation, and Fact-Finding

The meanings associated with the terms conciliation, mediation, and fact-finding can vary so much that these terms are sometimes used interchangeably. But however defined, all three typically involve procedures intended to reduce the frequency of strikes as mistakes by helping the parties to communicate more effectively, clarifying the issues, and/or persuading the parties to change their positions, either directly, or indirectly, through public pressure.

Of the three terms, conciliation is most closely associated with legislation first adopted in Canada in the first decade of the twentieth century and incorporated within the post-war system of labour law (see chapter four). In its traditional form it involves two stages, both of which are required before a strike can legally take place. In the first stage, the parties are required to make use of the services of a conciliator appointed by the ministry of labour. As the term implies, the conciliator's role is to assist the parties reconcile their differences, helping them reach a settlement that both can live with. If unsuccessful, the conciliator files a report with the minister of labour outlining the issues in dispute and the likelihood of a settlement. This triggers the second stage. In this stage, the minister appoints a conciliation board (usually tripartite, consisting of a neutral, a union representative, and a management representative), whose job it is to take a more activist role, eliciting presentations from the parties and then making formal recommendations as to the appropriate settlement. In theory this not only helps to clarify the issues, it also induces the parties to alter their positions in accordance with the board's recommendations. If a settlement is still not reached, however, a strike is legally permitted, in effect serving as a "last resort".

The traditional two-step conciliation procedure has come under considerable criticism over the years (Ponak and Falkenberg, 1990). As noted in chapter eleven, it can entail an intrusion into the bargaining process which is unwelcome by one or both parties and may simply further complicate and frustrate negotiations. It can also enable one or both sides to prepare for a strike both materially and psychologically, so that once the strike finally begins both sides are much more entrenched and much less willing to modify their positions. But even where this is not the case, conciliation can be both cumbersome and time-consuming, serving as an unwarranted constraint on the right of workers to voice their collective discontent through the act of striking. Because of these and other problems, the compulsory two-stage procedure is, at present, rarely used in any jurisdiction (Ponak and Falkenberg, 1990: 266). Often, the minister *does* send in a conciliator (first stage), but a conciliation board (second stage) is established only in high profile situations, where the potential economic or social consequences of a strike are substantial. Moreover, while a majority of jurisdictions continue to prohibit strikes until the conciliation process is complete, at least four (Alberta, Saskatchewan, Manitoba, and Quebec) do not. Hence, a strike is legal even while conciliation is taking place.

Despite these modifications, the conciliation process continues to be subject to criticism in principle, as an essentially bureaucratic intrusion into the "free" collective bargaining process. Its effectiveness is also not entirely clear. There *is* evidence that it is associated with a lower incidence of strikes (Gunderson, Kervin, and Reid, 1985, 1986). But whether this "positive" effect outweighs its negative implications is not clear. Moreover, the finding that it reduces strike incidence should not be taken as evidence that it should be applied more widely. It may be that, at present, it is most likely to be used in those circumstances conducive to its effectiveness. If so, to expand its use could be of little value.

Mediation and fact-finding are intended to play similar roles. Mediation is, by and large, a variant on the first stage of the conciliation process; indeed, this stage is actually referred to as mediation in at least one province (Alberta). However, mediation is typically differentiated from the first stage of the conciliation process in two ways. First, in contrast to the conciliation process, it often involves a voluntary arrangement, under which the two parties agree to hire a neutral third party to help them arrive at a settlement. Second, a mediator's role is usually far more "interventionist", with the mediator becoming actively involved in the negotiating process, mediating between the two parties and attempting to "cut a deal" which is satisfactory to both. This can involve a number of stages, from (1) meeting with the parties and attempting to establish what the problem is, to (2) acting as a go-between and attempting to establish what kind of settlement might be possible, to (3) actively pressuring, cajoling, and manipulating the parties into altering their positions so that a settlement is achieved (see Downie, 1989, for a more comprehensive discussion).

Fact-finding is, in turn, a variant of the second stage of traditional conciliation, though it is typically used to handle impasses in specific areas of the public sector and is subject to legislation specific to these areas. Though rare, it usually entails the appointment of a third party to determine what issues are outstanding and to write a formal report with recommendations. In theory, the fact-finder does not become involved in the bargaining process but rather puts pressure on the parties to reach a settlement through the release of his or her report to the general public. In practice, however, fact-finders may attempt to mediate a settlement before doing so, in which case the report may become unnecessary. These attempts are usually less intensive than is the case in conventional mediation, and tend to be subject to the fact-finder's own discretion, based upon his or her sense as to whether a settlement can be readily achieved. But they generally involve greater involvement than is the case in the first stage of the conciliation process, and they do not entail a separate report.

As is the case with conciliation, mediation and fact-finding also tend to be controversial. On the one hand, both can undoubtedly be expected to reduce the incidence and duration of strikes. Not only is the third party likely to lend considerable expertise to the negotiating process, she is also, as a neutral, more likely to convince one or both sides that their position is untenable. On the other hand, the extent to which an increase in the use of these techniques would prove to be successful is not readily determined, for the same reasons discussed with respect to conciliation.

More generally, conciliation, mediation, and fact-finding are all premised primarily on the assumption that strikes are, by and large, mistakes. Where the parties are strongly motivated to reach a settlement, and where a positive contract zone already exists, then they are likely to be effective (Kochan and Katz, 1988: 275–76), for under these circumstances a strike would indeed *be* a mistake. But where the parties do not wish to avoid a strike, or where a breakdown in negotiations occurs due to external pressures identified under the strikes as collective voice approach, these procedures are far less likely to be effective, and may only make matters worse. This is especially so if the third party mistakenly pushes for a resolution that is unacceptable to one of the parties, and as a result causes that party to become even more frustrated and inflexible.

It thus seems that, while these forms of third party intervention have a role to play within the Canadian industrial relations system, just how widespread this role should be depends in large part on the extent to which strikes occur due to mistakes. To the extent that they do, third party intervention may be of *some* use. To the extent that they do not, third party intervention may be an unwarranted and counter productive intrusion into the negotiating process.

Interest Arbitration

Interest arbitration is so named because it involves the arbitration of interest conflicts in negotiations rather than of grievances (see chapter fourteen). In contrast to conciliation, mediation, and fact-finding, it entails the imposition of a final settlement upon the parties rather than an attempt to facilitate a settlement by the parties themselves. In some cases it may follow such an attempt, and it may even be chosen by the parties themselves if such an attempt has failed. However, it typically involves a removal of the right to strike and is compulsory, required either by law or by government edict.

There are two general forms of interest arbitration: "**conventional arbitration**" and "**final offer selection**". Under conventional arbitration, either a single arbitrator or a tripartite arbitration board decides on the terms of the final settlement, based on submissions from the two sides and on the "norm" for settlements covering similar employees elsewhere. Under final offer selection, each side submits its "final offer", and the arbitrator selects the one which is deemed to be most reasonable. In some cases this may be done on an item-by-item basis, so that each side may "win" on some issues but "lose" on others. In others, it may be on a total package basis, so that there is only one winner (either the union or management), and this winner "takes all".

Though neither form of interest arbitration is particularly popular, conventional arbitration has been subject to the greatest criticism, on the grounds that it can inhibit genuine bargaining. Here, two arguments are often advanced: (1) the parties find it easier to rely on an arbitrator than to have to negotiate and take responsibility for their own settlement; and (2) the parties tend to withhold concessions in the belief that the arbitrator will be inclined to seek a middle ground between the final positions of the two parties, in which case the withholding of concessions may mean a more favourable outcome. The former is typically referred to as the **"narcotic effect"**, for the parties are thought to develop a dependency on arbitration, while the latter is typically referred to as the **"chilling effect"**, for the parties are discouraged from "warming up" to each other and making the kinds of concessions that might lead to an agreement.

Final offer selection is intended to overcome those problems associated with conventional arbitration, for the parties can no longer count on the arbitrator to choose a middle ground. As such, arbitration can be extremely risky, especially where final offers are selected on a total package basis, in which case each party risks losing completely. Moreover, each side is induced to make additional concessions, in the knowledge that the arbitrator will select those positions which appear to be most reasonable. Thus, final offer selection in theory offsets both the narcotic and the chilling effect by discouraging each party from relying upon arbitration and encouraging each to make as many concessions as they can in the negotiating process itself, before going to arbitration.

Research on the consequences of arbitration (see Rose and Piczak, 1996) generally finds that settlement rates (the percentage of negotiations where the parties settle on their own) are substantially lower where conventional arbitration is required than it is where the parties have a right to strike. It also finds that the settlement rate is higher under final offer selection systems than under conventional arbitration, but it is still lower than when the parties have a right to strike. This indicates that a chilling effect may occur with conventional arbitration but is less likely with final offer selection. The research suggests only limited support, however, for the narcotic effect. While some parties may become dependent on arbitration, as predicted by the narcotic effect, the majority does not appear to repeatedly use this process (Ponak and Falkenberg, 1990: 286).

There are also broader concerns about the implications of arbitration, especially where it is compulsory.[5] First, to require arbitration may be seen as contravening the democratic right of the parties to resolve disputes on their own terms. In effect, the arbitrator becomes an agent of the state, imposing the state's will onto the parties. Although an arbitrator-imposed settlement is certainly to be preferred over one that is directly imposed by a government (see chapter nine), this is still not what one would otherwise expect or desire in a free

---

[5] See Bok and Dunlop, 1970: 234–41 for a discussion of the problems with arbitration. For a positive view of arbitration, based largely upon a strikes-as-mistakes view of strike activity, see Winch, 1989.

society. It also contravenes the doctrine of free collective bargaining, which is central to the Canadian system (as discussed in chapter eleven).

Second, a major function of strikes is to encourage the parties to adjust their expectations and eventually reach a settlement that is more or less acceptable to both, as noted earlier. Arbitration undermines this function, forcing the parties to accept an agreement that may be unacceptable to one or both. Thus, the problems underlying a breakdown in negotiations are more likely to go unresolved and hence to fester during the life of the collective agreement that follows. Moreover, to the extent that one party perceives that it has "won" and the other that it has "lost", a damaging "win-lose" mentality may result. This may be especially the case when final offer selection has been used, given that this method requires the arbitrator to pick the winner, either overall or on the major issue in dispute. It may be particularly serious if the main issue in dispute is a complex one where a "middle ground" solution would make the most sense, because final offer selection prevents the arbitrator from imposing such a solution.

These two problems may be aggravated to the extent that either the chilling or the narcotic effect pertains. Where this is the case, arbitration can not only undermine democratic rights and aggravate conflicts in those cases where it is required, but it can also increase the number of such cases by lessening the likelihood that the parties will reach a negotiated settlement. Final offer selection may in this respect be more preferable, at least to the extent that it reduces chilling and narcotic effects. Yet any resulting gain may be more than offset if it aggravates unresolved conflicts, as just suggested.

Perhaps for these reasons, neither conventional arbitration nor final offer selection is popular among employers or unions in Canada. They are usually resorted to only if required by law,[6] as is often the case in the public sector. As discussed in chapter ten, such a legal requirement may be justified in some areas of this sector due to the problems a strike can potentially cause for public health and safety. Yet the case can be made that compulsory arbitration has some role to play in the private sector as well, especially where a union has recently been organized, where workers have little bargaining power, or

---

[6] One exception is the Experimental Negotiations Agreement (ENA) adopted by the United Steelworkers and major U.S. steel producers in the 1970s. Under this agreement, both sides agreed to arbitration in the event that a settlement could not be reached. However, it collapsed in 1982, and during the decade over which it existed, the parties were able to reach settlements without relying upon arbitration.

where there is undue hostility on one or both sides (Adams, 1986). Under these conditions, strikes may be unavoidable, with the final settlement requiring an almost total capitulation by one side. As such, arbitration may be the only viable option if a reasonable settlement is to be achieved. In recognition of this, there has been growing support for the use of arbitration as a last resort in private sector as well as public sector strikes, especially where an employer is attempting to break a union. As discussed in chapter eleven, first contract arbitration is already in place in most Canadian jurisdictions, to ensure that a first agreement is assured where a union is newly certified and negotiations have broken down. Presently, however, there are few provisions for arbitrated settlements in subsequent negotiations, with the possible exception of Manitoba, which has a "sixty day" rule, under which either party may request compulsory arbitration after a strike has lasted 60 days.[7]

III. CONCLUSIONS

This chapter has considered strikes and dispute resolution processes. However, regardless of whether either is relied on, it is rare that the parties fail to reach *some* form of agreement, even if this agreement is unsatisfactory to one or both sides. And, once it *is* signed, the union is by law prohibited from striking until such time that this agreement expires and a good faith attempt has been made to negotiate a new one. In the meantime, a number of disputes can arise over the administration of the agreement, or the way it is to be interpreted and applied and the willingness of the parties to adhere to it. The grievance and grievance arbitration processes serve as the primary means for resolving such disputes. These are thus addressed in the next chapter.

---

[7] In 1987, the Manitoba government enacted legislation under which unionized workers could request final offer selection. In theory, doing so would prevent an employer from attempting to break a union through a protracted strike. However, this option was eliminated in 1991, after a new, Conservative government was elected to office. For a discussion, see Black and Silver, 1990, and Grant, 1990.

The Grievance
and Grievance
Arbitration Processes

14

As noted in chapter twelve, collective bargaining in many respects forms the heart of the Canadian system of industrial relations, for in the absence of a strong collective agreement, the right to join a union and bargain collectively is virtually meaningless. Equally important are the grievance and grievance arbitration processes, for these provide the primary mechanisms by which the parties (especially the union) are able to ensure that the terms of the collective agreement are adhered to. These processes are especially important in view of the prohibition against striking during the term of an agreement, because in their absence, the employer would be able to violate the terms of the agreement with impunity, effectively rendering it useless. Thus, this chapter addresses these processes in greater depth, beginning with the nature of the processes themselves, then turning to their functions, and then to various problems associated with them.

I. GRIEVANCES AND THEIR RESOLUTION

It is common to distinguish between two types of grievance: (1) **individual grievances**, and (2) **policy grievances**. Individual grievances are filed by or on behalf of an individual or group within the bargaining unit, most often in disciplinary cases, which can involve anything from management's giving a worker a written warning to a worker's outright dismissal. However, they can be filed for virtually any alleged transgression of individual and group rights under the agreement, whether this has to do with conformance to seniority provisions, violation of work rule provisions, improper job classification or pay levels, and so forth. An example of such a grievance appears in Box 14–1.

BOX 14–1 The Cole Company Case

Background of the Case

Mr. Edward Dembow is a filler on the sulphuric acid packaging line of the company's operations. Because of the danger from contact with acid, all employees on this line wear protective clothing. For example: gloves, sleeves, aprons, goggles, and boots, furnished by the company. Allegedly the company was having some difficulty in getting its workers to be properly dressed in protective clothing ready to start work at 8:00 a.m., the normal starting hour. This was particularly serious with respect to the filler, since he occupies the first position on the packaging line and all other work on the line follows in sequence.

On October 7, 1994, Mr. Sidney Lester, president of the company, allegedly warned Mr. Dembow approximately ten minutes before the starting hour that he expected him to be ready to start work by 8:00 a.m. Mr. Lester visited the line again at 8:00 A.M. and believing that Mr. Dembow was not properly dressed and ready for work told him that he was docking him fifteen minutes pay for not being ready to start work at the regular starting hour. Apparently little, if any, work was accomplished since Mr. Lester returned in a few minutes and threatened to dock the entire shop if the employees did not begin work. He returned again in a few minutes and found Mr. Dembow sitting on an empty packing case some twenty-five feet away from his normal position on the sulphuric acid line.

On October 12, 1994, the company and the union tried to reach a settlement, but the terms of the settlement, namely reinstatement without back pay, were not acceptable to Mr. Dembow and the union demanded arbitration of the issue.

On October 14, 1994, the company wrote the grievant a letter which read, in part:

> You are hereby notified that you have been given an eight-day suspension without pay for repeated failure to begin work promptly. You are hereby notified to return to work on Friday, October 16, 1994.

The grievant returned to work on that date and the union is seeking a determination of the propriety of the disciplinary suspension.

Position of the Union

The alleged warnings given to the grievant were not warnings, but merely suggestions to all employees on the sulphuric acid line that they should be ready to start work at 8:00 a.m. At no time were the employees specifically warned that disciplinary action would be taken for failure to start work promptly at 8:00 a.m.

Continued....

BOX 14–1 (continued)

The company in the person of Mr. Lester did discipline the grievant when he docked him fifteen minutes of wages for not being ready to begin work promptly at 8:00 a.m. The refusal of the grievant to work during a period in which the company had refused to pay him does not amount to a wildcat strike, but is merely the normal reaction of an employee when wages are withheld.

Position of the Company

Although the position of the company is that the actions leading up to the instant issues were the result of a show of strength by each party, the matter of causation is irrelevant, and the narrow issue is whether the grievant was ready to perform his work at 8:00 a.m.

Contrary to the union's contention, a number of warnings had been given by the company over this issue in the past, and certainly on the day in question. Mr. Edward Dembow was specifically warned only ten minutes previous to the incident giving rise to this dispute.

The company agrees that discharge was too severe a penalty and as a result it substituted a more moderate disciplinary action. Despite disagreement by the parties over the length of the disciplinary suspension assessed, the conduct of the grievant certainly called for some disciplinary action, and an eight-day disciplinary suspension was not too harsh a penalty.

Source: From John R. Abersold and Wayne E. Howard, *Cases in Labor Relations: An Arbitration Experience*, 1st Edition, pp. 42–45 (Englewood Cliffs, NJ: Prentice Hall, 1967). Reproduced by permission of Pearson Education, Inc. Upper Saddle River, NJ.

In contrast, policy grievances are filed by the union against management (or in some cases, by management against the union) for policy-related actions which may or may not directly affect individuals, but are considered to be contrary to the terms of the agreement in a way that affects the bargaining unit as a whole. Thus, for example, management may contract out some work which, under the agreement, should be done in-house. Doing so may not have a direct effect on individual workers, but it may mean fewer new hires and hence fewer jobs within the bargaining unit. Thus, the union might file a grievance on policy grounds.

The Grievance Procedure

The actual procedure by which grievances are handled is specified in the collective agreement and hence established through the collective bargaining process. Although all jurisdictions except one (Saskatchewan) require that a grievance procedure be contained in the agreement, it is up to the parties to determine how this procedure is designed. As such, this procedure can vary considerably from one bargaining unit to another (see Gandz and Whitehead, 1989: 241–42). In small firms, the procedure may be only a single step, involving a meeting between a union representative and the owner. However, in larger workplaces it tends to involve three or even four steps.

In a three-step procedure, the first step may involve the aggrieved worker and her union representative attempting to resolve the matter informally, by discussing it with the worker's immediate supervisor. If unsuccessful, they then submit the grievance in writing, either to the supervisor or to some other management official. The grievance then goes to the second stage, where the union representative meets with a more senior manager, perhaps a foreman or general manager. If there is still no resolution, the grievance may go to the third stage, under which senior union and company officials (e.g., the local union president and the head of IR/HRM) become involved. If there is still is no settlement at this stage, the grievance mechanism is said to be exhausted, and the grievance becomes a matter for arbitration. A 1999 Statistics Canada survey found that about 30 percent of all grievances in union settings were settled at the first stage, informally. About 15 percent went all the way to arbitration (Akyeampong, 2003: 35).

Often, there are time restrictions for each stage, in order to prevent the process from becoming too drawn out. However, these restrictions may be waived for individual grievances if the parties so agree. For some grievances, especially those involving dismissal, the collective agreement may also allow the parties to bypass the stages in the grievance procedure and go directly to arbitration.

The Arbitration Procedure

Collective agreements in all Canadian jurisdictions are required to have a provision for arbitration in the event that the parties cannot resolve a dispute on their own during the life of the agreement. Normally, this calls for the appointment of a mutually agreed upon arbitrator or third party neutral — usually a lawyer or university professor who is qualified to conduct arbitration — and often a tripartite board, made up of the arbitrator, a representative of the union, and a representative of management. If, however, the parties cannot agree on an arbitrator, either may request the minister of labour or labour board (depending on the jurisdiction) to appoint one.

Once an arbitrator has been selected, a hearing is arranged at a time and location satisfactory to both sides. In arranging and holding the hearing, the arbitrator must ensure that "due process" is followed, providing each party with ample opportunity both to present its case and to rebut the other side's presentation of *its* case. This frequently involves the calling and cross-examination of witnesses, as well as reference to established precedent, based on arbitration decisions in similar cases elsewhere. As such, the process can be highly legalistic and so it is common for each side to be represented by a lawyer. The specific stages in a typical arbitration hearing appear in Box 14–2.

Where a specific violation of the collective agreement is alleged, the burden of proof is on the party filing the grievance — usually the union. In other words, it is up to the union to present evidence and arguments which establish that the agreement was indeed violated. However, in a discipline or discharge case, the burden of proof is on the employer. The employer must not only establish that it had "just cause" to discipline the person involved, but also that the penalty it imposed was fair, or consistent with principles of "natural justice".

Once the hearing has been concluded, the arbitrator weighs the arguments and evidence of both sides and, after consultation with other board members (if an arbitration board is established), submits his or her decision and the rationale underlying it in writing. In making his or her decision, the arbitrator is legally constrained by the terms of the collective agreement. If these terms are reasonably clear, then the decision may be straightforward. But this is rare, for if the decision *is* straightforward, the parties are likely to have resolved the grievance on their own, at an earlier stage. As such, it is up to the arbitrator to interpret the meaning of the agreement and establish whether, in view of that interpretation, the contract appears to have been violated and what the remedy should be. To do so, the arbitrator will normally take into account any precedents that have been set by arbitrators in similar cases, with both sides often submitting cases which they believe to support their arguments. Finally they consider evidence as to what the parties intended when they negotiated the agreement and how the agreement has been interpreted in the past.

BOX 14–2 Stages in a Grievance Arbitration Hearing

1. The parties introduce themselves and state any preliminary objections they may have to holding the arbitration. For example, it may be argued that the grievance procedure was not properly followed, or that the grievance was withdrawn, or that the issue in question is not covered under the collective agreement. Usually, the arbitrator will still proceed with the hearing, ruling on the objections at a later time.
2. Each party makes an opening statement, outlining the nature of the grievance and the remedy sought. Usually, the party with the burden of proof goes first. However, this party normally has an opportunity to respond to the other party's opening statement once it is made.
3. The party with the burden of proof presents its witnesses, who usually give evidence under oath. These witnesses are then cross-examined by the other party. The arbitrator and panellists (where appointed) may also ask questions of each witness.
4. The other party presents its witnesses, who are also subject to cross-examination.
5. The parties make their closing arguments, usually referring to other arbitration rulings of relevance to the case. Again, the party with the burden of proof normally goes first.
6. The arbitrator adjourns the hearing.

Also see: Peirce (2000: 480–81); Thornicroft and Eden (1995).

Where a disciplinary case is involved, the arbitrator's decision may be especially difficult, for though there is some clause in most agreements outlining management's right to discipline workers and specifying that it must be for just cause, there may be no specified disciplinary procedures or penalties. As such, the arbitrator must establish not only whether there has been "just cause" for discipline, but also whether the discipline meted out has been consistent with principles of natural justice. In making this determination, the arbitrator typically considers such things as previous offenses committed by the employee, the employee's length of service with the employer, the seriousness of the offense, whether there were mitigating circumstances (e.g., marital problems), and whether the employee is willing to admit to and apologize for any wrongdoing.

The arbitrator must also normally establish whether **progressive discipline** has been employed (see Eden, 1993). To meet this requirement, the employer must have first provided the employee with substantial warning that her behaviour or performance was unacceptable, and must have relied on penalties of escalating severity. For example, an employee who is regularly late for work may first receive a verbal warning. Then, if the behaviour continues, there may be a written warning, then perhaps a one-day suspension without pay, then a one-week suspension, and, finally, permanent discharge. Unless the employer has a strong justification for doing so, failure to proceed in this way is likely to result in a finding in favour of the griever, probably with the arbitrator imposing a lesser punishment. In the case of more severe offenses, progressive discipline becomes less important. Nonetheless, if a first offence, the arbitrator may still rule that discharge is too severe, and that the party deserves a second chance.

Because the facts of an arbitration case can be in dispute, it is often up to the arbitrator to evaluate the evidence (see Thornicroft and Eden, 1995). In most cases, the arbitrator will rely on the "balance of probabilities", which is the criterion used in civil law for resolving a case. In other words, she must only establish which version of the facts is *most likely* to be true, not whether this version *is* true. However, in discharge cases, the arbitrator may require "proof beyond a reasonable doubt", which is the criterion used in criminal law. This is especially likely if the case involves allegations of severe misconduct, such as theft or dishonesty.

Over the past few decades, arbitrators have had to increasingly take various employment laws into account. They have also been given the same jurisdiction as the courts to apply the Canadian Charter of Rights and Freedoms and to order whatever remedies they find appropriate, provided these remedies do not violate existing legislation.

Particularly important has been human rights legislation and the **doctrine of constructive discrimination** associated with it (see Carter, 1997). Under this doctrine, a collective agreement provision need not be intended to discriminate, but if it has a disproportionately negative impact on a minority designated for protection under human rights legislation, it can be said to meet this doctrine. For example, collective agreement provisions specifying Christian holidays (e.g., Christmas) or overtime for working on Sundays may discriminate against religious minorities if they do not also contain provisions for the religious holidays of these minorities, and a grievance may be filed on this basis. In deciding whether to rule in favour of the grievance, the arbitrator must take into account the **duty to accommodate**. As discussed in chapter nine, the party justifying the rule or practice in question must be able to establish that the individual or group adversely effected could not be reasonably accommodated without causing substantial disruption to the running of the workplace or undue hardship to others. If the party cannot do so, the arbitrator is likely to rule that the duty to accommodate has not been met, thus ruling in the individual's or group's favour.

Finally, if the arbitrator rules in favour of the griever she must then determine the appropriate remedy. This may involve simply issuing a directive stating who is in the right and how similar incidences are to be dealt with in the future. But it may (and often does) also involve making the aggrieved party "whole". This is especially the case in "wrongful dismissal" cases, where it has been held that a dismissal was not justified. In these cases, the employee may simply be reinstated with back pay. However, the arbitrator may also determine that some form of discipline is still called for, including temporary suspension or demotion. It is common, for example, for the arbitrator to order reinstatement, but without back pay for the period the griever was out of work.

An arbitrator's decision may be appealed to the courts, but in order for such an appeal to succeed, it must be established that the arbitrator either (1) exceeded his or her jurisdiction by going "outside of" or disregarding the collective agreement, (2) had a personal interest or bias that prejudiced the decision (e.g., was related to the griever or held stock in the company), (3) did not follow due process, or (4) substantially misinterpreted the collective agreement or applicable laws. In essence, then, unless there is a clear basis for questioning either the competence or the integrity of the arbitrator, the arbitrator's decision is final, and both parties are legally bound by it.

Probably the best way to develop a feel for arbitration is to read actual awards by arbitrators. Examples of these can be found in the quarterly periodical, *Labour Arbitration Cases*. One of the shorter awards to be found in this periodical appears in Box 14–3.

II. ASSESSING THE GRIEVANCE AND ARBITRATION PROCESSES

The grievance and arbitration processes can serve a number of functions, some of which are consistent with the purposes of labour law; others of which are not and may be more controversial. In addition, a

BOX 14–3 Arbitration Award

Re Algoma Steel Inc. and U.S.W.A., Loc. 2251

This is the discharge grievance of Karl Turner. Initially hired in September of 1979, the griever was terminated by the company on January 27th, 1999, on the basis of the "automatic termination" provisions of Article 7.03.10 of the collective agreement. Article 7.03.10 in particular in paragraph 4 provides:

Loss of Seniority

7.03.10 An employee's employment shall be considered terminated and his seniority and vacation credits permanently cancelled when:

....

4. he is absent from work for ten consecutive scheduled working days without reasonable excuse...

Following his lay-off from the Tube Division late in 1998, the griever was transferred to the Janitorial Department. The first of the material shifts missed by the griever was January 3rd, 1999, and there is no dispute that he was absent from there for the requisite 10 scheduled days stipulated by Article 7.03.10.4. The only issue in the case, therefore, is whether the griever's absence was with "reasonable excuse." Given that focus, only the griever testified, apart briefly from his supervisor, Don Mei (whose testimony in all material respects was exactly the same as the griever's). The griever testified that he began in the week of January 3rd to experience flu-like symptoms, including diarrhea and abdominal pain. Rather than subsiding, the diarrhea gradually became so severe as to result almost in nausea, and the griever began to consider that there might be something more to his problem than simple flu. The griever had called in to Security on January 3rd, 4th and 5th, reporting his condition and advising that he would not be in. By the 5th he wanted to make sure his supervisor, Mr. Mei, was apprised of his situation, and so spoke to him directly as well. The griever advised Mr. Mei of his symptoms and indicated that he thought he might have some kind of intestinal virus. The griever added that he was going to see his doctor, and that he would bring in a note upon his return to work. Mr. Mei testified that that essentially was the conversation as he recalled it also, and that, whoever raised the point, under the company Sick Pay Policy it was appropriate that the griever bring in a doctor's note on his return.

It was in that simple vein that the matter was left. Unfortunately, the practice of the griever's family doctor, Dr. Catania, had grown very busy in recent times, and when the griever called on the 5th, the best he could get for an appointment was

Continued....

BOX 14–3 (continued)

January 20th. The griever took that, but explaining the severity of his now alternating diarrhea and constipation, asked the nurse to call him if anything came open sooner. The griever explained that, notwithstanding his condition, rather than go elsewhere he preferred to take his chances and wait for Dr. Catania, who had "saved his life" in diagnosing his earlier heart condition, and in whom he had absolute faith. The griever noted that he had also followed the same practice with Dr. Catania before, and had always been successful in getting in earlier through a cancellation. As it turns out on the evidence, it, in fact, worked again this time, as the doctor's records show that the griever had been written in for an appointment on January 12th, that was subsequently cancelled. The griever had no initial recollection of that as part of the chronology, but testified that that must have been the date of the heavy snowstorm, which rendered roads in northern Michigan (where he lives) impassable. The griever in cross-examination acknowledged that, in spite of his extreme condition, he did not consider attending earlier at either a walk-in clinic or the hospital Emergency Department, because his experience with both was a wait for potentially several hours, and in the end the advice he was give previously was to "see your family doctor". The griever testified that at this point he was more or less "living his life in the bathroom", and was just not up to such a further experience in the waiting room.

By the time the griever did see his doctor, on the 20th, he was feeling considerably better. Dr. Catania gave him some medication and certified him able to return to work, as the griever requested. Dr. Catania also completed the form required to cover the payment of sick pay for the period from January 3rd to the 20th, based on the griever's reported symptoms, entering as the diagnosis "gastritis/flu." The griever immediately made an appointment for January 22nd with the company's Medical Department to obtain clearance to return on his next scheduled shift, being January 23rd. After initial success with the medication, however, the griever found himself in rapid relapse, and he cancelled the appointment for the 22nd (as well as his return to work for the 23rd). On January 27th, apparently without additional discussion, the griever received notification that his employment was terminated under the "10-day" provisions of Article 7.03.10. The griever was not able to piece together exactly when a return visit to Dr. Catania was arranged, but it appears it may have been brought on by the Notice of Termination. Dr. Catania referred him for an "Upper GI series" of tests, and the lab report indicated "considerable irritability and some deformity of the duodenal

Continued....

355

BOX 14–3 (continued)

cap." Dr. Catania referred the griever to a specialist for further assessment, but with the griever's medical coverage lapsing with his termination, he testified that he has not been able to proceed on that.

As the Court of Appeal made clear in its oral judgment involving this collective agreement twenty-four years ago, Article 7.03.10 is an "automatic" termination provision, and if its terms are found by an arbitrator to have been met, that ends the matter: there is no room for arbitral discretion beyond that, to decide whether the "penalty" for some reason ought to be mitigated. It does, however, remain to be determined whether an absence in excess of the 10-day trigger level was "without reasonable excuse." Article 7.03.10.4 does not say "in the company's opinion"; nor does it explicitly say "as certified by a physician." The question is simply one of fact and indeed, more often than not, of credibility. I agree with Mr. Peterson that Article 7.03.10.4 and the company's "Sick Pay Policy" can stand independently; Article 7.03.10.4 is essentially an "AWOL" provision (although with an unusually long trigger-period), and can come to apply in cases of extended absences on vacation or whatever. Where, to the company's knowledge however, the explanation given for the absence is illness, the backdrop of the "Sick Pay Policy" cannot be ignored. That is a joint policy-statement developed at the "new" Algoma (i.e., since the employee buy-out), and begins with the statement:

> The Company and Union share the fundamental belief that if you are too sick to go to work that you and your family should not be penalized on payday.

In the face of that fundamental statement of principle in particular, it obviously could not be said that an employee "too sick to go to work" was off "without reasonable excuse." The sole question in the matter therefore, is whether I am prepared to find on the balance of the evidence that the griever was too sick to go to work on the days in question, as he asserts.

The company does not disagree with that, but essentially bases its position on the fact that, in its view, the medical evidence submitted wholly fails to support the griever in his assertion. The cases cited by the company are helpful on the various issues around medical certificates; however, the ultimate issue is one of fact or credibility, and in each of the cases one can see why the arbitrator, apart from the persuasiveness (or otherwise) of the medical evidence, found difficulty with the griever's assertions. In

Continued....

BOX 14–3 (continued)

the original Court of Appeal case itself, the griever denied that he was medically fit even for the *light* duties being offered him (for close to a year), and the arbitrator, on the medical evidence, came to a different conclusion. In the parties' September 3rd, 1977 award (Rayner) the evidence tendered to explain the griever's absence was a medical note expressing "surprise" that the griever had not in fact been back to work earlier. In the September 1989 award (Barton), the company *sought* some medical explanation for the griever's absence (apart from his admitted alcohol and drug consumption), but got none. In *Re St. Jean de Brebeuf Hospital and C.U.P.E., Loc. 1101* (1977), 16 L.A.C. (2d) 199 (Swan), the griever's absence from work was preceded by an "argument" over staffing levels on her floor, with the griever threatening to go home if she were not provided with more help. The griever then consulted her doctor, and on her own decided it was necessary to stay home. Arbitrator Swan noted [at p. 206]:

> After five days spent off work, taking medication and being looked after by a daughter (the griever's evidence is that she moved to her daughter's home while she was ill) the griever might reasonably have been expected to consult her doctor again, and to seek further assistance. She did not, however; she chose instead to remain at home and to look after herself. This is unreasonable conduct in a person too ill to return to work after five days of rest, and it clearly places the griever outside of the principle of reasonable accommodation which I have mentioned above. The griever's failure to seek further medical advice when a minor, if unpleasant, illness failed to subside after five days of rest casts doubt on her entire story, and weakens considerably the value of her own evidence.

In *Re Fishery Products (Marystown) Ltd. and Newfoundland Fishermen, Food & Allied Workers, Loc. 1245* (1979), 22 L.A.C. (2d) 439 (Hattenhauer), the two grievers had announced "that they were going to take the night off", and "if necessary, they were going to get a doctor's statement to indicate that they were sick." In the unreported *York University* decision of Mr. O'Shea (January 1978), all of the evidence raised an overwhelming suspicion (the arbitrator found, the medical certification notwithstanding) that the griever had planned to overstay her vacation back home in Italy from the outset. Similarly, in *Re Salvation Army Grace Hospital and C.U.P.E., Loc. 100* (1980), 25 L.A.C. (2d) 241, the griever had previously requested and been denied the days in question as days off, and Arbitrator McLaren agreed that the company had "reasonable and probable grounds" to require formal medical certification in the circumstances. In the unreported decision of Gail Brent in *Consolidated Fastfrate* (issued January

Continued....

BOX 14–3 (continued)

7th, 1981), the medical evidence raised contrary inferences similar to the *Algoma* (Rayner) case, *supra*, and Arbitrator Brent noted that the griever's delay in returning to work when he did was not reasonably explained in the circumstances. In *Re Alcan Smelters and Chemicals Ltd. and C.A.W., Loc. 2301 (Pegley)* (1997), 62 L.A.C. (4th) 371, the griever was disciplined for failing to report after being involved in heavy drinking and being sprayed with mace in the course of being arrested, and Arbitrator Hope noted, in some obviously implicit criticism of the griever's role in the matter, the lack of any medical evidence to demonstrate that the cause of the absence was anything other than "self-diagnosed and self-inflicted."

Many of the cases also revolve around claims for sick pay, and the collective agreement often will cast an onus on an employee specifically to file appropriate medical evidence to substantiate the claim. In such circumstances, it is inevitable that the sole question will be the adequacy of the medical certificate. Even there, however, it is noteworthy that in the oft-quoted case of *St. Jean de Brebeuf Hospital*, referred to above, Arbitrator Swan observed, at pp. 205–206:

> Quite clearly, an employee does not have to demonstrate total physical incapacity to work. It is enough to show that, because of illness-produced discomfort, weakness or pain, it would be unreasonable to expect the employee to perform the work of the job.
>
> As a result, a medical certificate obtained following a cursory examination, or even after a telephone consultation, will not always be valueless to an employee. Depending on the nature of the complaint, the medical history of the employee, the likely value of a detailed examination for a better diagnosis or for prescribing a cure, *it may be quite reasonable for a physician to simply record the fact of a reported illness and leave the matter at that.* Without a certain amount of reasonableness on the part of employees, employers, medical practitioners and arbitrators, sick pay schemes would collapse in a morass of red tape. [Emphasis added.]

The question in the present case is whether, notwithstanding the indirect nature of the medical evidence, I am prepared to find that the griever was indeed ill enough to justify not being at work as he had reported, and as his supervisor appeared to accept, or whether, as a converse determination would mean, he was effectively "AWOL." Mr. Peterson in cross-examination did an admirable job establishing — indeed getting the griever to admit that he could, in hindsight, have done more to pursue immediate medical attention, and to protect himself in this matter. But the circumstances, I find, were not such as to demand that. Had the

Continued....

BOX 14–3 (continued)

company been exhorting the griever, either for an earlier return, or for immediate medical confirmation for his absence, his efforts (as in the previous *Algoma* case with Professor Barton, *supra*) might be viewed differently. But that was not all the case here. The Sick Pay Policy has provisions for the scrutiny of suspected "abusers", including the specific requirement for direct medical certification for each and every shift missed, but no issue of abuse was ever raised or relied on there. The griever had advised the company of his situation, as well as his proposed course of action, and his own supervisor had accepted it (as indeed, when called by the Union as a witness, Mr. Mei confirmed again at the hearing). In that context I do not find that the griever's decision to await an appointment with Dr. Catania, for the reasons given, to be unreasonable — or more to the issue, to create an overall lack of believability of his story. The griever's failure to initially recount the cancelled January 12th appointment I put down more likely to imprecise recollection (at a time when his absence was not in issue) than to guile: indeed, the fact that he had *gotten* the earlier cancellation slot but had to cancel because of the snowstorm would have provided a ready answer to much of Mr. Peterson's searching cross-examination as to why he had simply waited for the January 20th appointment. The griever did finally get in to see his doctor on the 20th, and at that point, obtaining the medical clearance required for his return, on his own initiative (i.e., without any urging from anyone in the company) arranged for his return to work. He testified that he then suffered a relapse and had to pull back. I find no objective cause on the evidence to disbelieve him. But the company decided, without, so far as I am told, discussion of the circumstances of his January 22nd/23rd about-face, to invoke Article 7.03.10.4 of the collective agreement, and "automatically" terminate him.

For the reasons set out in the foregoing paragraph, I find that the griever has been able to establish that he had "reasonable cause" for his failure to attend at work on the days in question, and that the conditions of Article 7.03.10.4 have not been met. More specifically, I find the griever's explanation as to the reasons for his delay in actually attending at his doctor's office to be believable, so that the delay in this case (versus some of the cases cited) does not leave an unanswered question: "If you were that sick, why didn't you see a doctor?" And again, while the medical evidence, because of that delay, did not provide *direct* support of the griever's condition, it was at least consistent with the situation as the griever has described it. In all of the circumstances here, including the lack of anything suspicious about

Continued....

BOX 14–3 (continued)

the timing of the absence to begin with, I find nothing in the objective evidence, or in the delivery of his testimony, that would cause me to conclude that the griever was in fact abusing the sick-pay policy when keeping himself at home (as the company's position would have to imply), as opposed to being too incapacitated to work on those days.

It follows that the termination of the griever, relying on the provisions of Article 7.03.10.4, was improper, and I so declare. The griever is to be reinstated to his former position forthwith, without loss of service or seniority, and is to be compensated for any monetary loss suffered as a result of the termination. I will remain seized as requested, in the event there are any problems between the parties with respect to the latter.

Source: 80 L.A.C. (4th) at 101.

number of problems and limitations have been identified with the processes themselves. In this section, each is addressed in turn.

The Functions of the Grievance and Arbitration Processes

At least six functions can be associated with the grievance and arbitration processes. The first, and most evident, is that they provide the only viable legal means of ensuring that the terms of the agreement are adhered to. As such, they function to maintain the integrity of the agreement. This function is of pivotal importance to the Canadian system of labour law and collective bargaining, as discussed in the introduction in this chapter.

The second function is to serve as a forum and basis for supplementary negotiations. In some cases, the terms of the collective agreement are intentionally left ambiguous in order to allow flexibility or to avoid a strike over the specific content and wording of a particular provision. The grievance process can serve as a mechanism for deciding how to interpret and apply ambiguous provisions, with either side being able to resort to arbitration if they deem it necessary.

Third, the grievance process may be viewed as a mechanism for conflict resolution. The multi-stage procedure is designed so that the parties have every opportunity to arrive at a mutually satisfactory solution on their own, rather than having a resolution imposed by an arbitrator. In this respect, the grievance process can be likened to the collective bargaining process, while resort to arbitration can be seen as a failure of this process, resulting in problems similar to those associated with interest arbitration (see chapter thirteen).

Fourth, the grievance mechanism provides workers with a vehicle for expressing discontent, either in general or with respect to specific treatment afforded them by management. As such, it can serve as a mechanism of individual or group voice, much as a strike can serve as a mechanism of collective voice. Not only does this provide a release for workers, it also serves as a form of communication and hence a source of information to management about problems in the workplace. This may be especially useful to management where these problems involve the actions of lower level managers and supervisors.

Fifth, grievances can be used as a pressuring device, to get management to change its policies on issues that may not be covered in this agreement. For example, management may decide to contract out work normally done by bargaining unit members, thereby resulting in less overtime or even layoffs. If there is no subcontracting clause in the agreement, the union may decide to file grievances having to do with a number of other aspects of the agreement. Whether these are well-founded or not, they can cause considerable inconvenience and disruption for management, resulting in a "rethinking" of the subcontracting decision.

Sixth, grievances may serve as political devices for resolving conflicts and problems within each organization. For example, union officials may pursue a grievance in order to "look good" to the membership in general or to placate an individual or internal faction within the membership, not because they believe that the grievance itself is of merit. They may also pursue a grievance because they have been implicitly or explicitly encouraged to do so by lower level managers, in order to pressure senior management to change a policy or decision which lower level managers and the union dislike.

Finally, and perhaps most important, the grievance and grievance arbitration processes provide a system of industrial jurisprudence under which individuals are protected from, or at least have recourse for, arbitrary or unjust treatment from their superordinates. Not only do these processes provide employees with protection and freedoms normally considered to be basic democratic rights outside of the workplace (as discussed in chapter seven), they also have positive implications for morale, for they help to ensure that individuals receive just treatment from their superordinates. Indeed, it is for this reason, coupled, perhaps, with a desire to avoid unionization, that more "progressive" firms often adopt "internal justice systems". As discussed in chapter five, these systems are essentially grievance systems, renamed for symbolic purposes ("justice" sounds less adversarial than "grievance"). However, as also discussed in chapter five, they are typically limited in scope and do not allow for binding arbitration.

Failings of the Grievance and Arbitration Process

Though the grievance and arbitration processes can *in theory* have a number of benefits for both employees *and* employers, they have been a source of considerable criticism, in both principle and application. Four general criticisms are of particular note.

The first criticism is relatively simple: that in practice the grievance and arbitration processes can be both cumbersome and costly. Filing a grievance and pursuing it all the way to arbitration can cost thousands of dollars. For example, the arbitrator alone may cost as much as or more than two thousand dollars, plus expenses, for each day that there are hearings (these costs are split between the parties), and in more complex cases, hearings can be spread over a number of days. There are also the costs of working time lost both in preparation and during a hearing, of legal representation, and of hiring expert witnesses (where used). Finally, where an arbitration board panel is used, the additional members must also be paid.

In addition, the elapsed time from filing a grievance to the arbitrator's decision averages roughly a year (Ponak et al., 1996: 106) and can be considerably longer in some cases. This is believed to have a number of negative consequences (see Ponak et al., 1996: 107). Perhaps most important, it means that the source of discontent leading to the grievance is left to fester, thus enhancing adversariness both in the workplace and between union and management representatives, and possibly resulting in higher levels of alternative forms of conflict, such as quits, sabotage, and even wildcat strikes. In the case of a discharge, it can also mean severe stress for the individual affected, and may substantially lower the individual's ability to return to work.

As noted earlier, only about 15 percent of grievances ever get to arbitration. This may indicate that the parties succeed in satisfactorily resolving most grievances without undergoing the time and expense of pursuing them to arbitration, and it may even indicate that this time and expense provides an incentive to seek an early resolution. But it may also mean that one or both parties find that pursuing a grievance to the arbitration stage is often not viable *because* of the time and expense involved. If so, legitimate grievances may not be pursued, or they may be dropped at an early stage even though they have not been satisfactorily resolved. For example, a union may be hesitant to spend thousands of dollars on a grievance over a few hundred dollars in pay or benefits denied a member, unless doing so is likely to serve some broader principle. Yet to the member involved, this may represent a substantial sum of money.

The second criticism is that, even where the grievance and arbitration processes *do* operate as intended, they may not be satisfactory from the point of view of individual workers. One reason is that individuals may fear retribution in the event that they file a grievance. In other words, a worker might find that she is suddenly assigned the most onerous tasks or is subject to disciplinary measures for infractions that her supervisor would normally ignore. Research in the United States seems to confirm this, finding that workers who file grievances subsequently receive lower performance ratings, have a lower likelihood of promotion, and are more likely to quit, even though (in this study) they tend to have *better* records than non-grievers prior to filing (Lewin and Peterson, 1988, 1999).

A further reason the grievance and arbitration processes may not prove satisfactory to individual workers has to do with union "ownership" of the grievance process. As discussed in chapter eleven, if the union decides not to pursue a grievance, there is little that an individual can do unless it can be clearly established that the union is violating its duty of fair representation or unless there is a provision which allows individuals to pursue grievances independently of the union. The former is extremely difficult to establish. As for the latter, the right to file grievances independently of the union would appear to be widespread only in the public sector, where it is in a number of cases mandated under the law. Moreover, where individuals pursue their own grievances, they are typically required to pay for their own representation and for their share of arbitration fees and expenses.

The third criticism has to do with restrictions on arbitral authority. As discussed in chapters nine and eleven, under the doctrine of residual rights anything that is not in the collective agreement is subject to the unilateral authority of management. While management may and often does accept grievances that are not covered in the agreement (Gandz and Whitehead, 1989: 241), arbitrators have little choice under the law but to rule in management's favour, unless there is evidence that management clearly led the griever (or the union) to believe that it would not assert certain of its rights pertaining to the grievance (Haiven, 1991: 94; Arthurs et al., 1993: 329). Moreover, over the life of an agreement management may take any number of actions which workers consider to be unfair and/or which substantially affect their well-being. But because everything not in the agreement is subject to managerial authority, there is normally little that an arbitrator can do, as long as these appear to be for legitimate business reasons and are not specifically prohibited in the contract.

Fourth, a key tenant of the grievance process is that of "obey now, grieve later". That is, employees are generally required to obey all management orders unless they have reason to believe that doing so would require a violation of the law or would jeopardize their health and safety. They can only grieve after the fact, and even then management can continue to issue the same orders until such time that the grievance is resolved or an arbitrator has been on it. In view of the time delays involved in the grievance and arbitration process, it may thus be a long time before anything can be done "to right past wrongs" — if, indeed, anything *can* be done. This can render the grievance process of limited value, for, as one author has noted, "justice delayed, at least to the employees involved, may be justice denied" (Haiven, 1991: 103).

These problems are undoubtedly important, especially because the development of labour law has involved an historical compromise, under which labour gave up the right to strike during the term of the agreement in return for the right to grieve and arbitrate, what lawyers refer to as a quid pro quo. Yet, as one author has commented: "the no-strike provisions of ... collective agreements constitute a quo considerably in excess of the quid of the agreement to arbitrate" (Feller, 1973: 760, as cited in Haiven, 1991: 105). Even more important, these problems mean that, no matter how much labour and management appear to confront one another as equals under collective bargaining, and no matter how much they appear to have developed a mature, cooperative relationship, management ultimately has the upper hand under the law.

In practice, of course, there may be a number of ways that disaffected workers can "get back at" management during the term of an agreement. These can include exiting, striking illegally, or engaging in various forms of recalcitrance in the workplace. But these involve essentially reactive behaviour, and their effectiveness (from the point of view of workers) can vary considerably depending upon their exit, strike, and job power. Moreover, they can clearly entail major costs for workers, especially because illegal striking and recalcitrance can result in disciplinary action or even dismissal. As a result, workers and their leaders may simply become passive over time, acquiescing to management in recognition of the reality in which they find themselves. Where this is the case, conflict is not resolved. Rather, it is merely repressed, and is likely to be manifest in negative attitudes and ultimately poor overall performance. Perhaps as a result, employers may decide to accept and attempt to find redress for grievances not covered by the collective agreement, even though they are not required to do so under the law.

Possible Alternatives

What can be done about this? With respect to the first criticism identified above (the time and expense involved), it has become popular to advocate some form of **"expedited arbitration"**, which entails altering the grievance and arbitration processes so as to increase their flexibility and reduce the length of time it takes to resolve a grievance. A number of possible modifications have been identified with this term. One is to rely on a single arbitrator rather than a tripartite board, thus shortening the length of time necessary to arrange and hold an arbitration hearing (Ponak and Olson, 1993). Another is to have the arbitrator issue an oral decision within one or two days of the hearing, followed by a written award at a later time, thus reducing the delay from the time of the hearing to the decision. Yet another is to have an arbitrator hear several cases at a single sitting, thereby addressing delays due to scheduling conflicts that can arise when parties with busy timetables are involved. A final modification advocated is to limit the number of witnesses that each side can call, instead relying on written witness statements wherever possible. This may reduce both the costs that may arise from paying witnesses and the length of time it takes to complete a hearing.

Although there is some research suggesting that expedited arbitration can indeed reduce time and expenses (e.g., Thornicroft, 1996), its effectiveness likely depends on the nature of the case or cases involved. In more complex or severe cases (e.g., dismissal), it may entail a short-circuiting of due process and a violation of the principle of natural justice. The financial interests of both the employer and the union may still be served, as costs are reduced, but the interests of the worker or workers involved may not be.

A related alternative for reducing the time and expenses involved is to bring in a neutral third party to mediate a resolution to grievances once they have reached the final stage prior to arbitration — something referred to as **grievance mediation** (see Elliot and Goss,

1994). Grievance mediation is similar in spirit to the cooperative bargaining approaches considered in the preceding chapter. The mediator attempts to get the parties to focus on their interests and needs rather than who is right or wrong in the dispute, and then pursues a problem-solving approach, in which the parties seek an agreeable solution rather than attempting to win at the other's expense. This approach is provided by the Department of Labour in some Canadian jurisdictions, and is most often used as a first stage in an expedited arbitration. Available research suggests that it can be effective and can save substantial amounts of money for the parties (see Elliot and Goss, 1994: 41–52; Peirce, 2000: 492). However, this may be because parties that are more predisposed to a settlement are more likely to choose it. Whether it represents a universal solution is uncertain.

As for the second criticism (retribution and union ownership), there does not appear to be a way to ensure that grievers are not subject to some form of retribution, though perhaps they could be provided with a right to file a complaint with the arbitrator if, subsequent to his ruling, some form of retribution could be established. It would also make sense to enact legislation providing all union (and for that matter, non-union) workers the right to file grievances independently of their union.

The third criticism (restrictions on arbitral authority) could be addressed by moving away from the doctrine of residual rights towards one of the alternative doctrines discussed in chapter eleven. For example, under the doctrine of shared rights, the grievance mechanism could be relied upon whenever management acted in a way which was contrary to established rules and understandings in the workplace. Under the doctrine of fair administration, the grievance mechanism could be relied upon whenever an employee was unjustly treated, regardless of whether explicit restrictions upon the offending management decision were in the agreement or not.

The fourth criticism (obey now, grieve later) could be remedied by lifting the ban on striking during the term of the agreement, so that workers are able to contest managerial orders at the time these orders are made, rather than forcing them to file a grievance and waiting a year or more before a decision reversing this order is handed down by an arbitrator. In other words, management would be under pressure to take worker concerns more fully into account at the time an order is issued, as also discussed in chapter eleven.

These options could, in theory, greatly enhance the effectiveness of the grievance and arbitration process. But, whether they are desirable is a matter for debate. In particular, management groups could be expected to oppose most of them on the grounds that they could substantially shift the balance of power in the workplace, with negative implications for order and efficiency. One can only speculate over the extent to which this would be the case. However, there is little question that, with the exception of the first option, they would be likely to generate substantial employer resistance if a government attempted to implement them. It is thus unlikely that we will ever know what their real implications would be.

III. CONCLUSIONS

This and the preceding two chapters have woven their way through what may be referred to as the "nitty gritty" of labour–management relations under collective bargaining: negotiations, strikes and dispute resolution procedures, and the grievance and arbitration processes. Because these topics are at the heart of the practice of labour–management relations in the union sector, they are of considerable relevance for the practically minded. But they are also at the heart of the Canadian system of industrial relations (however broadly defined) and hence are critical to the effectiveness of this system. As such, they have a much broader importance, one that goes to the heart of the Canadian system's ability to ensure meaningful democratic rights and protections at work. Also of considerable importance is the collective agreement itself, for it forms the focal point around which these processes revolve. The following chapter thus discusses the contents of collective agreements and the issues that surround their negotiation.

The Collective Agreement
Content and Issues

15

This chapter addresses the contents of collective agreements and the issues involved in their negotiation. One purpose in doing so is to provide a working knowledge of the general contents of these agreements. A second, and equally if not more important purpose, however, is to foster an *understanding* of why it is that unions often seek to negotiate various provisions and why it is that management often resists these provisions. As shall become apparent, many of the issues involved in the negotiation of collective agreements arise out of and reflect the underlying sources of conflict identified in chapter three. Thus, in pursuing this second objective, the intention is to provide not just an understanding of specific issues, but also an understanding of how the more abstract sources of conflict identified in chapter three come to be manifest in the interactions between labour and management — both at the bargaining table, and on a day-to-day basis in the workplace.

Collective agreements can be highly complex and can vary considerably in both their structure and their content. Thus, consistent with the approach taken in chapter eleven, this chapter does not attempt to discuss all of the specific clauses to be found in collective agreements. Rather, it begins by providing a broad overview of the contents of these agreements. It then discusses at a general level six aspects of collective agreements: (1) wages and benefits, (2) hours of work and overtime, (3) work rules, (4) job and income security, (5) seniority, and (6) union security and rights. As discussed in chapter twelve, the first four of these aspects can be thought of as "substantive", the fifth as "procedural", and the final one as "relational". Although a number of other aspects of collective agreements might also be addressed, these six aspects tend to be both the most important clauses in collective agreements and often the most controversial.

I. OVERVIEW OF COLLECTIVE AGREEMENTS

Collective agreements come in a variety of sizes, shapes, and colours, and their contents can vary considerably. Most often, however, they are printed in the form of small, pocket or purse-sized booklets, and are somewhere between ten and 100 pages in length. The front cover usually contains the names of the parties to the agreement (the employer and the union) and either the date that the agreement takes effect or its expiry date (or both). Inside, on the first page or two, there is usually a table of contents, with clauses listed in the order in which they appear in the agreement. There may also be an index, with the clauses listed alphabetically, in accordance with their topic area. An example of the former appears in the appendix at the end of this chapter.

On the next few pages, one usually finds a number of preliminary clauses, setting out in general terms the rights and obligations of the parties. Most notable are the "**union recognition**" and the "**management rights**" clauses, examples of which appear in Box 15–1. The former normally states that management "recognizes" the union as the sole bargaining agent of workers in the operations covered by the agreement; the latter normally states that management retains unilateral authority over all operations unless otherwise specified in the agreement. Both of these clauses are largely "formalities" in the sense that the former simply affirms the legal requirement for management to recognize the union (discussed in chapter eleven), while the latter simply affirms the doctrine of residual rights applied by arbitrators. Thus, the inclusion of these clauses often makes little real difference, except perhaps in the unusual case where the residual rights clause suggests a broader or narrower interpretation of managerial rights than is normally assumed under the residual rights doctrine.

In addition to these two clauses, there is usually a clause stipulating that the union will not strike during the term of the agreement. As is the case for management rights and union recognition clauses, the "**no strike clause**" merely affirms established labour law forbidding unions from striking during the term of the agreement and hence its inclusion is also largely a formality. Finally, it is common to find a clause or set of clauses stipulating that an employee will not be disciplined or discharged except for "just cause". In some jurisdictions this is also required by law, but even where this is not the case, the doctrine of just cause is central to the grievance and arbitration process, as discussed in the preceding chapter.

BOX 15–1 Sample Union Recognition and Management Rights Clauses

RECOGNITION

(1) Employees Covered

(a) Pursuant to and in accordance with all applicable provisions of the *Ontario Labour Relations Act*, as amended, Chrysler Canada Ltd., herein called the Corporation, does hereby recognize the Union as the exclusive representative for the purposes of collective bargaining in respect to rates of pay, wages, hours of employment, and other conditions of employment for the term of this Agreement of all employees of the Corporation included in the bargaining units described in Schedule "A"' appended to this Agreement.

(b) This Agreement shall extend automatically to production and maintenance employees at any new plant the Corporation builds that the parties shall agree, or, in the absence of agreement, that the Ontario Labour Relations Board shall determine, constitutes an accretion to the multiple-plant bargaining unit this Agreement covers, excluding such employees as the parties agree or the Board decides should be excluded.

(c) If the Union becomes the representative of employees at a plant that is not a part of such unit, the parties shall determine by negotiation whether this Agreement shall apply, in whole or in part, to such employees.

(2) Management Rights

The Corporation has the exclusive right to manage its plants and offices and direct its affairs and working forces, except as limited by the terms of this Agreement and any Memorandums, Letter Agreements or Supplementary Agreements that by their terms modify this Agreement.

Source: Courtesy of DaimlerChrysler Corporation.

Following these clauses are numerous clauses governing issues such as wages and benefits, job classifications, seniority rights, grievance processing, union security and rights, work rules, disciplinary procedures and penalties, job and income security, and a plethora of other considerations that can arise in negotiations. It is also not uncommon to find various "**letters of intent**" and separate provisions for different groups of workers in the bargaining unit. In the former case, for example, management may not be prepared to negotiate a clause protecting workers from technological change, but it may be willing to sign a letter stating that it will attempt to do so if technological change becomes necessary. Such a letter is usually not legally binding, but it often appears as an appendix to the agreement and provides union officials with a "moral" tool for holding management to its word.

Finally, in cases where union and employer negotiators engage in two-tier bargaining, there is a "**master agreement**" to cover all operations in the bargaining unit and separate "**supplemental agreements**" for various work settings within this unit. As discussed in chapter twelve, the former addresses broad issues of relevance to all workers (such as wages and benefits), while the latter address issues of specific concern at individual work settings (such as job classifications and work rules).

II.   WAGES AND BENEFITS

Wages and benefits are typically the most contentious issues in collective bargaining. Disagreements can arise not just over the level of wages and benefits, but also over the way in which they vary or are dispersed within the bargaining unit and the mechanisms by which they are adjusted during the term of an agreement. Contingent pay provisions have also become important in recent years. In this section, each of these issues is discussed in turn.

Wage and Benefit Levels

Wage and benefit levels represent one of the primary underlying sources of labour–management conflict identified in chapter three. For workers, wages and benefits can have critical implications not only for their standard of living at a particular time, but also for their future income (e.g., pensions). As such, it is in their interests to negotiate the most favourable wages and benefits possible, other things being equal. For employers, wage and benefit costs can have major implications for financial performance and for the economic viability of the operations involved. As such, it is in *their* interests to minimize wages and benefits, again other things being equal. It is thus not surprising that wages and benefits are major issues in negotiation or that they often appear to be a key sticking point.

At the same time, to assume that wages and benefits are *necessarily* highly contentious would be mistaken. As discussed in chapter twelve, management may, under some conditions, be quite prepared to grant a "reasonable" wage and benefit settlement. This may be the case, for example, where workers require high levels of training or where high levels of commitment are critical to performance and hence management is concerned with maintaining morale and keeping turnover to a minimum. Or it may be the case where major competitors are unionized and can be counted upon to grant similar increases, thereby "taking wages out of competition".

For their part, workers are often satisfied with moderate wage and benefit increases, provided that these meet with their expectations and fairness perceptions. These can vary for a number of reasons, though three considerations would appear to be most important: (1) wages and benefits granted by similar employers, (2) increases in the cost of living, and (3) the employer's ability to grant wage and benefit concessions without jeopardizing the health of the firm (or, in the public sector, the economy). Beginning in the 1980s, harsh economic conditions have made the latter of these especially important, so much so that there have been a number of incidences under which workers have actually conceded wage and benefit cuts in order to ensure the financial viability of their employer. But the point should be clear: wage and benefit levels may not always be as contentious as often assumed.

Why, then, do negotiations often appear to stumble over wage and benefit issues? There are a number of reasons, not the least of which is a simple belief by management that it is not in their interests to meet the expectations of workers and a concomitant unwillingness of workers to adjust their expectations downward. Another may be a misunderstanding by one or both parties as to the other's "bottom line", again as is discussed in chapter twelve. Yet, the real cause may not be wages and benefits per se, but rather underlying hostilities that have come to be expressed in the bargaining positions of one or both sides *as they pertain* to wages and benefits. Thus, for example, workers may be discontent with the exercise of managerial authority in the workplace, and they may attempt to "get back" at management by making excessive (at least from management's point of view) wage demands. Or, management may wish to undermine union officials (and, perhaps, the union in general) by refusing to grant meaningful wage and benefit increases, thus forcing them to strike until such time that worker morale is broken and they are forced to accept management's terms. But whatever the case, it should be evident that wages and benefit demands may be as much a pretext for a strike or lockout as they are a cause.

Wage Dispersion

In addition to the overall wage and benefit levels negotiated, conflict can arise over the distribution or dispersion of wages and benefits within the negotiating unit. Most workplaces are characterized by a variety of jobs, entailing different levels of complexity and responsibility and requiring different skill and experience levels. Jobs are often classified and graded in accordance with these differences, and those with higher grades are typically assigned a higher rate of pay. In larger workplaces, with high levels of differentiation, this can result in considerable variation in pay. This is especially true where job ladders have been established (see chapter five), so that workers can expect to move up to higher and better paying job classifications over time. Although it has become common to read that job ladders have been gradually eliminated, as employers have moved towards a more autonomic/consociative approach associated with the high performance paradigm, it would appear that they remain widespread.

The actual reasons for the establishment of job ladders, and for high levels of differentiation in general, are subject to some dispute in academic circles.[1] There is little doubt, however, that they can be cause for considerable disagreement in negotiations (and, for that matter, during the term of a collective agreement). One reason is that there is always room for disagreement over the level at which a particular job should be classified. This can have important implications for the amount that workers are paid. Also important is the overall degree of variation or inequality in wage levels across different grades. As is discussed in chapter seven, research findings would appear to indicate that management generally favours a higher degree of inequality than do union officials. Possibly, this is because management is more concerned with the morale and loyalty of workers in

---

[1] Some argue that they are established by management for reasons of efficiency in reflection of differences in worker experience and "firm-specific skills" (Doeringer and Piore, 1971). Others argue that they are established in order to divide workers among themselves and enhance control over them (Stone, 1975). Still others argue that they are established largely in response to union pressure, and hence reflect union strike power (Jacoby, 1985).

higher classifications, who tend to have higher skill levels and perform more critical work, while union officials are more concerned with improving the wages and benefits of those at lower levels, in part for social democratic reasons, but also because these workers tend to be more numerous and to have more votes. In any case, the result is that both the "wage spread" across classifications and the allocation of jobs to classifications can be matters for considerable dispute.

Wage Adjustment Clauses

A further issue, particularly in times of high inflation, is the magnitude of wage increases during the term of the agreement and the way in which these increases are calculated. When inflation is high, the absence of wage adjustment clauses can mean that workers will see their purchasing power substantially eroded over the life of a agreement. To protect their members against this, unions have four main options. One is to negotiate short-term agreements of a year or so in duration so that they can catch up on a year by year basis. Another is to have a "**reopener**" clause, under which it is agreed that wages will be subject to renegotiation at some point during the term of the agreement, by reopening the agreement on this issue only. The third is to refuse the effects of inflation by negotiating planned increases to take effect at periodic intervals (e.g., every six months) over the life of the agreement, based on the expected level of inflation.

The fourth, and most complicated option, is to negotiate a "**COLA**" or "**cost-of-living-adjustment**" clause. COLA clauses stipulate that employees will receive increases over the life of the agreement (usually every three or six months) but that the size of these increases will be tied to increases in the Consumer Price Index (CPI), which is a government produced measure of the rate of inflation. These clauses can be highly complex, but the magnitude of the wage adjustment is usually some fraction of (and hence smaller than) the rate of inflation, and often does not "kick in" until a pre-established level of inflation has been reached. It may also be subject to a "cap", or maximum level of adjustment, beyond which workers receive no further adjustment. Thus, for example, a clause might stipulate that workers will receive a .5 percent increase in their wages for every 1 percent increase in the CPI, provided that the rate of increase in the CPI equals or exceeds 3 percent, and subject to a maximum increase of 4 percent. But it is rare to find a COLA clause that is even this straightforward, as the representative clause in Box 15–2 indicates.

BOX 15–2 Sample COLA Clause

Article 35 Cost of Living Allowance

35.01 If the June 1992 Consumer Price Index (C.P.I.) exceeds the C.P.I. for June 1991 by more than 6.4, then all basic rates of pay in effect at August 31, 1992 will be increased effective September 1, 1992 by a percentage figure equal to the difference between:

(a) the percentage by which the June 1992 C.P.I. exceeds the June 1991 C.P.I.

and

(b) 6.4%

35.02 If the June 1993 Consumer Price Index (C.P.I.) exceeds the C.P.I. for June 1992 by more than 6.4, then all basic rates of pay in effect at August 31, 1993 will be increased effective September 1, 1993 by a percentage figure equal to the difference between:

(a) the percentage by which the June 1993 C.P.I. exceeds the June 1992 C.P.I.

and

(b) 6.4%

35.03 The Consumer Price Index used for the formula in sections 35.01 and 35.02 shall be the C.P.I.-Canada All Items (1986 = 100) as published by Statistics Canada or any successor department or agency.

35.04 Should the Consumer Price Index be amended or discontinued prior to January 1992, the parties agree to consult to determine a means by which rates of pay will be increased effective September 1, 1992, consistent with the formula in section 35.01.

35.05 Should the Consumer Price Index be amended or discontinued prior to January 1993, the parties agree to consult to determine a means by which rates of pay will be increased effective September 1, 1993, consistent with the formula in section 35.02.

Source: From the agreement between Bell Canada and the Communications and Electrical Workers of Canada, Craft and Services Employees, effective February 1, 1991. Reproduced by permission of S.C.E.P.

Management generally does not like any of these options, particularly when there is uncertainty about the rate of inflation (as is usually the case when inflation is high). In the case of the first two options, management can find itself subject to uncertainty not only as to wage and benefit costs, but also as to the likelihood of a strike. As such, it generally prefers long-term contracts with fixed wage increases (option three). The problem here, however, is that under conditions of uncertainty, it is difficult for the two sides to come to an agreement on the magnitude of these increases, for management fears granting an increase which turns out to be far in excess of the rate of inflation, while the union fears agreeing to increases which turn out to be far below the rate of inflation. COLA clauses help to avoid this, but they reintroduce the problem of cost uncertainty for management, and can have serious economic consequences if management is unable to raise its prices in line with COLA adjustments without harming its market position.

As a result of these difficulties, inflationary periods often complicate negotiations, because it is during these periods that wage protection issues are most salient. While it is rare that management will refuse to make some accommodation along these lines, there can be considerable acrimony over the nature and magnitude of this accommodation. At the time of this writing, inflation has been relatively low, so this issue has been less important. But, to assume that inflation will remain low and that this issue will not once again be a major one may be unduly optimistic.

Contingent Pay Provisions

Individual piece rate and commission systems have been common forms of compensation since the advent of industrial capitalism in Canada over a century ago. As discussed in chapter five, however, more group-based contingent pay schemes have received growing attention in recent years, especially with the growing popularity of high performance work practices. These can include group bonus systems, gainsharing, profit-sharing, and other systems. Most are not particularly new, dating back to the early decades of the twentieth century. But they are viewed by some as of central importance to the attainment of high performance levels.

Unions generally oppose these schemes, because they can render employee income uncertain and subject to employer decisions over which they have little influence. For example, to make employee income dependent on profits when employees have little or no say in decisions that determine profit levels is to, in effect, put them in a position where they can find themselves penalized for the mistakes of others. A recent, much publicized case, was that of the Saturn automobile plant in Tennessee, when workers found their bonuses dropping

BOX 15–3 Life and Profit on the Table in "Family-Friendly" Contracts

─── ♦ *Virginia Galt*

Brian Chetwynd is entering his third year in the jazz performance program at the University of Toronto — with a little backup from his mother's employer.

Mr. Chetwynd, a singer, gets $800 a year in tuition assistance, which he described as fantastic. "Every dime counts, let me tell you," he said. The tuition was $4,900 last year — and is increasing — and off-campus living costs in downtown Toronto are steep.

His mother's employer is the Canadian Auto Workers union, which extended postsecondary tuition assistance to the children of its own staff after negotiating the precedent-setting benefits for its members in the last round of contract negotiations with the Big Three automakers.

...

The provision is one of hundreds of innovative "family-friendly" contract clauses highlighted in a new Web site recently established by the federal Ministry of Labour....

... For instance, many employers grant employees a day off, with pay, to get married. A handful throw in an extra week for the honeymoon.

Both the CBC and the Canadian Union of Public Employees have agreed that "an employee going through divorce proceedings is entitled to one day of leave with pay if required to appear in court." And Telus Communications (Edmonton) Inc., a unit of Burnaby, B.C.-based Telus Corp., has agreed that, in the event of family breakup, family benefits will still be provided to ex-spouses who remain dependent on Telus employees for support.

It is common for employers to grant paid "celebration leave" for new dads, although most allow only one day, according to the new federal Web site.

Unions and employers have also negotiated a sweep of provisions aimed at helping employees meet their child-care and elder-care responsibilities.

These range from flexible working hours to child-care subsidies to telework arrangements that allow people to work from home and cut down on their commuting time — although the boss reserves the right to drop in on short notice (as little as 15 minutes' notice in one agreement between Bell Canada, a unit of Montreal-based BCE Inc., and the Communications, Energy and Paperworkers Union).

Continued....

BOX 15–3 (continued)

A collective agreement between the British Columbia government and its professional employees' association recognizes the special challenges of the teenage years, providing a day off with pay to accompany a child to youth court. Several agreements in Quebec allow for a paid moving day once a year.

But hours of work are often the most hotly contested bargaining issue, particularly in the growing number of operations that run 24 hours a day, seven days a week, the federal researchers report. Even a relatively short work week can cause work-family conflicts if an employee is scheduled to work during nights or weekends, researchers wrote on the Web site.

The Web site showcases a clause, negotiated between Casino Windsor in Windsor, Ont., and the Canadian Auto Workers, that states: "The parties acknowledge the employer's right to schedule employees to meet the demands of the business. The parties also acknowledge the right of employees to maintain a family life."

Casino Windsor never sleeps. Its peak times are on the weekends and over the Christmas holiday period, said Jim Mundy, communications director. But that's precisely the times when most family events take place, said Gerry Bastien, a CAW negotiator.

By way of accommodation, the parties have agreed to a formula that allows employees to book unpaid "commitment days" to help them cope with the conflicting demands on their time.

Modern life makes the juggle more difficult, said Peter Kennedy, a CAW official, because both parents frequently work outside the home "to maintain a quality of life." And these pressures are not restricted to union members.

At Ford, for instance, salaried employee Sandy Shaw is grateful for the $2,000-a-year reimbursement in child-care expenses that was first negotiated for CAW members, and then was offered to all staff.

Her three-year-old son, Matthew, is enrolled in the company's on-site daycare centre, and the reimbursement helps defray expenses, said Ms. Shaw, assistant to the vice-president of finance.

She said that after a year-long maternity leave, she "was having guilt feelings about returning," and that the company's family-assistance measures "made it a lot easier to come back to work."

Go to labour-travail.hrdc-drhc.gc.ca [now http://www.sdc.gc.ca/en/lp/spila/wlb/06worklife_balance.shtml] for more information on the federal government's work-life balance program.

Source: *The Globe and Mail* (July 16, 2001), A1, A6. Reproduced with permission from The Globe and Mail.

due to what they considered to be poor corporate decisions. In addition, unions have traditionally attempted to build fixed increases into collective agreements each negotiation, so that pay increases accumulate over time. Contingent pay systems typically do not allow for this, and so unions (and their members) are especially resistant if the employer advocates them at the expense of such increases. For example, General Motors attempted to negotiate profit-sharing provisions into their collective agreement in the early 1980s rather than providing for annual wage improvements it had agreed to throughout the post-war era. Although it had been successful in doing so in the United States, there was considerable resistance among its Canadian workers. Not only did a strike result, but pressures from the U.S. parent union to accept profit-sharing so that it (the parent) did not look bad to its U.S. members created a major rift in the union. As noted in chapter twelve, this rift became a major justification for the Canadian division to secede, creating its own, independent union, the Canadian Auto Workers.

III. HOURS OF WORK AND OVERTIME

Also of growing controversy in recent years have been provisions restricting management's right to assign hours of work and overtime. Most contracts make some reference to the number of hours per day and/or per week that employers can *require* workers to perform. Thus, for example, a collective agreement may specify that the normal working day is eight hours and that management can require a worker to work no more than one hour beyond that. Or, a collective agreement may specify that the normal work week is 40 hours, and that the employer cannot require workers to work more than five hours of overtime during that week. In addition, the agreement may place restrictions on the days of the week that employees can be required to work or the days of the week that they can be required to work overtime. Thus, it may stipulate that workers cannot be required to work weekends, or that they cannot be required to perform overtime on Friday afternoons.

Collective agreements can also include clauses restricting the way in which overtime is assigned. Often employers can require overtime, yet the agreement may specify that more senior workers can refuse provided that less senior workers are able to perform the required work. Or, it may specify that overtime is to be allocated on an even basis over some period of time, so that no workers find themselves having to work more overtime than others in their department or area.

Though unions seek restrictions on management's ability to assign involuntary overtime, overtime generally means extra income for workers, at a premium rate (e.g., one and a half times or twice the regular hourly rate). Because of this, worker representatives may also attempt to negotiate provisions dealing with the allocation of the right to work overtime voluntarily. Generally these provisions specify that either more senior workers or those with the least overtime offered to them in the past have the first choice or "right of refusal", again provided that they are capable of performing the work.

These sorts of provisions can restrict managerial flexibility considerably. This is especially the case with respect to limits on involuntary overtime. For example, there may be occasions when, for one reason or another, a work area or department falls behind schedule. If lost time cannot be made up through overtime work, then other areas of operations may be held up, and, indeed, customers may ultimately be inconvenienced. In addition, restrictions on involuntary overtime may force management to employ additional workers on a full-time basis in order to ensure it is able to meet fluctuations in demand. These workers can be laid off in periods of low demand and hired back when demand increases, but doing so can be cumbersome and impractical, especially if demand peaks are short-lived (e.g., a few weeks). Of course, from the union's point of view, greater management flexibility comes at the expense of unemployed or laid off workers. It can also represent an intrusion into the personal lives of workers, especially those with important family or other commitments that required overtime prevents them from honouring. Many workers may also simply find themselves too tired or stressed to handle overtime. But from management's point of view, restrictions or overtime can translate into a weakened ability to respond to demand peaks.

IV. WORK RULES

As discussed in chapter three, it is common for informal rules and understandings as to the amount of work to be performed and the way it is to be performed to emerge over time in the workplace. Generally, these rules and understandings represent the "effort" side of what is commonly referred to as the "wage-effort" bargain, under which workers implicitly agree to provide a certain amount of effort for a certain amount of pay (Baldamus, 1961). But they also reflect understandings as to the content of different jobs and the classifications assigned to them. For example, in a machine shop it may be understood that skilled mechanics have responsibility for machine maintenance and repair and that this function falls outside of the responsibility of machine operators. To ask machine operators to perform maintenance work would be to violate this understanding.

Though such rules and understandings may have been more or less agreed to by workers *and* their supervisors, management can, under the doctrine of residual rights, legally violate them if it sees fit unless they are codified in the collective agreement. Thus, for example, management may decide to "rationalize" operations by cutting down on the number of workers but not the overall workload. Or, it may keep the number of workers the same but increase the workload. Or, it may redesign or reallocate work so that unskilled or semi-skilled workers can perform tasks that were previously performed by skilled workers. In all three cases, management will have upset the effort-wage bargain. In the first and second case, workers find themselves performing more work but for the same pay, while in the third case, work is "deskilled", thereby reducing the level of skills required and, in most cases, pay levels.

In order to prevent management from taking these sorts of actions, unions have historically sought to negotiate what are commonly referred to as "**work rules**" into the collective agreement. These rules can vary considerably, but they often involve things such as minimum "crew sizes", workload or work pace restrictions, and job content limitations. Minimum crew sizes establish the minimum number of workers management can use to perform a certain task or function, while workload and work pace restrictions limit the amount of work individuals or work groups can be required to do in a specified time period or the pace at which this work is to be performed. In turn, job content limitations establish the task responsibilities that can be assigned to particular job types or classifications so that workers cannot be assigned tasks normally performed by other workers (e.g. skilled workers) or required to do work which is not normally part of their "job".

Work rules have been subject to widespread criticism in recent years, particularly from neoliberals and managerialists. These scholars believe that such rules not only infringe on the right of management to manage as it sees fit, but also that they result in considerable waste and inefficiency and prevent management from attaining the level of flexibility necessary to meet the challenges and uncertainties of a global marketplace (see Piore, 1986; Cappelli and McKersie, 1987). It is not unusual to hear of cases where, for example, only skilled electricians are allowed to replace light bulbs, even though this task could be performed by anyone in the workplace. Similarly, one often hears about so-called "**feather-bedding**", where individuals perform totally obsolete or unnecessary tasks simply because they are required by work rules in the collective agreement.

Though it is not clear just how widespread they are, these sorts of excesses clearly give work rules (and unions in general) a bad name. The real problem, however, is that the employment contract can be a highly ambiguous one, in which it is difficult to specify the precise nature of most jobs. As such, work rules that may be only minimally acceptable from the point of view of workers may be unduly restrictive and cumbersome from the point of view of management. But as long as the doctrine of residual rights prevails, work rules would appear to be the only way in which unions can protect their members against violations of the work-effort bargain and the erosion of worker skill levels. The elimination of work rules might well enhance efficiency and in the long run even save jobs, but it also means a loss of this protection.

V.   JOB AND INCOME PROTECTION

Job and income security have long been a major concern of unions, especially in periods of economic instability, as has been the case for much of the last decade. To some extent, it is reflected in the negotiation of work rules and seniority provisions, the former of which protect workers from skill downgrading, and the latter protect more senior workers from job loss in the event of a layoff, as discussed below. It is also reflected in the negotiation of union shop arrangements, as also discussed below. But in addition to these provisions are a number of more specific provisions intended to protect the income and jobs of union members. Three are of particular relevance: (1) subcontracting clauses, (2) layoff notice and technological change clauses, and (3) supplemental unemployment benefits (SUBs).

Subcontracting

Unless otherwise specified in the collective agreement, the doctrine of residual rights enables management to subcontract work so that it is performed by workers outside of the bargaining unit and hence not covered under the collective agreement. As discussed in chapter five, this can involve outsourcing, which typically entails the purchase of parts and accessories from outsiders rather than producing them in-house, or it can involve contracting out, which typically entails the use of outside firms or contractors rather than workers within the bargaining unit to perform various services for the employer.

Subcontracting is a relatively innocuous practice when it involves work that cannot be done or is not normally done by workers in the bargaining unit. But where this is not the case, it can generate a considerable amount of acrimony. Not only can it mean less work for workers in the bargaining unit and hence either layoffs or reduced overtime, it can also violate the integrity of the collective agreement by enabling management to have work done at a lower wage and benefit rate than would apply if it was done in-house. For these reasons, unions often attempt to negotiate restrictions on management's ability to subcontract.

Although subcontracting restrictions would appear to be relatively common, they are typically weak, specifying only that management is not allowed to contract out work that could be performed in-house if it leads to layoffs or a failure to recall workers already on layoff. Nonetheless, as is the case with other restrictions on management flexibility, they have been increasingly criticized in recent years, with critics claiming that they prevent employers from realizing important cost savings that are necessary for the economic viability of the establishment involved. Though the extent to which this argument is, in fact, a genuine one remains uncertain, there does appear to have been a trend towards increased subcontracting in both the union and non-union sectors. It would also appear that, in the face of employer attempts to reduce costs, unions have become increasingly amenable to doing so as one alternative to wage and benefit concessions, especially where there is a genuine threat to job security.

Layoffs and Technological Change

Closely related to subcontracting issues are those pertaining to layoffs and major technological changes, both of which can have highly deleterious consequences for affected workers. This is most obvious with respect to layoffs, which not only mean an immediate loss of income, but can also have serious psychological consequences, with workers losing their sense of self-worth and their self-identity. Moreover, while most workers eventually find alternative employment, they may undergo considerable uncertainty and stress in the meantime, and even once they do become re-employed, they have to, in effect, "start over", with no seniority and in many cases lower income.

Technological change can also be highly traumatic, for even if it does not result in immediate layoffs, it too can create considerable uncertainty and stress among workers, who (often with good reason) fear that it may mean layoffs in the future or a downgrading of their skills and a lower paying job classification. Workers also may fear that they will be unable to master any new skills required and/or that they will be reassigned to less satisfactory jobs. More generally, major technological changes can undermine the established collective agreement, especially because they can mean a major reclassification of jobs, with implications for the number of jobs at higher pay levels and hence for the average wage rate in the bargaining unit.

For these reasons, unions often attempt to negotiate provisions which restrict management's ability to lay workers off or implement technological change, or which at minimum cushion the impact of such decisions. These sorts of provisions are not particularly widespread and where they are negotiated they also tend to be weak. Usually they require only adequate advance notice and/or consultation with union officials, though in some cases they also provide for such things as severance pay, retraining, early retirement, workforce reductions through attrition (i.e. not replacing workers who quit or retire), the payment of workers displaced into lower job classifications at a level commensurate with their previous job (referred to as "red circling"), and even employment in other company operations. Finally, management may agree, or be required, to reopen the collective agreement in the event of major technological changes, in the recognition that such changes may render the established agreement obsolete. Indeed, in a number of jurisdictions, this is required by law.

The third issue having to do with job and income protection involves **supplementary unemployment benefits**, or **SUBs**. Generally, these involve employer- (and in some cases, worker-) funded plans that are drawn on to "top up" the employment insurance benefits (for example, to 90 percent of their regular earnings) received by workers who have been temporarily laid off or are away from work for reasons of parental leave, training, illness, or injury. The length of time for which a worker may be eligible is limited, and the amount of money she receives is often tied to the amount of money remaining in the fund at a particular time. But SUB plans are clearly a boon for individual workers because they minimize their income loss in the event of a layoff.

VI. SENIORITY PROVISIONS

There are two general types of seniority: "**benefits status seniority**" and "**competitive status seniority**". Benefits status seniority involves the use of seniority to determine an employee's status with respect to accrued benefits. The most common form of benefits status has to do with vacations, under which the number of weeks of vacation entitlement increases with the number of years that an individual has worked for the employer. Thus, for example, after five years of service an employee may be entitled to three weeks of vacation, after ten years to four weeks, and so forth. However, benefits status seniority can also be used as a basis for establishing the date at which individuals become eligible to retire with pension (e.g., after 35 years of service), the amount of severance pay to which they are entitled in the event of layoff, and other benefits.

While benefits status seniority is relatively straightforward and non-controversial, the opposite is generally true of competitive status seniority, which can require employers to take an employee's seniority into account on matters having to do with promotions, layoffs and recall, job transfers, work assignment, shift preference, choice of vacation dates, the allocation of time off, and, as discussed earlier, overtime. In contrast to benefits status seniority, competitive status seniority is usually not the *sole* factor in determining an employee's status but is instead usually combined with other factors, most notably ability and qualifications. With respect to seniority in promotion, for example, most collective agreements either stipulate that (1) the applicant with the highest seniority receive the promotion *provided* that he/she is able to demonstrate, or develop, sufficient ability over some reasonable period of time, or (2) that the employee with the highest ability receives the promotion unless two or more employees are equally qualified, in which case the position goes to the employee with highest seniority. This is an important distinction, for the extent to which management must take seniority into account is clearly lower in the latter than in the former case. But in both cases, ability clearly plays an important role. Both are illustrated by the sample clauses in Box 15–4.

In addition, many collective agreements place limits on the "breadth" of seniority units, or the units over which competitive status seniority applies. In some contracts, for example, seniority may be only department-wide, in which case the amount of seniority workers are credited with is limited to the length of time that they have been in a particular department, even though they may have a number of years

BOX 15–4 Sample Seniority Provisions

Seniority before ability:

Any employee covered by this Agreement may apply ... and the vacancy shall be filled by the applicant who has the most seniority. In the case of vacancies involving tradesmen, the senior applicant who has the required certification, skills and/or experience shall be selected. The man selected will be given a reasonable trial period to prove his suitability. He will have the right to return to his former job within ten (10) days for relief postings and within fifteen (15) days for permanent postings....

Source: From the Collective Agreement between Molson Breweries and Brewery, Winery and Distillery Workers Union, Local 300, May 2006–April 2012. Reproduced with Permission of Molson Coors Canada and Local 300.

Ability before seniority:

114.05   In considering such applicants, the factors which shall be considered are related ability, education, attitude, job performance with the Corporation and related experience with the Corporation. The Corporation is not necessarily obliged to consider the application of an employee:

(a)   Where the employee has moved geographically at Corporation expense with less than two (2) years at his present location, or

(b)   Where no promotion is involved with less than one (1) year in his present position.

With reference to point (a) and (b), in the event that an employee's application was not considered by the Corporation, the Corporation shall communicate in writing to the employee the reason(s) why his application was not considered. For the purpose of this Article, a position with a higher calculated hourly rate of pay shall be considered as a promotion. In the case of progression positions, the calculated hourly rate of pay of the position of automatic progression shall be utilized to determine whether or not a promotion is involved. In the event there is no applicant suitable for the job posted, the Corporation reserves the right to hire from outside the organization.

114.06   When making promotions or transfers, the above outlined procedure and criteria of selection shall apply and when the overall assessment, based on the above stated factors, is equal for two or more of the applicants, the applicant with the greater length of service shall be selected for the posting.

Source: From the Plant Unit Agreement with the Natural Gas Employees' Benefit Association, 1991–1992. Used by permission of ATCO Gas and Pipelines Ltd.

of additional service in another department. In other cases, highly specific seniority provisions are negotiated, under which only workers in specified positions are eligible for promotions into more advanced positions (also see chapter five). These sorts of limits are generally sought by management, apparently in the belief that workers within a particular unit are more likely to be familiar with the work done and to be integrated into the work group, making it easier for them to take over more advanced jobs.

Finally, most contracts with seniority restrictions on layoffs contain something known as "**bumping rights**". There are essentially two types. The first is "**chain bumping**", under which an employee whose job has been eliminated (temporarily or permanently) has the right to "bump" (take the job of) any person with less seniority. The person bumped is in turn able to bump any other person in the seniority unit with even less seniority, and so forth until the bottom of the chain is reached and the person with the least seniority is displaced and laid off. The other type of bumping right involves what is referred to as a "**labour pan**", whereby a displaced employee is allowed to bump only that employee with the lowest seniority, in which case he waits in the "pan" until a better job becomes available.

The use of a bumping chain can clearly cause difficulties for management, as the elimination of a more senior worker's job can set in motion a chain reaction throughout the seniority unit. For this reason management typically prefers to negotiate a labour pan provision, a narrow seniority unit for purposes of bumping, and a clause which requires employees who have bumped other employees to demonstrate adequate ability in their new position within a minimal period of time. Unions, however, generally resist such restrictions in the belief that they are unfair. For example, an employee with high seniority may pass up a job for which she is eligible, only to find sometime later that her own job (which may have been a "better" one) is to be eliminated. From the employee's point of view, it would be unfair if she was now laid off or assigned to one of the worst jobs in the seniority unit, especially if the person in the job she passed up has far less seniority.

Seniority clauses appear to be sought by unions for two reasons. The first is the belief that more senior workers, by virtue of their length of service, have earned the rights associated with their seniority, and that they should not have to fear displacement by more junior workers as they age. Second, seniority provides an objective, impersonal basis for promotion, layoff, and other decisions related to the deployment of workers. In contrast, attempts to determine ability can be highly subjective, leaving workers subject to favouritism or arbitrary management decisions. In the absence of reasonably strong seniority provisions, workers can find themselves subject to considerable coercion and fear, as employers choose to promote those workers with whom they are (for whatever reason) most satisfied and lay off those with whom they are least satisfied. As such, workers find themselves constantly under pressure to be obsequious to superordinates, with negative implications for their dignity and self-respect.

Despite the reasons for their negotiation, competitive status seniority clauses have come in for considerable criticism. The first and perhaps the most widespread criticism is that, by restricting management's ability to allocate workers in accordance with their ability and past performance, seniority provisions ultimately impair efficiency. They also restrict management's flexibility when it comes to layoffs, imposing a cost burden which would otherwise not exist (see Piore, 1986). A second, related criticism, is that seniority provisions impair work performance and initiative, for workers generally become discouraged when they learn that loyalty and hard work are not in themselves sufficient to "get ahead". Third, it is sometimes argued that seniority provisions protect the mediocre in the case of layoffs, for management is required to keep more senior workers even though they may be inferior performers compared to those laid off. A final argument is that seniority provisions discriminate against women and minorities, who, despite employer attempts to remedy past discrimination by hiring them, are unable to qualify for good jobs because they have not acquired sufficient seniority. According to critics, they are also first to be laid off, again because of their low seniority.

Though these arguments may contain a certain amount of truth, a number of arguments have also been advanced to counter them. The first is that, because seniority reduces the role of personal biases in managerial decisions, these decisions are more likely to be seen as objective and hence fair, with positive implications for morale. Second, it has been argued that seniority helps to reduce competition and rivalry among workers, resulting in more cooperation within the workplace and a greater willingness by more senior workers to help train their more junior counterparts, in the knowledge that doing so will not jeopardize their own job security or advancement opportunities in the future (see Freeman and Medoff, 1984). Third, proponents of seniority argue that more senior workers tend in any case to be of higher ability, for they have greater experience and are likely to have a better knowledge and understanding of operations, thus having higher levels of what is referred to as "firm-specific skills" (Doeringer and Piore,

1971). A fourth argument is that, where the seniority principle is established, workers can look forward to advancement into "better" jobs and can expect to be protected against layoff if they remain with the employer, and that this in turn both reduces the quit rate (Block, 1978) and enhances morale (Edwards, 1979). A final argument is that, while seniority may prevent women and minorities from qualifying for good jobs in the short run, it in fact protects them against discrimination over the long run, as it is less possible for managers to base decisions upon personal prejudices.

Whether seniority clauses are good or bad is not something that can be resolved here. However, their implications are likely to vary considerably, depending on the strength of the seniority provisions negotiated and, perhaps more important, on the context within which they are negotiated. For example, there is some evidence to suggest that, in large establishments where high levels of firm-specific skills are required, the benefits of strong seniority provisions may outweigh their costs for management, while in smaller establishments with low levels of firm-specific skills, the opposite may be the case (see Godard, 1993a). Also of note is research evidence suggesting that seniority has traditionally seen an important determinant of promotion and layoff decisions in non-union firms (albeit not as important as in union firms; see Abraham and Medoff, 1984, 1985). This would appear to indicate that, even in many non-union firms, managers see some merit to the seniority principle. Finally, research findings in the United States indicate that seniority provisions do not appear to have harmed employment opportunities for women and minorities (Leonard, 1985). In Canada, one study actually found that the probability of being laid off is actually lower for these groups in the union than the non-union sector (other things equal), suggesting that union seniority systems may indeed protect minorities from discrimination (Singh and Reid, 1998).

VII. UNION SECURITY AND RIGHTS

The mere certification of a union does not mean that the union's existence is secure or that it will be able to serve its members effectively, for management may continue to resist the union, and a number of workers may avoid paying union dues or refuse to go on strike. As such, the union may find itself undermined both externally and internally, lacking either the strength or the resources to negotiate improvements in the terms and conditions of employment or to represent its members adequately during the term of an agreement. Union security and rights provisions are intended to help prevent this from occurring.

Union security clauses specify whether workers are required to be union members and to pay dues. To the extent that they are, unions are generally considered to be more secure, for they have greater control over workers and are less susceptible to attempts by employers to undermine the union by encouraging workers to avoid paying dues. Traditionally, there have been four basic types of union security arrangement: (a) a "closed shop", (b) a "union shop", (c) an "agency shop", and (d) an "open shop". Under a **closed shop** arrangement, the collective agreement specifies that workers must be union members *before* they can be hired by the employer; in other words, the "shop" (i.e., workplace) is "closed" to non-union workers. Under a **union shop** arrangement, workers need not be union members to begin with, but are required to join the union within a specified period (e.g., three months) once hired. An **agency shop** arrangement does not require workers to join the union, but it does require that they pay the equivalent of membership dues to the union in return for services rendered. Finally, an **open shop** arrangement requires neither that individuals join the union nor that they pay the equivalent of dues.

In addition to these four types of arrangement are two variants: (a) the maintenance of membership shop and (b) the modified union shop. Under a **maintenance of membership** clause, workers are not required to join the union, but if they do, they must maintain that membership for as long as they are employed within the bargaining unit. Under the **modified union shop**, union members must maintain their membership *and* new employees must join the union, but those already employed in the unit prior to unionization and choosing to remain non-union can do so.

As with most of the issues considered in this chapter, union security provisions have been a source of some controversy. Perhaps most controversial are closed shop arrangements. Though relatively rare, these arrangements enable union officials to control the supply of labour and to determine who will and will not be considered eligible for employment. Under these arrangements, employers are usually required to phone a union hiring hall if they need to hire workers. The union then assigns workers to the employer, usually giving more senior workers first priority. Though employers often have some right to refuse those workers they consider to be inappropriate for the tasks involved, they have little control over the overall composition of their workforce, and workers unable to obtain union membership find themselves having to look elsewhere for work. Yet these clauses are usually adopted in occupations characterized by unstable employment (e.g., construction trades, longshoring) and help to ensure that union members laid off from one job will be hired for subsequent jobs, thus providing them with greater income security and ensuring the continuity and stability of union membership. They also protect more senior workers against age discrimination and displacement by younger workers. In addition, union hiring halls in effect serve as free employment agencies for employers, saving them the time and expense of seeking out qualified employees on their own. Because of this, employers are often quite happy to use them.

A further issue, raised with respect to both closed and union shop arrangements, is that, in a free and democratic society, individuals should have a right to work without being required to join a union against their will. As noted in chapter eleven, this argument is especially popular in the United States, where twenty-one states have so-called right-to-work laws, under which both closed and union shop arrangements are illegal. Yet proponents of compulsory union membership argue that unions provide an "indivisible" service, from which workers benefit whether they pay for it or not, in the same way that government services often benefit the general population. As such, workers should not be allowed a "free ride" any more than should citizens who benefit from government services. Not only would doing so be unfair, it would induce other workers to follow suit, thereby weakening the union considerably.

Agency, maintenance of membership, and modified union shop provisions represent compromise positions between those who favour compulsory union membership and those who favour right to work laws. Agency shop provisions address the free rider problem by requiring workers to pay for union services but not requiring them to join the union. Maintenance of membership clauses go somewhat further, for workers are required to be union members only if they have at some point already done so of their own accord. Finally a modified union shop only requires union membership of new workers, who are in theory free not to accept the job if they are opposed to being a union member.

Closely associated with union security provisions is something referred to as a "**dues check off**" clause. With this clause, management agrees to regularly deduct union dues from workers' pay and remit these to the union. These deductions are in some cases voluntary, subject to the approval of individual workers, but they are usually compulsory. Not only does such an arrangement save union officials the time and expense of soliciting dues directly from workers, it also prevents individual workers from attempting to avoid dues payment. The result is a more secure union and ultimately a more stable union-management relationship. Because of this, a number of jurisdictions require compulsory dues check off by law.

Between them, agency shop provisions and dues check-off provisions comprise the Rand Formula, named after Justice Ivan Rand, who first proposed them in 1946 as a compromise position over union security.

Finally, many contracts contain union "rights" provisions, which allow paid time off for union officials on union business and provide what is known as "**superseniority**". With respect to paid time off, union officials are paid for time taken off work for grievance handling, negotiations, and other aspects of their representational function. In some cases they may even receive paid time off for attending union functions, and in some large work places, union officials may be allowed paid leaves of absence from their job so that they can work full-time on union-related business. In turn, superseniority clauses generally stipulate that union officials are to be treated as if they have the highest competitive status with respect to such things as layoff and recall, overtime, and shift selection. In effect, this discriminates against workers who are not active in the union, and it is illegal in the United States. The justification for it, however, is that it ensures that union officials are able to be on site at all times, and hence available if they should be needed by their constituents.

VIII. CONCLUSIONS

As should now be apparent, collective agreements can be highly complex, and the provisions included in them can be highly contentious. Arguably, this reflects both the difficulties posed by the residual rights doctrine and the sources of conflict underlying the labour–management relation. As a result, the process of negotiating a collective agreement and "administering" that agreement can also be extremely complex and contentious. This explains (at least in part) why the relations between union and management officials often seem to be so adversarial and, more important, why it is that negotiations often break down, resulting in a strike or some form of third party intervention.

APPENDIX 15–1 The Collective Agreement: Sample Table of Contents

Continued....

Continued....

APPENDIX 15–1 (continued)

Continued....

APPENDIX 15–1 (continued)

Source: Courtesy of DaimlerChrysler Corporation.

Contemporary Problems, Challenges, and Alternatives

16

As discussed in chapter four, the post-World War II era, from the late 1940s to the early 1970s, was one in which Canadians enjoyed substantial economic growth and social progress. Among other things, unions came to be well-established within the institutional status quo, the large majority of workers came to enjoy considerably improved standards of living, and the rights and protections afforded workers increased markedly — both within the employment relationship and in society in general. This period was not without its problems, but there was a general perception that these could be readily addressed and that the future was full of economic and social promise.

Beginning in the mid-1970s, things began to change. Harsh economic conditions, coupled with shifts in government policies, created an environment far more hostile to workers and their unions. But by the late 1990s, it appeared that Canada was entering yet another new era. Unemployment levels began to drop, and economic growth began to increase. Income levels began to recover, and by the mid-to-late 2000s, they finally came to equal and then exceed levels reached roughly a quarter of a century earlier. There was reason to think that, at long last, the pain of the 1980s and much of the 1990s had ended, and that the future was bright once again. The global economic crisis of 2008, and what seems to be increasing instability within the global economy in general, suggest that such optimism may have been premature. Yet even if we can assume that Canada has turned a corner, and that the policies and changes of the 1990s will continue to pay off into the foreseeable future, a number of problems and challenges of relevance to work and employment remain. This chapter discusses these problems and challenges. It then addresses possible alternatives for the future.

I.   CONTEMPORARY PROBLEMS AND CHALLENGES

Many of the problems and challenges facing work and employment in Canada have been identified in earlier chapters. However, they are reviewed and elaborated on here. In doing so, the intention is not to imply that the experience of work and employment is inherently a negative one for most Canadians or that the Canadian system is without merit. But it is important to be familiar with these problems, because their resolution is important to advancing the well-being of Canadians and ultimately to ensuring that work and employment in Canada are fully consistent with what one might expect of a truly advanced, democratic society.

The Work and Labour Market Experience. As discussed in chapter three, a great majority of employed Canadians — close to 9 in 10, agree that they are satisfied with their job and that they find their work to be challenging. Yet as many as half believe that what happens to them at work is beyond their control and that they have little choice but to simply go along with things. Seven in ten find their job stressful and are worn out by the end of the day, and four in ten report that they are too tired to do things with others when they come home from work. Three-quarters feel pressure to adopt employer goals as their own and constant pressure to perform at high levels. Four in ten report that they are worried that things could change for the worse at work and three in ten worry that they could soon find themselves out of a job. Quite apart from the implications that these conditions may have for conflict, they represent important problems in and of themselves, problems that are contrary to what one might expect of an advanced democratic society.

Employee Rights and Protections. In addition, employee rights and protections are weak in a number of areas. As discussed in chapter nine, the minimum wage is set so low that, in most if not all jurisdictions, full-time workers can still find themselves earning below the poverty level. In addition, employees in all but one jurisdiction are legally entitled to only two weeks of vacation per year, unless they have accumulated seniority of at least five years, in which case they may qualify for three weeks. This compares to six weeks of vacation in a number of European countries.

Canadian workers also have only weak protections against termination and layoffs. Indeed, unless they are in managerial or professional jobs or represented by a union, most can be arbitrarily dismissed, without cause, and are only entitled to from two to eight weeks notice or pay in lieu of notice, depending on their length of service. Moreover, only four in ten of those who find themselves out of work qualify for employment insurance benefits at any point in time, and these benefits are at most 55 percent of pay or just over 450 dollars per week, whichever is lowest (as of July 2010).

New parents can now take up to a year of leave, yet during this period they are legally entitled only to employment insurance benefits, which at most amount to only a little more than half of their normal earnings. Employers are not legally required to even supplement these benefits. Overall, only 20 percent of employers actually do so, and when they do, it is typically for a limited period, averaging 19 weeks. In the private sector, only 8 percent do so, for an even more limited period, averaging 12 weeks (Marshall, 2010). Moreover, weak protections against unjust dismissal mean that employers may still arbitrarily dismiss employees when or shortly after they return from leave. New parents also face a lack of affordable day-care facilities in most if not all provinces, and have few, if any, rights to alter their work hours so as to manage their family responsibilities.

Finally, workers have few, if any, a priori (i.e., automatic) information-sharing, consultation, or co-decision making rights, even though management decisions can have major implications not just for their economic well-being, but also for their work experience and hence their social and psychological well-being. In more democratically advanced, European nations, such rights are often taken-for-granted. Yet, in Canada, any such rights are generally limited to health and safety issues. As discussed in chapter three, work organizations can, in this respect at least, be compared to authoritarian states. Workers have few meaningful legal rights to participate in decisions that affect them, and those who make these decisions are neither elected by nor legally accountable to them.

Income Inequality and Stagnation. As mentioned in the introduction, the incomes of Canadians began to improve in the late 1990s, catching up to and passing previous levels by the mid-2000s. Yet, although average family income was fourteen percent higher in 2008 than it had been in 1980, the median earnings of full-time, full-year workers were still only 2.5 percent above their 1976 level, despite an increase in average labour productivity of close to 50 percent (see chapter three).

Moreover, income inequality continued to increase in the late 1990s and early 2000s. As revealed in Table 16–1, those in the upper income quintile enjoyed the largest increases in income after taxes, fol-

TABLE 16–1 After Tax Income by Income Quintiles, 1980, 1997, and 2008

	All quintiles	Lowest quintile (lower income)	Second quintile (lower-middle income)	Middle quintile (middle income)	Fourth quintile (upper-middle income)	Highest quintile (upper income)
1980	51,400	12,800	30,300	47,000	64,200	102,700
1997	47,000	11,900	25,600	39,700	57,800	100,000
2008	59,500	14,500	31,500	48,500	71,200	131,900
1980–2008	+8,100	+1,700	+1,200	+1,500	+7,000	+29,200
% Change	+16%	+13%	+4%	+3%	+11%	+28%

Source: CANSIM table 202-0701.

lowed by those in the upper-middle income quintile. Overall, these groups enjoyed gains of almost 28 percent and 11 percent, respectively. The lowest-income quintile also did reasonably well, likely due to increased employment opportunities. They enjoyed a gain of 13 percent, although in absolute terms this amounted to only 1,700 dollars, or one seventeenth that of their upper-income counterparts. Of greatest note, however, are the gains for the middle and lower-middle quintiles. They were only 3 and 4 percent, respectively. So, as of 2008, not only were middle- and lower-middle income Canadians not appreciably better off than their equivalents three decades ago, they had actually fallen further behind their upper-middle and high-income counterparts. These data do not reflect the 2008 crisis, which occurred late in the year. The crisis resulted in a 50 percent increase in the unemployment rate in 2009, to 9 percent. It was still 8 percent in mid-2010 (as of this writing). The implications of this crisis for pay and for inequality have yet to be established, but it is not likely that they have been pretty.

Trends in both pay and income inequality matter, and not just for their possible implications for conflict (see chapter three). The preponderance of research now shows that increasing pay levels do not in themselves make much difference to overall well-being in developed economies. But, indirectly, they can mean more tax revenues for governments, enabling them to meet growing financial pressures caused by an aging population without cutting programs or increasing taxes.

Moreover, the preponderance of research does show that income inequality makes a significant difference. Higher levels of inequality have been found to be associated with a broad range of negative outcomes, from more mental and physical health problems to lower educational performance and to higher levels of violence and crime (Wilkinson and Pickett, 2009). High levels of inequality are also, of course, contrary to the very values on which modern democracies are founded.

Collective Bargaining and Union Representation. In theory, the right to join unions and bargain collectively enables workers to address most of the above problems. But unions represent only one in three employed Canadians. Thus, the greater majority of workers have remained non-union and, as such, do not enjoy the rights and protections associated with collective bargaining. What makes this especially noteworthy is the finding, reported in chapter nine, that a third of all non-union workers report that they would vote in favour of a union if they had a chance, and an additional one in ten would do so if they did not have to worry about employer reprisals.

Even where a union is established, its ability to win favourable terms of employment and provide workers with various rights and protections can vary considerably, depending in large part upon its bargaining power. This is made especially important by the long-standing doctrine of management rights, under which many of the rights and protections associated with unions must be negotiated into a collective agreement. Thus, if union bargaining power is low, these rights and protections are less likely to be obtained (Beatty, 1983), and it makes little sense to join a union and pay dues if the union lacks sufficient power to "make a difference".

As discussed in chapter twelve, Canada's decentralized (i.e., workplace or employer level) bargaining structure may contribute to this problem. This structure makes it difficult for unions to take wages out of competition and hence to achieve gains for their members. It also enhances adversariness, because negotiating conflicts are more likely to spill over into the day-to-day relationships between parties, and because bargaining is likely to be less professional and more prone to impasse.

In addition, unions tend to find themselves in a largely reactive position relative to management, limiting their effectiveness and often forcing them to adopt a more adversarial posture than otherwise. Part of the problem is, again, the doctrine of management rights. Even where unions are able to negotiate restrictions on the exercise of management authority, they are rarely able to achieve meaningful information-sharing, consultation, or co-decision rights and hence to play a meaningful role in management decision processes.

A further part of the problem, however, may be the certification process itself (see Adams, 1993b, 1995). As discussed in chapter nine, this process is typically adversarial, with employers tending to view unionization as an attack on their authority rather than an expression of a legitimate desire of workers for collective representation, and resisting it accordingly. In anticipation of this, employees are less likely to exercise their right to union representation, except where very dissatisfied with employer practices. This, coupled with the typical employer response, helps to explain why union organizing drives often involve a high degree of acrimony, effectively poisoning the relationship between the parties once certification has occurred.

The reactive position in which unions are placed, coupled with the poisoned atmosphere that the certification process can create, means that union representatives often find themselves treated as the "enemy", and as such are unable to obtain adequate information from management, frozen out of decisions that impact their members, and frustrated at the bargaining table. It is not surprising under these conditions that union leaders appear to be "unnecessarily" adversarial. But these conditions may also sharply limit a union's effectiveness, particularly with respect to its integrative role, and may ultimately provide yet another explanation for low union density.

Making matters worse have been the economic conditions to which unions have been subject. These conditions have been worsened — if not in considerable measure caused — by government economic policies and by a general weakening of labour laws in the 1990s (particularly the elimination of card certification in a number of jurisdictions). These policies, combined with the economic conditions associated with them, have tended to weaken union power, intimidate workers, and foster an ideological environment hostile to trade unions. These conditions have not only made it more difficult for unions to organize workers, they have also meant that unions were able to capture few, if any, of the gains from the productivity growth during the 1980s and 1990s. In the private sector, major union wage settlements exceeded the rate of inflation by only 5 percent (compared to a 30 percent productivity increase), and this was offset by losses in the public sector, with the result that overall wage gains were on net slightly below the rate of inflation. Beginning in 1998, major union wage settlements began to exceed the rate of inflation in both the public and private sectors, but the average yearly gain from 1998 to 2009 was still only 0.5 percent after inflation (Statistics Canada, 2009a: 7). This was roughly the same as for non-union workers. But it was less than half the rate of growth in labour productivity.

Strike activity also dropped to less than a quarter of its 1970s levels during the 1990s and 2000s. Although low unemployment rates have in the past increased worker use of the strike weapon as a means to win their share of economic gains, this did not happen in the 2000s, even though unemployment dipped to as low as 6 percent. The reason for this is unclear, but it likely reflected diminished worker expectations and confidence.

Finally, union density continued its slow decline, dropping from 32.5 percent in 1998 to 29.6 percent as of 2010.[1] This decline has been relatively small compared to the decline in a number of other nations (especially the United States). But coupled with the relatively low wage gains and low levels of strike activity, it reflects an inability of labour unions to recapture any of the momentum that they once enjoyed. It also suggests that, barring a major change in labour movement strategy and ultimately in economic and political conditions, they will be unlikely to do so in the future.

One may or may not view these developments as necessarily bad, and there may be a number of plausible additional explanations for them. But they would seem to indicate that the ability of unions to fight and win gains for their members has been eroded, albeit perhaps largely by government policies rather than by market forces per se. There is also reason to believe that unions have become increasingly marginalized in government policy circles (Godard, 2003b).

Shifting Sands. Complicating matters have been shifts in workforce composition and in the nature of employment. The Canadian system of work and employment developed in an era in which the overwhelming majority of workers were of European descent, the male was the primary breadwinner in the household, and most jobs were permanent and full-time, often in large, industrial establishments or government offices that lent themselves to bureaucratic terms and conditions of employment. Unions and collective bargaining developed largely to serve these workers, enabling them to win good wages and benefits and democratic rights and protections on the job.

---

[1] Table 4–1 suggests that density was actually 34.1 percent in 1997, but this likely reflects a change in data collection methods. See Godard (2005: 415).

Over the past few decades, however, it has become commonplace to argue that these conditions no longer hold (see Arthurs, 2006). First, Canada is becoming increasingly multicultural. Visible minorities, often recent immigrants from diverse religious and cultural backgrounds and from countries with repressive governments and weak (if any) labour movements, now make up 13 percent of the Canadian population (Tran, 2004).[2] Members of these minorities often find themselves at the fringes of the labour market, subject to poor jobs, poor working conditions, and even outright discrimination. But unions and collective bargaining are often foreign to them, and they are frequently either unaware of their rights, or fearful of exercising them.

Second, there has been a substantial increase in female labour force participation since the 1970s. Women now account for half of the labour force, and there are now many households with either two breadwinners or with a single, female parent breadwinner. Although this has been good for the economy and ultimately for society, it has become increasingly difficult for many to balance the demands of their job with those of their personal life — especially in families with young children. Women may also possess somewhat different work orientations, valuing the quality of both their working and personal lives more highly than the pursuit of high pay or advancement. Yet they too often have little alternative but to work in traditional career-type jobs if they wish to obtain employment that is appropriate to their knowledge and skills levels (Bailyn, 2006).

Third, there have been increases in "non-standard" jobs, defined as jobs in which workers are employed on a temporary or part-time basis. Both these increases and their implications have often been overstated. But almost one in five (19 percent) is now in a part-time job (defined as less than 30 hours per week), and almost one in eight is in a temporary job.[3]

The reasons for the high portion of non-standard jobs tend to be complex. In some (if not many) cases, workers are quite happy with them. Nonetheless, these jobs are often more precarious than their full-time, permanent counterparts. Both part-time and temporary workers tend to have fewer benefits and much lower security than those in full-time, permanent jobs. In the case of part-time jobs, workers can

---

[2] Immigration now accounts for 70 percent of population growth in Canada, up from under 20 percent in the 1970s; nearly three-quarters of recent immigrants are members of a visible minority (Arthurs, 2006: 18).

[3] Statistics in this and the next two paragraphs are from Statistics Canada, 2009a: 70–71.

find their hours arbitrarily reduced or their working times changed, rendering them unable to meet financial (e.g., rent) or family (e.g., child care) commitments. In the case of temporary jobs, which are often stepping stones to permanent employment, workers often have to worry that they will not be hired on after their contract expires, and they normally have little recourse should they be arbitrarily replaced at that time.

In both part-time and full-time jobs, workers are less able to fight if dissatisfied with the way they are treated, and in the case of part-time work, less able to afford to pay union dues that are sufficient for a union to represent them effectively, given the legalistic nature of the Canadian system. Perhaps as a result, part-time workers are less likely to be represented by a union (one in four, compared to one in three full-time workers). Temporary workers are almost as likely as are their permanent counterparts to be in a union workplace (30.4 percent, compared to 31.8 percent for permanent workers), but still typically do not enjoy the same rights and protections as their permanent counterparts.

Fourth, and closely related, has been an increase in self-employment, which now accounts for almost one in six jobs (Statistics Canada, 2010b). Working for one's self can provide considerable autonomy and control, and is consistent with values of "free enterprise" that many hold dear. The reality, however, is that workers in this status can have difficulty getting steady work and ultimately in making ends meet (Arthurs, 2006: 61). In some cases (e.g., trucking), they may find themselves employed as independent contractors, doing work that at one time would have been done in-house, but is now contracted out on the employer's terms. They often have little bargaining power or clout should they be unhappy with these terms. Moreover, they have no recourse to employment insurance should they lose their contract or go out of business, and they lack the kinds of benefits often taken for granted in more traditional work settings (e.g., pensions).

Fifth, there has been an increase in the share of jobs in the so-called "new economy", a term which is often ill-defined but usually refers to any jobs not in a traditional industrial or governmental setting. Again, the extent and importance of this increase may be overstated. But a third of jobs are now accounted for by the trade (retail and wholesale), accommodation and food, professional services, and financial (and related) services sectors (Statistics Canada, 2010b). None of these sectors lend themselves as readily to the bureaucratic model that came to dominate in the mid-twentieth century. Thus, employers in these sectors may be more intensely anti-union, and workers less likely to consider union representation as an effective alternative. Perhaps as a result, union density is low in these sectors (13, 7, 5, and 10 percent, respectively).

Finally, there have been shifts in the work and HRM practices adopted by employers. As discussed in chapter five, the extent and nature of these shifts is uncertain, and it does not appear that the so-called "high performance" model has become particularly widespread. Yet a large number of employers appear to have adopted various components of this model, whether in the form of increased teamwork (albeit non-autonomous), better systems for communicating with workers, or even the establishment of joint worker-management committees. There also appears to have been an increase in the "new HRM", especially a movement towards various forms of performance monitoring and incentives. As also discussed in chapter five, the implications of these shifts for workers and their unions can be complex. But they do suggest that the traditional bureaucratic model on which unions and collective bargaining were built may not be well suited to a significant portion of the Canadian economy.

In combination, these developments are sometimes pointed to as evidence that the established system is obsolete and that there is need of a new model for representing workers and ensuring fairness and justice at work. Some have seemed to argue that the labour movement can and should play a major role in this respect and that, if the right combination of innovations is adopted, it would not only be good for the workers involved, but for the labour movement itself (e.g., Yates, 2008). The Canadian labour movement has in this respect made various efforts, not just within the confines of the present system of collective bargaining, but outside of them as well, through various forms of both advocacy and representation (Hebdon and Brown, 2008: 372–75; McQuarrie, 2006: 575–78). But progress has been limited. The problem is that labour unions have both limited political influence and limited resources with which to pursue these initiatives. While doing so may be consistent with their social-democratic role and the "social unionism" that has distinguished the Canadian labour movement from its U.S. counterpart, the first responsibility of labour leaders is to their current members, the large majority of whom are in relatively traditional employment settings. Given the Canadian system and challenges unions currently face, just effectively representing these members poses a major challenge in itself.

Finally, a large proportion of Canadian workers continue to hold relatively traditional jobs in traditional "old economy" sectors. These jobs have likely undergone substantial change, and workers who occupy them face some of the problems identified above. Yet the established system would appear to work reasonably well for them, its limitations notwithstanding, especially because unions appear to have been adjusting reasonably well within these sectors given the constraints to which they are subject. To suggest that the current system is obsolete would thus be mistaken, at least in the case of the large proportion of workers in these sectors. To suggest that it is ill-suited to the circumstances of a large number of workers outside of these sectors and that there is a need for reforms that address these circumstances may, however, be justified.

Overall. A great many working Canadians are presently in jobs where they experience some combination of powerlessness, stress, fatigue, psychological coercion, and insecurity. Workplace rights and protections appear to fall far below what one might expect in an advanced democratic society. Income levels have increased for families at the top of the income hierarchy, but they have been stagnant or have even declined for the rest. Only three in ten employed Canadians is represented by a union, and the ability of unions to win gains for their members appears to have declined, reflecting a combination of problems with the Canadian system of labour law and collective bargaining and of the economic policies adopted over the past two decades. It thus seems that Canada falls considerably short of what one might expect of a truly advanced democratic society. It also appears that, in the absence of major reforms, it is likely to continue to fall short. Indeed, in view of emerging challenges, it is likely to fall further behind. The question is, therefore, "What can be done?"

II. CONTEMPORARY ALTERNATIVES

It can be argued that, although the developments of the past three decades may have had negative implications for workers and their unions, there is little that could have been done. In an era of globalization, governments have little option but to adopt essentially neoliberal policies, and failure to do so would only have made matters worse, as reflected in lower levels of investment, poor productivity growth rates, even higher unemployment, and ultimately declining living standards. Rather than rejecting the neoliberal model, there is thus need to embrace it even further, through additional tax cuts, privatization of government services, continued weakening of labour and employment laws, and adoption of other policies that in theory allow for a more flexible, dynamic economy. If anything, the problems identified above reflect a failure to go far enough in adopting neoliberal policies, not a problem with these policies per se.

Although these arguments may seem compelling, there is little evidence that neoliberal policies can address the problems currently experienced by Canadian workers. Indeed, the opposite may be the case. This is especially so when one compares Canada to the United States, which is typically viewed as the exemplar of modern neoliberalism. As revealed in Table 16–2, GDP per capita is roughly 20 percent higher than in Canada after differences in the purchasing power of a Canadian and a U.S. dollar are taken into account (see column d). Yet Canadians also work, on average, about 65 fewer hours per year than do their U.S. counterparts (see column h) and a 2005 Statistics Canada study found that only a third of the difference in GDP per capita can be accounted for by differences in labour productivity. The remainder is attributable to fewer hours worked per job and fewer jobs per capita in the population (Statistics Canada, 2005). Moreover, income inequality and poverty tend to be much lower in Canada (columns k to m), as is the percentage expected to die before they reach 60 years of age (column n). Indeed, a Statistics Canada study found that those in the bottom half of the income distribution in the United States are no better off than their Canadian counterparts, and those in the bottom third are actually worse off (Wolfson and Murphy, 1998). The apparent gains from the U.S. system would thus appear to go primarily to those at the top.

Making matters worse, workers in the United States have even fewer rights and protections at work than do their Canadian counterparts. There are no mandated vacation rights under federal law, and although individual states may legislate such rights, they often do not. The same is the case with respect to dismissal. There are some legal restrictions on the reasons for dismissal, but these tend to be weak and difficult to enforce. In most U.S. states, employees can be dismissed "at will", with no prior notice or pay in lieu of notice. Moreover, although public support for unions is as high as in Canada (see chapter nine), weak labour laws have created a circumstance under which union density has dropped to only 12 percent overall, and only 7 percent in the private sector (as of 2009).

It would thus appear that a U.S.-style system may generate higher levels of GDP per capita, but is not necessarily superior to alternative models once social outcomes such as inequality, poverty, and life expectancy are considered. As revealed in Table 16–2, this applies not just relative to the Canadian case, but also with regard to numerous

TABLE 16-2 Canada in Comparative Perspective: Selected Countries

	(a) tax receipts as % of GDP 2008	(b) social spending as % of GDP 2005	(c) annual GDP growth 1998–2008	(d) GDP/capita 2008 (purchasing-power parities)	(e) labour productivity as % of the USA	(f) unemployment 2008	(g) labour force participation rate 2008
Canada	32	17	1.9	38,600	78	5.3	79
U.S.A.	27	16	1.5	47,300	100	5.8	75
U.K.	36	21	2.2	36,300	81	5.7	77
Australia	31	17	1.9	36,900	81	4.2	77
New Zealand	35	19	1.9	25,000	55	4.2	78
Japan	28	19	1.2	35,300	69	4.0	74
Germany	36	27	1.5	36,000	91	7.5	76
France	43	29	1.4	33,300	96	7.5	70
Italy	43	25	0.7	30,700	74	6.8	63
Netherlands	38	21	1.9	40,000	100	2.8	78
Sweden	47	29	2.4	37,800	83	6.2	81

a, b,c, d, f = *OECD Factbook, 2010* edition
g = *OECD Employment Outlook,* 2009 edition
e = *OECD Statextracts,* July 2010

Continued....

TABLE 16–2 (continued)

	(h) hours worked/year 2008	(i) union density/ coverage 2003	(j) annual days lost to strikes, per 1,000 workers 1997–2006	(k) low-paid employment 2008	(l) inequality (top 20% ÷ bottom 20%)	(m) poverty (% earning under 50% of median)	(n) % not expected to live to 60[n]
Canada	1,729	30/32	186	22	5.5	11.0	7
U.S.A.	1,792	13/14	347	25	8.4	15.0	10
U.K.	1,653	31/33	21	21	7.2	15.0	8
Australia	1,721	25/83	46	13	7.0	12.0	6
New Zealand	1,753	23/28	16	—	6.8	—	8
Japan	1,772	22/18	1	15	3.4	12.0	6
Germany	1,432	25/68	4	18	4.3	10.0	8
France	1,542	10/93	—	—	5.6	11.0	8
Italy	1,802	35/83	88	—	6.5	13.0	7
Netherlands	1,389	23/83	15	—	5.1	7.0	7
Sweden	1,625	81/93	20	6	4.0	6.0	6

h = OECD Employment Outlook, 2009 edition
i = OECD Employment Outlook, 2004
j = annual average from Dominic Hale, Economic and Labour Market Review (2008) 4(2): 33; Statistics for the United States are only for strikes of over 1,000 workers
k = full-time employees earning less than 2/3 of median earnings for all full-time employments; from OECD Employment Outlook, 2009 edition
l, m, n = from U.N. Human Development Report, 2009

other developed countries, many of which perform even better than Canada on such outcomes.

It is also possible that the apparent successes of the U.S. economy do not reflect the superiority of its economic model so much as they do unique conditions under which the U.S. economy has developed (e.g., abundant arable land and resources) and its superior power within the world economy. For example, the U.K. implemented U.S.-style neoliberal policies beginning in the early 1980s, yet its per capita GDP continued to lag Canada's for the almost two decades that they were in place.

In addition to the failings of the U.S. model, there is little evidence of widespread movement towards this model, at least among developed nations (Whitley, 1999; Hirst and Thompson, 1999; Fligstein, 2001; Godard, 2004c). This is also evident in Table 16–2, especially with regard to differences in tax and social spending levels (columns a and b), and union coverage levels (column i). Moreover, although many of these nations have lower per capita GDP, much of this difference is explained by a stronger preference in these nations for leisure time, as reflected in fewer hours worked per year (column h). Thus, the neoliberal imperatives associated with globalization may not be as strong as many pundits have suggested.

It can be argued that the constraints faced by Canadian employers and governments may be greater than those faced by other developed nations (e.g., in Europe) due to Canada's location next to the United States and the growing integration of these two countries under the North American Free Trade Agreement. For example, neoliberals argue that failure to achieve the productivity levels of the United States poses a threat to Canadian competitiveness and ultimately to living standards and that this failure is proof of the need for further integration into the U.S. economy. As revealed in Table 16–2, both France and the Netherlands have similar levels of labour productivity (column e), yet they could not be much farther from the neoliberal model. In addition, the U.S. experience, coupled with the Canadian experience over the past two decades, suggests that, in and of itself, high productivity may do little to help those in the bottom half of the income distribution, who are most in need of such help. The mantra that productivity growth is the key to rising living standards may thus have some truth to it, but it begs the question of "living standards for whom?" It appears that, under a neoliberal regime, the answer is "those at the top".

It follows that Canadians may have far more room for choice than they are often led to believe, and hence that many of the problems currently experienced by employed Canadians may involve politics as much as they do economics. This is not to suggest that Canadians do not face important constraints. But it is to suggest that there are alternatives to the neoliberal model. A number of such alternatives can be considered.

The High Performance Alternative. Within the fields of industrial relations and human resources management, many have argued not only that the high performance paradigm has been transforming the workplace, but also that it represents the best solution for addressing problems at work, allowing for the provision of higher quality jobs, with better pay and higher levels of empowerment, and a new, "partnership" role for unions. What makes this paradigm especially ideal is that it also promises performance gains for employers. Thus, in theory it represents a positive sum solution to work and employment problems, making it possible to address these problems not through stronger legal rights for workers or unions, but rather through the encouragement of employers to adopt practices that also happen to enhance performance.

As discussed earlier in this chapter and in chapter five, the research literature suggests that, in practice, the high performance model has not been fully adopted by more than a small minority of employers, and the evidence as to its implications for employers, workers, and unions is mixed. According to proponents, these findings do not reflect any inherent flaws to the high performance alternative. Rather, they reflect either managerial failings, due to the wrong values or a lack of expertise, or inappropriate incentive structures for management. Thus, there is need for policies that overcome these barriers. In particular, proponents argue that they can be addressed by more aggressive government programs designed to support managers with the needed expertise and resources and to provide the right incentive structures for adoption, particularly assistance for training.

To date, such programs have been of uncertain success. It could be that they have not had sufficient time to take hold or that they require more resources. Yet, the problem may be more basic than this, involving the nature of the employment relation itself within the Canadian economy. Because this relation is one of subordination to employer authority, and employer authority is exercised to serve ownership interests, it generates problems of trust and interest conflicts. These problems limit the effectiveness of the high performance model and the extent to which it makes sense for employers to adopt it (Godard, 2004a).

Thus, it may be that the high performance model is unlikely to ever represent a particularly effective alternative, at least without broader changes that alter the nature of the employment relation and the purposes to which authority is exercised. Even if this was not the case, the high performance model can do little to ensure that workers have meaningful democratic rights at work. Indeed, within the current Canadian context, this model may be seen as an alternative to the provision of such rights, one that is implemented at the behest of the employer and is in this sense largely paternalistic. This is not to suggest that promotion of the high performance alternative is of no value. It is, however, to suggest that this alternative falls far short of what is needed to address the problems faced by many Canadian workers.

The Human Capital Alternative. A second alternative, one that now seems to be popular in some policy circles in Canada (see Courchene, 2002; Chaykowski, 2002) and may also be seen as largely consistent with the high performance model, argues for government programs to promote higher levels of human capital development (i.e., education and skill levels) within the Canadian economy. The primary concern of those advocating this alternative appears to be to enhance productivity levels as much as it is to improve the circumstances of workers. Yet, in theory, higher levels of human capital encourage the creation of higher quality jobs and ultimately translate into more favourable terms and conditions of employment.

The assumption underlying this alternative is that the main barrier to high quality, high value-added jobs at present is an insufficiently skilled and trained workforce. Thus, there is need of government programs to foster higher levels of human capital, both through initial skill development before individuals enter into the labour market, and through life-long learning opportunities after they have done so. As human capital improves, employers will in turn be able to design jobs accordingly.

Although this strategy is undoubtedly of some merit and could form part of an alternative policy regime, it would, in itself, appear to hold only limited promise for addressing the problems identified earlier. Some might be able to imagine a utopia in which most or all workers had sufficiently high skill levels that they would be able to qualify for high quality, high pay jobs and in which employers responded by providing such jobs. But the practical reality is that there are always likely to be significant numbers of Canadians who, for any number of reasons, are unable to achieve such levels and, even if they do, are unable to find jobs in which they are able to fully utilize such skills (see Livingston, 1999). Indeed, one in four participants in a 1997 Angus Reid poll reported that the required skills in their job were significantly *below* either their expertise or experience (Lowe, 2000: 57). There may simply be too many jobs which, by their nature, do not lend themselves to particularly high skill levels (e.g., many jobs in the retail, restaurant and accommodation sectors). Moreover, any attempt to minimize the number of employees who fall into the low skill category would likely require massive additional expenditures on training and education and the establishment of elaborate programs to ensure that this expenditure yielded the desired results. Canada's experience with such programs has proven uneven at best to date. But even if such an effort could succeed, it would also not likely resolve a number of the problems faced by Canadian workers, particularly the lack of meaningful rights and protections in the workplace. It would thus need to be complemented by additional reforms.

Conventional Labour Law Reforms. From the perspective of orthodox pluralists, union representation and collective bargaining represent the primary means through which the problems faced by workers can be addressed. To this end, the solution is generally one of strengthening the current system, largely through legal reforms. In this regard, there are a number of possible such reforms. One such reform is the introduction of more centralized, industry-level bargaining, especially in sectors that are characterized by high numbers of small employers and often autocratic/exploitive practices. As discussed in chapter twelve, this would help to ensure that unionized employers did not find themselves at a competitive disadvantage, thus potentially reducing their opposition to unionization and increasing their willingness to grant meaningful concessions where a union is established.

A second such reform is the introduction of automatic card certification in those jurisdictions that, at present, require a ballot in all cases. As discussed in chapters nine and ten, provision for card certification greatly reduces the opportunities for an employer to interfere in a union certification drive. This would in turn appear to be critical to minimizing the level of intimidation felt by workers during a drive. As a result, the right to card certification has been found to be of major importance for union organizing success and ultimately the level of union density within Canadian jurisdictions.

Yet a third option is to weaken the management rights doctrine so that the ability of unions to provide basic rights and protections becomes less dependent on bargaining power. This could also help to reduce adversariness, as unions would no longer find themselves in a largely reactive role.

Although these and related reforms could be expected to improve the ability of unions to gain certification and to represent their members, they do not address what many see as more fundamental problems with the Canadian labour law system, as discussed above. This is especially true with respect to the majority requirement for certification and, indeed, the certification process itself. As long as these are not addressed, a sizeable majority of workers are likely to find themselves without union representation and hence potentially subject to all of the problems identified earlier in this chapter. In addition, the process by which unions become established is likely to remain unduly adversarial, with negative implications for the relationship that develops between a union and management where certification has occurred.

Conventional labour law reforms also do not address the broader problems faced by labour unions over the past two decades due to government economic policies. Neither the demand for nor the effectiveness of unions is likely to improve in an environment where workers have reason to fear job losses due to foreign competition for both markets and investment, where they can expect only weak government assistance if they lose their job, and where many have limited alternatives due to relatively high unemployment levels. Although there may be some room for improvement on these policies, major changes do not seem possible except perhaps in the distant future.

A further, related problem is that, although a number of such reforms (e.g., sectoral bargaining) are consistent with practices adopted in most European countries, attempts to implement such reforms have in recent years generated massive resistance within the employer community on the grounds that they are intended only to serve the "special interests" of labour unions and are only likely to have negative economic effects, ultimately harming rather than helping workers. As a result, such attempts have either failed or entailed substantial political costs for governments.

Finally, it may simply be that this model is not likely to prove satisfactory for the challenges associated with new forms of employment and new economy jobs.

Employment Law Reforms. Proponents of employment law reforms generally proceed from more of a liberal-reformist perspective than do proponents of conventional labour law reform, especially those who promote only labour law reform. Specifically, although proponents of employment law reforms tend to be favourable towards labour law reforms and a strong labour movement, they also tend to view the post World War II, orthodox pluralist model as ineffective and even out-moded. Hence, they argue for the creation of universal rights and protections for workers, regardless of whether they are in a union or not. Such rights and protections include: substantial increases to mini-mum wage laws; improved human rights protections, especially for women, gays, and minorities; improved support and rights for working parents (e.g., day care, a right to reduced hours); stronger and more effectively enforced health and safety laws; and stronger protections against dismissals, layoffs, and plant closings.

Contrary to what one might expect, there is little evidence that these sorts of reforms need to have particularly negative economic effects. For example, the evidence suggests that moderate increases (i.e., 10 to 15 percent) in the minimum wage may result in a decline in teen employment of from only 1 to 3 percent, and even this may take a number of years to occur (e.g., Campolieti et al., 2006). It would appear to make no significant difference in adult employment overall, and may even increase employment for older workers (Fang and Gunderson, 2009). In addition, much depends on whether teens and other more vulnerable groups (e.g., high school dropouts) are sub-ject to a special sub-minimum and on whether there are programs in place to assist such groups in developing job skills and finding employment (see Neumark and Wascher, 2004). This is generally con-trary to neoliberal theory, which assumes that any increase in the cost of labour is likely to be met by a decrease in demand for it. Thus, it suggests not only that moderate increases to the minimum wage may not have particularly negative effects, but also that similar laws improving other aspects of the employment experience also may not have such effects. However, whether larger increases have more severe effects is uncertain, suggesting that any such increases would at mini-mum need to be implemented with considerable caution.

In addition, a major problem with employment law is that it can be unduly rigid and hence harmful to efficiency on the one hand, yet difficult and unduly costly for governments to enforce on the other. In an era in which flexibility has become a major concern of employers, and government budgets a major concern of politicians, traditional employment laws can seem unwieldy and hard to enforce without major budget increases, thus rendering them largely ineffective. Making matters worse, workers are often not well informed about their rights and may be fearful of employer retribution if they try to exercise them. Finally, substantial increases in workplace rights and protections would again be likely to meet with massive employer resistance on the grounds that they only increase employer costs, although such resistance could possibly be muted if such increases could be justified under a clear alternative paradigm, one that established a strong normative case for reforms. To date, proponents of stronger employment laws do not seem to have advanced such a paradigm.

Institutional Restructuring. More radically minded liberal reformists would agree on the need for stronger employment laws. But they also have argued for more fundamental reforms, ones that alter the institutions associated with the employment relation (e.g., Adams, 1995, 2001). One such reform that has been proposed is for all workers to be given an automatic right to collective bargaining in some form, thus eliminating the union certification process altogether and helping to ensure universal or virtually universal representation at work (see Adams, 1992b, 2001). Although this may at first seem extreme, it is premised on the argument that, just as citizens have an automatic right to be represented in their government, so should workers have an automatic right to be represented in their workplace. Proponents of this option have also argued that establishing such a right would effectively normalize collective bargaining and help to eliminate the adversariness generated by the current certification system.

Another proposed reform is to introduce alternative forms of representation, that go beyond traditional union representation to include **works councils** and worker representatives on company boards (Weiler, 1990; Adams, 1985, 1995). Works councils are committees of employee (and sometimes employer) representatives with information-sharing, consultation, and/or joint decision-making rights. In theory, these mechanisms not only enhance democratic rights at work, they also make for more inclusive decision processes at the workplace level, so that workers and their representatives are in a more proactive (rather than reactive) position. This in turn helps to facilitate a more consensual relationship, with potentially positive economic implications (Freeman and Lazear, 1996). It also helps to ensure that worker interests are more fully incorporated into workplace level decisions, in theory helping to overcome problems of trust and short-term employer thinking that can occur when employers unilaterally introduce new forms of work organization (Godard, 2004a: 369–70). Worker representatives on company boards are believed to have similar effects, albeit at the company level. As suggested in chapter nine, these two forms of representation can help to alter the way in which the employment relation is constituted, rendering management decision-makers accountable to workers as well as owners and possibly even ensuring that worker interests are considered of equal importance to those of owners.

For those advocating these sorts of reforms, Sweden and Germany are often invoked as exemplars (e.g., Adams, 1995). In the Swedish case, workplace-wide union recognition is automatic if so requested by only one or a few workers. This helps to ensure high levels of union representation, so much so that union coverage exceeds 90 percent of all employees. Bargaining is also at the industry level, and there is a high degree of co-ordination across industries. Unions are thus able to negotiate more favourable wages and working conditions for virtually all members of the Swedish labour force, although the tradition has been for them to focus on improving the circumstances of those in lower paying jobs. Moreover, unions have extensive consultation and participation rights, with the result that worker interests are incorporated into the way work is designed. This, in theory, helps to ensure that workers are protected against high levels of stress and work overload, and are at the same time truly empowered in the workplace. Unions also have extensive say in layoff and dismissal decisions, and, indeed, a worker who is to be dismissed for poor performance or behaviour may remain in his or her job until such time as that there has been a proper hearing to establish just cause. Finally, Sweden is famous for its generous social and labour market programs, including extensive retraining opportunities in the event that a worker is laid off, unemployment and parental leave benefits that amount to 80 percent of regular pay, and a free day care system. Of all of the nations included in Table 16–2, it has the highest spending on social programs on the one hand, and the lowest levels of both inequality (with the exception of Japan) and poverty on the other.

In the German case, bargaining is also almost entirely at the industry level. Although employers may opt out of the agreement for their industry, roughly two-thirds of all employees are explicitly covered by a collective agreement, and employers who opt out still typically follow the agreement for their industry. Depending on the size of their employer, employees are able to elect between one-third and one-half of the members of their employer's supervisory board (the equivalent of a board of directors). They also have a right to elect a works council for their workplace. Where established (usually in mid- to large-sized workplaces), works councils have extensive information-sharing, consultation, and co-decision rights, and can effectively veto employer decisions on matters pertaining to the design of work and employer human resource practices. There is also an extensive system of labour standards governing working hours, dismissals and layoffs, employment status (e.g., the use of temporary workers), and related concerns. Finally, unions and employers are considered to be "social partners", with both participating in the administration of various labour market and social programs, including Germany's vocational training system, which is widely credited for helping to the support the existence of a high skill, high pay workforce.

As revealed in Table 16–2, the per capita GDP of both Sweden and Germany are somewhat lower than Canada's, although the extent to which this can be attributed to their stronger laws and protections for workers is not clear. In particular, both Swedes and Germans work substantially fewer hours per year than their Canadian counterparts, but labour productivity in both countries is higher than in Canada. Thus, GDP differences may reflect national preferences for leisure over labour. Indeed, workers in both countries typically enjoy six weeks of vacation per year. In addition, these two countries also have lower levels of inequality and poverty than does Canada, thus suggesting that those in the bottom half are likely to be as well off economically as their Canadian counterparts. This may be especially true of Sweden, where the poverty rate is only half that of Canada's, and the top 20 percent make only 4.0 times that of the bottom 20 percent, compared to 5.8 times in Canada. Finally, it is worth noting that the days lost due to strikes per thousand workers is far lower in both of these countries, even though the percent covered by collective bargaining is far higher. In both countries, this likely reflects the advantages of industry level bargaining, coupled with an environment in which there is far less animosity between labour and management.

These two countries reinforce the argument that there are clear alternatives to the neoliberal model. Although both have undergone a number of changes over the past decade or so, some of which may be considered consistent with such a model, both remain distinct from the United States in fundamental ways. Indeed, Germany is considered by many to represent a distinctive form of capitalism, one that is based on extensive co-ordination and cooperation between firms, unions, and governments, rather than on the high levels of competition and adversariness associated with U.S.-style capitalism (e.g., Hall and Soskice, 2001).

It follows that much might be learned from both Sweden and Germany. Yet, it would be misguided to expect that the institutional structures associated with either country could be readily adopted within the Canadian context, except perhaps over the long run — unless, perhaps, there was some sort of fundamental crisis within the Canadian economy. Not only would employer resistance likely be massive, potentially creating an outflow of investment to the United States, but the broader economic, political, and social systems within which these structures function differ in important ways from their Canadian counterparts. It would thus be necessary to usher in broader, more fundamental reforms before such structures could be expected to function effectively. In addition, the norms and traditions that underpin these institutional structures differ in fundamental ways, thus limiting their transferability to the Canadian context.[4]

Institutional Revolution. A further alternative, as advanced by many radicals, is to effectively dismantle the institutions of capitalism as they now exist and to replace them with alternative, more fundamentally democratic institutions. Radicals generally believe that the differences between countries like the United States and Canada, on the one hand, and Sweden and Germany, on the other, are too often overstated and that the sorts of problems experienced by Canadian workers are increasingly characteristic of all capitalist economies. They also believe that these problems have been worsening in recent decades, as various trade agreements and the institutions of global capitalism (e.g., the World Trade Organization) have increased the pressures on nations to adopt neoliberal policies. These pressures are believed to not only account for the problems identified in the previous section of this chapter, but also to have undermined the very institutions of democracy within nations (e.g., unions, governments), rendering them even more ineffectual as means of serving the interests of working people than they have been in the past. At the same time, the global economy has become increasingly fragile, as reflected by the crisis of 2008.

According to radicals, this situation is only likely to worsen until such time that the people and their organizations have become fully aware of the root causes of the problems they are facing and develop the capacities to attack them head on, essentially replacing capitalism with a truly democratic alternative. At the centre of such a system would be democratic control of investment, so that capital is allocated in a way that is consistent with public rather than private goals. At the local level, for example, there could be "democratic planning boards"

---

[4] For example, German firms tend to be financed primarily by large banks and viewed as essentially "social" institutions, to be managed in society's interests. Thus, institutions that provide strong rights and protections for workers are more broadly supported than in Canada, where firms tend to be financed through stock markets and are viewed as purely economic institutions.

vested with the responsibility of ensuring that investment is done in a way that ensures everyone in their catchment area is gainfully employed (Panitch and Swartz, 2003: 234). Labour unions would play a key role in helping to bring this state of affairs about, but would first need to broaden their mandate beyond simply workplace issues to "become more inclusive of workers' full life experiences, as producers, as family members, and as citizens" (Panitch and Swartz, 2003: 237). They would also need to become part of a broader "structured movement" which included other social groups and movements and was dedicated towards the development of a democratic alternative to capitalism (Panitch and Swartz, 2003: 236).

Although this alternative is indeed radical, there is some precedent for an alternative to capitalism as we understand it. The Mondragon system centred in the Basque region of Spain consists of over 250 enterprises and has its own financial and educational institutions, all of which are worker owned and controlled. It faces a number of challenges, many of which arise from its position within a broader capitalist economy (see Cheney, 1999). But it has continued to survive and grow since its founding in 1956. As of 2009, it employed 85,000 workers and had assets worth the equivalent of 44 billion Canadian dollars, with sales worth the equivalent of 23 billion Canadian dollars (www.mondragon-corporation.com).

Despite the apparent success of the Mondragon system, the prospects for and likely effectiveness of such an alternative in Canada would appear to be limited. The Mondragon system began essentially as a strategy for economic development. It is highly unlikely that a similar system could be developed in an advanced economy, where conventional capitalist institutions are already strongly entrenched — except perhaps under very unusual circumstances. It is always possible that the sorts of strategies advanced by radicals could help to create such circumstances, and it is always too easy to under-estimate the possibilities for change. But such strategies have not borne much fruit to date, and it is not very likely that they will in the future, except possibly over the very long run. The underlying problem may be that radicals seriously underestimate the difficulties involved in not only mobilizing support for such changes, but also creating the kinds of institutions necessary for these changes to succeed. There would seem to be little alternative at present but to seek to improve on the design and functioning of established institutions.

Nonetheless, this system could hold important lessons for the Canadian system. Particularly relevant in this regard is a 2009 agreement between the Mondragon Corporation and the U.S. union, the

United Steel Workers to collaborate by adapting principles of the Mondragon model to the North American economy. This agreement appears in Box 16–1.

The Good Practice Alternative. Each of the alternatives considered to this point has been found to be either too limited or unrealistic in view of contemporary circumstances. A final alternative, one that seeks to avoid both of these criticisms, entails what has been referred to as the "good practice paradigm". As developed in greater detail elsewhere (Godard, 2003b), this paradigm is founded on three basic principles that one would expect to observe at work in any advanced democracy yet are often violated due to the nature of the employment relation and the conflicts that underlie it: (1) dignity and freedom, (2) fairness and equality, and (3) representation and voice. It advocates employer practices that serve these principles and have always, in varying degrees, been considered to represent "good" management practice. However, it does not assume that it is necessarily in the interests of employers to adopt such practices or that their adoption should be a matter for employer choice. Nor does it assume that such practices should be the subject for collective bargaining. Rather, it is based on the argument that the three principles represent basic rights. Hence, there is need of government policies and laws to ensure that they are realized in virtually all workplaces regardless of employer volition or union bargaining power.

The good practice paradigm also assumes that it is possible to achieve basic levels of these three principles without unduly negative economic implications. Although the attainment of these principles can have costs for employers, their violation can result in employee deprivation, resentment, and distrust (respectively), all of which can also have negative performance implications. Addressing these potential problems could thus have benefits for employers that at least partly offset any costs. A further assumption is that the magnitude of any such costs or of any resulting benefits is likely to depend in consider-able measure on matters of design and implementation, something that is often overlooked in debates over the likely effects of stronger labour and employment laws.

Unions could be expected to play a critical role in this respect, a role that would extend to workplaces where they are not certified for collective bargaining purposes. First, unions could provide workers with "institutional backup", or in other words, the information, exper-tise, and resources needed to ensure that they are able to effectively assert their rights and that they can do so without fear of employer

BOX 16–1 Framework Agreement between
                The United Steelworkers (USW) and
                MONDRAGON Internacional, S.A.

The Unitied Steelworkers (USW) and MONDRAGON Internacional, S.A. intend to collaborate in the United States/Canadian market-place by adapting collective bargaining principles to the MONDRAGON cooperative model and worker ownership principles.

The goals of the collaboration are to develop and grow manu-facturing jobs in the United States and Canada, to improve the quality of life of workers, and to create sustainable jobs in a sus-tainable economy that supports stronger communities and sustain-able environmental practices.

This collaboration further intends to demonstrate that the MONDRAGON worker-ownership model can be highly effective as adapted to an organized workforce and North American culture.

Specifically the USW/MONDRAGON Internacional, S.A. collabora-tion aims to:

1. Increase participative "one class" employee ownership of businesses through understanding, adopting, and practicing the MONDRAGON Corp. cooperative model as it may apply in hybrid combinations for USW-represented compa-nies.

2. Integrate collective bargaining with MONDRAGON Corp's cooperative practices and model, such as having the Union's Bargaining Committee also serve as the Social Council.

3. Further explore next generation hybrid approaches to col-lective bargaining that allow deeper worker participation and union/management collaboration.

4. Explore co-investing models and opportunities using success-ful precedents such as the USW's participation in the Que-bec Solidarity Fund, which invests back into the greater Quebec community, and the MONDRAGON Corp. Eroski Foundation, which has similar goals and a fully integrated community ownership structure.

Agreed and signed this __27th__ day, month of __October__, 2009.

For the United Steelworkers: For MONDRAGON Internacional, S.A.

_____   _____

Leo Gerard   Josu Ugarte
International President   President
                                MONDRAGON Internacional, S.A.

Note: Reproduced with permission.

retribution. Second, they could be instrumental in the establishment of more flexible "framework" rights and protections, where government policies and laws allow for a high degree of discretion in how they are implemented, provided that workers have union representation in the implementation process to ensure that this discretion is not abused (e.g., Ozaki, 1999: 55–60). Third, unions could play an important role in helping to enforce these rights and protections, thus reducing enforcement costs traditionally borne by governments.

To further these ends, workers would be provided with a universal right to union representation with regard to the implementation and enforcement of good practice policies and laws, regardless of whether there was majority support for a union in their workplace. However, this right would not necessarily extend to include traditional collective bargaining rights, for which majority support and certification might still be required. Thus, there would be no necessary change to the established labour law system, only an expansion of this system to include a right for workers to be represented on matters pertaining to good practice laws, a right that would be protected by unfair labour practice laws similar to those currently in place.

With regard to the terms of employment, good practice laws could include, for example, substantial improvements to the minimum wage and related benefits (e.g., vacation times). Decent minimum wage and benefit levels can be seen as critical to ensuring minimum levels of dignity and economic freedom, even for those workers who live in relatively well-to-do households. In particular, no adult should be expected to work for a poverty-level wage, regardless of their family circumstances. A decent minimum wage is also important to the attainment of fairness and equality, especially where low wages reflect a surplus of workers competing for the same jobs, rendering these workers subject to exploitation in the labour market. Thus, the minimum wage could be set at a level sufficient for an individual to earn the equivalent of the Statistics Canada LICO for a full-time, full-year employee (also see Arthurs, 2006: 249). To minimize any negative economic consequences from such increases, there could be a lower minimum wage for workers most likely to suffer such consequences (e.g., those under 18, with limited experience, or with learning deficiencies). Government programs could also be established to assist disadvantaged workers in improving their human capital levels to ensure that they are able to produce at a level equalling or exceeding the new minimum, and there could be forms of government assistance for those unable to reach this level (see Godard, 2002).

In addition to decent pay and benefits, workers could be provided with stronger, although possibly more flexible, rights with regard to health and safety, working time, and parental leave. They could also be provided with universal grievance and arbitration rights on selected issues, backed up by the right to legal representation, including union representation, in the exercise of these rights. Such rights would be based on codes of "good practice" promulgated by governments, and designed to ensure basic levels of fairness and equality at work, especially with regard to discipline and dismissal, but also, perhaps, to promotions, layoffs, and related issues. In this respect we might refer to violations of these rights as "unfair employment practices", thus paralleling what we now refer to as "unfair labour practices".

A further possibility would be a right for all employees in uncertified workplaces to some form of signed contract with their employer. Employees might be given the right not only to negotiate such a contract at the time of hiring, but also to renegotiate this contract at subsequent intervals, and to do so through a legal representative of their choice, either as individuals or, for those who wish to do so, collectively. This contract would be more specific and confer more rights and obligations on the parties than is currently the case under the law or under most non-union employment contracts. In the event that the negotiations did not succeed or there was a perception that an established contract had been violated, either side would have a right to file a grievance and go to either arbitration or some form of government tribunal.

As a final example, workers could be provided with universal communication and participation rights on selected issues (e.g., training), thus ensuring representation and voice in decisions that affect their well-being. To advocate German-style works councils, as some liberal reformists have done, is unlikely to be taken seriously given Canadian traditions. But universal information-sharing and consultation rights on selected issues, such as training, layoffs, and changes to work design, might be.

Combined, these sorts of rights could entail a substantial advance beyond the orthodox pluralist model that has dominated labour policy in Canada since the second world war. But rather than replacing this model, their adoption would extend many of the legal rights and protections typically assumed to exist in union workplaces to all workers. It would also possibly shift the main role of unions away from having to fight for certification and various attendant rights to one of simply helping to implement and enforce such rights. Moreover, because this role would not require workers to go through the certification process, the presence of a union would be less likely to be viewed as an attack on management or a threat to management's competitive position. Ideally, this would result in less conflictual relations, and unionization would come to be seen as normal, even if with a somewhat different role.

Although these rights would entail a substantial shift, they are not without precedent. In particular, the U.K. has long had a system of employment tribunals for workers that believe they have been unfairly disciplined or dismissed, and in 1999 it implemented a minimum wage regime similar to the one proposed here. It has also adopted mandatory consultation laws with regard to training and layoffs, and, most recently, legislation to substantially extend information-sharing and consultation rights to matters involving employer strategy and workplace change (albeit largely in response to a European Union directive requiring all member states to do so). Although it is difficult to gauge the effectiveness of some of these laws, they do not appear to have had any significant negative economic effects, and employer opposition to them appears to have been limited.

The U.K. experience may be especially relevant given similarities in its traditions and institutions to those of Canada. Nonetheless, good practice rights would need to be implemented gradually and in a way designed to minimize both employer opposition and any negative economic consequences, a task made more difficult by Canada's proximity to the United States and by what would appear to be a more hostile employer culture. Yet the good practice paradigm could be promoted not as serving the interests of any particular group (e.g., labour unions) but rather as advancing Canadian society so that it is more consistent with principles that should be basic to any advanced democracy and that are already widely adhered to in Europe. It could also be promoted on the grounds that it is simply consistent with what has always been thought of as good management practice and that any negative effects would likely be small at best, as borne out by the U.K. experience.

It is, of course, not at all certain that such a modest alternative could effectively address the problems currently faced by Canadians at work. But it would ideally help to move things in the right direction, setting Canada on a path or "trajectory" that would gradually lead to the kind of quality of life and working experience that one would hope to see for all Canadians. It could also help to lay the foundation for a more fundamentally democratic culture in the economy and in Canadian society in general. Regardless of whether one agrees with the arguments advanced by radicals as to the need to democratize control over investment, few could disagree with the development of a more democratic culture at work as a basic requirement for any truly advanced civilization.

Bibliography

Abraham, K., and J. Medoff. 1985. "Length of Service and Promotions in Union and Nonunion Work Groups". *Industrial and Labor Relations Review* 38: 408–20.

———. 1984. "Length of Service and Layoffs in Union and Nonunion Work Groups". *Industrial and Labor Relations Review* 38: 87–97.

Ackroyd, Stephen, and Paul Thompson. 1999. *Organizational Misbehaviour*. London: Sage Publications.

Adams, Roy. 2001. "Choice or Voice? Rethinking American Labor Policy". *Employee Rights and Employment Policy Journal* 5(2): 521–48.

———. 1998. "The Human Right to Bargain Collectively: A Review of Documents Supporting International Consensus". Working Paper, Society for the Promotion of Human Rights in Employment, McMaster University (http://mericleinc.com/Sphre).

———. 1995. *Industrial Relations Under Liberal Democracy*. Columbia, S.C.: University of South Carolina Press.

———. 1994. "Union Certification as an Instrument of Labor Policy: A Comparative Perspective". In S. Friedman et al. (Eds.), *Restoring the Promise of American Labor Law*, pp. 260–69. Ithaca, NY: ILR Press.

———. 1993a. "'All Aspects of People at Work': Unity and Division in the Study of Labour and Management". In R. Adams and N. Meltz (Eds.), *Industrial Relations: Its Nature, Scope, and Pedagogy*. Metuchen, New Jersey: Scarecrow Press.

———. 1993b. "The North American Model of Employee Representational Participation: 'A Hollow Mockery'". *Comparative Labor Law Journal* 15(4): 4–14.

———. 1992a. "The Role of the State in Industrial Relations". In D. Lewin et al. (Eds.), *Research Frontiers in Industrial Relations and Human Resources*. Madison, WI: IRRA.

———. 1992b. "The Right to Participate". *Employee Responsibilities and Rights Journal* 5(2): 91–99.

———. 1988. "The 'Old Industrial Relations' and Corporate Competitiveness: A Canadian Case". *Employee Relations* 10: 3–7.

———. 1986. "Two Policy Approaches to Labour–Management Decision Making at the Level of the Enterprise". In C. Riddell (Ed.), *Labour Management Cooperation in Canada*. Toronto: University of Toronto Press.

———. 1985. "Should Workers Councils Be Used As Industrial Relations". *Monthly Labor Review* July: 25–29.

Adams, Roy J., and Ray Markey. 1997. "How the State Affects Trade Union Growth". In J. Browne (Ed.), *The Role of the State in Industrial Relations* (Vol. 3 of the Official Proceedings of the European Industrial Relations Congress). Dublin: Oak Tree Press.

Addison, John and Clive Belfield. 2004. "Union Voice" *Journal of Labour Research* 25(4): 563–96.

Adell, B. 1986. "Establishing a Collective Employee Voice in the Workplace", in *Essays in Labour Relations Law*. Papers Presented at the Conference on Government and Labour Relations: The Death of Voluntarism. Don Mills: CCH Canadian.

Adell, N. 1988. "Law and IR in Common Law Canada". In G. Hébert et al. (Eds.), *The State of the Art in Industrial Relations*. Kingston: Queens University Industrial Relations Centre.

Aglietta, M. 1979. *A Theory of Capitalist Regulation: The U.S. Experience*. London: New Left Books.

Akard, P.J. 1992. "Corporate Mobilization and U.S. Economic Policy in the 1970s". *American Sociological Review* 57: 597–615.

Akerlof, G., and J. Yellon. 1986. *Efficiency Wage Models of the Labor Market*. Cambridge: Cambridge University Press.

Akyeampong, Ernest. 2003. "Unionization and the Grievance System". *Perspectives on Work and Income* 15(3): 31–37.

Anderson, J. 1989a. "The Structure of Collective Bargaining". In J. Anderson, M. Gunderson, and A. Ponak (Eds.), *Union–Management Relations In Canada*, 2nd Ed. Toronto: Addison Wesley.

———. 1989b. "The Strategic Management of Labour Relations". In J. Anderson, M. Gunderson, and A. Ponak. *Union Management Relations in Canada*, 2nd Ed. Toronto: Addison-Wesley.

Applebaum, H.A. 1981. *Royal Blue: The Culture of Construction Workers*. New York: Holt Rinehart and Winston.

Arthurs, Harry. 2006. *Fairness at Work: Federal Labour Standards for the 21st Century*. Gateneau: Human Resources and Skill Development Canada.

Arthurs, Harry, D.D. Carter, J. Fudgge, H.J. Glasbeek, and G. Trudeau. 1993. *Labour Law and Industrial Relations in Canada*, 4th Ed. Markham, ON: Butterworths.

Ashenfelter, O., and G. Johnson. 1969. "Bargaining Theory, Trade Unions, and Industrial Strike Activity". *American Economic Review* 59: 35–49.

Asher, Martin, and Robert DeFina. 1997. "The Impact of Changing Union Density of Income Inequality". *Journal of Labor Research* 18(3): 425–38.

Bacharach, S., and E.J. Lawler. 1981. *Bargaining: Power, Tactics, and Outcomes*. San Francisco: Jossey Bass.

Bailyn, Lotte. 2006. *Breaking the Mold*, 2nd ed. Ithaca: Cornell Press.

Bakke, E.W. 1945. "Why Workers Join Unions". *Personnel* 22: 2–11.

Baldamus, W. 1961. *Efficiency and Effort*. London: Tavistock.

Baron, J., P. Devereaux Jennings, and F. Dobbin. 1988. "Mission Control? The Development of Personnel Systems in U.S. Industry". *American Sociological Review* 53: 497–514.

Baron, J., F. Dobbin, and P. Devereaux Jennings. 1986. "War and Peace: The Evolution of Modern Personnel Administration". *American Journal of Sociology* 92: 350–83.

Batstone, E., A. Ferner, and M. Terry. 1984. *Consent and Efficiency*. Oxford: Blackwell.

Batstone, E., I. Boraston, and S. Frenkel. 1978. *The Social Organization of Strikes*. Oxford: Blackwell.

Beatty, D. 1984. "The Role of the Arbitrator: the Liberal Version". *University of Toronto Law Review* 34: 136–69.

———. 1983. "Ideology, Politics, and Unionism". In K. Swan and K. Swinton (Eds.), *Studies in Labour Law*. Toronto: Butterworths.

Becker, Brian, and Craig Olson. 1992. "Unions and Firm Profits". *Industrial Relations* 31(3): 395–416.

Beer, Michael, and B. Spector, 1985. "Corporate Wide Transformation in Human Resource Management". In R.E. Walton and P.R. Lawrence (eds.), *Human Resource Management: Trends and Challenges*. pp. 219–53. Boston, MA: Harvard Business School Press.

Bell, D. 1973. *The Coming of the Post-Industrial Society*. New York: Basic Books.

———. 1967. *The End of Ideology*. New York: Free Press.

Bemmels, B. 1987. "How Unions Affect Productivity in Manufacturing Plants". *Industrial and Labor Relations Review* 40: 241–53.

Bemmels, B., E.G. Fisher, and B. Nyland. 1986. "Canadian-American Jurisprudence on 'Good Faith' Bargaining". *Relations Industrielles* 41: 596–621.

Bender, Keith, and Peter J. Sloane. 1998. "Job Satisfaction, Trade Unions, and Exit-Voice Revisited". *Industrial and Labor Relations Review* 51(2): 222–40.

Bendix, R. 1956. *Work and Authority in Industry*. New York: Wiley.

Bennis, W. 1967. "The Coming Death of Bureaucracy". *Management Review* 56: 19–24.

Bercusson, D. 1974. *Confrontation at Winnipeg*. Montreal: McGill University Press.

Berggren, Christian. 1992. *Alternatives to Lean Production*. Ithaca, NY: ILR Press.

Berglof, E. 1990. "Capital Structure as a Mechanism of Control". In M. Aoki, B. Gustafasson, and O.E. Williamson (Eds.), *The Firm as a Nexus of Treaties*. London: Sage.

Berle, A. 1959. *Power Without Property*. New York: Harcourt, Brace, and Company.

Berle, A., and G. Means. 1932. *The Modern Corporation and Private Property*.

Bernstein, I. 1972. *The Lean Years*. New York: Houghton-Mifflin.

Black, Erol, and Jim Silver. 1990. "Contradictions and Limitations of Final Offer Selection: the Manitoba Experience". *Relations Industrielles* 454(1): 146–64.

Blackburn, R., and M. Mann. 1975. "Ideology in the Non-Skilled Working Class". In M. Bulmer (Ed.), *Working Class Images of Society*. London: Routledge and Kegan Paul.

Blanchflower, Danny, and Alex Bryson. 2003. "Changes Over Time in Union Relative Wage Effects in the UK and US Revisited". In John T. Addison and Claus Schnabel (eds.), *International Handbook of Trade Unions*. Cheltenham: Edward Elgar.

Blanchflower, David G., and Richard B. Freeman. 1992. "Unionism in the United States and Other Advanced OECD Countries". *Industrial Relations* 31: 56–80.

Blauner, R. 1964. *Alienation and Freedom*. Chicago: Chicago University Press.

Block, Fred. 1994. "The Roles of the State in the Economy". In Neil Smelser and Richard Swedberg (Eds.), *Handbook of Economic Sociology*. Princeton: Princeton University Press.

––––––. 1987. *Revising State Theory: Essays in Politics and Postindustrialism*. Philadelphia: Temple University Press.

Block, R. 1978. "The Impact of Seniority Provisions on the Manufacturing Quit Rate". *Industrial and Labor Relations Review* 31: 474–81.

Blouin, Rodrique. 1995, "Minority Opinion". In Andrew Simms, Rodrique Blouin, and Paula Knopf, *Seeking a Balance*, pp. 140–50. Ottawa: Minister of Public Services.

Bluestone, B. and I. Bluestone. 1992. *Negotiating the Future: A Labor Perspective on American Business*, New York: Basic Books.

Bok, D., and J. Dunlop. 1970. *Labor and the American Community*. New York: Simon and Schuster.

Borins, S.F. 1988. "Public Choice: 'Yes Minister' Made It Popular, But Does Winning the Nobel Prize Make It True?" *Canadian Public Administration* 31: 12–26.

Bowles, S. 1985. "The Production Process in a Competitive Economy". *American Economic Review* 75: 16–36.

Bowles, S., D. Gordon, and T. Weisskopf. 1983. *Beyond the Waste Land*. Garden City, NY: Anchor Press.

Bowles, S., and H. Gintis. 1976. *Schooling in Capitalist America*. New York: Basic Books.

Bratsberg, Bernt, and James Ragan, Jr. 1997 "Have Unions Impeded Growing Wages Dispersion Among Young Workers". *Journal of Labor Research* 18(4): 593–612.

Braverman, H. 1974. *Labor and Monopoly Capital*. New York: Monthly Review Press.

Breshin, F. Curtis, Peter Smith, Mieke Koeboorn, and Hyunmi Lee. 2006. "Is the Workplace Becoming Safer?" *Perspectives on Labour and Income* 18(3): 36–41.

Bronars, Stephen, Donald Deere, and Joseph Tracy. 1994. "The Effects of Unions on Firm Behaviour". *Industrial Relations* 33(4): 426–51.

Bronfenbrenner, Kate. 1997. "The Role of Union Strategies in NLRB Certification Elections". *Industrial and Labor Relations Review* 50(2): 195–211.

––––––. 1992. "Seeds of Resurgence: Successful Union Organizing Strategies". Paper presented at the 1992 Annual Meetings of the American Sociological Association.

Brown, R. 1983. "Towards A General Theory of Fair Representation in Contract Administration". In K. Swan and K. Swinton (Eds.), *Studies in Labour Law*. Toronto: Butterworths.

Buchanan, J., and G. Tullock. 1962. *The Calculus of Consent*. Ann Arbour: University of Michigan Press.

Burawoy, M. 1985. *The Politics of Production*. London: Verso.

––––––. 1979. *Manufacturing Consent: Changes in the Labour Process Under Monopoly Capitalism*. Chicago: University of Chicago Press.

Burke, Mike, and John Shields. 1999. *The Job Poor Recovery*, Research Report, Toronto, Ryerson Social Reporting Network, Ryerson Polytechnic University.

Burns, T., and G. Stalker. 1961. *The Management of Innovation*. London: Tavistock.

Burstein, M., N. Tienharra, P. Hewson, and B. Warrander. 1975. *Canadian Work Values: Findings of a Work Ethic Survey and a Job Satisfaction Survey*. Ottawa: Information Canada.

Byrman, A. 1984. "Organization Studies and the Concept of Rationality". *Journal of Management Studies* 21: 391–408.

Calmfors, L., and J. Driffill. 1988. "Bargaining Structure, Corporatism, and Macro-economic Performance". *Economic Policy* 6: 13–61.

Campbell, R.M. 1991. *The Full-Employment Objective in Canada, 1945–1985: A Study Prepared for the Economic Council of Canada*. Ottawa: Minister of Supply and Services.

Campolieti, Michele, Morley Gundeson, and Chris Riddell. 2006. "Minimum Wage Impacts from a Prespecified Research Design: Canada 1981–1997" *Industrial Relations* 45(2): 195–216.

Campolieti, Michele, Chris Riddell, and Sara Slinn. 2007. "Labor Law Reform and the Role of Delay in Union Organizing: Empirical Evidence from Canada". *Industrial and Labor Relations Review* 61(1): 32–58.

Canada Health Monitor. 1998. *Stress, Illness, and Injury in the Workplace and Their Consequences*, Report prepared for Homewood Health Centre, Guelph, Ontario.

Canadian Council on Social Development (CCSD). 2003. *Personal Security Index 2003*. Ottawa: CCSD.

Canadian Labour Congress (CLC). 2003. Canadians Talk About Unions. unpublished report.

Canadian Policy Research Networks (CPRN). 2003. "How Canada Stacks Up: the Quality of Work — An International Perspective" Ottawa: CPRN.

Cappelli, P., and R. McKersie. 1987. "Management Strategy and the Redesign of Workrules". *Journal of Management Studies* 24: 441–62.

Cappelli, Peter, and David Neumark. 2001. "Do 'High Performance' Work Practices Improve Establishment Level Outcomes?" *Industrial and Labor Relations Review* 54(4): 737–76.

Carey, A. 1967. "The Hawthorne Studies: A Radical Criticism". *American Sociological Review* 32: 403–16.

Carter, Donald. 1997. "The Duty to Accommodate: Its Growing Impact on the Grievance Arbitration Process". *Relations Industrielles* 52(1): 185–207.

Cavanaugh, Joseph. 1998. "Asset-specific Investment and Unionized Labor". Industrial Relations 37(1): 9–34.

Chaison, G., and J. Rose. 1991a. "The Macrodeterminants of Union Growth and Decline". In G. Strauss et al. (Eds.), *The State of the Unions*. Madison, WI: IRRA.

———. 1991b. "Continental Divide: The Direction and Fate of North American Unions". In D. Lewin and D. Sockell (Eds.), *Advances in Industrial and Labor Relations*, Vol. 5, pp. 169–205. Greenwich, CT: JAI Press.

———. 1989. "Unions, Growth, Structure, and Internal Dynamics". In J. Anderson, M Gunderson, and A. Ponak (Eds.), *Union — Management Relations in Canada*. Don Mills, ON: Addison-Wesley.

Chamberlain, N., and James Kuhn. 1965. *Collective Bargaining, 2nd Ed.* New York: McGraw-Hill.

Chandler, A. 1977. *The Visible Hand: The Managerial Revolution in American Business*. Cambridge, MA: Harvard University Press.

Chaykowski, Richard. 2002. "Globalization and the Modernization of Canadian Labour Policy". *Canadian Public Policy* 28(1): 81–91.

———. 1998. "The Role of Sector Initiatives in the Canadian Industrial Relations System". In Morley Gunderson and Andrew Sharpe (Eds.) *Forging Business-Labour Partnerships: The Emergence of Sector Councils in Canada*. Toronto: University of Toronto Press.

———. 1995. "The Structure and Process of Collective Bargaining". In Morley Gunderson and Allen Ponak (Eds.), *Union-Management Relations in Canada*. Don Mills, ON: Addison Wesley.

Chaykowski, Richard, and George Slotsve, 2002. "Earnings Inequality and Unions in Canada". *British Journal of Industrial Relations* 40(3): 493–519.

Cheney, George. 1999. *Values at Work*. Ithaca: Cornell University Press.

Child, J. 1985. "Managerial Strategies, New Technology, and the Labour Process". In D. Knights, H. Willmott, and D. Collinson (Eds.), *Job Redesign*. Brookfield, Vermont: Gower.

Clawson, D. 1980. *Bureaucracy and the Labor Process*. New York: Monthly Review Press.

Clegg, H.A. 1976. *Trade Unionism Under Collective Bargaining: A Theory Based Upon Comparisons of Six Countries*. Oxford: Blackwell.

———. 1975. "Pluralism in Industrial Relations". *British Journal of Industrial Relations* 13: 306–21.

Cohen, M.D., J.G. March, and P. Olsen. 1972. "A 'Garbage Can' Model of Organizational Choice". *Administrative Science Quarterly* 17: 1–25.

Cohen-Rosenthal, E., and C.E. Burton. 1992. *Mutual Gains: A Guide to Union-Management Cooperation*. Ithaca, NY: ILR Press.

Cohn, S., and A. Eaton. 1989. "Historical Limits on Neoclassical Strike Theories: Evidence from French Coal Mining, 1890–1935". *Industrial and Labor Relations Review* 42: 649–62.

Colander, D.C. 1984. *Neoclassical Political Economy: The Analysis of Rent-Seeking and DUP Activities*. Cambridge: Ballinger Publishing.

Collins, R. 1986. *Max Weber: A Skeleton Key*. Beverly Hills, CA: Sage.

Commons, John R. 1909. "American Shoemakers, 1648–1895". *The Quarterly Journal of Economics*, Vol. 24.

Compa, Lance. 2001. "Free Trade, Fair Trade, and the Battle for Labor Rights". In Lowell Turner, Harry Katz, and Richard Hurd (Eds.), *Rekindling the Labor Movement*, pp. 314–23. Ithaca: Cornell University Press.

Corry, Dan. 1997, "Macroeconomic Policy and Stakeholder Capitalism". In Gavin Kelly, Dominic Kelly, and Andrew Gamble (Eds.), *Stakeholder Capitalism*. London: Macmillan Press.

Coughlin, D.C. 1985. "Domestic Content Legislation: House Voting and the Economies of Regulation". *Economic Inquiry* 23: 437–48.

Courchene, T.J. 2002. "Human Capital in an Information Era". *Canadian Public Policy* 28(1): 73–80.

Cousineau, J.M., and R. Lacroix. 1986. "Imperfect Information and Strikes: An Analysis of the Canadian Experience, 1967–1982". *Industrial and Labor Relations Review* 39: 377–87.

Coutts, Jane. 1998. "Workplace Stress More Prevalent Than Illness, Injury". *Globe and Mail*. April 8.

Craven, P. 1980. *An Impartial Umpire: Industrial Relations and the Canadian State, 1900–1911*. Toronto: University of Toronto Press.

Cully, Mark, Stephen Woodland, Andrew O'Reilly, and Gill Dix. 1999. *Britain at Work: As Depicted by the 1998 Workplace and Employee Relations Survey*. London: Routledge.

Cutcher-Gershenfeld, Joel, Thomas Kochan, and John Calhoun Wells. 2001. "In Whose Interest? A First Look at National Survey Data on Interest-Based Bargaining in Labor Relations". *Industrial Relations* 40(1): 1–21.

Cutcher-Gershenfeld, Joel, Donald Power, and Maureen McCabe-Power. 1996. "Global Implications of Recent Innovations in U.S. Collective Bargaining". *Relations Industrielles* 51(2): 281–301.

Cyert, R.M., and J.G. March. 1963. "A Behavioral Theory of Organizational Objectives". In M. Haire (Ed.), *Modern Organization Theory*. New York: John Wiley and Sons.

Dachraoui, Kais, Tarek Harchaoui, and Faouzi Tarkhani. 2003, "Productivity and Prosperity in the Information Age". *Perspectives on Labour and Income* 15(3): 43–46.

Davies, Jack. 2000. "International Comparisons of Labour Disputes in 1998". *Labour Market Trends* (U.K. Office of National Statistics), April.

Dahl, R. 1961. *Who Governs: Democracy and Power in An American City*. New Haven: Yale University Press.

Dahrendorf, R. 1957. *Class and Class Conflict in Industrial Society*. Stanford: Stanford University Press.

Delaney, John, and John Godard. 2001. "An Industrial Relations Perspective on the High Performance Paradigm". *The Human Resource Management Review (U.S.)* 11: 395–429.

DiNardo, John, and Thomas Lemieux. 1997. "Diverging Male Wage Inequality in the United States and Canada. 1981–1988". *Industrial and Labor Relations Review* 50(4): 629–51.

Doeringer, P., and M. Piore. 1971. *Internal Labor Markets and Manpower Analysis*. Lexington, MA: Heath Lexington.

Domhoff, W. 1983. *Who Rules America Now?* Englewood Cliffs, NJ: Prentice Hall.

Donaldson, Lex. 1995. *American Anti-Management Theories of Organization*. Cambridge: Cambridge University Press.

——. 1990. "The Ethereal Hand: Organizational Economics and Management Theory". *Academy of Management Review* 15: 369–81.

Dore, Ronald. 1997. "The Distinctiveness of Japan". In Colin Crouch and Wolfgang Streeck (Eds.), *Political Economy of Modern Capitalism*. London: Sage.

Doremus, Paul, William Keller, Louis Pauly, and Simon Reich. 1998. *The Myth of the Global Corporation*. Princeton, NJ: Princeton University Press.

Doucouliagos, Christos, and Patrice Laroche. 2003. "What Do Unions Do to Productivity? A Meta-Analysis". *Industrial Relations* 42(4): 650–91.

Doucouliagos, Christos, and Patrice Laroche. 2009. "Unions and Profits: A Meta-Regression Analysis". *Industrial Relations* 48(1): 146–84.

Downie, B. 1989. "Third Party Assistance in Collective Bargaining". In A.S. Sethi (Ed.), *Collective Bargaining in Canada*. Toronto: Nelson.

Downs, A. 1957. *An Economic Theory of Democracy*. New York: Harper Brothers.

Drache, Daniel, and Harry Glasbeek. 1992. *The Changing Workplace*. Toronto: Lorimer and Company.

Drago, Robert. 1996. "Workplace Transformation and the Disposable Workplace: Employee Involvement in Australia". *Industrial Relations* 35(4): 526–43.

Drolet, Marie. 2011. "Why Has the Gender Gap Narrowed?" *Perspectives on Labour and Income* 23(1): 3–13.

Drucker, P. 1989. *The New Realities*. New York: Harper and Row.

Dubofsky, Melvin. 1994. *The State and Labor In Modern America*, Chapel Hill, NC: University of North Carolina Press.

Dunlop, J. 1958. *Industrial Relations Systems*. New York: Holt.

——. 1944. *Wage Determination Under Trade Unions*. New York: Macmillan.

Durkheim, E. 1964 [1893]. *The Division of Labour in Society*. New York: The Free Press.

Dye, T. 1986. *Who's Running America Now?* Englewood Cliffs, NJ: Prentice Hall.

Eaton, J.K. 1975. "The Growth of the Canadian Labour Movement". *Labour Gazette* 75: 643–49.

Eden, G. 1993. "Industrial Discipline in the Canadian Federal Jurisdiction". *Relations Industrielles* 48(1): 163–79.

Edwards, P.K., and Colin Whitson. 1989. "Industrial Discipline, the Control of Attendance, and the Subordination of Labour". *Work, Employment, and Society* 3(1): 1–28.

Edwards, R. 1979. *Contested Terrain*. New York: Basic Books.

Ehrenberg, R., and R. Smith. 1985. *Modern Labor Economics*. Glenview, IL: Scott Foresnan.

Elliot, David, and Joanne Goss. 1994. *Grievance Mediation: How and Why it Works*. Aurora, ON: Canada Law Books.

England, G. 1983. "Some Observations on Selected Strike Laws". In K. Swan and K. Swinton (Eds.), *Studies in Labour Law*. Toronto: Butterworths.

England, Geoffery. 2005. "The Individual Employment Contract and Employment Legislation in Canada". In Morley Gunderson, Allen Ponak, and Daphne Taras (Eds.), *Union-Management Relations in Canada*, 5th Ed. Toronto: Pearson.

Etzioni, A. 1988. *The Moral Dimension: Toward A New Economics*. New York: The Free Press.

Evans, Martin, and Dan Ondrack. 1990. "The Role of Job Outcomes and Values in Understanding Union's Impact on Job Satisfaction: A Replication". *Human Relations* 43(5): 401–18.

Evans, W.M. 1993. *Organizational Theory: Research and Design*. New York: Macmillan.

Fang, Tony, and Morley Gunderson. 2009. "Minimum Wage Impacts on Older Workers: Longitudinal Estimates From Canada". *British Journal of Industrial Relations* 47(2): 371–87.

Fang, Tony, and Anil Verma. 2002. "Union Wage Premium". *Perspectives on Labour and Income* 14(4): 17–23.

Fantasia, R. 1988. *Cultures of Solidarity*. Berkeley: University of California Press.

Fantasia, R., D. Clawson, and G. Graham. 1988. "A Critical View of Worker Participation in American Industry". *Work and Occupations* 15: 468–88.

Farrar, Ann Layne. 2009. "An Empirical Assessment of the Employee Free Choice Act: The Economic Implications" <http://ssrn.com/abstract=1353305>.

Feller, David E. 1973. "A General Theory of the Collective Bargaining Agreement". *California Law Review* 61(3): 663–856.

Ferguson, Jean-Paul. 2008. "The Eyes of the Needles: A Sequential Model of Union Organizing". *Industrial and Labor Relations Review* 62(1): 3–21.

Fiorito, Jack, Paul Jarley, and John Thomas Delaney. 1995. "National Union Effectiveness in Organizing". *Industrial and Labor Relations Review* 48(4): 613–35.

Fligstein, N. 2001. *The Architecture of Markets*. Princeton, NJ: Princeton University Press.

Fisher, E.G., and Brian Willimas. 1989. "Negotiating the Union-Management Agreement". In John Anderson, Morley Gunderson, and Alan Ponack (Eds.), *Union Management Relations in Canada*, 2nd Ed. Toronto: Addison Wesley.

Fisher, R., and W. Ury. 1983. *Getting to Yes: Negotiating Agreement Without Giving In*. New York: Penguin Books.

Fligstein, Neil. 1996. "Markets as Politics: a Political-Cultural Approach to Market Institutions". *American Sociological Review* 61: 6556–673.

Forbath, W.E. 1991. *Law and the Shaping of the American Labor Movement*. Cambridge, MA: Harvard University Press.

Form, W. 1985. *Divided We Stand*. Urbana: University of Chicago Press.

Fox, A. 1974. *Beyond Contract: Work, Power, and Trust Relations*. London: Faber and Faber.

———. 1971. *A Sociology of Work in Industry*. London: Macmillan Company.

Freeman, Richard. 2007. "Do Workers Still Want Unions? More Than Ever". EPI Briefing Paper#182. Washington DC. Washington DC: Economic Policy Institute.

———. 1986. "Effects of Unions on the Economy". In S.M. Lipset (Ed.), *Unions in Transition*, pp. 177–200. San Francisco: ICS Press.

———. 1982. "Union Wage Practices and Wage Dispersion Within Establishments". *Industrial and Labor Relations Review* 36(1): 3–39.

———. 1980. "Unionism and the Dispersion of Wages". *Industrial and Labor Relations Review* 34: 3–23.

———. 1976. "Individual Mobility and Union Voice in the Labor Market". *American Economic Review* May: 234–62.

Freeman, Richard, and Edward Lazear. 1996. "An Economic Analysis of Works Councils". In Joel Rogers and Wolfgang Streeck (Eds.), *Works Councils: Consultation, Representation, and Cooperation in Industrial Relations*. Chicago: University of Chicago Press.

Freeman, Richard, and Morris Kleiner. 1999. "Do Unions Make Enterprises Insolvent?" *Industrial and Labor Relations Review* 52(4): 510–27.

Freeman, Richard, and Joel Rogers. 1999. *What Workers Want*. Ithaca, NY: Cornell University Press.

Freeman, R., and M. Kleiner. 1990. "Employer Behavior in the Face of Union Organizing Drives". *Industrial and Labor Relations Review* 43: 351–65.

Freeman, R., and J. Medoff. 1984. *What Do Unions Do?* New York: Basic Books.

———. 1979. "The Two Faces of Unionism". *The Public Interest* 57: 69–93.

Friedman, A. 1977. *Industry and Labour*. London: Macmillan.

Frost, Ann and Anil Verma. 1999. "Restructuring in Canadian Steel: the Case of Stelco Inc". In Anil Verma and Rick Chaykowski (Eds.), *Contract and Commitment: Employment Relations in the New Economy*, Kingston: IRC Press.

Fryer, John. 1995. "Provincial Public Sector Labour Relations". In Gene Swimmer and Mark Thompson (Eds.), *Public Sector Collective Bargaining in Canada*. Kingston, ON: IRC Press.

Gallie, D. 1978. *In Search of the New Working Class*. Cambridge: Cambridge University Press.

Gandz, J., and J.D. Whitehead. 1989. "Grievances and Their Resolution". In M. Gunderson et al. (Eds.), *Union-Management Relations in Canada*, 2nd Ed. Toronto: Addison Wesley.

Garrett, Geoffery. 1998. "Global Markets and National Politics: Collision Course of Virtuous Circle?" *International Organization* 52(4): 787–825.

Gennard, John, and Graham Judge. 1997. *Employee Relations*. London: Institute of Personnel and Development.

Giddens, A. 1971. *Capitalism and Modern Social Theory: Marx, Durkheim, and Max Weber*. London: Cambridge University Press.

Giles, A. 1989. "Industrial Relations Theory, The State, and Politics". In J. Barbash and K. Barbash (Eds.), *Theories and Concepts in Comparative Industrial Relations*. Columbia, SC: University of South Carolina Press.

Giles, A., and H. Jain. 1989. "The Collective Agreement". In M. Gunderson et al. (Eds.), *Union Management Relations in Canada*. Toronto: Addison Wesley.

Gilson, C.H.J., I. Spencer, and S. Granville. 1989. "The Impact of a Strike on the Attitudes and Behavior of a Rural Community". *Relations Industrielles* 44: 785–804.

Gindin, Sam. 1997. "Notes on Labor at the End of the Century: Starting Over?" *Monthly Review* 39(3): 140–57.

Glyn Andrew. 2006. *Capitalism Unleashed*. Oxford: Oxford University Press.

Glynn, Sean, and Howard Gospel. 1993. "Britain's Low Skill Equilibrium: A Problem of Demand?" *Industrial Relations Journal* 24(2): 112–25.

Godard, John. 2011. "The Correlates of Union Voting Propensity: A Union Organizing Approach". *Industrial Relations*, forthcoming.

———. 2010. "What's Best for Workers? The Implications of Work and Human Resource Practices Revisited". *Industrial Relations* 49(3) (July): 465–87.

———. 2009a. "Institutional Environments, Work and Human Resource Practices, and Unions: Canada Versus England". *Industrial and Labor Relations Review* 62(2): 173–99.

———. 2009b. "What Has Happened to Strikes?" Paper presented at the British Journal of Industrial Relations Symposium in Honour of Richard Hyman, June 28–29, 2009.

———. 2008. "Union Formation". In Paul Blyton, Nicolas Bacon, Jack Fiorito, and Edmund Heery (eds.), *The Sage Handbook of Industrial Relations*, pp. 377–405. London: Sage Publications.

———. 2005. *Industrial Relations, the Economy, and Society*, 3rd ed. Scarborough ON: Captus Press.

———. 2004a. "A Critical Assessment of the High Performance Paradigm". *British Journal of Industrial Relations* 42(2): 349–78.

———. 2004b. *Trade Union Recognition: Statutory Unfair Labour Practice Regimes in the USA and Canada*. Employment Relations Research Paper Series No. 29, Department of Trade and Industry, UK Government.

———. 2004c. "The New Institutionalism, Capitalist Diversity, and Industrial Relations". In Bruce Kaufman (Ed.), *Theoretical Perspectives on Work and the Employment Relationship*. Urbana-Champaign, Ill: Industrial Relations Research Association.

———. 2004d. "Work and the Quality of Democracy in Canada". Unpublished working paper, University of Manitoba.

———. 2003a. "Do Labour Laws Matter: The Union Decline and Convergence Thesis Revisited". *Industrial Relations* 42(3): 458–92.

———. 2003b. "Labour Unions, Workplace Rights, and Canadian Public Policy". *Canadian Public Policy* 29(4): 449–67.

———. 2003c. "Manitoba: Beyond the Class Divide?" In Mark Thompson, Joe Rose, and Anthony Smith (Eds.), *Beyond the National Divide*. Montreal: McGill-Queen's University Press.

———. 2002. "Institutional Environments, Employment Practices, and the State in Liberal Market Economies". *Industrial Relations* 41(2): 249–86.

———. 2001. "The Transformation of Work *and* High Performance? The Implications of Alternative Work Practices for the Experience and Outcomes of Work". *Industrial and Labor Relations Review* 54(4): 776–805.

———. 1999a. "Post-Industrial Society? Work and Alienation in Late Twentieth Century Canada". Working Paper, Faculty of Management, the University of Manitoba.

———. 1999b. "Do Implementation Processes and Rationales Matter? The Case of Workplace Reforms". *Journal of Management Studies* 36(5): 679–704.

———. 1998a. "An Organizational Theory of Variation in the Management of Labor". In David Lewin and Bruce Kaufman (Eds.), *Advances in Industrial and Labor Relations*, Vol. 8, pp. 25–66.

———. 1998b. "Strikes and the Law: A Critical Analysis". *Relations Industrielles* 53(2): 258–77.

———. 1997a. "Managerial Strategies, Labour and Employment Relations, and the State". *British Journal of Industrial Relations* 35(3): 399–426.

———. 1997b. "Whither Strategic Choice: Do Managerial IR Ideologies Matter?" *Industrial Relations* 36(2): 206–28.

———. 1997c. "Beliefs About Unions and What They Should Do: A Survey of Employed Canadians". *Journal of Labor Research* 18(4): 621–40.

———. 1996, "In Search of Managerial Ideologies". *Proceedings of the 1996 Annual Meeting of the Industrial Relations Research Association (IRRA)*. Madison, WI: IRRA.

———. 1993a. "Structural Inequality and the Management of Labour". *Work and Occupations* 20(3): 337–67.

———. 1993b. "Beyond Empiricism: Toward A Reconstruction of IR Theory and Research". *Advances in Industrial and Labor Relations* 6: 1–35.

———. 1992a. "Education vs. Training in Business Schools". *Canadian Journal of Administrative Science* 9: 238–52.

———. 1992b. "Strikes as Collective Voice: A Behavioral Analysis of Strike Activity". *Industrial and Labor Relations Review* 46: 161–75.

———. 1992c. "Strikes as Collective Voice: Towards An Integrative Theory of Strike Activity". *Proceedings of the 44th Annual Meetings of the Industrial Relations Research Association*.

———. 1991. "The Progressive HRM Paradigm: A Theoretical and Empirical Re-examination". *Relations Industrielles* 46: 378–99.

Godard, John, and John Delaney. 2000. "Reflections of the High Performance Paradigm's Implications for IR as a Field". *Industrial and Labor Relations Review* 53(2): 482–502.

Godard, John, and Carola Frege. 2010. "Union Decline, Alternative Forms of Representation, and Workplace Authority Relations in the United States". Accepted for the competitive papers session of the Annual Meetings of the Labor and Employment Relations Association (LERA), Denver, Colorado, January 6–9, 2011.

Gomez, Raphael, Morley Gunderson, and Noah Meltz, 2002. "Comparing Youth and Adult Desire for Unionization in Canada". *British Journal of Industrial Relations* 40(3): 521–42.

Gordon, D., R. Edwards, and M. Reich. 1982. *Segmented Work, Divided Workers*. Cambridge: Cambridge University Press.

Gordon, D.M. 1976. "Capitalist vs. Socialist Efficiency". *Monthly Review* 28: 19–39.

Gordon, Michael, and Angelo DeNisi. 1995. "A Re-examination of the Relationship Between Union Membership and Job Satisfaction, *Industrial and Labor Relations Review* 48(2): 222–36.

Gospel. Howard, and Andrew Pendleton. 2003. "Finance, Corporate Governance, and the Management of Labour". *British Journal of Industrial Relations* 41(3): 557–82.

Gouldner, A. 1954. *Wildcat Strike*. Yellow Springs, OH: Antioch Press.

Gramm, C., W. Hendricks, and L. Kahn. 1988. "Inflation, Uncertainty, and Strikes". *Industrial Relations* 27: 114–29.

Gramsci, A. 1971. *Selections from Prison Notebooks*. New York: International Publishers.

Grant, Hugh. 1990. "Contradictions and Limitations of Final Offer Selection: the Manitoba Experience: A Comment". *Relations Industrielles* 454(1): 164–66.

Groshen, Erica, and David Levine. 1998. "The Rise and Decline (?) of U.S. Internal Labor Markets". Federal Reserve Bank of New York, Research Paper #9819.

Gunderson, M. 1988. "Labor Economics and Industrial Relations". In G. Hébert, H.C. Jain, and N.M. Meltz (Eds.). *The State of the Art in Industrial Relations*. Kingston, ON: Industrial Relations Centre, Queens University.

Gunderson, M., J. Kervin, and F. Reid. 1986. "Logit Estimates of Strike Incidence from Canadian Contract Data". *Journal of Labor Economics* 4(2): 257–76.

———. 1985. *The Effect of Labour Relations Legislation on Strike Incidence*. Toronto: University of Toronto Centre for Industrial Relations.

Gunderson, Morley. 1998. "Harmonization of Labour Policies Under Trade Liberalization". *Relations Industrielles* 53(1): 24–54.

Haiven, Larry. 1995. "On Bringing Back the Right to Strike and Lockout In Midterm". In C. Gonick, P. Philips, and J. Vorst (Eds.), *Labour Gains, Labour Pains: Fifty Years of PC 1003*. Toronto: Fernwood.

———. 1991. "Hegemony and the Workplace: The Role of Arbitration". In L. Haiven et al. (Eds.), *Regulating Labour*. Toronto: Garamond Press.

Haiven, L., S. McBride, and J. Shields. 1991. "The State, Neo-Conservatism, and Industrial Relations". In L. Haiven, S. McBride, and J. Shields (Eds.), *Regulating Labour*. Toronto: Garamond Press.

Hale, Dominic. 2008. "International Comparisons of Labour Disputes". *Economic and Labour Market Review* 2(4): 32–39.

Hall, Peter, and David Soskice. 2001. "An Introduction to Varieties of Capitalism". In Peter Hall and David Soskice (Eds.), *Varieties of Capitalism: Institutional Foundations of Comparative Advantage*. Oxford: Oxford University Press.

Hammer, Tove Helland, and Ariel Avgar. 2005. "The Impact of Unions on Job Satisfaction, Organizational Commitment, and Turnover". *Journal of Labor Research* 26(2): 241–66.

Harris, H.J. 1982. *The Right To Manage*. Madison: The University of Wisconsin Press.

Harvey, D. 1982. *The Limits to Capital*. Oxford: Basil Blackwell.

Hayes, B. 1984. "Unions and Strikes with Asymmetric Information". *Journal of Labor Economics* 2: 57–78.

Headley, B.W. 1970. "Trade Unions and National Wage Politics". *Journal of Politics* 32: 407–39.

Hebdon, Robert. 2005. "Toward a Theory of Workplace Conflict: The Case of US Municipal Bargaining". *Advances in Industrial and Labor Relations* 14: 33–65.

Hebdon, Robert, and Travor Brown. 2008. *Industrial Relations in Canada*. Toronto: Nelson.

Hebdon, Robert, and Robert Stern. 2003. "Do Public-Sector Strike Bans Really Prevent Conflict?" *Industrial Relations* 42(3): 493–512.

———. 1998. "Tradeoffs Among Expressions of Industrial conflict: Public Sector Strike Bans and Grievance Arbitrations". *Industrial and Labor Relations Review* 50(2): 204–21.

Heckscher, C. 1988. *The New Unionism: Employee Involvement in the Changing Corporation*. New York: Basic Books.

Hepple, Bob. 1986. "Introduction". In Bob Hepple (Ed.), *The Making of Labour Law in Europe*. London: Mansell Publishing Ltd.

Heron, C. 1989. *The Canadian Labour Movement*. Toronto: Lorimer.

Heron, C., and B. Palmer. 1987. "Through the Prism of the Strike: Industrial Conflict in Southern Ontario. 1901–1914". In D. Bercuson (Ed.), *Canadian Labour History*. Toronto: Copp Clark Pitman.

Hicks, J.R. 1932. *The Theory of Wages*. London: Macmillan.

Hirsch, B. 1992. "Firm Investment Behavior and Collective Bargaining Strategy". *Industrial Relations* 31: 95–121.

Hirsch, B., and M. Berger. 1984. "Union Membership Determination and Industry Characteristics". *Canadian Journal of Economics* 50: 665–79.

Hirsch, Barry, David MacPherson, and J. Michael Dumond. 1997. "Workers' Compensation Recipiency in Union and Nonunion Workplaces". *Industrial and Labor Relations Review* 50(2): 213–36.

Hirst, Paul and Grahame Thompson. 1999. *Globalization in Question*. Oxford: Polity Press.

Hodgson, G. 1988. *Economics and Institutions*. Philadelphia: University of Philadelphia Press.

Hodson, R. 1984. "Corporate Structure and Job Satisfaction". *Social Science Quarterly* 66: 266–80.

Hodson, R., and T. Sullivan. 1990. *The Social Organization of Work*. Belmont, CA: Wadsworth.

Hooks, G. 1993. "The U.S. State's Dominance of the World War II Investment Process". *American Sociological Review* 58: 37–53.

Human Resource Development Canada (HRDC), Workplace Information Directorate. 2000. *Labour Legislation in Canada* <http://www.hrsdc.gc.ca/en/gateways/nav/top_nav/program/labour.shtml>.

———. 1999. *Directory of Labour Organizations in Canada*, Ottawa: Minister of Industry.

Human Rights Watch. 2000. *Unfair Advantage: Workers' Freedom of Association in the United States Under International Human Rights Standards*. New York: Human Rights Watch.

Hunter, L.W., and R.B, McKersie. 1992. "Can Mutual Gains Training Change Labor-Management Relationships? *Negotiation Journal* 8: 319–30.

Hutton, W. 1995. *The State We're In*. London: Jonathon Cape.

Hyman, R. 1987. "Strategy or Structure? Capital, Labour, and Control". *Work, Employment, and Society* 1(1): 25–55.

———. 1977. *Strikes*, 2nd Ed. Glasgow: Fontana/Collins.

———. 1975. *Industrial Relations: A Marxist Introduction*. London: The Macmillan Press.

Hyman, R., and I. Brough. 1975. *Social Values and Industrial Relations*. Oxford: Basil Blackwell.

Isaac, J.C. 1988. *Power and Marxist Theory*. Ithaca, NY: Cornell University Press.

Jacoby, Sanford. 2000. "Melting into Air? Downsizing, Job Stability and the Future of Work". *Chicago-Kent Law Review* 76: 1195–34.

———. 1997. *Modern Manors: Welfare Capitalism Since the New Deal*. Princeton, NJ: Princeton University Press.

———. 1985. *Employing Bureaucracy*. New York: Columbia University Press.

Jamieson, S. 1968. *Times of Trouble: Labour Unrest and Industrial Conflict in Canada, 1900–66*. Ottawa: Minister of Supply and Services.

Jessop, Bob. 1990. *State Theory: Putting Capitalist States in Their Place*. University Park, PA: Pennsylvania State University Press.

Johnson, Holly. 1994. "Work-Related Sexual Harassment". *Perspectives on Labour and Income* 6(4): 9–12.

Johnson, Susan. 2009. "Comments on *An Empirical Assessment of the Employee Free Choice Act: The Economic Implications* by Ann Layne Farrar". *Just Labour* 15 (Nov.): 46–59.

Jones, S. 1990. "Worker Interdependence and Output: The Hawthorne Studies Reevaluated". *American Journal of Sociology* 55: 176–90.

Kalecki, Michael. 1971 [1943]. "Political Aspects of Full Employment". In Michael Kalecki (Ed.), *Selected Essays on the Dynamics of the Capitalist Economy, 1933–1970*. Cambridge, UK: Cambridge University Press.

Katz, H., and T. Kochan. 1992. *An Introduction to Collective Bargaining and Industrial Relations*. New York: McGraw Hill.

Kaufman, Bruce. 2010. "SHRM Theory in the Post-Huselid Era: Why it is Fundamentally Misspecified?" *Industrial Relations* 49(2): 286–313.

——. 1992. "Research on Strike Models and Outcomes in the 1980s". In D. Lewin et al. (Eds.), *Research Frontiers in Industrial Relations and Human Resources*. Madison, WI: IRRA.

——. 1991. "Labor's Inequality of Bargaining Power: Myth or Reality?" *Journal of Labor Research* 12: 151–65.

——. 1981. "Bargaining Theory, Inflation, and Cyclical Strike Activity in Manufacturing". *Industrial and Labor Relations Review* 34: 333–55.

Kealey, G. 1986. "1919: The Canadian Labour Revolt". In B. Palmer (Ed.), *The Character of the Class Struggle: Essays in Canadian Working Class History, 1850–1985*, pp. 90–114. Toronto: McClelland and Stewart.

——. 1973. *Canada Investigates Industrialism*. Toronto: University of Toronto Press.

Kealey, G., and B. Palmer. 1986. "The Bonds of Unity: The Knights of Labour in Ontario, 1880–1900". In B. Palmer (Ed.), *The Character of the Class Struggle: Essays in Canadian Working Class History, 1850–1985*, pp. 90–114. Toronto: McClelland and Stewart.

Kelly, John. 1998. *Rethinking Industrial Relations*. London, UK: Routledge.

Kerr, C., J.T. Dunlop, F.H. Harbison, and C.A. Myers. 1964. *Industrialism and Industrial Man, 2nd Ed.* New York: Oxford University Press.

Kerr, C., and A. Siegel. 1954. "The Interindustry Propensity to Strike". In Kornhauser et al. (Eds.), *Industrial Conflict*. New York: McGraw-Hill.

Klare, K.E. 1988. "Workplace Democracy and Market Reconstruction: An Agenda for Legal Reform". *Catholic University Law Review* 38(1): 1–49.

Knight, T. 1987a. "Tactical Use of the Union's Duty of Fair Representation". *Industrial and Labour Relations Review* 40: 180–94.

——. 1987b. "The Role of the Duty of Fair Representation". *Relations Industrielles* 42: 716–36.

Kochan, Thomas A. 1991. *Transforming Industrial Relations: A Blueprint for Change*. Kingston: Queen's University Industrial Relations Centre.

——. 1980. *Collective Bargaining and Industrial Relations*. Homewood, IL: Richard D. Irwin Inc.

——. 1973. "Correlates of State Public Employee Bargaining Laws". *Industrial Relations* 12: 322–37.

Kochan, Thomas A., and R. Block. 1977. "An Interindustry Analysis of Bargaining Outcomes". *Quarterly Journal of Economics* 32: 431–52.

Kochan, Thomas A., and P. Cappelli. 1983. "The Transformation of the Industrial Relations/Human Resources Function". In P. Osterman (Ed.), *Internal Labor Markets*. Cambridge, MA: MIT Press.

Kochan, Thomas A., and H. Katz. 1988. *Collective Bargaining and Industrial Relations*, 2nd Ed. Homewood, IL: Irwin.

Kochan, Thomas A., R. McKersie, and P. Cappelli. 1984. "Strategic Choice and Industrial Relations Theory". *Industrial Relations* 23: 16–39.

Kochan, Thomas A., and H. Wheeler. 1975. "Municipal Collective Bargaining: A Model and Analysis of Bargaining Outcomes" *Industrial Relations* 29: 53–72.

Kochan, Thomas A., H. Katz, and R. McKersie. 1986. *The Transformation of Industrial Relations*. New York: Basic Books.

Kochan, Thomas A., and Paul Osterman. 1994. *The Mutual Gains Enterprise*. Boston, MA: Harvard Business School Press.

Kohn, M. 1979. *Class and Conformity: A Study of Values*, 2nd Ed. Chicago, IL: University of Chicago Press.

Kohn, M., A. Naoi, C. Shoenbach, C. Schooler, and K. Slomczynski. 1990. "Position in the Class Structure and Psychological Functioning in the U.S., Japan, and Poland". *American Journal of Sociology* 95(4): 964–1008.

Korpi, W. 1983. *The Democratic Class Struggle*. London: Routledge and Kegan Paul.

——. 1974. "Conflict, Power, and Relative Deprivation". *American Political Science Review* 68: 569–78.

Korpi, W., and M. Shalev. 1980. "Strikes, Power, and Politics in the Western Nations, 1900–1976". In Maurice Zeitlin (Ed.), *Political Power and Social Theory, I*, pp. 301–34. Greenwich, CT: Jai Press.

Kotz, David M., Terrence McDonough, and Michael Reich. 1994. *Social Structures of Accumulation: the Political Economy of Growth and Crisis*. Cambridge: Cambridge University Press.

Krahn, H.J., and G.S. Lowe. 1998. *Work, Industry, and Canadian Society*, 3rd Ed. Scarborough, ON: Nelson.

Krahn, H., and G. Lowe. 1984. "Public Attitudes Toward Unions: Some Canadian Evidence". *Journal of Labor Research* 5: 149–64.

Kumar, Pradeep, and Noah Meltz. 1992. "Industrial Relations in the Canadian Auto Industry". In Rick Chaykowski and Anil Verma (Eds.), *Industrial Relations in Canadian Industry*. Toronto: Holt, Rinehart, and Winston.

Lacroix, R. 1986. "Strike Activity in Canada". In C. Riddell (Ed.), *Canadian Labour Relations*, pp. 161–209. Toronto: University of Toronto Press.

Landsberger, H. 1958. *Hawthorne Revisited*. Ithaca, NY: Cornell University Press.

Landsbergis, Paul, Janet Cahill, and Peter Schnall. 1999. "The Impact of Lean Production and Related New Systems of Work Organization on Worker Health". *Journal of Occupational Health Psychology* 4(2): 108–30.

Laporta, Pasquale, and Alexander Jenkins. 1996. "Unionization and Profitability in the Canadian Manufacturing Sector". *Relations Industrielles* 51(4): 756–77.

LaRochelle-Côté, Sebastian and Claude Dionne. 2009. "International Differences in Low-Paid Work". *Perspectives on Labour and Income* 21(3): 5–13.

Lazear, E.P. 1992. "Compensation, Productivity, and the New Economics of Personnel". In David Lewin et al., *Research Frontiers in Industrial Relations and Human Resources*. Madison, WI: IRRA.

———. 1986. "Salaries and Piece Rates". *Journal of Business* 59: 405–31.

Leap, T.L., and D.W. Grigsby. 1986. "Power and the Bargaining Process". *Industrial and Labor Relations Review* 39: 202–13.

Legge, Karen. 1995. *Human Resource Management: Rhetorics and Realities*. London: Macmillan.

———. 1989. "Human Resource Management — A Critical Analysis". In John Storey (ed.), *New Perspectives in Human Resource Management*, pp. 19–40. London: Routledge.

Leiserson, W. 1973. "Employment Management, Employee Representation, and Industrial Democracy". In A. Nash and J.B. Miner (Eds.), *Personnel and Industrial Relations: An Evolutionary Approach*. New York: Macmillan.

Lennin, E. 1976. "Organizing the Unorganized: Unionization in the Chartered Banks of Canada". *Osgoode Hall Law Journal* 18: 177.

Leonard, J. 1992. "Unions and Employment Growth". *Industrial Relations* 31: 80–94.

———. 1985. "The Effects of Unions on the Employment of Blacks, Hispanics, and Women". *Industrial and Labor Relations Review* 39: 115–32.

Lester, R.A. 1958. *As Unions Mature*. Princeton, NJ: Princeton University Press.

Lewchuk, Don, and Don Wells. 2006. "When Corporations Substitute for Adversarial Unions: Labour Markets and Human Resource Development at Magna". *Relations Industrielles* 61(4): 639–56.

Lewin, David, and Richard Peterson. 1999. "Behavioral Outcomes of Grievance Activity". *Industrial Relations* 38(1): 554–76.

Lewin, D., and R. Peterson. 1988. *The Modern Grievance Procedure in the American Economy*. Westport, CT: Quorum.

Lichtenstein, N. 1985. "UAW Bargaining Strategy and Shop-Floor Conflict, 1946–1970". *Industrial Relations* 24: 360–81.

Lin, Jane. 2008. "Trends in Employment and Wages". *Perspectives on Labour and Income* 20(4): 5–15.

Lipietz, A. 1987. *Mirages and Miracles*. London: Verso.

Lipset, Seymour M. 1960. *Political Man*. New York: Doubleday.

Lipset, Seymour M., and Noah Meltz. 2000. "Estimates of Nonunion Employee Representation in the United States and Canada". In Bruce E Kaufman and Daphne Gottlieb Taras (eds.), *Nonunion Employee Representation*, pp. 223–30. Armonk NY: ME: Sharpe.

———. 1998. "Canadian and American Attitudes Toward Work and Institutions". *Perspectives on Work* 1(3): 14–19.

Littler, C. 1990. "The Labour Process Debate: A Theoretical Review, 1974–88". In D. Knights and H. Wilmott (Eds.), *Labour Process Theory*. London: Gower.

Livingstone, D.W. 1999. *The Education-Jobs Gap: Underemployment or Economic Democracy*. Toronto: Garamond Press.

Lowe, G. 1984. "The Rise of Modern Management in Canada". In G. Lowe and H.J. Krahn (Eds.), *Working Canadians*. Toronto: Methuen.

———. 1979. "The Rise of Modern Management in Canada". *Canadian Dimension* 14(3): 32–38. Reprinted in G. Lowe and H. Krahn (Eds.), 1984. *Working Canadians*. Toronto: Methuen.

Lowe, Graham. 2000. *The Quality of Work. A People Centred Agenda*. Don Mills, ON: Oxford University Press.

MacDowell, Laurel Sefton. 1993. "After the Strike — Labour Relations in Oshawa, 1937–1939". *Relations Industrielles* 48(4): 691–711.

MacPherson, C.B. 1973. *Democratic Theory*. London: Oxford University Press.

Mahoney, Karen, and T. Decktop, 1986. "Evolution of Concept and Practice in Personnel Administration/Human Resource Management". *Journal of Management* 12(2): 223–41.

Maranto, C., and J. Fiorito. 1987. "The Effects of Union Characteristics on the Outcomes of NLRB Certification Elections". *Industrial and Labor Relations Review* 40: 225–40.

March, J. 1981. "Decisions in Organizations and Theories of Choice". In A. Van de Ven and W. Joyce (Eds.), *Perspectives on Organization Design and Behavior*. New York: Wiley.

March, J., and J.P. Olsen. 1976. *Ambiguity and Choice in Organizations*. Bergen, Norway: Universitetsforlaget.

March, J., and H. Simon. 1958. *Organizations*. New York: John Wiley.

Marshall, Katherine. 2010. "Employer Top-ups". *Perspectives on Labour and Income* 22(1): 43–50.

Martin, C.J. 1989. "Business Influence and State Power: The Case of U.S. Corporate Tax Policy". *Politics and Society* 17: 189–223.

Martin, Ross. 1989. *Trade Unionism: Purpose and Forms*. Oxford: Clarendon Press.

Marx, K. 1967 [1867]. *Capital, Vol. 1*. London: Lawrence and Wilhart.

———. 1959 [1844]. *Economic and Philosophic Manuscripts of 1844*. Moscow: Progress Publishers.

———. 1958 [1865]. "Wages, Prices, and Profit". In K. Marx and F. Engels, *Selected Works, Vol. 1*. Moscow: Progress Publishers.

———. 1953 [1858]. *The Grundisse*. Harmondsworth: Middlesex.

Marx, K., and F. Engels. 1972 [1848]. "The German Ideology: Part I". In R.C. Tucker (Ed.), *The Marx-Engels Reader*. New York: Norton.

———. 1958 [1847]. "Wage Labour and Capital". In K. Marx and F. Engels, *Selected Works, Vol. 1*, pp. 92–93.

Mayo, E. 1933. *The Human Problems of an Industrial Civilization*. New York: The MacMillan Company.

McConnell, S. 1989. "Strikes, Wages, and Private Information". *American Economic Review* 79: 801–13.

McDonald, David. 2010. "Success is No Accident". *CCPA*, April 2010.

McQuarrie, Fiona. 2010. "In Good Faith? An Analysis of the Features and Outcomes of Duty of Fair Representation Cases". *Relations Industrielles* 65(1): 118–33.

———. 2006. *Industrial Relations in Canada*. Toronto: John Wiley and Sons.

McKinlay, Alan, and Phil Taylor. 1996. "Power, Surveillance, and Resistance: Inside the factory of the Future". In Peter Ackers, Chris Smith, and Paul Smith (Eds.), *The New Workplace and Trade Unionism*. London: Routledge.

Meltz, N. 1989. "Industrial Relations: Balancing Efficiency and Equity". In Jack and Kate Barbash (Eds.), *Theories and Concepts in Comparative Industrial Relations*. Columbia, SC: University of South Carolina Press.

Meng, R.A. 1990. "Union Effects on Wage Dispersion in Canadian Industry". *Economic Letters* 32: 399–403.

Michels, Robert. 1959 [1911]. *Political Parties*. New York: Dover.

Miliband, R. 1969. *The State in Capitalist Society*. New York: Basic Books.

Mills, A., and S. Murgatroyd. 1991. *Organizational Rules*. Philadelphia: Open University Press.

Mills, C. Wright. 1956. *The Power Elite*. New York: Oxford University Press.

———. 1948. *The New Men of Power*. Englewood Cliffs, NJ: Harcourt Brace.

Mishel, L. 1986. "The Structural Determinants of Union Bargaining Power". *Industrial and Labor Relations Review* 40: 90–104.

Mitchell, Daniel, and Mahmood Zaidi. 1996. "A Too Narrow Report on American Labor Policy". unpublished manuscript.

Mitroff, Ian. 1983. *Stakeholders of the Organizational Mind*. San Francisco: Jossey Bass.

Morisette, Rene, and X. Zhang 2007. "Revisiting Wealth Inequality." *Perspectives* 19(1): 6–17.

Morissette, R., and J.M. Rosa. 2003. "Alternative Work Practices and Quit Rates: Methodological Issues and Empirical Evidence for Canada". Ottawa: Statistics Canada Business and Labour Market Analysis Division, Catalogue no. 11F0019MIE — No. 199.

Morrill, Calvin, Mayer N. Zald, and Hatagreeva Rao. 2003. "Covert Political Conflict in Organizations". *Annual Review of Sociology* 29: 391–415.

Morton, D. 1989. "The History of the Canadian Labour Movement". In J. Anderson, M. Gunderson, and A. Ponak (Eds.), *Union-Management Relations in Canada*. Don Mills: Addison Wesley.

Mosca, G. 1939 [1896]. *The Ruling Class* (H.D. Kahn, Trans.). New York: McGraw Hill.

Mueller, D.C. 1989. *Public Choice II*. Cambridge: Cambridge University Press.

Murphy, Brian, Paul Roberts, and Michael Wolfson. 2007. "High-income Canadians". *Perspectives on Labour and Income* 19(4): 7–20.

Murray, G., and A. Giles. 1988. "Towards an Historical Understanding of Industrial Relations Theory in Canada". *Relations Industrielles* 43(4): 780–811.

Naisbitt, J. 1982. *Megatrends: Ten New Directions Transforming Our Lives*. New York: Warner.

Nelson, D. 1975. *Managers and Workers: Origins of the New Factory System in the U.S., 1880–1920*. Madison: University of Wisconsin Press.

Nelson, R., and S. Winter. 1982. *An Evolutionary Theory of Economic Change*. Boston: Belknap Press.

Neumark, David, and William Wascher. 2004. "Minimum Wages, Labor Market Institutions, and Youth Employment: A Cross-National Analysis". *Industrial and Labor Relations Review* 57(2): 223–48.

Nyland, Chris. 1998. "Taylorism and the Mutual-Gains Strategy". *Industrial Relations* 37(4): 519–42.

O'Toole, J., et al. 1974. *Work in America: A Report To The Secretary of Health, Education, and Welfare*. Cambridge, MA: MIT Press.

Offe, C. 1985. "The Political Economy of the Labour Market". In C. Offe, *Disorganized Capitalism*. Cambridge, MA: MIT Press.

———. 1984. *Contradictions of the Welfare State*. London: Hutchison.

Ogders, Cameron W., and Julian Betts. 1997. "Do Unions Reduce Investment? Evidence from Canada". *Industrial and Labor Relations Review* 51(1): 18–36.

Ollman, B. 1971. *Alienation: Marx's Conception of Man in Capitalist Society*. Cambridge, U.K.: Cambridge University Press.

Olsen, Gregg. 2002. *The Politics of the Welfare State: Canada, Sweden, and the United States*. Don Mills, ON: Oxford University Press.

Organisation for Economic Co-operation and Development (OECD). 2004. *OECD Employment Outlook*. Paris: OECD.

Orum, A.M. 1988. "Political Sociology". In N. Smelser (Ed.), *Handbook of Sociology*. Newbury Park, CA: Sage Publishing.

Ozaki, M. 1999. *Negotiating Flexibility*. Geneva: International Labour Office.

Palmer, B. 1992. *Working Class Experience: Rethinking the History of Canadian Labour, 1800–1991*. Toronto: McClelland and Stewart.

Panetta, Alexander. 2001. "Canadians Feeling Poorer". *Winnipeg Free Press*. September 24: B1.

Panitch, L., and D. Swartz. 1985. *From Consent to Coercion: The Assault on Trade Union Freedoms*. Toronto: Garamond Press.

Panitch, Leo, and Donald Swartz. 2003. *From Consent to Coercion: the Assault on Trade Union Freedoms*, 3rd. Ed. Aurora, ON: Garamond Press.

Pareto, V. 1935 [1915–1919]. *The Mind and Society, Vols I–IV*. London: Jonathon Cape.

Parkin, F. 1982. *Max Weber*. London: Tavistock.

Parsons, T., and N. Smelser. 1956. *Economy and Society*. Glencoe, IL: Free Press.

Peach, D., and P. Bergman. 1991. *The Practice of Labour Relations*. Toronto: McGraw-Hill Ryerson.

Peirce, Jon. 2000. *Canadian Industrial Relations*. Scarborough: Prentice Hall.

Perlman, Selig. 1949 [1928]. *A Theory of the Labor Movement*. New York: Augustus Kelly.

Pfeffer, Jeffrey. 1998. *The Human Equation*. Boston, MA: Harvard Business School Press.

———. 1994. *Competitive Advantage Through People*. Boston, MA: Harvard Business School Press.

Pfeffer, J., and G. Salancik. 1978. *The External Control of Organizations: A Resource Dependence Perspective*. New York: Harper and Row.

Pierson, Paul and Theda Skocpol. 2002. "Historical Institutionalism in Contemporary Political Science". In Izra Katznelson and Helen Milner (Eds.), *Political Science: the State of the Discipline*. New York: W.W. Norton & Company.

Piore, M. 1986. "Perspectives on Labor Market Flexibility". *Industrial Relations* 25: 146–66.

Piven, F.F., and R. Cloward. 1979. *Poor People's Movements*. New York: Random House.

Polanyi, K. 1944. *The Great Transformation*. Boston, MA: Beacon Press.

Polsby, N. 1980. *Community Power and Political Theory*, 2nd Ed. New Haven: Yale University Press.

Ponak, A., and C. Olson. 1993. "Time Delays in Grievance Arbitration". *Relations Industrielles* 47: 690–708.

Ponak, A., and L. Falkenberg. 1990. "Resolution of Interest Disputes". In A.S. Sethi (Ed.), *Collective Bargaining in Canada*, pp. 260–94. Toronto: Nelson.

Ponak, Allen, and Mark Thompson. 2001. "Public Sector Collective Bargaining". In Morley Gunderson, Allen Ponak, and Daphne Gottlieb Taras (Eds.), *Union-Management Relations in Canada*, 4th ed. Toronto: Addison-Wesley Longman.

Ponak, Allen, Wilfred Zerbe, Sarah Rose, and Corliss Olson. 1996. "Using Event History Analysis to Model Delay in Grievance Arbitration". *Industrial and Labor Relations Review* 50(1): 105–21.

Poole, M. 1981. *Theories of Trade Unionism: A Sociology of Industrial Relations*. London: Routledge and Kegan Paul.

Porter, Michael. 1992. "Capital Disadvantage: America's Failing Capital Investment System". *Harvard Business Review* Sept.–Oct.: 65–82.

———. 1990. *The Competitive Advantage of Nations*. New York: Free Press.

Poulantzas, N. 1978. *Political Power and Social Classes*. London: Verso.

Prechel, H. 1990. "Steel and State: Politics and Business Policy Formation, 1940–1989". *American Sociological Review* 55: 648–68.

Quan, N. 1984. "Unionism and the Size Distribution of Earnings". *Industrial Relations* 23: 270–77.

Reder, M., and G. Neumann. 1980. "Conflict and Contract: The Case of Strikes". *Journal of Political Economy* 60: 371–82.

Reed, M. 1989. *The Sociology of Management*. New York: Harvester Weatsheaf.

———. 1985. *Redirections in Organizational Analysis*. London: Tavistock Publications.

Rees, A. 1952. "Industrial Conflict and Business Fluctuations". *Journal of Political Economy* 60: 37–82.

Renaud, Stephane, 2002. "Rethinking the Union Membership/Job Satisfaction Relationship: Some Empirical Evidence from Canada". *International Journal of Manpower* 23(2): 137–50.

———. 1998. "Unions, Wages and Total Compensation in Canada: An Empirical Study". *Relations Industrielles* 53(4): 710–29.

Reshef, Yonatan, and Sandra Rastin. 2003. *Unions in the Time of Revolution*. Toronto: University of Toronto.

Reynolds, M. 1991. "The Myth of Labor's Inequality of Bargaining Power". *Journal of Labor Research* 12: 167–83.

Reynolds, M. 1984. *Power and Privilege: Labor Unions in America*. New York: Universe.

Riddell, Chris. 2010. "The Causal Effect of Election Delay on Union Win Rates". *Industrial Relations* 49(3): 371–86.

Rinehart, James. 1996. *The Tyranny of Work*, 3rd Ed. Toronto: Harcourt Brace.

Robbins, S.P. 1992. *Essentials of Organizational Behavior*, 3rd Ed. Englewood Cliffs, NJ: Prentice Hall.

Robinson, Ian. 1992. *Organizing Labour: The Moral Economy of Canadian-American Union Density Divergence, 1963–1986*. Queen's Papers in Industrial Relations, 1992–2. Kingston, ON: Queen's University.

Roe, Mark J. 1994. *Strong Managers, Weak Owners*. Princeton: Princeton University Press.

Rose, A. 1967. *The Power Structure*. New York: Oxford University Press.

Rose, Joseph. 1992. "Industrial Relations in the Construction Industry". In Richard Chaykowski and Anil Verma (Eds.), *Industrial Relations in Canadian Industry*. Toronto: Holt, Rinehart, and Winston.

Rose, Joseph and Michael Piczak. 1996. "Settlement Rates and Settlement Stages in Contemporary Interest Arbitration". *Relations Industrielles* 51(4): 643–64.

Ross, Arthur. 1948. *Trade Union Wage Policy*. Berkeley: University of California Press.

Rousseau, Denise M. 1995. *Psychological Contracts in Organizations*. Thousand Oaks, CA: Sage Publishing.

Roy, D. 1959. "'Banana Time': Job Satisfaction and Informal Interaction". *Human Organization* 18: 158–68.

Russell, B. 1990. *Back to Work? Labour, State and Industrial Relations in Canada*. Toronto: Nelson Press.

Russell, Ellen, and Mathieu Dufour. 2007. "Rising Profit Shares, Falling Wage Shares". *CCPA*, June 2007.

Sack, J., and T. Lee. 1989. "The Role of the State in Canadian Labour Relations". *Relations Industrielles* 44(1): 195–223.

Sass, R. 1989. "The Art of Collective Bargaining". In A. Sethi (Ed.), *Collective Bargaining in Canada*. Toronto: Nelson.

Schlaifer, R. 1980. "The Relay Assembly Test Room: An Alternative Statistical Interpretation". *American Sociological Review* 45: 995–1005.

Sennett, Richard. 1998. *The Corrosion of Character*, London: W.W. Norton.

Shalev, M. 1980. "Trade Unions and Economic Analysis". *Journal of Labour Research* 1: 133–74.

Shorter, E., and C. Tilly. 1974. *Strikes in France, 1930–1968*. Cambridge: Cambridge University Press.

Siebert, S.W., and J.T. Addison. 1981. "Are Strikes Accidental?" *Economic Journal* 91: 389–404.

Sims, Andrew, Rodrique Blouin, and Paula Knopf. 1995. *Seeking a Balance*. Ottawa: Minister of Public Services.

Simons, H. 1948. *Economic Policy for a Free Society*. Chicago: University of Chicago Press.

Singh, Gangaram, and Frank Reid. 1998. "Are Seniority-Based Layoffs Discriminatory?" *Relations Industrielles* 53(4): 730–49.

Skocpol, T. 1985. "Bringing the State Bank In: Strategies of Analysis in Current Research". In P. Evans et al. (Eds.), *Bringing the State Bank In*. Cambridge: Cambridge University Press.

Slichter, S. 1941. *Union Policies and Industrial Management*. Washington, D.C.: the Brookings Institution.

Smart, B. 1992. *Modern Conditions, Postmodern Controversies*. London: Routledge.

Soskice, David. 1990a. "Reinterpreting Corporatism and Explaining Unemployment: Co-ordinated and Non-co-ordinated Market Economies". In R. Brunetta and Carla Dell'Aringa (Eds.), *Labor Relations and Economic Performance*. New York: New York University Press.

Soskice, David. 1990b. "Wage Determination: the Changing Role of Institutions in Advanced Industrialized Economies". *Oxford Review of Economic Policy* 6: 36–61.

Soule, G. 1952. *Economic Forces in American History*. New York: Viking Press.

Sran, Garry, and Jim Stanford. 2009. "Further Tests of the Link Between Unionization, Unemployment, and Employment: Findings from Canadian National and Provincial Data". *Just Labour* 15 (Nov.): 29–45.

Statistics Canada. 2010a. Unionization 2010. *October 2010 Perspectives*. Catalogue no. 75-001-X.

———. 2010b. *Labour Force Information* — June 13–19, 2010. Catalogue no. 71-001-X.

———. 2009a. Unionization. *Perspectives on Labour and Income* 21(3): 67–75.

———. 2009b. *The Daily* for June 3 2009.

———. 2006a. *The Daily* for April 6, 2006.

———. 2006b. *The Daily* for April 13, 2006.

———. 2006c. *The Daily* for December 13, 2006.

———. 2005. *The Daily*. January 13 <www.statcan.ca>.

———. 2004. *Workplace and Employee Survey Compendium*. Ottawa: Statistics Canada catalogue 71-585.

———. 2003a. "Key Labour and Income Facts: Unionization". *Perspectives on Labour and Income* 15(3): 48–55.

———. 2003b. "Working Hours in Canada and the United States". *The Daily*. September 11 <www.statcan.ca>.

———. 1992. *Quality of Work in the Service Sector* (Prepared by H. Krahn). Ottawa: Ministry of Supply and Services.

Stern, R. 1976. "Intermetropolitan Patterns of Strike Frequency". *Industrial and Labour Relations Review* 29: 218–36.

Stone, K. 1975. "The Origins of Job Structures in the Steel Industry". In R. Edwards, M. Reich, and D. Gordon (Eds.), *Labor Market Segmentation*. Lexington, MA: Lexington Books.

Storey, R. 1987. "Unionization Versus Corporate Welfare: The Dofasco Way". In D. Bercuson (Ed.), *Canadian Labour History*. Toronto: Copp Clark Pitman.

Strauss, George. 1991. "Union Democracy". In G. Strauss, D. Gallagher, and J. Fiorito (Eds.), *The State of the Unions*. Madison, WI: IRRA.

Streeck, Wolfgang. 1997. "German Capitalism: Does it Exist? Can it Survive?" in Colin Crouch and Wolfgang Streeck (Eds.), *Political Economy of Modern Capitalism*. London: Sage.

Stultz, E. 1987. "Organizing the Unorganized Farm Workers in Ontario". In R. Argue et al. (Eds.), *Working People and Hard Times*. Toronto: Garamond Press.

Sugiman, P. 1984. "The Sales Clerks: Worker Discontent and Obstacles to its Collective Expression". In G. Lowe and H. Krahn (Eds.), *Working Canadians: Readings in the Sociology of Work and Industry*, pp. 74–86. Toronto: Methuen.

Swedberg. R., U. Himmelstrand, and G. Brulin. 1990. "The Paradigm of Economic Sociology". In S. Zukin and P. DiMaggio (Eds.), *Structures of Capital*. Cambridge: Cambridge University Press.

Swimmer, G. 1989. "Critical Issues in Public Sector Industrial Relations". In A.S. Sethi (Ed.), *Collective Bargaining in Canada*. Toronto: Nelson.

Taft, P. 1956. *The Structure and Government of Trade Unions*. Cambridge, MA: Harvard University Press.

Tannenbaum, F. 1951. *A Philosophy of Labor*. New York: Knopf.

——. 1921. *The Labor Movement: Its Conservative Functions and Social Consequences*. New York: G.P. Putnam's Sons.

Taras, Daphne. 1997a. "Collective Bargaining Regulation in Canada and the United States: Divergent Cultures, Divergent Outcomes". In Bruce Kaufman (Ed.), *Government Regulation of the Employment Relation*, pp. 295–342. Madison, WI: IRRA.

——. 1997b. "Company Unionism in Canada". *Proceedings of the Forty-Ninth Annual Meeting of the IRRA*. Madison, WI: IRRA.

Taras, Daphne, and Jason Copping. 1998. "The Transition From Formal Nonunion Representation to Unionization: A Contemporary Case". *Industrial and Labor Relations Review* 52(1): 22–44.

Taras, Daphne, and Bruce Kaufman. 2006. "Non-union Employee Representation in North America: Diversity, Controversy and Uncertain Future". *Industrial Relations Journal* 37(5): 513–42.

Taras, Daphne, and Allen Ponak. 2001. "Mandatory Agency Shop Laws and an Explanation of Canada-U.S. Union Density Divergence". *Journal of Labor Research* 22(3): 541–68.

Taylor, F. 1947 [1903]. "Shop Management". In *Scientific Management*. New York: Harper.

Thelen, Kathleen. 2002. "The Political Economy of Business and Labor in the Developed Democracies". In Izra Katznelson and Helen Milner (Eds.), *Political Science: the State of the Discipline*. New York: W.W. Norton & Company.

Thompson, J.D. 1967. *Organizations in Action*. New York: McGraw-Hill.

Thornicroft, Ken. 1996. "The Timeliness of Expedited Arbitration in B.C: the First Two Years". *Labour Arbitration*. Vancouver, B.C.: Continuing Legal Education Society of B.C.

Thornicroft, Ken, and Genevieve Eden. 1995. "Grievances and their Resolution". In J. Anderson, M. Gunderson, and A. Ponak (Eds.), *Union-Management Relations in Canada*. Don Mills: Addison Wesley.

Toffler, A. 1972. *Future Shock*. New York: Bantam Books.

Tomlins, C. 1985. *The State and the Unions*. London: Cambridge University Press.

Tourraine, A. 1971. *The Post-Industrial Society*. New York: Random House.

Tracy, J. 1987. "An Empirical Test of the Asymmetric Information Model of Strikes". *Journal of Labor Economics* 5: 149–73.

Tran, K., 2004. "Visible Minorities in the Labour Force: 20 Years of Change". *Canadian Social Trends*. Statistics Canada, cat. no. 11-008: 7–11.

Traxler, Franz. 2003. "Bargaining (De)centralization, Macroeconomic Performance, and Control over the Employer Relationship". *British Journal of Industrial Relations* 41(1): 1–28.

Troy, L., and N. Sheflin. 1985. *Union Sourcebook*. W. Orange, NJ: Industrial Relations Data and Information Services.

Veblen, T. 1921. *The Engineers and the Price System*. New York: Viking.

Vitols, Sigurt. 2001. "The Origins of Bank-Based and Market-Based Financial Systems: Germany, Japan, and the United States". In W. Streeck and Kozo Yamamura (Eds.), *The Origins of Nonliberal Capitalism: Germany and Japan in Comparison*. Ithaca: Cornell University Press.

Vogel, D. 1989. *Fluctuating Fortunes: The Political Power of Business in America*. New York: Basic Books.

Voss, Kim. 1993. *The Making of American Exceptionalism: the Knights of Labor and Class Formation in the Nineteenth Century*. Ithaca, NY: Cornell University Press.

Waligorski, C.P. 1990. *The Political Theory of Conservative Economists*. University of Kansas Press.

Walsworth, Scott. 2010. "Unions and Employment Growth: the Canadian Experience". *Industrial Relations* 49(1): 142–56.

Walton, R.E., and R.B. McKersie. 1991 [1965]. *A Behavioral Theory of Labor Negotiations*. Ithaca, NY: ILR Press.

Warskett, R. 1988. "Bank Worker Unionization and the Law". *Studies in Political Economy*, Vol. 25.

Watson, Tony. 1987. *Sociology, Work and Industry*, 2nd Ed. London: Routledge and Kegan Paul.

Waxman, Jason A. 2009. "The Stelco Restructuring Paradox". *Just Labour: A Canadian Journal of Work and Society* 13 (Spring): 48–55.

Weber, M. 1968 [1922]. *Economy and Society* (G. Roth and K. Wittich, Eds.). New York: Bedminster.

——. 1961 [1922]. *General Economic History* (F.H. Knight, Trans.). New York: Collier-Macmillan.

——. 1930 [1905]. *The Protestant Ethic and the Spirit of Capitalism* (T. Parsons, Trans.). New York: Scribner's.

Weil, David. 1999. "Are Mandated Health and Safety Committees Substitutes for or Supplements to Labor Unions?" *Industrial and Labor Relations Review* 52(3): 339–60.

Weiler, P. 1990. *Governing the Workplace: The Future of Labor and Employment Law*. Cambridge, MA: Harvard University Press.

Wells, D. 1987. *Empty Promises*. New York: Monthly Review Press.

Wheeler, H., and J. McClendon. 1991. "The Individual Decision to Unionize". In G. Strauss et al. (Eds.), *The State of the Union*. Madison, WI: IRRA.

Whitener, Ellen M. 2001. "Do High Commitment Human Resource Practices Affect Employee Commitment?" *Journal of Management* 27: 515–35.

Whitley, Richard. 1999. "Globalization and Business Systems". In Richard Whitley (Ed.), *Divergent Capitalisms: The Social Structuring and Change of Business Systems*. Oxford: Oxford University Press.

Whyte, William F. 1999. "The Mondragon Cooperatives in 1976 and 1998". *Industrial and Labour Relations Review* 52(3): 478–81.

Wilkinson, Richard, and Kate Pickett. 2009. *The Spirit Level: Why More Equal Societies Almost Always Do Better*. London: Allen Lane.

Williamson, O.E. 1975. *Markets and Hierarchies: Analysis and Antitrust Implications*. New York: Free Press.

Williamson, O., and W. Ouchi. 1981. "The Markets and Hierarchies and Visible Hand Perspectives". In A. Van de Ven and W. Joyce (Eds.), *Perspectives on Organizational Design and Behaviour*. New York: Wiley.

Winch, D. 1989. *Collective Bargaining and the Public Interest: A Welfare Economics Assessment*. Montreal: McGill-Queen's Press.

Wolfson, Michael, and Brian Murphy. 1998. "New Views on Income Inequality Trends in Canada and the United States". Statistics Canada Paper 11F0019MPE No. 124.

Wood, E.M. 1986. *The Retreat From Class*. London: Verso.

Wood, S. 1982. "Introduction". In S. Wood (Ed.), *The Degradation of Work*. London: Hutchison.

Wood, Stephen, and John Godard. 1999. "The Statutory Recognition Procedure in the Employee Relations Bill: A Comparative Perspective". *British Journal of Industrial Relations* 37(2): 203–45.

Woods, H.D. 1973. *Labour Policy in Canada*, 2nd Ed. Toronto: Macmillan.

Woodward, J. 1965. *Industrial Organization*. Oxford: Oxford University Press.

——. 1958. *Management and Technology*. London: HMSO.

Workplace Information Directorate. 2003. "Union Membership in Canada". *Workplace Gazette* 6(3): 40–46.

Wright, E.O. 1985. *Classes*. London: Verso.

Yalnizyan. Armine. 1998. *The Growing Gap*. Toronto: Centre for Social Justice.

Yates, Charlotte. 2007. "Missed Opportunities and Forgotten Futures: Why Union Renewal in Canada Has Stalled". In Craig Phelan (ed.), *Trade Union Revitalization: Trends and Prospects in 34 Countries*, pp. 9–16. New York: Peter Lang.

Zeitlin, J. 1985. "Shop Floor Bargaining and the State: A Contradictory Relationship". In S. Tolliday and J. Zeitlin (Eds.), *Shop Floor Bargaining and the State*. Cambridge: Cambridge University Press.

Zeytinoglu, I. 1992. "Reasons for Hiring Part-Time Workers". *Industrial Relations* 31: 489–99.

———. 1991. "A Sectoral Study of Part-Time Workers Covered by Collective Agreements". *Relations Industrielles* 46: 401–19.

———. 1989. "The ILO Standards and Canadian Labour Legislation". *Relations Industrielles* 42: 292–306.

Glossary

A

accommodative managerial orientation: A managerial orientation under which it is recognized that employees have legitimate needs and concerns and that these should be accommodated to the extent that they are deemed "reasonable".

administrative approach: Principles for managing complex organizations, including the establishment of a clear hierarchy of authority, of separate departments to deal with specific functional areas (e.g., industrial relations), and of elaborate organizational planning and control systems.

adversarial participation: Unions participate in high performance work systems without disregarding their adversarial role. Unions are able to serve as independent representatives on which workers can count to ensure that high performance practices are not simply ploys to intensify the work process, undercut skills levels, or reduce employment with worker interests, as a result, worker distrust is likely to be lower.

agency shop clause: A collective agreement clause specifying that workers are not required to join the union, but that they are required to pay the equivalent of membership dues to the union. (Also *see* Union security clause.)

alienation: A condition under which individuals lack a sense of meaning or purpose in life and feel estranged from both their inner selves and their fellow human beings.

allied trade federations: "Inter-union" bodies comprised of locals from different unions but with members in the same industry, which serve both to coordinate local activities and to resolve jurisdictional disputes. (Also *see* Joint union councils.)

amalgamated union locals: Union locals that represent workers at a number of locations within a geographical area (e.g., a city); these locals are particularly prevalent where workers have no fixed employer and, thus, become members of the same local regardless of their employer or whether they are, in fact, employed.

American Federation of Labor (AFL): A U.S.-based labour federation consisting predominantly of craft or trade unions; founded in 1886 and merged with the Congress of Industrial Organization in 1955 to form the AFL-CIO.

American Federation of Labor-Congress of Industrial Organization (AFL-CIO): The largest national labour federation in the United States.

anomie: A term employed by Emile Durkheim to express a state of normlessness, under which individuals have little sense of belonging or moral purpose in life.

arbitration: The imposition, by a single arbitrator or a tripartite arbitration board, of a final settlement upon labour and management in the event that the parties are unable to reach a settlement on their own; it can apply to contract negotiations, in which case it is referred to as interest arbitration, or to the resolution of a grievance, in which case it is referred to as grievance arbitration.

attitude surveys: A traditional information-sharing practice, which involves conducting internal surveys of employee opinions and concerns, sometimes followed up by group interviews.

authority: The authorization to make decisions or act on behalf of others.

autocratic authority structure: An authority relationship where employees are subject to personal directives from superordinates, have little job discretion, and are subject to arbitrary discipline.

autocratic workplace structure: A workplace structure where superordinates personally allocate and direct the work, monitor and evaluate workers, and determine rewards and discipline.

autocratic/exploitive practices: Management practices and policies that essentially involve management through personal edict, entailing low tolerance for "misconduct", arbitrary treatment of employees, and disciplinary measures lacking in due process.

autonomic/consociative practices: Management practices and policies aimed at creating a consensual and cooperative relationship between management and labour, including the provision of good wages and benefits, ensuring that workers are treated fairly and equitably, and implementing various workplace participation and employee involvement programs. (Also *see* Progressive HRM practices.)

autonomous teams: Workers work together in small groups (e.g., six to twelve members), are given a measure of autonomy over the pace at which they work and the allocation of tasks among members, are not subject to direct supervision, and are ideally responsible for an identifiable output or service.

B

"back-to-work" legislation: Government legislation enacted to unilaterally end a labour strike.

"bad faith" bargaining: A circumstance under which a party engages in negotiations but has little intention of making meaningful concessions or arriving at a settlement. (*See* Surface bargaining.)

Bank of Canada: A quasi-autonomous Crown corporation operated by government-appointed officials and is responsible for issuing all cash reserve assets for the banking system and, hence, for regulating the supply of money in the Canadian economy.

bank rate: The rate of interest at which chartered banks (members of the Canadian Payments Association) are able to borrow money from the government (the Bank of Canada).

bargaining power: The direct and indirect costs of a strike to each party to the collective bargaining process. (Also *see* Relational power.)

bargaining unit: Encompasses all employees covered by a specific collective agreement and represented in a specific labour–management bargaining relationship.

benefits status seniority: The use of seniority to determine an employee's status with respect to accrued benefits. (Also *see* Seniority and Competitive status seniority.)

Boulwarism: An illegal negotiation tactic whereby management attempts to circumvent the union and make an offer directly to union workers — named after Lemuel Boulware of General Electric, who first engaged in this tactic in the 1950s.

bounded rationality: The notion that rationality in the managerial decision process is bounded or limited by limited information, limited time, and limited cognitive capacity.

bourgeoisie: A class of individuals, as defined by Marxist theory, that own or control productive assets or the "means of production".

British North America (BNA) Act: A statute enacted on March 29, 1867 by the British Parliament providing for Canadian confederation.

bumping rights: Situation in which a displaced employee is allowed to "bump" (take the job of) another employee with less seniority. (Also *see* Chain bumping, Labour pan, and Seniority.)

burden of proof: The responsibility to present evidence and arguments proving the other party is in the wrong.

bureaucracy: Defined by Max Weber as an organization that is characterized primarily by a high degree of specialization in the way work is performed, a clearly established hierarchy of authority, a well-developed system of rules and procedures, selection and promotion based upon impersonal standards (qualifications, merit, seniority), and lifetime employment with career advancement opportunities.

bureaucratic/accommodative practices: Management practices and policies that are characterized by a high degree of "functional specialization" within management and where organizational activities are typically carried out in accordance with well-established rules and procedures, implemented by personnel/IR specialists in accordance with norms of calculative rationality.

bureaucratic authority structure: An authority relationship where employees are constrained to act in accordance with formally established rules and procedures, work roles are clearly defined, and procedures for discipline are well-established.

bureaucratic workplace structure: A workplace structure where employees are subject to a lower degree of direct authority but are constrained by the technical design of work and by formally established rules and procedures, conformity to which, in turn, forms the basis on which workers are monitored, rewarded, and disciplined.

business agents: *See* Union business agents.

business unionism philosophy: An essentially conservative approach to union operations, directed primarily at protecting and advancing the immediate economic interests of union members rather than seeking broader economic or social reforms.

C

calculative rationality: A Weberian term that denotes the use of rational calculation in order to ascertain the most efficient means to a given end.

Canadian Congress of Labour (CCL): A labour federation created in 1940 out of a merger of the All-Canadian Congress of Labour and the Canadian section of the Congress of Industrial Organization (CIO); merged with the Trades and Labour Congress (TLC) in 1956 to create the Canadian Labour Congress.

Canadian Federation of Labour (CFL): A national labour federation founded in 1902 by the Knights of Labor and the national unions of shoemakers, cigarmakers, painters, and carpenters; reformed in 1982 by a number of trade unions discontented with the policies of the Canadian Labour Congress.

Canadian Labour Congress (CLC): The largest national federation in Canada, accounting for roughly 60 percent of all unionized workers in Canada; formed in 1956 in a merger of the Canadian Congress of Labour and the Trades and Labour Congress of Canada.

Canadian Labour Union (CLU): The first national labour federation formed in Canada, founded in 1873 and collapsing in 1878.

capital: As employed by proponents of the capitalism thesis, a term that denotes the ownership and control of the means of production.

capital intensity: A dimension of technology that refers to the amount of capital invested per worker.

capitalism thesis: A theory that attributes the nature and development of the western economies primarily to the underlying nature of capitalism, and, in particular, to the private ownership of work organizations.

certification: The process by which a union obtains the legal right to represent a group of workers as their exclusive agent.

chain bumping: A form of "bumping right" in which an employee whose job has been eliminated (temporarily or permanently) has the right to "bump" (take the job of) any person with less "seniority"; the person bumped is in turn able to "bump" any other person with even less seniority, and so on. (Also *see* Bumping rights and Labour pan.)

chilling effect: A commonly identified problem with interest arbitration, whereby the parties in the collective bargaining process withhold concessions in the expectation that an arbitrator will be inclined to seek a middle ground between the final positions of the two parties.

class: Social groupings that differ primarily with respect to their command of economic or material resources.

class conflict/revolutionary function: A function of unions that involves the expression of class conflict and/or the revolutionary overthrow of an established economic and political system; traditionally associated with the radical perspective in general and with syndicalism in particular. (Also *see* Syndicalism.)

closed shop clause: A collective agreement clause that specifies that workers must be union members before they can be hired by the employer. (Also *see* Union security clause.)

coercive drive system: The system of industrial relations established during the "early industrialization era" in which a middle strata of supervisors and gang bosses were provided with almost total authority over the hiring, disciplining, and payment of workers under their direction, and were often paid on the basis of output, thus encouraging them to extract as much labour from workers as possible at as low a cost as possible.

collective agreement: A contract outlining the terms and conditions of employment and the rights of each party, as negotiated in the collective bargaining process. (Also *see* Labour–management contract.)

collective bargaining: The process by which labour unions represent their members through formal negotiations with management representatives.

commitment variant of the high performance model: A variant of management practice in which the employer seeks to achieve high performance by adopting job design reforms, participatory reforms, and progressive employment practices intended to maximize employee motivation and commitment.

common law: Law that has evolved through tradition and, more broadly, established norms.

communism: An economic and political system under which productive assets are owned and controlled by the state.

communist theory of revolution: Belief that the overthrow of capitalism can only occur once workers in general have developed a revolutionary consciousness and have become organized for mass political action, and that unions can play only a limited role in this process. (Also *see* Union class conflict function and Union revolutionary function.)

company unions: A management-instituted union or association under which worker representatives meet periodically with management representatives to discuss various issues and problems, but under which workers have no legal collective bargaining rights. (Also *see* Work councils.)

competitive status seniority: Provisions that require employers to take an employee's seniority into account on matters having to do with promotions, lay-offs and recall, job transfers, work assignment, shift preference, choice of vacation dates, the allocation of time off, and overtime. (Also *see* Benefit status seniority and Seniority.)

comprehensiveness thesis: A thesis under which reforms must be fully or comprehensively implemented if their real potential is to be realized.

complementarities thesis: A thesis under which high performance practices are thought to complement one another; that is, while each practice can be expected to have some positive effect in and of itself, this effect is enhanced to the extent that it is implemented *in combination* with other practices.

concentrated industries: Industries where a small number of firms (e.g., four or less) account for most of the output (e.g., 70 percent or more) and, hence, are able to exert considerable control over their markets.

concession bargaining: Situations in which workers concede wage and benefit cuts in order to ensure the financial viability of their employer.

conciliation: This involves the services of a conciliator, as appointed by the ministry of labour, to help the parties reconcile their differences in the event that an impasse is reached in collective bargaining.

Confederation of National Trade Unions (CNTU): A national labour federation (largely based in Quebec) founded in 1921 and representing 6.2 percent of unionized workers in Canada.

conferences: As applied to unions, an intra-union body comprised of locals of a national union that join together in a particular area in order to coordinate their bargaining, their organizing, and their political activities. (Also *see* District councils and Joint boards.)

conflict: When the interests, goals, and expectations of one party differ from those of another and this party's pursuit of these interests, goals, and expectations negatively affects the other's outcomes.

congresses: Associations of unions, established primarily to represent, coordinate and provide services to member unions at the provincial and national levels. (Also *see* Labour federations.)

Congress of Industrial Organizations (CIO): A U.S.-based labour federation founded in 1938 and comprised largely of industrial unions; merged with the American Federation of Labor to form the AFL-CIO in 1955.

consociative managerial orientation: A managerial orientation characterized by the appearance of high concern for employee welfare and the adoption of extensive programs to ensure employee identification with and loyalty to the organization.

constructive discrimination: *See* Doctrine of constructive discrimination.

constructive dismissal: An unjust dismissal where an employee is induced to quit her job due to an action of the employer rendering continued employment untenable (e.g., reassignment to a job with substantially lower status and pay).

Consumer Price Index (CPI): The average level of prices of goods and services bought by consumers; used to generate a measure of inflation (changes in the average household's cost of living). (Also *see* Inflation.)

context: The conditions and constraints under which labour–management relations take place (e.g., economic, technological, legal-institutional, political, socio-cultural contexts).

contextual sources of conflict: Sources of labour–management conflict that are external to the labour–management relation and tend to vary across employers and over time. (Also *see* Underlying sources of conflict.)

contingency theory: An organizational theory that maintains that the most effective form of organization is contingent upon (depends upon) the size, technology, and environment of the organization, and that management adopts organizational structures, policies, and practices accordingly; typically distinguishes between "mechanistic" and "organic" organizational forms.

contingent pay systems: A progressive personnel and employment practice that links pay to individual, work group, or even plant and employer-wide performance. (Also *see* Gainsharing plans, Profit-sharing plans, and Employee stock ownership plans.)

continuous improvement committee: *See* Joint steering committee.

contract zone: The area in which the range of acceptable settlements for both sides of the collective bargaining process overlap, thus making an agreement possible.

contracting out: The use of "outside" workers to perform work which could otherwise be done by a firm's own workers. (Also *see* Outsourcing and Subcontracting.)

control: The extent to which various sources of "influence" are systematically brought to bear by one party in a way that increases the likelihood that the actions of another party will conform with the first party's goals or interests.

control variant of the high performance model: A variant of management practice in which the employer seeks to achieve high performance by enhancing control over and intensifying the work process and, as such, only partially adopts the high performance model.

conventional interest arbitration: The imposition of a final settlement upon the parties in the collective bargaining process by a single arbitrator or a tripartite arbitration board, based upon submissions from the two sides and upon the "norm" for settlements covering similar employees elsewhere.

cooperation: A social relation that both labour and management function jointly to produce particular goods or services, acting largely in accordance with a system or "web" of rules to which each party expects the other to adhere.

coordinated bargaining: Separate agreements are negotiated based on the understanding that all will reach essentially the same settlement, with only minor modifications at most.

core sector: That sector of the economy consisting of large, capital intensive employers with more dominant positions in their product. Core sector employers are believed to provide substantially more favourable terms of employment and adopt more progressive practices. They are better able to absorb or pass on additional costs and workers have much higher relational power with which to retaliate if they do not do so.

corporatism: The establishment of national level structures that incorporate both business and labour within the policy processes of the state.

cost-of-living-adjustment (COLA) clause: A collective agreement clause which stipulates that employees receive wage increases over the life of the agreement (usually every three or six months) but that the size of these increases will be tied to increases in the Consumer Price Index (CPI).

craft unions: Unions that have traditionally claimed workers in a specific trade or craft as constituting their jurisdiction. (Also *see* Trade unions.)

cross-training: *See* Multi-skilling.

crowding effect: The notion that union wage gains result in lower employment in the union sector, thus resulting in an increased number of workers seeking employment in the non-union sector and, hence, in lower wages and benefits in this sector.

cultural disenchantment: A Weberian term that denotes the development of a culture that is cold, depersonalized, and devoid of meaning or moral purpose; it results from the growth of calculative rationality as a predominant ethos.

D

decertification: Removal by a labour board of a union's legal right to represent a group of workers for purposes of collective bargaining; this usually occurs if a union has become inactive or if a majority of workers within an established bargaining unit vote in favour of decertification.

decision process theory: A model of management that argues that managerial rationality is often limited by time constraints, incomplete information, and limited cognitive capacity. (Also *see* Bounded rationality.)

democratization function of unions: A function of unions that involves the representation of workers to management and the provision of various worker rights and protections in the workplace, thereby introducing an element of democracy into the employment relation; most developed by proponents of the orthodox-pluralist perspective.

"de-skilling" of the labour process: A process by which management designs work so as to reduce the skill levels required, thus making it possible to rely upon lower paid unskilled and semi-skilled workers, who tend to have lower labour market and relational power. (Also *see* Labour process theory.)

discretionary certification: When a labour relations board decides that employer unfair labour practices have so undermined support for a union that the union should be certified regardless of whether a majority of workers still support it.

disemployment effects: The argument that union wage and benefit gains either (a) induce employers to raise prices, thereby lowering demand for their output, or (b) use more capital intensive technologies than otherwise; the result is lower employment, either because employers lay off workers or because they hire fewer workers in the future.

disposable workplace thesis: Argues that, where workers have reason to fear job loss, high commitment can, in effect, be coerced, thus enhancing the effectiveness of the control approach to high performance practices.

distributive issues: Negotiating issues in which a gain for one side entails a loss for the other.

district councils: An intra-union body comprised of locals of a national union that join together in a particular area in order to coordinate their bargaining, organizing, and political activities. (Also *see* Joint boards and Conferences.)

district labour councils: Bodies established by a labour federation that represent the labour movement in general within individual cities and municipalities (e.g., the Kingston and District Labour Council). (Also *see* Local labour councils.)

doctrine of constructive discrimination: A collective agreement provision that can have a disproportionately negative impact on a minority designated for protection under human rights legislation, even though the provision is not intended to discriminate.

doctrine of shared rights: A legal doctrine predicated on the belief that an informal or implicit contract exists between workers and management, based upon various understandings and customs that have developed over time as to the nature of work and the obligations and duties of each party. This doctrine is normally advanced as an alternative to the doctrine of management rights, which suggests that management should have unilateral authority over all decisions not explicitly restricted by a collective agreement.

dues check-off clause: A collective agreement clause that stipulates that management agrees to regularly deduct union dues from workers' pay and remit these to the union.

"duty of fair representation" doctrine: The notion (often legally defined) that a union has an obligation to represent all workers in a bargaining unit equally, even if they are not actually members of the union.

duty to accommodate: Refers to the requirement of employers to accommodate those individuals who cannot fully comply with employer requirements because of their sex, religion, or some related characteristic if compliance would constitute an undue hardship for these individuals and any performance implications of accommodating them is not sufficient to justify this hardship.

E

early industrialization era: The period of Canadian history characterized by the widespread growth in factory work, and with it the emergence of what has come to be referred to as the "coercive drive system" of labour relations (circa 1870–1900).

economic context: The economic conditions and constraints under which labour and management interact; includes "micro" conditions and constraints such as employer size and product market concentration, and "macro" conditions and constraints such as unemployment levels, interest rates, and economic growth rates.

economic democracy: The system under which employees collectively own and/or exert effective control over the "means of production".

economic function of unions: A function of unions which involves improving the wages and benefits of workers; most fully developed under the neoclassical perspective.

economic rents: As employed in this book, the ability of workers to win wage and benefit settlements in excess of the productive value of their labour; also refers to the ability of employers to obtain profits in excess of the normal costs of production.

employee involvement schemes: Programs designed to foster greater employee involvement in, or commitment to, their work by allowing them to participate in decision processes and to exchange ideas on how to improve working conditions and product quality. (Also referred to as EI involvement schemes; also *see* Quality circles.)

employee stock ownership plans (ESOPs): A system under which employees purchase or are awarded ownership shares in the company for which they work.

employer and establishment size: The number of people employed by a given employer or establishment.

employer associations: Formal and informal associations created for the advancement of employer interests.

employment equity legislation: Legislation intended to ensure that individuals are not intentionally or unintentionally discriminated against on the basis of race, sex, religion, or other personal characteristics unrelated to ability.

employment standards legislation: Government legislation addressing concerns such as minimum wage levels, minimum annual vacation entitlements, statutory holidays, maternity leaves, and the minimum notice period employees are entitled to in the event of termination.

enterprise unions: *See* Local independent union.

exclusivity: The notion that a single union should represent workers in a given work situation, serving as their exclusive "agent".

exit power: A form of "relational power" that varies with the costs to management of hiring and training replacements in the event that workers quit or "exit" from the employment relation (i.e., permanent withdrawal).

expedited arbitration: The agreement to skip various steps within the process in the case of grievances that are of particular urgency or importance, such as employee dismissals.

exploitive managerial orientation: A managerial orientation under which management displays little or no concern for employees, seeking only to get the most work out of them for the lowest possible wage.

external inequalities: A term, conceived by Emile Durkheim, that refers to economic inequalities attributable to social and economic background rather than "internal" characteristics (e.g., intelligence).

F

fact-finding: A variant of the second stage of the traditional conciliation process; entails the appointment, normally by a labour board or equivalent body, of a third party to determine what issues are unresolved in negotiations and to issue a formal report with recommendations for the resolution of these issues.

"fair administration" doctrine: The notion that workers are entitled to "fair and reasonable" treatment regardless of the provisions of the collective agreement.

feather-bedding: A situation where individuals perform obsolete or unnecessary tasks simply because they are required by work rules in the collective agreement.

final offer selection (F.O.S.):   The imposition of a final settlement upon the parties in the collective bargaining process under which an arbitrator chooses between the "final offers" presented by each side, either on an issue by issue or a total package basis.

first agreement arbitration: In Canada, where the parties are unable to negotiate an agreement on their own, often regardless of whether bad faith bargaining can be established, a neutral arbitrator is appointed by either the minister of labour or the labour board.

first contract arbitration: The imposition of a final settlement upon the parties in the collective bargaining process in a situation where a union is newly organized and unable to negotiate a first agreement.

fiscal policy: Government policies having to do with taxation and spending levels and methods.

flexible employment arrangements: Employment arrangements that provide employers with greater flexibility in the assignment and allocation of work and pay; can involve extensive use of temporary and part-time employees, "contracting out", and "outsourcing", and "contingent pay systems".

flexible specialization: Adaptable and flexible work systems that shorten set-up times in manufacturing and make it possible to program production to meet with the specific requirements of individual customers.

forced division of labour: A term used by Emile Durkheim to describe a condition where external inequalities are able to persist, thereby preventing disadvantaged individuals from attaining positions that utilize their true potential.

Fordism: A system prevalent in the post-war era, under which economic growth was sustained by providing workers with wage increases commensurate with their productivity gains, thus ensuring demand for their output.

formal subordination: A Marxist term used to denote the state in which workers are formally under the authority of capitalists, but may retain considerable control over the process by which they perform their work.

free collective bargaining: Circumstance when both labour and management are able to negotiate a settlement on their own terms, free from government interference.

free riders: Individuals who receive the benefits of union representation (e.g., higher wages) without undergoing the costs (e.g., paying dues, suffering lost wages during a strike).

functionalist theory of the state: A theory of the state, consistent with "managerialist theory", which assumes that the state's primary purpose is to maintain order and stability, and that this serves the interests of society and the social system as a whole. (Also *see* Systems theory of the state.)

G

gainsharing plans: A "contingent pay system" in which workers receive some form of bonus tied to productivity gains. (Also *see* Profit-sharing plans and Employee stock ownership plans.)

general shop steward: A shop steward that presides over a "shop steward's committee" representing workers in a particular establishment or area. (Also *see* Shop steward and Shop stewards' committee.)

"good faith" bargaining: The opposite of bad faith bargaining. (Also *see* Bad faith bargaining.)

Greenfield sites: Locations in provinces, regions, or countries where the likelihood of unionization is perceived to be lower due to weak labour laws and conservative, anti-union values.

grievance: A formal (normally written) complaint stating an issue in dispute over the adherence to a "collective agreement" or "labour–management contract". (Also *see* Individual grievance and Policy grievance.)

grievance arbitrator: An outside "neutral" paid to adjudicate a grievance in the event that the parties are unable to resolve this grievance on their own.

grievance mediation: The introduction of a neutral third party in the grievance process to mediate a resolution once it has reached the final stage prior to arbitration.

H

"hard-line" bargaining: Employer refusal to grant meaningful concessions so that the union's credibility will be undermined unless a strike is called. (Also *see* Good faith negotiations.)

Hawthorne experiments: A series of experiments conducted by Elton Mayo and his associates in the Hawthorne plant of Western Electric from 1924 to 1933, which concluded that problems of employee motivation and commitment were largely explained by an inability to fulfil their social needs at work and by poor "human relations" on the part of management. (Also *see* Human relations movement.)

high performance work systems: "New" forms of work and HRM practices associated with the autonomic/consociative management approach and including job design reforms, participatory reforms, and progressive employment practices.

human relations movement: In the 1930s, this movement emerged to improve labour–management relations by encouraging employers to engage in better human relations, based upon the belief that problems of motivation and commitment largely reflected inappropriate managerial policies and practices rather than underlying interest conflicts; served both as an anti-union ideology and as a foundation for the fields of Organizational Behaviour and Human Resources Management.

human rights legislation: Government legislation enacted to prevent discrimination against individuals on the basis of personal characteristics (e.g., race, sex), beliefs (e.g., religion), and affiliations (e.g., political party).

I

ideologies: Frameworks of interconnected values, beliefs, and assumptions upon which individuals draw in order to assess the functioning and legitimacy of established institutional arrangements (e.g., labour law) and the desirability of reforms.

IDIA: *See* Industrial Disputes and Investigation Act.

ILO conventions: International standards, set by the United Nations International Labour Organization (ILO), which serve as guidelines for member countries.

"implied obligations" doctrine: The legal doctrine that maintains that management has an implied obligation to consult with and obtain the agreement of union officials before making major changes that are relevant to the collective agreement; typically proposed as an alternative to the doctrine of management rights.

independent local unions: Unions that have membership restricted to a single locale (and usually a single employer).

individual grievance: A formal (normally written) complaint stating an issue in dispute over the adherence to a "collective agreement" filed by, or on behalf of, an individual or group within the bargaining unit.

industrial capitalism thesis: A thesis that attributes the nature and development of western economies to the nature of capitalism and to processes of industrialization combined.

Industrial Disputes and Investigation Act (IDIA): Federal government legislation (1906) that compelled all unions and employers in the transportation, resource, and utilities industries to submit their disputes to an ad hoc three-person board of conciliation, wait for the board to issue its report, and then go through a cooling out period before a strike or lockout could legally occur; incorporated in modified form into post-World War II labour legislation.

industrial relations: The study of the "relations" between "labour" and "management", and the "context" within which labour and management interact.

Industrial Relations and Disputes Investigations Act: Federal government legislation (1948) combining the provisions of Order in Council PC 1003 (1944) with those of the Industrial Disputes and Investigation Act (IDIA) of 1906.

industrial society thesis: A variant of the "industrialism thesis" that argues that industrialization processes have eradicated many of the sources of conflict underlying labour–management relations in earlier times, based upon the belief that the traditional working class-capitalist class dichotomy has become outmoded, that the separation between the ownership of firms and their management in large part has meant that owners no longer exert much effective control over the way corporations are run, and that labour unionism and collective bargaining enable workers to confront management as equals and hence introduce democracy into the workplace.

industrial unions: Unions that have traditionally claimed workers in a specific industry as constituting their jurisdiction.

industrialism thesis: A theory that attributes the nature and development of the western economies primarily to the processes of industrialization over the past century or so, making little reference to the role of capitalism in these processes.

industry level: The level of labour–management interaction involving senior employer as well as worker representatives in an industry.

industry organizations: Industry-based employer associations that do not directly involve themselves *in* labour–management relations, but that often engage in extensive political activities, advocating policies and legal reforms with important implications *for* labour–management relations (e.g., "free" trade). (Also *see* Trade organizations.)

inflation: The rate of change in the average price level per year. (Also *see* Consumer Price Index.)

institutionalist tradition: An industrial relations tradition that focuses upon the institutions of labour unionism, labour law, and collective bargaining, and is primarily descriptive in nature.

institutionalization of conflict era: A period in Canadian history during which unions and collective bargaining came to be accommodated within the status quo, thus institutionalizing and containing conflict within the economic sphere (circa 1930–1950).

instrumentalist view of the state: A "radical" perspective, which views the state as little more than an instrument of the capitalist class, due to capitalist political contributions, close personal and professional ties between senior corporate and senior government officials, and the capitalist domination of the media.

integrative function: A function of unions that involves the integration of workers into the workplace and the fostering of labour–management harmony; most associated with the "managerial perspective".

integrative issues: Negotiating issues the resolution of which both parties potentially benefit from.

intensification of the labour process: A Marxist term used to denote attempts by capitalists to increase the amount of labour extracted from workers.

inter-industry pattern bargaining: Occurs when collective agreements reached in one sector or industry tend to be followed in other sectors or industries, thus setting a "pattern".

interest arbitration: The imposition by an appointed arbitrator (or arbitration board) of a final settlement upon the parties in the collective bargaining process in the event that the parties are unable to reach an agreement on their own accord. (Also *see* Conventional interest arbitration and Final offer selection.)

internal justice system: Formal mechanism by which workers in non-union operations are able to register a complaint in the event that they believe themselves to have been unfairly treated; similar to a union grievance system, but implemented by management and typically lacking any legal right to third party arbitration.

internal labour market: A job allocation system within a single workplace or employer that provides workers with the opportunity to advance without having to switch employers.

International Labour Organization (ILO): A tripartite agency of the United Nations, consisting of governments, trade union federations, and employer organizations, and which is responsible for the collection and dissemination of information pertaining to the conditions of employment and the rights afforded workers throughout the world.

international unions: Unions with a membership in both Canada and the United States, thereby transcending national boundaries.

intra-organizational bargaining: The process in which individuals within the bargaining process find themselves negotiating with their own constituents in an attempt to get them to modify their expectations.

iron cage of bureaucracy: A condition that sees individuals inescapably immersed in and constrained by bureaucratic systems and norms of calculative rationality, resulting in a state of cultural disenchantment within society in general; associated with Max Weber's concerns about the development of industrial capitalist societies.

Iron Law of Oligarchy: A theory proposed by Robert Michels which argues that as political parties become established and begin to accomplish their initial objectives, a small elite is able to entrench itself and undermine democratic processes that could threaten their tenure.

J

job design reforms: Changes to the nature and organization of work which entail increased autonomy, variety, and team work; associated with the "high commitment" variant of the high performance model.

job enlargement: A progressive HRM program that broadens tasks in order to provide workers with greater variety and more "meaningful" units of work.

job enrichment: A progressive HRM program under which jobs are "enriched" so that they entail greater challenge, discretion, and responsibility, thereby appealing to the need for personal growth and fulfilment.

job ladders: A formal or informal system that allows workers to advance into progressively better jobs as they accumulate seniority and experience, with each job serving as a prerequisite to the next, much like climbing a ladder.

job power: A form of "relational power" that varies with the costs to management of worker mistakes or recalcitrance in the workplace (i.e., partial withdrawal).

job rotation: A progressive HRM program under which workers are rotated among different jobs, enabling them to develop a better understanding of the entire operation, providing them with greater variety, and introducing the challenge of learning different tasks.

joint boards: An intra-union body comprised of locals of a national union that join together in a particular area in order to coordinate their bargaining, their organizing, and their political activities. (Also *see* District councils and Conferences.)

joint steering committees: A labour–management problem-solving and decision-making mechanism where employee representatives meet with management personnel to discuss broad developments in the workplace and upcoming workplace changes.

joint union councils: "Inter-union" bodies comprised of locals from different unions but with members in the same industry; the primary functions of these councils are to coordinate local activities and to resolve jurisdictional disputes. (Also *see* Allied trade federations.)

jurisdiction: The category of workers that a union claims the exclusive right to represent.

just-in-time (JIT) inventory systems: A system in which firms minimize inventory levels by arranging to have required inputs delivered only as needed, reducing inventory build-ups within the production process itself, and scheduling production so that goods are completed only as they are needed by customers.

K, L

Keynesianism: An economic doctrine associated with the British economist John Maynard Keynes that argues that governments are able to smooth out the business cycle by increasing spending and, hence, the level of economic activity during downturns, and decreasing spending and, hence, the level of economic activity, during upturns.

Knights of Labor: A predominantly U.S.-based working class organization was founded in Philadelphia in 1869; it became involved with Canadian labour in the late 1870s, and largely disappeared by the early 1900s.

labour: Refers to all of those working Canadians who are in an employment relation and *do not* exercise a substantial degree of authority over others, but are instead in positions of subordination to those who do.

labour board: A tripartite administrative tribunal appointed by a minister of labour to interpret and administer laws pertaining to the right of workers to organize unions and engage in collective bargaining; found in all Canadian jurisdictions with the exception of Quebec (which has labour commissioners and a labour court).

labour congresses: Associations of unions, established primarily to represent, coordinate, and provide services to member unions at the provincial and national levels. (Also *see* Labour federations.)

labour federations: Associations of unions, established primarily to represent, coordinate, and provide services to member unions at the provincial and national levels. (Also *see* Congresses.)

labour laws: Laws pertaining to the right of workers to organize unions, engage in collective bargaining, and strike.

labour–management committees: Committees comprised of worker and management representatives, the function of which is to address concerns such as health and safety, worker training and development, and workplace design. (Also *see* Scanlon plans.)

labour–management contract: An agreement outlining the terms and conditions of employment and the rights of each party, as negotiated in the collective bargaining process (Also *see* Collective agreement.)

labour market power: The amount of power workers or employers have vis-à-vis each other in the labour market; worker labour market power varies in accordance with the extent to which employers value the skills and abilities of workers, while employer labour market power varies in accordance with the extent to which workers value the job opportunities offered by employers.

labour movement: Labour unions and their members, as well as related associations such as "labour federations" or "congresses". (Also *see* Organized labour.)

labour pan: A form of "bumping" arrangement whereby a displaced employee is allowed to "bump" (take the job of) only that employee with the lowest seniority, in which case he/she waits in the "pan" until a better job becomes available. (Also *see* Bumping rights and Chain bumping.)

labour process theory: A school of thought that suggests that, with capitalist relations of production, management attempts to minimize skill requirements and/or maximize control (through direct or indirect means) over workers rather than maximize efficiency per se; closely associated with, though not restricted to, the work of Harry Braverman and the radical perspective on industrial relations.

labour unions: Organizations of workers intended primarily to represent and advance the interests and values of their members.

layoff: Circumstance under which employees are dismissed by their employer (either permanently or temporarily) because of a lack of work.

lean production systems: Production systems involving "just-in-time inventory" and in which work is performed in non-autonomous teams (i.e., with supervision); they also typically entail a total quality management program.

legal-institutional context: That aspect of the industrial relations context that encompasses the system of labour and employment law in Canada and the agencies that administer this system. Primarily refers to laws and enforcement mechanisms intended to regulate the actions of the parties, particularly **labour laws,** or laws pertaining to collective bargaining and unions, and **employment laws,** or laws pertaining to basic employee rights and working conditions, such as minimum wages, health and safety regulations, and human rights standards.

legitimation: The process by which management attempts to establish its right to hold and exercise its authority based upon established social norms and values, and thereby to elicit voluntary compliance or consent of those over whom authority is exercised.

letters of intent: A letter that is not legally binding but that is appended to the collective agreement, usually stating management's intent to consider the interests and concerns of workers or their representatives in the event that certain decisions or changes become necessary (e.g., technological change).

liberal-reformist perspective: A critical approach to industrial relations concerned with reducing or eliminating inequalities and injustices in the treatment afforded workers, and generally entailing a focus upon such problems as discrimination, layoffs and plant closings, inadequate wages and benefits, hazardous working conditions, or weaknesses in the established system of labour law and collective bargaining; proceeds from the assumption that workers are often at a disadvantage relative to management and that collective bargaining is often not sufficient to offset this disadvantage.

living agreement: An agreement between labour and management under which, rather than negotiating formal rules and procedures into a union contract, management is to consult with worker representatives prior to making workplace level decisions; associated with General Motors' Saturn plant in Tennessee and advocated by some proponents of the progressive HRM paradigm.

local labour councils: Bodies established by a labour federation that represent the labour movement in general within individual cities and municipalities (e.g., the Kingston and District Labour Council). (Also *see* District labour councils.)

local union: A union representing workers in a specific establishment or locale; can be independent, but is usually affiliated with a parent union. (Also simply referred to as a "local".)

lockout: An act in which management refuses workers access to their jobs until a dispute over the negotiation of a new collective agreement is settled.

M

maintenance of membership clause: A collective agreement clause that stipulates that workers are not required to join the union, but if they do, they must maintain their membership for as long as they are employed within the bargaining unit. (Also *see* Union security clause.)

majoritarianism: The notion that the majority should rule with respect to worker decisions about joining a union or going on strike.

make whole remedy: A non-punitive remedy for violations of law, under which the guilty party is required to right past wrongs by restoring the offended party to the position he/she would have been in if an offence had not been committed.

management: All individuals in positions of substantial authority over others within work organizations.

management era: A period in Canadian history during which management responded to growing labour conflict by adopting increasingly coercive union avoidance practices, developing techniques for rationalizing and gaining control over the work process, and adopting paternalistic practices in an attempt to establish relations of trust and loyalty (circa 1900–1930).

management rights clause: Collective agreement clauses that stipulate that management retains unilateral authority over all operations unless otherwise specified in the agreement.

managerial paradigm: Set of values, beliefs, and assumptions that guide managerial decisions.

managerial revolution thesis: The notion that professional managers rather than owners operate and effectively control the "modern" corporation, with managerial goals coming to displace ownership goals.

managerialist perspective: An ideology concerned primarily with the maximization of worker motivation and commitment through the adoption of progressive HRM practices, and based upon the belief that conflict is largely a result of inappropriate managerial policies.

master agreement: A term, usually in the context of two-tier bargaining, that refers to an overarching collective agreement that addresses broad issues of relevance to workers (such as wages and benefits) in all locales within a given bargaining unit, but that leaves more specific issues to be revolved through separate negotiations at each locale. (Also *see* Supplemental agreements and Two-tier bargaining.)

maturation of industrial relations era: The period of Canadian industrial development during which collective bargaining came to be widely accepted by both labour and management and under which this process came to be rationalized and bureaucratized (circa 1950–1965).

mature Fordism: A term that refers to an implicit accord between labour and management in the post-war era, under which labour agreed to maintain stability and help to foster productivity increases in return for steady improvements in wages and working conditions, thereby fostering the increased consumption levels necessary to absorb increases in output. (Also *see* Virtuous circle and Fordism.)

mechanical solidarity: A concept, conceived by Emile Durkheim, that refers to the social order that results from the development of a common identity and "collective conscience", consisting of a "totality of beliefs and sentiments common to average citizens"; characteristic of pre-industrial societies.

mediation: A process by which a neutral third party becomes involved in negotiations in an attempt to induce the parties to reach a settlement; similar to the first stage of the "conciliation process" but is usually entered into voluntarily and tends to be more "interventionist".

memorandum of agreement: A document signed by union and management officials once an agreement has been reached, outlining everything that has been agreed to (although the precise wording of individual clauses may have yet to be worked out).

minority unionism: An arrangement under which a minority of workers in an election unit are allowed to form their own union; usually advocated as an option to be provided workers if a majority chooses not to be represented by a union.

modified union shop clause: A collective agreement clause that stipulates that union members must maintain their membership and new employees must join the union, but those already employed in the unit and choosing to remain non-union can do so. (Also *see* Union security clause.)

monetarism: A number of economic theories underpinned by the notion that the general level of prices in the economy can be controlled or altered through the manipulation of the supply of money within the economy, and thus can be used as an instrument to minimize harmful business cycles.

monetary policy: Government policies that affect the supply of money in the economy and the rate at which chartered banks are able to borrow from the Bank of Canada.

multi-skilling: Employees are trained so that they have a broader variety of skills than that required for their own jobs, making them able to do different jobs. This makes employees more interchangeable in addition to providing employees with a more thorough understanding of how their work fits into the overall picture.

mutual benefit function: Union provision of financial support to members and/or their dependents in the case of mishap or death; characteristic of unions in preindustrial times.

N

narcotic effect: The notion that the parties in the collective bargaining process find it easier to rely on an arbitrator than to have to negotiate and hence take responsibility for their own settlement; identified as a problem with compulsory arbitration, for it is thought to reduce the likelihood of the parties reaching an agreement of their own accord.

National Labor Relations Act (NLRA): The benchmark federal U.S. legislation implemented in 1935, which provided workers with the legal right to organize a union free from employer intimidation and required employers to recognize the union and bargain with it in good faith once certified. (Also referred to as the Wagner Act.)

national unions: Unions that have members in a number of locales within a given country, and hence transcend a number of provincial or regional boundaries.

neoclassical perspective: An ideology concerned primarily with the maximization of economic efficiency, that focuses upon the role of market forces; generally proceeds from the assumption that workers as individuals are not at a power disadvantage relative to management and that unions are both unnecessary and detrimental to the economy. (Also referred to as the neoliberal perspective.)

negative settlement zone: When two parties' bottom lines do not overlap.

neoclassical theory of the firm: A theory of the firm that assumes that managers serve as "agents" of owners and investors (if they are not themselves the owners), and that as agents, they continually strive to enhance the efficiency and competitive position of the firm, thereby maximizing profits and ownership wealth.

new deal legislation: Legislation enacted under Franklin Delanor Roosevelt in order to quell conflict and establish a basis for rebuilding the U.S. economy.

new militancy era: The period of Canadian history characterized by increased labour militancy and a growth in the labour movement (circa 1965–1980).

new realities era: The period of Canadian history characterized by an increasingly hostile environment for the Canadian labour movement and workers in general, featuring an apparent increase in global competition, and the negotiation of both the U.S.-Canadian Free Trade Agreement and the North American Free Trade Agreement (circa 1980–present).

Nine-Hour Movement: A drive by workers, beginning in Hamilton in 1872, to secure a reduction in the standard work day from twelve to nine hours.

no strike clauses: Collective agreement clauses under which the parties agree to submit unresolved negotiating issues to arbitration rather than undergo a strike or lockout.

O

One Big Union (OBU):   A radical (syndicalist), predominantly Western Canadian union founded in 1919; included both craft and industrial workers and was instrumental in the Winnipeg General Strike.

open door policy: A management policy where individuals are free to take their concerns or grievances directly to senior management officials, whose door is "always open".

open shop clause: A collective agreement clause that specifies that workers are not required to join the union, nor pay union dues or the equivalent of dues. (Also *see* Union security clause.)

Order-in-Council PC 1003:   A federal government order-in-council issued in 1944, providing workers with the legal right to organize a union free from employer intimidation and requiring employers to recognize the union and bargain with it in good faith once certified; modelled after the National Labor Relations Act passed in the U.S. in 1935.

organic solidarity: A concept, conceived by Emile Durkheim, that refers to the social order that results from the development of interdependence between individuals, thus giving rise to the need for coordination and cooperation; believed by Durkheim to emerge in developed industrial societies.

organization theory: A field of study that focuses upon the relationships between the environment, the structure, and the processes of organizations.

organize: The process by which workers choose to be legally represented by a union.

organized labour: Labour unions and their members, as well as related associations such as "labour federations" or "congresses". (Also *see* Labour movement.)

orthodox-pluralist perspective: An ideology concerned primarily with finding a balance between the need for efficiency in the economy and the need for equity and fairness in employment relations, and traditionally focusing upon the institutions of labour law, labour unionism, and collective bargaining; it proceeds from the assumption that workers as individuals are often at a disadvantage relative to management but that unions remedy this disadvantage and enable them to confront their employers as equals.

outsourcing: The decision to purchase inputs to the production process (i.e., parts and accessories) from outside sources rather than producing them in-house. (Also *see* Contracting out and Subcontracting.)

P

paradigm: An established system of values and beliefs about the way things work.

parent union: Consists of a number of local unions that are affiliated under the same name and are subject to a common overarching constitution and structure, both of which supersede the constitution and structure of the locals themselves; it may be provincial, national, or international in scope.

parent union staffers: Employees of a parent union whose job it is to perform one or more of the parent union functions identified in chapter eight.

participatory reforms: Programs designed to foster greater employee involvement in, or commitment to their work by allowing them to participate in decision processes and to exchange ideas on how to improve working conditions and product quality. (Also referred to as involvement schemes; also *see* Quality circles.)

paternalistic management: The adoption by management of a number of "progressive" measures intended to reduce discontent and enhance worker identification with their employer, without providing workers any real rights or responsibilities; based upon the pre-industrial assumption that management has a responsibility to look after the welfare of workers and determine what is in their best interests.

pattern bargaining: When collective agreements reached in one workplace, firm, or industry tend to be followed by other firms or industries, thus setting a pattern.

pay-for-knowledge schemes: Payment schemes under which workers are paid bonuses based on the number of tasks they can perform, thereby inducing them to become more knowledgeable about different tasks and able to be reallocated to different jobs if need be; closely associated with the progressive HRM paradigm. (Also *see* Progressive personnel and Employment practices.)

PC 1003: *See* Order-in-Council PC 1003.

performance-based pay system: *See* Contingent pay system.

periphery sector: That sector of the economy consisting of small, labour intensive employers operating in more competitive markets. Periphery sector employers are believed to provide substantially less favourable terms of employment and to adopt less progressive practices.

pervasive egoism: A term used by Emile Durkheim to denote a condition where individuals and groups pursue only their own interests, with little concern for the interests or needs of others; according to Durkheim, this condition is caused by the "forced division of labour".

planned obsolescence: As employed in this book, an anti-union strategy in which employers cease to invest in union sites, instead directing new investments to non-union operations and allowing union establishments to become obsolete; once it can be established that the union establishment is no longer economically viable, it can be legally shut down, without fear of an unfair labour practice charge.

policy grievance: A grievance filed by the union against management (or in some cases, by management against the union) for policy-related actions that may or may not directly affect individuals, but are considered to be contrary to the terms of the agreement in a way that affects the bargaining unit as a whole.

political context: The characteristics of the national and provincial political systems within which labour and management interact. Generally includes government policies and programs, including monetary and fiscal policies, employment insurance programs, education and training programs, and others.

political economy: As employed in this book, a function that underlies managerial decision processes in industrial relations and that entails minimization of the costs associated with the essentially political problem of motivating and controlling workers.

political economy approach: As developed in this book, an approach to industrial relations that attempts to foster a more critically oriented, sociological understanding of industrial relations and that places emphasis upon the interconnections between industrial relations and broader issues of economy and society.

positive settlement zone: When two parties' bottom lines overlap.

post-industrial society: An extension of the industrialism thesis that argues that we are moving into a post-industrial era, where traditional-blue collar/industrial work (as we know it) will virtually disappear and large, bureaucratic organizations will give way to smaller, more participative "adhocracies", characterized by high levels of flexibility and adaptiveness.

post-war era: The period of time encompassing, roughly, the late 1940s to the mid-1970s.

post-war industrial relations system: The institutions of labour law, labour unionism, and collective bargaining as they developed in the post-war era.

post-war system: The system of economic and political institutions and arrangements that were established in the post-war era, including, but not limited to, the institutions of labour unionism, labour law, and collective bargaining system.

power: As employed in this book, a term denoting the ability to affect the outcomes of others — whether these outcomes are economic (e.g., money), social (e.g., friendship), or psychological (e.g., praise).

precarious work arrangements: Jobs which are on a part-time or temporary basis, often providing employees with little income or job security.

principle of job rights: The principle that states that workers accrue certain rights pertaining to their job over time, and that these rights balance off against managerial property rights.

problem solving groups: *See* Quality circles.

profit rationality: Managerial decisions and actions that are conducive to the rational pursuit of profit. (Also *see* Calculative rationality.)

profit-sharing plans: A "contingent pay system" in which workers receive some form of bonus tied to their employer's profitability. (Also *see* Gainsharing plans and Employee stock ownership plans.)

progressive employment practices: Employment practices designed to maximize employee motivation, commitment, and performance, including performance based pay, intensive training, a no-layoff policy, sophisticated selection practices, minimization of status distinctions, and others.

progressive/high commitment HRM practices: Management policies aimed at creating a consensual and cooperative relationship between management and labour, including the provision of good wages and benefits, ensuring that workers are treated fairly and equitably, and implementing various workplace participation and employee involvement programs. (Also *see* autonomic/consociative practices.)

progressive discipline: Penalties of escalating severity for unacceptable behaviour or performance.

proletariat: A class of working individuals, as defined by Marxist theory, that do not own or control productive assets or the "means of production" and, hence, are coerced to sell their labouring capacity to capitalists if they are to earn a living.

psychological contract: Unwritten expectations and understandings that have developed over time.

public choice theory: A theory of the state, consistent with the neoclassical perspective, which views politicians as rational, self-interested utility maximizers who are primarily concerned with maintaining their status and power, and who do so through the implementation of policy choices aimed at maximizing their re-election prospects. (Also referred to as rational choice theory.)

Public Service Staff Relations Act (PSSRA): Federal government legislation (1967) that provided federal government workers with collective bargaining rights.

Q, R

quality circles: Progressive HRM participation schemes held on company time anywhere from once a day to once a month, in which workers discuss any problems or concerns they have in the work process and put forth ideas on how these can be remedied and, hence, quality can be enhanced. (Also *see* Production quality meetings and Employee involvement schemes.)

radical crisis theorists: A variant of the radical perspective that argues that as capitalism develops it becomes increasingly difficult to maintain a healthy economy due to broader contradictions built into the system, with the result that the economy becomes increasingly susceptible to crises.

radical perspective: An ideology that, in terms of the economy in general, views the interests of labour (as represented by workers) and those of capital (as represented by those who own and manage work organizations) as on the whole diametrically opposed and that considers workers to be at an inherent disadvantage relative to management, whether they are unionized or not.

radical/labour process school: *See* Labour process theory.

rational choice theory: *See* Public choice theory.

real subordination: A Marxist term used to denote the state in which workers are not only formally under the authority of capitalists, but in which capitalists have also gained control over the actual methods and processes by which work is performed.

recalcitrance: As employed in this book, a term referring to work-related behaviour that is contrary to managerial interests and/or reflects underlying sources of conflict, including slacking, sabotage, and absenteeism.

re-engineering committees: *See* joint steering committees.

relational power: The extent to which permanent, temporary, or partial withdrawal from the labour–management relation by one party entails costs for the other; it refers to power acquired by each party once in the relationship and is, therefore, distinguished from labour market power. It consists of three subtypes: exit power, strike power, and job power. The focus in this book is upon the relational power of workers rather than of management.

remedy: An action taken by a court or administrative agency (e.g., labour board) to right past wrongs by an offending party. (Also *see* Make whole remedy.)

reopener clause: Collective agreement clause that stipulates that wages will be subject to renegotiation at some point during the term of the agreement, by "reopening" the agreement on this issue only.

replacement workers: A term used to refer to the replacement of striking workers in order to maintain operations; it can involve hiring new workers on a temporary basis or the use of employees not on strike. (Also *see* Scabs.)

residual rights: A doctrine stipulating that anything that is not specifically included within the collective agreement remains, by default, under the sole authority of management.

right-to-work doctrine: The doctrine that states that an individual should have the "right" to work without having to join a union or being required to pay union dues.

S

scabs: A derogatory term used to refer to replacement workers utilized by employers during a strike. (Also *see* Replacement workers.)

Scanlon plan: A progressive HRM program intended to enhance productivity through the establishment of "labour–management committees" and the implementation of an employee bonus system based upon productivity gains. (Also *see* Labour–management committees.)

scientific management: An approach to management associated with Frederick Winslow Taylor that involves the application of scientific principles to both the design of work and the resolution of labour–management disagreements; viewed by labour process theorists as a method for de-skilling work and intensifying the labour process. (Also *see* Labour process theory.)

secondary picketing: When striking workers picket suppliers or customers of their employer.

sector councils: Councils involving unions and employers from within the same industry, potentially serving a number of purposes, but in Canada intended primarily to foster joint, industry wide training and education initiatives.

self-directed/autonomous work teams: Workers in group are given considerable autonomy over the pace at which they work, decide how tasks are allocated among members, and are not subject to direct supervision, instead selecting their own "team leader" and taking joint responsibility for each other's performance.

seniority: The length of time that an employee has worked for an employer or in a department, calculated for the purpose of establishing employee benefits and rights relative to other employees.

shop steward: Member of union local who represents workers in specific departments or areas of the workplace but normally remains in his or her regular job, performing his or her duties as shop steward on a part-time basis.

shop stewards' committee: A committee, normally comprised of all shop stewards in a work establishment and presided over by a "general shop steward".

shutdown: The closing down of a union or non-union establishment.

single team bargaining: A "progressive" approach to collective bargaining in which workers and employers attempt to go beyond the "we-they" atmosphere of most negotiations by viewing issues in negotiations as problems to be solved jointly, with representatives from both sides working together as a single team.

slacking: A term used to denote the partial withdrawal of one's labour by providing less effort than would normally be the case; referred to by one author as the "withdrawal of efficiency".

social democratic function: A function of unions that involves the promotion of social democratic reforms within both the economy and society in general, such as an improved "workers' compensation" system, reduced wage inequality within and across firms, and support for human rights concerns in developing nations; most closely associated with the liberal-reformist perspective.

Social Justice Fund: A fund negotiated by the Canadian Auto Workers, under which participating employers are required to donate one cent for each straight time hour worked by each worker in the bargaining unit to a designated charity, food bank, or international relief effort.

social unionism: Union adherence to strong social democratic values and the perception that the union mission is one of furthering the well-being of workers as a whole.

socio-cultural context: The values, beliefs, customs, and understandings that predominate within a particular community or society and form part of the context within which labour and management interact. Consisting of predominant traditions, values, and beliefs which vary by country, province, region, or workplace.

spillover effect: The notion that because of unions, non-union employers have historically been compelled to provide more favourable wages and benefits than they would have otherwise.

stakeholder theory: An organizational theory that views work organizations as "coalitions" of "stakeholder" groups, each of which contributes resources to the firm in return for various inducements, and each of which can hence be said to have a "stake" in the firm.

state, the: A federal or provincial government and its agencies.

strategic choice school of management: A model of management that disputes the assumption that managerial actions are determined by the context in which they take place and places emphasis on the role of strategic choices born out of the values, beliefs, and (ultimately) philosophies of senior management.

strike: The collective withdrawal of labour by a group of individuals in order to protest established (managerial or governmental) policies or conditions and to pressure those in authority to change these policies and conditions; usually involves actions taken by unionized workers once negotiations over a collective agreement have failed, but can also involve actions by workers during the term of an agreement and/or in a non-union workplace, to protest either managerial or governmental policies.

strike breaking: Employer attempts to undermine a strike through the use of replacement workers and through various forms of intimidation.

strike fund: Financial resources accumulated by a union (generally from membership dues) for use during strikes and lockouts.

strike pay: The provision of financial assistance to workers in the event of a strike or lockout, drawn from an accumulated union "strike fund"; typically amounts to only a fraction of the striker's normal income.

strike power: A form of "relational power" that varies with the costs to management of a strike (i.e., temporary withdrawal).

structural antagonism: Term employed by radical theorists and adherents to the capitalism thesis to refer to an inherent conflict between the interests of workers as sellers of labour and those of capitalists and their "agents"(management) as buyers of labour.

structural inequality literature: A body of literature associated with the liberal-reformist perspective that generally argues that the terms of employment and the treatment afforded workers depends in large part upon structural variables such as employer size, workplace technology, and product market concentration.

structuralist view of the state: A radical perspective on the state which argues that, while the state is constrained over the long run to enact policies and laws conducive to the general interests of capitalists, divisions within the capitalist class provide it with a certain amount of relative autonomy and, hence, choice over the policies and laws it enacts.

subcontracting: The management practice of having work performed by independent workers or firms rather than by workers in-house; sometimes used as a strategy for bypassing the collective agreement. (Also *see* Outsourcing and Contracting out.)

suggestion system: A traditional information-sharing practice under, which employees can hope to receive some form of award if they contribute a suggestion which enhances performance.

superseniority clause: A collective agreement clause that stipulates that union officials are to be treated as if they have the highest competitive status with respect to such things as layoff and recall, overtime, and shift selection.

supplemental agreement: Collective agreement operating in conjunction with "master agreement" in "two-tier bargaining", that offer a greater measure of specificity with regard to particular concerns at individual work settings (such as job classifications and work rules) within a bargaining unit. (Also *see* Master agreement and Two-tier bargaining.)

supplementary unemployment benefits (SUBs): Employment provisions that draw money from employer- (and in some cases, worker-) funded plans in order to supplement or top up the unemployment insurance benefits of workers who have been laid off.

surface bargaining: Frustration of the bargaining process by a party that partakes in contradictory demands or simply goes through the motions with no intention of making meaningful concessions.

surplus value: The proceeds of production left over after all of the costs of production are paid; associated with Marx's argument that a worker's first few hours on the job produce enough value to pay for his or her wages, with the rest of the day (the surplus work) being appropriated by the employer.

syndicalism: An early twentieth-century ideology that generally argues that unions are the only true instruments of the working class, and that, as such, they should play the primary role in the overthrow of capitalism and in the formation of a new economic order. (Also *see* Union class conflict/revolutionary function.)

systems theory of the state: A theory of the state, consistent with managerialist theory, which assumes that the state's primary purpose is to maintain order and stability, and that this serves the interests of society and the social system as a whole. (Also *see* Functionalist theory of the state.)

T

Taylorism: Application of the principles of "scientific management", as associated with the work of Frederick Taylor. (Also *see* Scientific management.)

team briefings: An information and consultation process which involves regularly scheduled meetings through which work teams or groups are informed about developments relevant to their work and subsequent plans which may affect them.

technical economy: A function that underlies managerial decision processes in industrial relations and entails minimization of the costs associated with the technical requirements of production.

technological context: The forms of technology available for the transformation of inputs into outputs and/or characteristic of a particular workplace. It includes the means and methods by which a good or service is produced, including the extent to which they entail high capital intensity (capital invested per worker), are fragile or susceptible to break-downs, and are complex, requiring high levels of knowledge or skills.

time and motion studies: An aspect of scientific management conceived by Frederick Taylor, under which trained experts systematically observe the activities of workers, break them down into specific tasks and motions, and time how long it takes to do each one.

timeliness restrictions: Legal conditions that must be met before a strike is deemed to be timely and, hence, legal.

think-do dichotomy: Frederick Taylor's belief that conception (thinking) is management's job, while execution (doing) is a worker's job; thus the two should be separated.

Total Quality Management (TQM):   Programs that are intended to procure improvements in all aspects of quality, based upon the idea that quality is something for which all employees should share responsibility (rather than relegating quality-related concerns to specific individuals or departments); closely associated with the progressive HRM paradigm.

town hall democracies: A form of direct democracy under which meetings are held frequently, attendance is high, debate and disagreement are encouraged, and all members/citizens feel both free to run for election and are able to mount a credible challenge to incumbent officers.

Trades and Labour Congress (TLC):   A Canadian labour federation founded in 1886 and, after 1902, consisting primarily of craft unions; eventually merged with the Canadian Congress of Labour (CCL) in 1956 to create the Canadian Labour Congress.

Trade Union Act of 1872:   An Act that recognized the right of workers to form unions and exempted them from conspiracy charges, but provided them with few positive rights and protections.

trade unions: Unions that have traditionally claimed workers in a specific trade or craft (rather than industry) as constituting their jurisdiction. (Also *see* Craft unions.)

two-tier bargaining: Negotiations that set forth a "master agreement" to cover all operations in the multi-establishment bargaining unit and separate "supplemental agreements" for various work settings within this unit. (Also *see* Master agreement and Supplemental agreements.)

U

underlying sources of conflict: Sources of conflict, which for all intents and purposes appear to be fundamental to the labour–management relation in industrial capitalist economies. (Also *see* Contextual sources of conflict.)

unfair labour practice: A management or union practice that is considered under the law to unfairly undermine the other party's ability to represent its constituents and, hence, is considered to be illegal; applies most often to employer attempts to undermine a union organizing attempt through intimidation or coercion.

unfair labour practice complaint: A complaint filed with a labour board by one party (usually a union) claiming that another party (usually management) has acted in a way that contravenes labour laws; most often filed in connection with management attempts to undermine a union organizing drive.

union business agents: Full-time union employees whose role it is to help deal with the day-to-day functions of union locals.

union class conflict/revolutionary function: A function of unions that involves the expression of class conflict and/or the revolutionary overthrow of an established economic and political system; traditionally associated with the radical perspective in general and with syndicalism in particular. (Also *see* Syndicalism.)

union council: A term sometimes used to refer to a union district. (Also *see* Union district.)

union democratization function: A function of unions that involves the representation of workers to management and the provision of various rights and protections for workers, thereby introducing an element of democracy into the employment relation; most developed by proponents of the orthodox-pluralist perspective.

union density: The percentage of non-agricultural paid workers who are members of a union in a given occupation, industry, or geographical area (e.g., country).

union district: Subdivision of national or international unions that coordinate union activities and provide union services in different geographical regions, hence bringing the parent union closer to the local level and enabling it to address the needs and problems specific to a particular area. (Also *see* Union council.)

union economic function: A function of unions that involves improving the wages and benefits of workers; most closely associated with the neoclassical perspective.

union executive council: Groupings of elected union officers and some senior staff specialists that meet periodically (e.g., once a month) to map out strategy and make policy decisions concerning the day-to-day operation of the union, organizing activities, bargaining strategies, and so forth.

union integrative function: A function of unions that involves the integration of workers into the workplace and the fostering of labour–management harmony; most associated with the "managerialist perspective".

union local: *See* Local union.

union raiding: A situation in which one union attempts to encourage workers who are already in another union to change their union affiliation.

union recognition clauses: Collective agreement clauses that stipulate that management agrees to recognize the union as the sole bargaining agent of workers in operations covered by the agreement.

union revolutionary function: *See* Class conflict/revolutionary function.

union security clause: A collective agreement clause that specifies whether workers are required to be union members and whether they are required to pay dues. (Also *see* Closed shop clause, Union shop clause, Agency shop clause, Open shop clause, Maintenance of membership clause, and Modified union shop clause.)

union shop clause: A collective agreement clause that specifies that workers need not be union members at the time that they are hired, but are required to join the union within a specified period thereafter (e.g., three months) once hired. (Also *see* Union security clause.)

union social democratic function: A function of unions that involves the promotion of social democratic reforms within both the economy and society in general, such as an improved workers compensation system, reduced wage inequality within and across firms, and support for human rights concerns in developing nations; most developed by proponents of the liberal-reformist perspective.

union substitution: In a non-union workplace, when management adopts many of the practices associated with union settings and provides wages and benefits that are comparable to those offered by union employers in the same industry or region.

unofficial strikes: Situations in which workers go on strike without the formal or official approval of union leaders.

V

virtuous circle: A term used to describe the post-war era, during which rising incomes ensured that the demand for consumer goods and services increased at a rate necessary to sustain increased production levels and, hence, economic growth.

voluntarism: The notion that unionized workers and their employers should be encouraged to resolve disputes and disagreements voluntarily and to the mutual satisfaction of both sides, through a process of "free collective bargaining" rather than through government intervention.

voluntary arbitration: The situation in which management and labour agree in advance of negotiations to submit any unresolvable differences to an arbitrator rather than undergo a strike.

W, Y

wage and price restraints: Government policies that limit the magnitude of wage increases that unions are allowed to negotiate and the magnitude of employer price increases.

wage-effort bargain: The level of pay workers can expect for a given level of effort.

wage-employment trade-off: *See* Disemployment effects.

Wagner Act: *See* National Labor Relations Act (NLRA).

Weber's iron cage: *See* Iron cage of bureaucracy.

welfare capitalism: The era in which paternalistic management practices came to be predominant; began in the early 1900s, but especially prevalent in the 1920s.

whip of hunger: An expression used by Max Weber to refer to worker acceptance of the terms and conditions imposed upon them as the only alternative to abject poverty.

wildcats/wildcat strikes: Strikes that take place during the term of a collective agreement and, hence, are normally considered to be illegal.

Winnipeg General Strike: One of the most famous Canadian labour disputes (1919), where virtually all workers in the city of Winnipeg staged a six-week walkout.

Woodward/Blauner thesis: Maintains that industrial conflict is largely a product of the fragmented and routinized work characteristic of mass production processes, and that it will dissipate as more automated production processes become more prevalent; closely associated with the post-industrial society thesis.

working class organizations: *See* Labour federations and Labour congresses.

workplace re-engineering: A term often used to refer to workplace change programs involving (in theory) radical restructuring of work relations so as to cut costs and improve flexibility.

work rules: Collective agreement provisions that place restrictions upon the exercise of managerial authority in the workplace, applying to such things as "crew sizes", workload or work-pace restrictions, and job content.

works councils: Workplace level committees of employee (and sometimes employer) representatives, with information-sharing, consultation, and/or joint decision-making rights.

work-to-rule: A situation, usually found in the context of labour–management conflict, where workers refuse to do anything not explicitly allowed for in the collective agreement.

yellow dog contract: A contract drawn up by management and signed by workers as a condition of employment, stipulating that they are not members of a union and will not join one; popular in the early decades of the twentieth century, but currently illegal.

Index

INDEX

About the Author

John Godard holds a B.Comm. (Hons.) and an MBA from the University of Manitoba, and a PhD in industrial relations from Cornell University. His work focuses on the nature and institutions of the employment relation, employer practices and the organization of work, and cross-national variation in both of these areas. Professor Godard's work has been widely published, appearing in a number of edited books and in leading journals in Canada, the United States and the United Kingdom. He is both a past editor of the *British Journal of Industrial Relations* and past president of the Canadian Industrial Relations Association. He is currently a professor at the Asper School of Business of the University of Manitoba.